FRIEDRICH NIETZSCHE
and
THE POLITICS OF
TRANSFIGURATION

Friedrich Nietzsche and the Politics of Transfiguration

Expanded Edition

Tracy B. Strong

UNIVERSITY OF CALIFORNIA PRESS

Berkeley • Los Angeles • London

University of California Press
Berkeley and Los Angeles, California

University of California Press, Ltd.
London, England
First paperback printing and expanded edition, 1988

Much of Chapter X appeared previously as "Texts and Pretexts: Reflections on Perspectivism in Nietzsche," Political Theory, XIII, no. 2 (May, 1985), 164–182. Permission to reprint is gratefully acknowledged.

Library of Congress Cataloging-in-Publication Data

Strong, Tracy B.
   Friedrich Nietzsche and the politics of transfiguration / Tracy B. Strong. – Expanded ed.
     p.   cm.
   Bibliography: p.
   Includes index.
   ISBN 0-520-06449-6 (cloth : alk paper)
   ISBN 0-520-06347-3 (pbk. : alk. paper)
   1. Nietzsche, Friedrich Wilhelm, 1844–1900.   I. Title.
B3317.S76 1988
193 – dc19   88-4767

Printed in the United States of America
1   2   3   4   5   6   7   8   9

*Also I doubt if I could ever become a true philologist;
unless I become one by the way, as if by accident, there
is no hope for it. The misfortune is this: I have no model
and am in danger of making a fool of myself by my own
hand.*

—Nietzsche to Rohde, 1870

*Sing me a new song, the world is transfigured and all the
skies rejoice.*

—Nietzsche to Gast, 1889

PREFACE

The pages of this preface are, in a sense, not the beginning of this book, but only precisely what a preface is: it comes before and surveys what I have to say. I play here, perhaps, the role of guide, in no way a substitute for the journey itself, but sometimes able to point out in advance some of the landscapes, some sections of the city which may be of particular interest. I wish to take this preliminary opportunity to overview some of the concerns and problems which Nietzsche raises, and which are raised for all students of Nietzsche by their study. In the metaphor I borrow from Wittgenstein for use in chapter i, Nietzsche is a bit like a foreign city. Though it *looks* like all other cities, it *is* like none, and whatever knowledge we may have from previous experience will, very likely, be of little use in getting around.

I have tried to write this book with as little animosity toward other commentators as possible. This has not always been easy; indeed, traces of the possessiveness I feel about my thoughts remain in some footnotes. I hope that such *widersagen* serves a useful purpose. Nietzsche, as anyone who has read him knows, is an author who engenders the most intense and personal feelings. All interpretations seem possible: between the racial enthusiasms of national socialism, the still encountered dedication of those trying to live, a la

Demian, a "Nietzschean" life, the bright individualism of most Anglo-American interpretations, and the dark cosmic mysteries offered by Continental philosophers, the new reader knows not where to turn. A case *can* be made for each interpretation. Generally speaking, most interpreters have found passages that, in context, do appear to support their understanding (though, from the quarrels among Nietzsche scholars, one might suspect that *ressentiment* was a prerequisite for admission to the guild).

I deal specifically with some of the best and standard interpretations in the course of the book. In each case, I think that the interpretations are not so much wrong, as missing some elements of Nietzsche's thought which, if their authors were to take them seriously, would force them to cast their whole analysis in a different light. Nietzsche is to some degree responsible for this, again as all who have looked into his works must realize. He does not write in any of the standard philosophical forms, the treatise and the essay, nor even in an older one, the dialogue. Instead, we have aphorisms, poetry, vindicative, confessions; where the argument seems more sustained, as perhaps in *On the Genealogy of Morals*, the coherence we feel is at best that of a musical composition, of an interior pattern repeatedly manifesting itself in different forms, always again new.

I have tried in this book to take Nietzsche *seriously* and at the same time to make sense of all his claims. Most previous interpreters have, I believe, in their conviction that they understood Nietzsche, managed to blind themselves to what they did not want or need to see. I realize that my claims to have partially avoided such exegetical cecity may be presumptuous. Nietzsche warns his readers: "This is, in the end, my ordinary experience, and, if you will, the *originality* of my experience. Whoever has believed he understood something of me, has made himself something of me in his own image — not rarely an opposite to me . . . ; who has understood nothing of me, denied that I needed to be considered at all."[1] My only justification for the claim that I have escaped his accusation must come in the writing that follows. I can indicate in advance that I was helped in my endeavor by an almost accidental decision, to take at face value those claims in Nietzsche which appear the most histrionic and exasperating. Among these are his demands for "master races" and "breeding," his assertions that he "breaks the world in two," and so forth. For many commentators, these form the fringe of Nietzsche's megalomania. Such pronouncements get treated a bit in the conde-sending manner one would treat an interesting and important person who had "spent too long a time in the bush"; they are ignored, as not really part of civilized discourse. For me, however, Nietzsche must have had a reason for saying such things, and a reason beyond the rather feeble excuse of the "rhetoric of the times." As an example: it is sometimes claimed that we must be careful in inter-preting what Nietzsche says in favor of war, since his experience of war in the nineteenth century was so different from ours. Yet, Nietzsche speaks specifically of "wars such as no man has ever seen." It seems, then, that any interpretation of Nietzsche must deal with all the seemingly "unpleasant" sides of his teaching.

Let me rehearse, then, what I have to say. I focus on Nietzsche's claim that Western culture, in all its aspects, is coming to an *end*. Though this process be not yet accomplished, for Nietzsche it will form the history of the twentieth and twenty-first centuries, cen-turies that he believes or hopes will be informed by his thought. Western culture has, Nietzsche argues, hollowed itself out, and men, the "last men," are left blinking in a world devoid of all meaning. This is what Nietzsche calls nihilism, that men continue to pursue in their lives and intelligence that which their intelligence and lives make impossible to attain. Contrary to those such as Marx, who also saw an era drawing to an end but hoped for the birth of a new world from the demise of the old, Nietzsche does not associate the advent of nihilism with the necessary birth of another world, but only with nothing.

I draw in this work upon all of Nietzsche's writings, but avoid chronological exegesis of them. It is my conviction, based on the demonstration of what follows, that Nietzsche's works are all (or almost all) of a piece. From his earliest writing, he remains concerned with questions of an ultimate and almost eschatological nature: the meaning of truth, the justifiability of existence, the future of the human race. These sorts of areas, with their ancillary topics of inquiry, form consistent and ongoing problems for Nietzsche. His answers, if properly understood, must, I think, be faced. They are profound and explicit, and sound a continuous note throughout his philosophical activity.

Nietzsche sees his first task as effectuating a diagnosis of present conditions which will permit men to make a break with their past.

Our genealogy, the soil from which our "nature" springs, holds the roots of the growth of nihilism. It has many subtle ways of retaining a grip on men, even, and perhaps especially, when they think themselves freed from it. By his critique, Nietzsche would present to mankind a picture of their lot such that it can be broken. This is no easy task: the first men whom Zarathustra tries to warn of their own existence laugh at him, and demand precisely that to which Zarathustra would alert them.

There is, then, a preliminary problem for Nietzsche: his "originality," as he calls it. He will not be able simply to tell men what he has to say. The events he would make known still lie beyond the language of most of his potential listeners.[2] Nietzsche is not, as so many commentators have said, "obscure"; in fact, I think that he generally means exactly what he says. If we find him obscure or mystical, this says something about us, for it is not until we are able to cast off the pictures that hold us prisoner to a traditional way of seeing moral, political, social, and epistemological problems that we will be able to face directly what Nietzsche says.

Here Nietzsche's task is preliminarily destructive. He essays a *tractatus politicus* to break the hold he sees in the structure of language and conceptual patterns, in the nature of moral interactions, and in our inheritance from Socrates and Christ. Men, says Nietzsche, do not want to be freed from their illusions, not because those illusions are "comforting," but because those illusions are all there is. If the illusions are broken, then there will be nothing. For Nietzsche, the ensuing chaos is a necessary risk; it permits that all things be made new, but it does not ensure how they will be made, or that they will be made at all. Nothing can provide men with an example in the chaos which lies beyond the edge of nihilism. Not even ancient Greece, a culture often understood as Nietzsche's ideal, can be a model any longer. "We must," he proclaims, "surpass even the Greeks."[3] And, as we cannot go backward, we will also not naturally go forward: mankind is threatened with a *folie circulaire*, the madness of the compulsive repetition of a life void of meaning.

Men are "human-all-too-human." The faults and errors in so being human affect and infect everything men do: it is their *nature* to move into nihilism. If so, then there can be no answer but to change the very stuff of humanity, to eradicate that which makes men human-all-too-human and transfigure them into "overmen." The doctrine of eternal return and the lessons of the will to power form the center of Nietzsche's attempt to accomplish such a revaluation. This provides us with a clue to Nietzsche's so-called amorality. It is a mistake to think that Nietzsche criticizes morality, or politics, or any other traits of Western man, as "simply" illusions, which can be wiped away with bold words. His critique is of *us*, the men and women for whom that morality is *not* "childish" nonsense, but actual. Morality is real because of the sort of people we are. A critique of morality, or of politics, or religion, cannot stop with the institution or practice; for Nietzsche, it must continue on to the beings of whose life it is a necessary part.

Nietzsche then forces us to know ourselves. But, contrary to much of later psychiatry, he does not think we can stop there. There is no reason that self-knowledge should be a satisfactory stopping point — but now I do more than anticipate. What follows does, I hope, what I claim for it here. May it at least provoke a reader to the necessity of having to know such things.

A version of chapter vii was printed in *Nietzsche*, edited by Robert Solomon, in the Doubleday Series in Modern Philosophy (New York: Doubleday, 1973). Permission to reprint it here is gratefully recognized.

An early version of chapter vii was given at the Northeastern Political Science Association Meetings in 1970; portions of chapters vi and ix were given at the Columbia Philosophy Colloquium in 1971; a portion of chapter viii was given at the University of Chicago Political Science Colloquium, 1973. I am grateful for the comments received on these occasions.

The writing of an early draft of this book was partly supported by a Summer Research Grant from the University of Pittsburgh in 1970.

Many thanks to Linda Perkins for typing and other help.

Though few of my friends and teachers are mentioned in the notes, the debts I owe them are together personal and intellectual; they cannot be repaid through the publication of this book. I was first instructed in political theory, and shown the integrity of that vocation by John D. Lewis at Oberlin College. His recognition of something of merit in my obscure struggles with political thought and his encouragement remain a central motivation in my pursuits since that time. At Oberlin, I also came to know Wilson Carey McWilliams, to whom I owe only that which one can owe to a teacher who has known how to break away from the seductiveness of that position and become a companion. The initial writing of this book in the form of a dissertation was supervised by Judith N. Shklar; when I look back upon that original manuscript, of which a word remains buried here and there in this present work, I can only marvel at what she put up with, and at the quiet and completely precise encouragement and assistance she gave. I should also mention here the understanding and example of Stanley Hoffmann, who, though not a political theorist, made my stay at Harvard much more productive than it would otherwise have been.

The chapters of this book have been written and rewritten at the promptings of a number of friends. I should mention particularly Timothy Gould, whose comments on the last chapter showed me what I meant to say; Alexander Nehamas, whose readings of chapters vi and ix forced me to rethink many inconsistencies; Robert Eden, who kept the picture of what I was trying to do always in front of me; Anne Kreilkamp, who prompted me on Wittgenstein and grace during a period when my ideas were beginning to take shape; and, last, Ingrid Lorch Turner, without whom this would not have been written when it first was, and who, when she came into my life a second time, confirmed my confidence in the last chapters of this book.

The entire manuscript, in close to final form, has been read by a number of people, to whom I owe very different sorts of debts. Walter Kaufmann shared his knowledge of Nietzsche in an extended commentary and saved me from many foolish mistakes. Wilson Carey McWilliams provided the support he always has. Hanna Fenichel Pitkin read the entire book with an intelligence and care born from the feeling that we were struggling toward the same clarity, and that it was better to struggle together. Finally, Helene Keyssar not only taught me about semicolons, but, during this time we have been together, taught me more about myself, and thus more about what I was attempting to write. That it is with her that I finally break away from Nietzsche is as it should be.

Many conversations and criticisms are silently present in these pages. Foremost among these, and most important, are those with Alexander Keyssar and Barry O'Connell. I ask them to stand for the others.

Much of this material has been presented in earlier forms to students in various courses and discussions. Their responses have influenced direction and emphasis in manners both direct and subtle. I single out here Ellen Pearlman, with whom many conversations and exchanges have helped me to sharpen and focus my thoughts.

Finally, I owe to my parents the knowledge and experience of what it means to live a life where moral imperatives are daily made flesh in activity. Their support, criticism, and love made and make my life possible.

Acknowledgments, as a form of confession, are a temptation. Let me add that the confusions and opacities in what follows are mine alone. I regret only that all the times, loves, and pains could not erase them.

Tracy B. Strong

Wellfleet, Massachusetts
August 6, 1974

CONTENTS

Chapter I

INTRODUCTION: ON APPROACHING NIETZSCHE

A voice said, Look in me the stars
And tell me truly, men of earth,
If all the soul and body scars
Were not too much to pay for birth.

— Robert Frost, "A Question"

And the end of all our exploring
Will be to arrive where we started
And know the place for the first time.

— T. S. Eliot, *Little Gidding*, V

When Nietzsche stepped into clinical insanity shortly after the new year in 1889, he left behind him a dismaying and disparate array of accomplishments. Twenty years before he had appeared to be on the brink of a brilliant career in German universities. Without even the benefit of a completed doctorate, he had been appointed to the prestigious chair of classical philology at the University of Basel, then one of the centers of European culture. However, his study of the origins of Greek drama, *The Birth of*

Tragedy Out of the Spirit of Music, published in 1872, appeared to the academic world as the writing of a man obsessed with the most dubious of contemporary artistic phenomena, Richard Wagner, and Nietzsche was immediately cast as a man who had given up scholarship for propaganda. There was, of course, a partial truth to the accusation. While I intend to show that *The Birth of Tragedy* must be taken seriously as an understanding of the Greeks, there is no doubt that Nietzsche's concerns did go far beyond the world of the university. He sought to find the artistic basis of the rejuvenation of a German culture which he believed to be in the final stages of decadence.

Nietzsche was greatly disheartened by the reception of his first work; he stayed on at the university, nonetheless, devoting himself to teaching, and wrote a series of essays which he hoped would further the task he had set himself with the *Birth*. These pieces, the *Untimely Considerations*, addressed themselves to the major cultural symbols of the day, and sought to direct the attention of German youth away from false symbols (especially David Strauss and Hegel), and toward more difficult and creative masters (Schopenhauer and Wagner). These were the so-called "Wagner years"; Nietzsche appeared to have persuaded himself that the new music-drama could provide the basis of renewed culture, with Wagner performing the artistic role and he, Nietzsche, providing philosophical direction.

In the middle and late 1870's Nietzsche remained publicly cast as a propagandist for Wagner. His academic promise was unfulfilled and his health increasingly poor. By 1876 his health had become so bad that he was forced to obtain sick leave from Basel. This was not the only break in his life at that time. He was in the process of composing *Human, All-Too-Human* and was increasingly conscious of his ineradicable differences with Wagner. He attended the first Wagner music festival in Bayreuth[1] and, dismayed with what he saw as Wagner's pandering to the spirit of the times, fled in disgust. Within a year, the break with Wagner was public and irrevocable; Nietzsche's health continued to deteriorate; he resigned his post in Basel and was granted a small pension.

At this point in his life, Nietzsche had cut himself off from most "normal" institutional attachments. For the rest of his coherent life he wandered back and forth in Switzerland and Italy, rarely, if ever, setting foot in Germany, almost always in execrable health. Despite his physical condition (he claimed 118 days of migraine headaches in 1879), his output was constant and large; in the last ten years of his life he published eleven books and several new prefaces to old ones. When he collapsed in Turin in 1889, he left an immense amount of unpublished material, known as the *Nachlass*, and plans for major philosophical works; his work up until then, he claimed, had been a necessary preparatory ground-clearing for what was to follow.

The shape of these writings, both published and unpublished, constitutes a problem for the reader. On occasion, Nietzsche seems to take an aesthetic delight in being outrageous; at times, he simply is outrageous. He writes to provoke and jolt, perhaps to mislead. Even, for instance, of one of the most organized and coherent of his works, *On the Genealogy of Morals*, he notes: "Every time a beginning that is *calculated* to mislead: cool, scientific, even ironic, deliberately foreground, deliberately holding off. Gradually more unrest; sporadic lightning; very disagreeable truths are heard rumbling in the distance — until eventually a *tempo feroce* is attained in which everything rushes ahead in tremendous tension. Every time in the end, in the midst of perfectly gruesome detonations, a *new* truth becomes visible between thick clouds."[2]

That Nietzsche's intention never was to give us a systematic doctrine is clear. Nor, with few exceptions, does he write discursive essays. Indeed, a major work, *Thus Spoke Zarathustra*, is in a peculiar form of verse and contains some of the best poetry by a modern German stylist (and some of the worst). On the other hand, one cannot correctly say about reading Nietzsche what one might say about reading La Rochefoucauld, that these books are simply associations of more or less well polished lapidary aphorisms and epigrams. In reading a book like *Beyond Good and Evil* or *The Gay Science*, one has the general sense that a whole number of things are happening at the same time. The cloth of the text shows now this thread, now that. The numbered sections are not precisely separate; rather, they intertwine. If one remains too close to the text, the overall effect is undefined; yet, and this is of major importance, what distance one should assume from the text to see what it is about is not immediately apparent.

Yet no matter what distance one assumes, Nietzsche seems to make *some* sense. Hence, the answer to the question, "Do you understand Nietzsche?" is too often and from too many people,

"Yes." He has been judged a muddleheaded romantic irrationalist; or the forerunner of positivism, or of pragmatism, or of Freud; or an aristocrat cultural critic on the lines of Arnold and Ruskin; or an ideologist decrying the demise of the bourgeois order; or an Aryan racist, and so forth. The list can go on for a very long time. Nietzsche has been linked somehow with almost every development of importance in contemporary philosophy, art, politics, and society.

Nietzsche is, perhaps purposively, somewhat responsible for the motley of his interpreters. The writings he leaves us lend themselves to a whole series of immediate interpretations, depending on what portion rings changes in the reader. This is due to the nature of the work itself; it never seems to tell what is being said, but at the same time, one has in reading it the inescapable feeling that it does (somewhere, somehow) mean something. Erich Heller writes very well about this problem.

There are philosophies which, however difficult they may be, are in principle easy to teach and easy to learn. Of course, not everyone can teach or learn philosophy — any more than higher mathematics; but the philosophies of certain philosophers have this in common with higher mathematics: they present the simple alternative of being either understood or not understood. It is, in the last analysis, impossible to *mis*understand them. This is true of Aristotle, or St. Thomas Acquinas, or Descartes, or Locke, or Kant. Such philosophies are like mountains: you climb to their tops or you give up. In either case, you will know what has happened and "where you are." But this is not so with the thought of Plato, or St. Augustine, or Pascal, or Kierkegaard, or Nietzsche. Their philosophies are like human faces on the features' of which are inscribed, disquietingly, the destinies of souls; or like cities rich in history. "Do you understand Kant?" is like asking "Have you been to the summit of Mont Blanc?" The answer is *yes* or *no*. "Do you understand Nietzsche?" is like asking "Do you know Rome?" The answer is simple only if you have never been there.[3]

Taking these warnings to heart and mind, I do not propose in this book to give an *interpretation* of Nietzsche. I propose rather, in the language Wittgenstein was to use some decades after Nietzsche, to go there and "look and see."[4] Getting to know Nietzsche is a bit like getting to know a new town: I walk the streets, again and again, and only when I have encountered the same spot from a number of different backgrounds and approaches will it fall into place. In a very important way, I do not then conceive of this book as offering a new interpretation of Nietzsche, anymore than I would think of offering

a new interpretation of Paris, though I know the city well. Nietzsche's writings may appear chaotic and without order; so does a new
city at first glance. What one finds in coming to know a new city is
not that it *has* an order, nor that it is laid down on the basis of some
abstract logic, but that *it can be known*. When I know Paris, the fact
that Paris is not organized along some principle (except perhaps the
most general ones of streets, buildings, and intersections) does not
stop me from knowing my way about there; nor can it stop someone
else, if that person spends enough serious time there, from learning
his or her way about.

I should note here two things which I am, then, *not* claiming.
Firstly, I am not claiming that Nietzsche is "obscure," and that I am
trying to make him clear. Everything one needs to know is directly
there; being able to find one's way about does not involve looking
behind the surface; there is no hidden doctrine in Nietzsche. The
problem, rather, is to identify what counts and how it stands in
relation to the other material available. By and large, Nietzsche
means what he says. But, as if he were for us a new town, he will
often write of "events which lie altogether beyond the possibility of
a frequent or even rare experience — as the *first* language for a new
series of experiences."[5] If his claim is accepted, as I think it must be
in some cases, it does not, however, follow that to comprehend what
Nietzsche is talking about is simply impossible. One might be
tempted here to make an analogy to some putative anthropological
encounter with an entirely new tribe. It is wrong to conclude, no
matter how strange the tribe be, that one cannot come to know and
understand it (though, as the history of anthropology shows, there
are many dangers). Similarly one can *come* to know Nietzsche. The
danger is that a reader may venture forth too soon on the assumption
that he knows his way about. Recognition that one knows one's way
about comes when *all* elements one encounters make sense.

The metaphor can be pushed one step further. While some of
Nietzsche's thoughts are of greater importance than others, it is
wrong to conclude that any portion is necessarily an accident to be
discounted. For instance, it is commonplace now to assume that
Nietzsche is not a racist. (Walter Kaufmann is generally accorded the
credit in the Anglo-Saxon world for having rescued Nietzsche from
the moral abyss of the latter's supposed association with the Nazis.)[6]
As shall appear, however, in the course of his book, while Nietzsche

clearly is not a racist, he paradoxically might also clearly be a racist. I could, as could anyone if so inclined, so through the corpus and produce a picture, with quotes in context, which would seem to indicate that, if perhaps only at the beginning of his life an anti-Semite, he was nonetheless committed to the proposition of "superior races." Most modern commentators have generally ignored these portions of Nietzsche, or transfigured them into "rhetoric." This simply won't do. It is as if, after visiting happily on the East Side, one decided that Harlem were not part of New York, because, while the rest of the city appeared appealing, there simply was nothing like Harlem back home. In reading Nietzsche, the problem then is to find a way of understanding his apparently "racist" comments together with his apparently "anti-racist" comments. This, of course, will probably mean abandoning the sobriquet racist, but *not* in favor of anti-racist; rather, for something entirely else.

Nietzsche cannot then simply *tell* his readers what his discoveries might be. So also I will never learn my way around a new town if I am only *told* where things are. It is, perhaps, a bit like this. Assume a man who has never seen Jastrow's duck-rabbit before. He says "That's a duck"; if I respond "Well, don't you see a rabbit too?" he has to *go back and look again*; if he still cannot see it as a rabbit, I might help with "Here, look at it *like this*." Pretty soon, he will be able to see it that way for himself. In this process, nothing has been revealed to him which was previously secret. He has only come to be able to see the material so that it made sense also as a rabbit. I am suggesting a similar proposition about Nietzsche: I hope to be giving the reader a proper nudge so that the vast and apparently disparate corpus of Nietzsche's writings and teachings may be seen as a whole.

This forces my second disclaimer. I am not claiming that Nietzsche has a system; I am also not claiming that he did not have one. Starting with the city metaphor again: Does Paris have a system? The question seems silly. When one knows Paris, one knows one's way about; one has not acquired an algorithm which allows one to make sense of any part of a whole. But, one also does not know it as one knows a memorized series of random numbers. The city has, one might say, a certain coherence. With Nietzsche, the case is the same. Nietzsche does not have a system, in the sense of a structure on which to hang his philosophical outer garments. Yet, most all that he writes is of a piece, cut from a common cloth. I thus shall not be occupied with trying to *make* Nietzsche coherent, nor with showing that he *is* coherent; rather, I wish to make manifest the (coherent) thrust of his enterprise. By and large, Nietzsche's thought does not build on itself; it is a series of explorations, or "experiments," as he calls it. Much the same terms apply to Nietzsche, it seems to me, as Wittgenstein applies to himself in the preface to his *Philosophical Investigations*.

The best I could write would never be more than philosophical remarks; my thoughts were crippled if I tried to force them on in any single direction against their natural inclination. – And this was, of course, connected with the very nature of the investigation. For this compels us to travel over a wide field of thought criss-cross in every direction. – The philosophical remarks in this book are, as it were, a number of sketches of landscapes which were made in the course of these long and involved journeyings.[7]

The proof of all this will have to come out in the acknowledgment of what follows. Two preliminary questions do arise. What about divisions in Nietzsche's own writing? How can I justify the divisions which I have at least implied in my chapter titles? In terms of the first question, the following seems likely. It is commonplace to assume that there is a more or less important tripartite composition to Nietzsche's life and writings. Many authors see an early Basel-Wagner period, followed by a middle "positivist" period, which generally extends from *Human, All-Too-Human* through *The Gay Science*, and, finally, a mature period, reaching from *Zarathustra* to the end. Occasionally a final period of "collapse" (1888: *Nietzsche Contra Wagner, Antichrist, Ecce Homo*) is appended. There is nothing particularly wrong (or right) with this classification, except that it naturally tends to lead authors into following it. There are numerous books which simply proceed in a chronological, narrative fashion, spliced with a few "Nietzsche and'"s (Marx, Dewey, Freud, Valéry, etc.), or which select one of the periods for more "intensive" study. Such a procedure tends to leave the impression that Nietzsche's writings are "going" in some definite direction, or that his thought is "developing."

In a fashion, it is, of course, true that Nietzsche evolves over the period of twenty years during which he is actively writing, but to emphasize this seem perilous. It makes very difficult an examination of the thrust of Nietzsche's enterprise as a whole.[8] If I adopt a position that Nietzsche is constantly changing and hits in an almost ad hoc way on new ideas only through the fury of his attack, it will be hard to find an answer to the question "What is Nietzsche trying to do?" Certainly, Nietzsche himself did not think of his own work as divided into evolutionary periods. In later books he reasserts his attention to themes from early books. In 1888, for instance, he is still discussing the apollonian in some of his notes. In the *Genealogy*, he calls attention to the fact that the essential ideas of the book had already been formulated in *Human, All-Too-Human*. More importantly, themes from his last books are already prefigured in his earlier ones. This is significant in that while he only plays out the full implications of a particular question in a late work, the logic of his analysis in an earlier piece had already then led him to see the matter as problematic. As we shall see, his reflections on history and consciousness in the *Untimely Considerations* and *The Gay Science* lead him to conclusions there which foreshadow the problems of the overman in *Zarathustra* and other later works. The same is even more true of eternal return. Nietzsche himself declares that *Dawn of Day* and *The Gay Science* are commentaries, before the fact, on *Zarathustra*.[9] Late in his life, he writes to his sister that his works are all of a piece. In his commentary on each of his books in *Ecce Homo* he makes no divisions, and forcefully claims that what appears to look like a change in him (the rejection of Schopenhauer and Wagner) is merely the result of misunderstandings (some his own) of his earlier position on them.

Nietzsche himself does propose another division of his life. In a letter sent to Franz Overbeck on February 11, 1883, he writes of his "eerie, deliberately secluded secret life, which takes a step every six years, and actually wants nothing but the taking of this step . . . ." The six-year phases (which Christopher Middleton insightfully uses in his organization of the *Letters*) are: 1864-1870, student days; 1870-1876, Basel until the break with Wagner; 1876-1882, *Freigeisterei* and Lou Salomé; 1883-1889, presciently, *Zarathustra* until the end. This division has a lot to recommend it, not the least of which is that Nietzsche proposed it. But one must also say exactly what it is a division of. I read it as a division of his personal and philosophical life, with each step being a signal that he has moved more and more into separateness and solitude.[10] (The rest of the letter tends to bear this out.) Nietzsche moves out of recognized institutions, and then away from Wagner and cultural redemption; he abandons his dream of the early 1880's for a "brotherhood of the *Gaya Scienza*" as well as his relationship with Lou; he gradually cuts himself off from discourse. And, at the end of his life, he stands alone in his autobiography, which he entitles with the shout by which Pilate presented Christ to the crowd. He will even insist in his last mad letters that Georg Brandes "lose him," that he has paid his debts to Overbeck, and his respects to Jacob Burckhardt.

This division seems then to make sense along important lines. In it, we see a man becoming more and more alone in the world and we catch a glimpse of the marvelous paradox of Nietzsche as both Pilate and Christ. It is, after all, *his* autobiography in which he proclaims himself to the crowd by *his Ecce Homo*. The division is suggestive *not* because it gives us time periods by which to categorize Nietzsche's life, but rather because it presents a pattern which Nietzsche himself sees as repeating again and again. The problem Nietzsche sees as posed in himself is that of a man becoming more and more alone, without words for companions, nor companions to hear them. This breakdown, which Nietzsche finds in himself, is, for him, a reflection of the world; it is a vision of the increasing meaninglessness of human activity and pursuits, and of the extraordinary difficulty in finding a form of life in which he could live freed from the captivity of the prisons of his contemporary world. Much of the work that Nietzsche hopes to accomplish, and some of what he did, is aimed at the creation of precisely just such a new and transfigured world, where men would no longer be the prisoners of the old (of the "human-all-to-human"). This, at least, is how I read his last letter to Burckhardt: "In the end, I would rather be a Basel professor than God; but I have not ventured to carry my private egoism so far as to desist from creating the world on its account."[11] One might read this only as testimony to Nietzsche's onrushing madness, and indeed the universal identifications which Nietzsche makes here ("I am Prado, . . . I . . . [am] Lesseps . . . I am . . . Chambige . . . I am every name in history . . .") can be read as symptoms of schizophrenia. But this letter can also be read seriously, as Nietzsche's final realization that the inability to be oneself afflicts even him. The pervasiveness and danger of the possibility of being God is Nietzsche's great and true insight into our entire cultural and social condition. Even he did not finally break its attraction.

The divisions or chapters in my book respond to this understanding of Nietzsche's aim. As far as I have been able, they make manifest Nietzsche's enterprise: to show that that which had bound men and women together into Western society and culture has necessarily broken down; to further demonstrate why Nietzsche thinks it so difficult for men to reach an exit from the impasse into which he sees them headed; and finally, to indicate how he suggests that men possibly might find a new goal, and what the dangers involved in the discovery will be. My enterprise is necessarily manifold, as is Nietzsche's. My exploration of an area of his work at a time tries to keep these aims of Nietzsche in mind.

I have no intention, by and large, of dealing with Nietzsche's psychic disturbances. It is generally known that he went insane sometime around the end of 1888 and spent the last ten years of his life in madness. No matter how one understands the psychological processes, [12] Nietzsche moves to gradual isolation from the world around him because, in his understanding of it, he has less and less in common with that world. He finds that what he has to say cuts him off from the past; indeed he makes a necessary virtue of this for the success of his enterprise. In the chapter "Why I Am so Wise" in his autobiography he will go so far as to claim that he lives on "only in his mother," that is, that he has engendered himself and stands without normal parentage or genealogy in the world which he is attacking.

For Nietzsche, this break is necessary. Mankind is, and remains, pushed by an abysmal and abyss-making logic. "What I recount," he writes in the early part of 1888, "is the history of the next two centuries. I describe what is coming, what can no longer come differently: *the advent of nihilism*. This history can already be recounted: for the necessity itself is here at work. This future speaks already in a hundred signs, this destiny announces itself everywhere . . . . . For some time now our entire European culture moves itself as toward a catastrophe, with a tortured tension [*Tortur der Spannung*], which grows from decade to decade . . . . . For why is the arrival of nihilism *necessary*? Because our previous values themselves draw it in their wake; because nihilism is the logical result of thinking through our greatest values and ideals until the end — because we must experience nihilism first, to be able to uncover precisely what the worth of these values was . . . ."[13]

Nietzsche says here that all of past history (or all that counts) is inevitably making for nihilism, that the things we have valued the most are the main contributors to this process, and that we have no choice but to live through this, if there is ever to be anything else. One is tempted, on reading this, to assume that Nietzsche's psychic disturbances had, by this time, taken the upper hand and to dismiss such extravagant claims. Indeed, this passage from the *Nachlass* is not his only such world-historical posture. Nietzsche claims to be a "destiny," "dynamite," which "breaks the history of the world in two"; in a draft of a letter to his sister, he writes that "quite literally" he holds "the future of mankind in the palm of (his) hand" and that it was with him that "the question of millenniums had been decided."

Such claims are bewildering from the perspective of the present. Despite the experience of two world wars and the constant threat of a general conflagration, the notion that everything is necessarily dissolving into catastrophe may seem exaggerated. It is, perhaps, true that, as André Malraux points out, Nietzsche did understand that the twentieth century would be the time of ideological and universal wars ("for the domination of the earth"); is this, however, a reason for thinking that all of the "highest values" of the West are responsible for the disasters of this century? To me, if Nietzsche is to mean anything at all, claims such as this one must be taken seriously. I shall argue in what follows that the only understanding of Nietzsche which makes any sense is precisely one informed by his consciousness that everything dominant in Western culture — politics, religion, morality, and so on — has been of a piece and that no one part of it can pass away without the rest eventually following suit. Such events form one of the meanings of his famous aphoristic recognition of the "death of God." Nietzsche is not simply saying that "God is dead"; such, after all, was no news, since Hegel had announced it some seventy-five years before. Nietzsche is also claiming that "we killed Him," and that the news of the murder has not yet reached the consciousness of the general public, who continue to live on "in the shadows of the dead God." The consequences of this death, Nietzsche claims, are cosmic and catastrophic. "Who gave us the sponge to wipe away the whole horizon? What did we do when we unbound this earth from this sun? Where does it move now? Where do we move? Does not the night and only the night come constantly on? Shall we not light lanterns in the morning?"[14]

These images should not be dismissed as empty rhetoric. According to Nietzsche, after the death of God, we will not know how we stand toward anything that used to give us constancy and meaning. There are no natural limits any more (no "horizon"), regularity has disappeared (the earth is "loosed from the sun"). We cannot see any more, for night comes on and we are forced to rely on artifice for preserving our normal life patterns (to "light lanterns in the morning"). The crisis of the time, as signaled in the death of God, announces a time when men no longer know their way about with themselves, or with others. The history of the "next two centuries" will be the gradual discovery of this *fact*.

For Nietzsche, this comes about, I suggested before, because of a pattern inscribed in the Western way of doing things, which, when pushed to the limit, leads to nihilism. It is important here to be clear about exactly what Nietzsche is saying. He is not trying to say that in the past men thought they based their actions on God (or another authority), but that, in fact, they were "really" operating on the basis of something else. If this were all he were doing, such a revelation should make men more, rather than less, secure in their lives. Nietzsche rather is saying that, in the past, men based their lives on (for example) God, that this foundation is, for particular historical and logical reasons, no longer available, *and that there is nothing else*. For instance, in *The Dawn of Day*, Nietzsche writes that there are "two manners of denying morality." On the one hand, one might deny that the moral motives men advance to explain their actions actually lead to those actions. Morality, in this perspective, would merely be a form of self-deception, an illusion from which one might simply awaken. Such Voltairian criticism is not Nietzsche's. Nietzsche denies morality "as he would alchemy." This is not a denial that there have been alchemists, nor an assertion that alchemists were somehow lying to themselves; it recognizes that they were persuaded to their experiments by alchemical motives. It says, instead, that the *whole* operation was based on erroneous perspectives.

This makes precise the focus and nature of Nietzsche's attack. He does not deny that there is, for example, moral behavior, nor even that it has a definition on which men could agree. Rather, he asserts that it can only exist if certain other premises are held true, much in the way that alchemy can exist only if certain presuppositions are held to be true. The problem confronting modern times, then, is for

Nietzsche that the presuppositions, which made, for example, morality possible, no longer exist. The reasons for this have not been examined; they will form the focus for much of the investigations that follow here. There is also no assurance, as the parable of the death of God makes clear, that men immediately recognize that the life they live and the values they espouse are becoming, in an increasingly sharp way, incompatible. The "wars the like of which have never yet been seen on earth" which Nietzsche forsees in *Ecce Homo* [15] will be the results of this last self-discovery.

To criticize Nietzsche for being an "immoralist" is then to miss a very important point. By going "beyond good and evil" he means to deny not only morality, but also immorality. In fact, his focus turns away from behavior and concentrates on that which makes morality (for instance) "possible," or, in his language, "the soil" from which it springs. In the passage cited from *Dawn* above, he continues:

I deny also immorality: *not* that countless men feel themselves to be immoral, but rather that there be a ground in *truth* that one should feel this way. I do not deny that which is self-evident — presuming that I am no fool — that many acts, which are called immoral, are to be avoided and fought against, and that many which are called moral, are to be pursed and accomplished. I do mean: *the one, as the other, but on other grounds than before.* We must *change our thoughts around* [*umzulernen*], in order at last, and perhaps very far from now, to reach even more: in order to *learn to feel newly* [*umzufühlen*] . [16]

The clear indication is that our present grounds have led first to the death of God and now push us onward toward coming catastrophies.

I am suggesting here, in a preliminary fashion, that Nietzsche sees the source of the problems besetting Western civilization as incarnate in humans themselves, or, at least, in humans as they are now. This, I presume, is the source of his strictures against the "human-all-too-human," and the grounds for his call for something or someone who is not human-all-too-human, but rather "overman." Implicit here is the notion that to deal with the problems besetting the civilization (what these are, I shall investigate), men will require not the discoveries of answers nor of new ways of dealing with the problems, but rather the development of beings who simply do not live as human-all-too-human. If "slave morality" leads mankind down the path to nihilism, as Nietzsche claims it does, his answer will not seek for a manner of dealing with the path, but rather try to eliminate the path. Some other journey must be undertaken.

This portion of Nietzsche is the dimly understood basis for the oft encountered contention that Nietzsche is a "romantic." I understand "romantic" to describe a person who believes that somewhere under the shellac of modern civilization lies a natural man, who requires only liberation to come into full play in the world. A variation on the "Nietzsche as romantic" thesis is the notion that he wants to somehow "return" to the Greek heroes, and that they are the models who provide examples for contemporary man. Both contentions are almost always wrong. As we shall see on several occasions, Nietzsche claims that return is impossible. Rather he wishes to (selectively) break the hold of the past over the present. To use psychological language, he sees our past as the source of the neuroses and psychoses besetting the present, much as Freud saw the past of a person as the source of ongoing patterns of behavior that underlay adult neuroses, and, in *Civilization and Its Discontents*, attempted a similar diagnosis of the entire culture. For Nietzsche, the problem will then be to change the person or society in such a manner that the basis of the neurosis is eliminated.[17]

What this means for Nietzsche and how it is to be achieved is the subject of this book; it is a continuing theme in Nietzsche. In a passage in the early *On the Use and Disadvantage of History for Life*, to which I shall return several times, he writes: "Men are the resultant of previous generations, also . . . of the errors, passions and crimes; it is impossible to shake off this chain." There is, he continues, no escape from our criminal ancestry; it constantly afflicts us, the more we continue to learn about it. To be rid of it we will have to "plant a new way of life, a new instinct, a second nature that withers the first." This will be "an attempt to gain a past a posteriori from which we might spring, as against that from which we do spring. . . . [To those who succeed] there is the consolation of knowing that this first nature was also once a second nature and that each conquering second nature became once the first."[18]

We are, for Nietzsche, chained to our past so strongly that the tie cannot simply be broken. Nietzsche does not advocate a blithe *écrasez l'infâme de l'autorité*. Simply to *deny* the past would not mitigate the fact that it will live on in those very ones who deny it. Nietzsche wants rather to "plant a new way of life" (*Gewohnung*) which will "wither" the first. This forms the basis for the "new problem" he sees dawning in a hardly yet recognizable manner over the human race. Only those who "have grasped that until now we have only embodied our errors" can begin to see this new task and "to embody knowledge and make it instinctive." [19]

It is important not to mistake the direction of these considerations. Nietzsche is not asserting that the whole range of questions that one might associate with traditional Western philosophy and especially metaphysics are useless or inappropriate questions. Such an attitude might be closer to that taken by the logical positivists in the early part of the twentieth century, who in their passion for accurate knowledge, rejected as simply muddleheaded many of the enterprises of traditional philosophy. Nietzsche's stance is quite other. For him, because traditional philosophy *did* more or less accurately describe people's lives, it is to be rejected, along with those lives. Human moral reasoning *did* speak of human moral concerns. It is the moral concerns themselves and the lives which give rise to them that Nietzsche is concerned to attack. He sees them as a problem in the manner in which one might see alchemy as a problem: the extirpation will be of a kind as to simply eliminate the option of being an alchemist. Once again, for Nietzsche the source of human discontents goes so deep as to be bound up in the very stuff of what it is to be human-all-too-human. Extirpation, in fact, a new "soil," is needed.

The process is not, and will not be easy. The logic by which the past lives on to always inform the present is the logic of *genealogy*. I shall have opportunity to go into this central Nietzschean concept at length. It suffices to note here that by this logic there is no automatic transformation of one stage into another. Marx, writing around the same time, had diagnosed many of the same crises in bourgeois civilization as Nietzsche. He, too, thought that a final transformation was needed, such that men and society could come to operate on the basis of a quite different logic. In Marx's term, men were to pass from "prehistory," where they were controlled and shaped by a harmful class struggle, into "history," where the dynamic of class warfare would no longer exist. The men of Marx's *German Ideology* who can hunt in the morning, fish in the afternoon, and criticize after dinner, without "ever thereby becoming a hunter, a fisherman, or a critical critic," are men undriven by logics external to themselves. They do not become what society would have them be, for their society does not so drive them. Marx had thought that this happy situation might be arrived at as the culmination of the forces of history. In Nietzsche, however, history provides no such helping hand. The same genealogical kernel continues to inform the whole development of the West, from Socrates to the present, and even, he indicates, for some centuries to come. Hence, it is not because we have arrived at a crisis point that a transfiguration will occur. In Marx, there is a point in history when all things become new. In Nietzsche, this change is not ordained in the process of our development;[20] thus, if it is to occur at all, it will have to be *made* from whole cloth.

The immediate question is, of course, Who will make it? The obvious answer is that it will be those men and women who have managed to eliminate even the roots of "slave morality" from themselves. To engender such beings is, I believe, what Nietzsche intended by the doctrine of eternal return. I can do no more here than indicate this; the exploration of this doctrine in Nietzsche is the subject of the whole book. What is certain is that Nietzsche intended his teaching and philosophy to reshape and consciously remold the very stuff of humanity.

What might this mean? I read Nietzsche's intention to refer to the following problem. He sees the period of Western civilization extending roughly from Socrates until the present as beset with an impossible dilemma. We are, in Nietzsche's diagnosis, beholden to a double conviction: we should continue to look for answers to the discontents of our civilization, yet we must despair of finding them. Kant had noted this in the Preface to the first edition of the *Critique of Pure Reason*, one hundred years before Nietzsche. He wrote there, in a famous passage, to which we shall return in a number of contexts, that "Human reason has this peculiar fate, that in one species of its knowledge it is burdened by questions which, as prescribed by the very nature of reason itself, it is not able to ignore, but which, as transcending all its powers, it is also unable to answer."[22] Kant saw this dilemma limited to one species of human reason, and thought he found a solution. For Nietzsche, however, this "peculiar fate" is endemic to the whole of the human condition. This problem is then more than the "problem of metaphysics," and is, for Nietzsche, manifest in all aspects of human life. Everywhere, man is pushed by constantly trying to reach that which he increasingly knows to be impossible. This state, known to Nietzsche as "nihilism," expresses more and more a life of "hatred against the human, even more against the animal, still more against the material, this horror of the senses, of reason itself, the fear of happiness and beauty, this demand to get out of all appearance, change, becoming, death, wish, from demanding itself. . . ." [22] This goal is never reached, for the desire to reach it has made it unattainable, and, at the last, Nietzsche sees men preferring and having to "will the void, rather than be void of will." "The first question," writes Nietzsche, "is not at all whether or not we are happy with ourselves, but instead whether we are happy with anything at all." [23]

The problem, then, is for men to shed this "will to the void." To achieve this is a complicated and multifarious task. Nietzsche says man must first "evaluate that portion of existence which has until now alone been valued": he must, that is, formulate an accurate analysis of precisely what the form of existence is that the West has lived under. Then he must "grasp from what this valuation springs," discover why the West has the values that it does, whether they are "natural," or if they spring from a series of events which might or might not be. He must "stop short and grasp exactly what . . . in fact says Yes (for one, the instinct to suffer; for another, the instinct of the herd; and, for a third, the instinct of the majority in contradiction to the exceptions . . .)." Once these genealogical stables are set in order, he will then be able to see "how little a dionysian dimension of value for existence is obliged to it." [24] "Dionysian" is Nietzsche's word for what he is trying to bring about. I shall investigate its precise meaning; more important here is his insistence that a form of life is possible which shares little or no common characteristics with that which afflicts men at present.

What Nietzsche gives us is not, in my reading, a new set of philosophical answers to particular problems; it is, instead, more a form of human archeology, an analysis of the particular "soil" from which these problems have sprung. The philosophical problems men have met and set for themselves in the past two and one-half thousand years are, in Nietzsche's analysis, related to the sorts of beings these men were. This is not true only of those who call themselves philosophers; after all, the problems are not limited to those who thought about them, but are endemic to the condition of human-all-too-human. Nietzsche does not propose a new philosophical answer to these problems; indeed, such an attempt would be foolhardy. The problem lies in the kinds of beings who saw these sorts of problems as necessary. The proper response is not an answer, but the development of a form of life in which these matters are no longer problems. Nietzsche continues on in the passage cited above: "I hit upon the extent to which another stronger type of man would necessarily have to conceive of the elevation and enhancement of men as going in another direction: higher beings, as beyond good and evil, as beyond those values that cannot disown their origin in the sphere of suffering, the herd, and the majority. . . ."

What does it mean to make all of human history a problem? At the very least, it would seem to be to see human history as the result of certain choices and acceptances which need not be. It is, after all, only in the sphere of necessity that a given question cannot become problematic. If, for instance, there is such a thing as a more or less fixed "human nature," then, once a given practice has been shown to be grounded firmly in that human nature, that is all that can be said about it. To make something a problem means to show that there is no necessity that it be or not be, and to produce questions that have to be taken seriously. It is perhaps an indication of the force and originality of Nietzsche's enterprise that, while we do not always immediately understand his questions, nor see perfectly clearly what he is calling into question, we nonetheless often continue to walk within his town.

If one allows oneself this seduction, the first knowledge gained will be knowledge of self; Nietzsche forces upon his readers questions about beliefs that one may have thought secure. But, and it is this that keeps him from being merely *épatant pour la bourgeoisie*, there is never an indication in Nietzsche that self-knowledge is a legitimate stopping point. One may find that the self one comes to know is radically flawed and must then be changed. The problem arises: If the self as we have known it is flawed, then so also must be all that it knew and did, even what it called truth. If, however, all "horizons are erased," then one, literally, does not know one's way about, and what will count as a question, or an answer, or indeed as truth itself, is not clear. Not knowing one's way about was for Wittgenstein the paradigm of a philosophical problem; it arose in connection with finding oneself in unfamiliar and extraordinary circumstances. Nietzsche, as I trace his enterprise, seeks to show us that a world we have thought familiar has, in fact, become strange, even though we have yet to fully acknowledge this. Then, having shown us that we have and will become strangers to ourselves, he would show us a world where we might, once again, and for the first time, come to be ourselves. What follows here is an attempt to retrace the complexity of the journey he sketches.

Chapter II

THE NECESSITY AND POSSIBILITY OF TRUTH

It might be imagined that some propositions having the form of empirical propositions were hardened and functioned as channels for such empirical propositions as were not hardened but fluid; and that this relationship altered with time, in that fluid propositions hardened and hard ones became fluid.

— Ludwig Wittgenstein, *On Certainty*, par. 96

The First World War marked a turning point in the confidence Westerners were able to express in the world around them. This conflict revealed to an almost incredulous Europe that the course of political and social events had acquired a logic and power all its own, neither subject to the restraints imposed by a preexisting moral community among nations and their leaders, nor attributable, as conceivably had been the case with the French Revolution, to the actions of one deviant nation. A century that had started with the anticipation of the possibility of men at last possessing the capacity and knowledge to control and shape their own destinies ended with the insane frightfulness of Verdun and the Machiavellian idealism of Versailles, and for the first time, men in all walks of life faced the possibility of knowing that existence did not present itself meaningfully to them. Not only was the violence and oppression of the social, political, and moral world obvious — which is after all nothing new — but men and women began to believe that such a state of affairs could not be judged in terms of any external standard. "Man had died," wrote Ezra Pound, "for an old bitch gone in the teeth, for a botched civilization," and the world emerged from the war with all faith in old gods gone and no sense that the future mattered. This was a time "after Utopia,"[1] when the promise of actualizing an ideal society faded in the long aftermath of the French Revolution. By 1920 — Nietzsche foresaw it as much as fifty years earlier — the failure of nerve of bourgeois society was becoming painfully destructive.

In 1919, in his great lecture "Politics as a Vocation," Max Weber defined politics as "the monopoly of the legitimate means of violence inside a given territory." The definition may appear cynical, but Weber at least accurately reflected some of the changes that had gone on in Europe over the previous century. Twenty years prior, Friedrich Nietzsche also called the politics of his time "organized violence."[2] This definition, too, portrays the transformations which, having brewed throughout Europe during the previous centuries, had finally erupted into their first major political form with the First World War.

For Nietzsche, such definitions mark not so much a permanent "fact" as a process of historical change which has roots in times far removed even from the turn of the eighteenth century. He sees them as the increasingly immanent culmination of the whole of what we call "Western Civilization": a crisis of truly unprecedented world-historical proportions. In Chapters III through VII, I examine Nietzsche's account and analysis of this development. I wish now only to investigate in a preliminary fashion the situation sketched above.

That men no longer feel the world about them to be meaningful marks some sort of change, but it is not clear of what sort. I am interested here in tracing Nietzsche's analysis of the alterations in the relation of men to themselves, to others, and to the world around them such that they now apparently inevitably come to such hopelessness. The matter is complicated: after all, one cannot simply decide that there is no sense to the universe. Anyone who seriously holds such a position, individually or in a group so characterized, must be convinced of it. To move from a state of belief that the actual world might be understood in terms of some potentially universal categories to a position that sees no sense or meaning anywhere, presupposes that something has happened.

Turgenev, and others after him, call this change nihilism. This is not the methodological doubt of Descartes, nor the relaxed and universal skepticism of Hume; nihilism does not only describe the questioning of old truths and values. Such questioning, after all, goes on constantly in one form or another. It is rather a consciousness that there is no meaning or truth to be found *at all*. As Nietzsche notes in the winter of 1888: "The feeling of *valuelessness* was reached when one realized that the basic character of existence could not be understood with either the notion of *purpose*, or that of *unity*, or that of *truth*. With such interpretations, nothing is reached or attained: the encompassing unity of events is missing in the multiplicity of occurrences: the character of existence [*Dasein*] is not 'true,' is *false* . . . , one has absolutely no more ground to convince oneself of a true world."[3] In this definition, there is the sensibility that nihilism is a historical development, not a philosophical (or anti-philosophical) position accessible at any period. "Before," remarks Kirsanov in *Fathers and Sons*, "there were Hegelians, now there are only nihilists."

That Nietzsche sees the characteristic of the modern age as nihilism is hardly open to question.[4] It implies however that consciousness and public knowledge of "truth" are no longer held to be possible. If this is in fact the state in which men find themselves, then they have changed from a previous sensibility in which they believed not only that truth might be arrived at, but that in fact some moral and physical facts *were true*. One could expect that two or more people, in fact that most people, might arrive at agreement as to what categories applied to particular data, and as to how they applied. To assert then, as Nietzsche does, that "the character of existence is . . . *false*" is to note the consciousness of a change from a form of life which understood events and experiences as epiphenom-enally rooted in a larger and unquestioned context, to one which saw them without any unifying common ground. For Hegel, this unifying common ground had been World History; for Kant, it was the structures of pure reason; for Emerson and the transcendentalists, the reality of human emotions. Earlier there had been natural law.

Even the aesthetic despair of Diderot in *Rameau's Nephew* reflected, as Hegel noted acutely, a form of raising oneself above a "torn and shattered condition."[5] For Hegel, Kant, and the others, the world makes available to men a structure independent of human subjectivity and thus potentially permits "objective" agreement. Nihilism denies there is any such overarching or underlying scheme: events simply *are*, and, at least for those who are "human-all-too-human," nothing can be called more true or meaningful than anything else.

In the beginning of *Beyond Good and Evil* Nietzsche recapitulates what he believes to be his new and ultimate question about "truth." "We finally came to a complete stop before a still more basic question. . . . The problem of the value of truth came before us — or was it we who came before the problem;"[6] It is difficult to deal with this query in a direct fashion. It presupposes an understanding of a particular historical rendezvous of men and world history which at first glance rings false. What *is* the value of truth? One is tempted to simply say that this is not a question one can ask.

Here, and in other circumstances when Nietzsche seems not to be making sense, we must resist the temptation to dismiss his questions. Instead, we should ask why it is that this question rings false to us. After all, it appears to be of the same superficial form as queries we have no difficulty understanding, such as, What is the value of being cured of an illness? In such cases, the answer will come in making reference to some other value, itself accepted and of obvious importance, for instance, to have control over one's life, or, to remain alive, or, health as preferable to illness. The particular reason doesn't matter: the fact that we can easily make such answers is of importance here. With the "problem of truth," however, matters seem to change. We are tempted to refer it to itself and say that "truth is what one seeks, because one seeks what is true." Nietzsche's question implies that what we actually mean by true is in some fashion analogous to what we mean by (in the example above) being cured. It implies that there must be some preconditions which have been generally accepted before something can be called "true."

Thus, when nihilists despaired of truth, they were in fact despairing of the commonly acceptable understandings that permitted the value of truth. In order to approach the question of the value of truth we must first understand how Nietzsche thinks it is *possible* for something to be true. What actually has *occurred* when we come to the conclusion that something is in fact the case? What spiritual and intellectual acts have we performed? Are there conceivable conditions under which we no longer could perform such acts? For what reasons? What would be the consequences of not being able to do so?

Preconditions for Truth: Preliminaries

The embarrassment that one feels with the question of the "value of truth" is due to a "prejudgment and prejudice [which] give away the metaphysicians of all ages."[7] Men *need* to feel that some values are not subject to question and are beyond it. In a note from the spring of 1888 Nietzsche writes: "All kinds of imperatives have been employed to make moral values appear permanent: they have been commanded for the longest time: — they *seem* instinctive, like inner commands. They impress [*drücken*] themselves as *conditions for the existence of society*, such that moral values are felt *to be beyond discussion.* . . . Every means is employed to paralyze reflection and criticism in this field."[8]

Here, as well as in the section on "The Prejudices of Philosophers" in *Beyond Good and Evil*, there is an implied distinction between two types of statements having to do with morality and truth. While the distinction I am about to draw is not specifically made by Nietzsche, it is certainly latent in his proposition that "moral values are felt to be beyond discussion." I would argue that there is in Nietzsche an important distinction between that which is un-question*ed* and that which is unquestion*able*.[9] If a truth-statement is unquestion*able*, men (some men, for some time) refrain from moral compulsion. One simply refuses to talk about it and admit it into consciousness.

Such conclusions are fragile. For instance, when Wagner in *Lohengrin* proposes a situation in which the salvation of the kingdom of Brabant depends on the heroine refraining from asking the unknown knight his name — *Das sollst du mich nicht fragen* — the resultant moral structure is quickly and necessarily destroyed by the fatal question. Nietzsche, of course, refuses to let Wagner even suggest such moral adolescence. He knows full well that such warnings rarely work with the rebellious children against whom they are habitually directed, let alone with a society.

Unquestion*able* considerations may then emerge into conscious-ness at any time. Indeed a considerable part of moral education has been devoted to elevating barriers against such questions. The guilt that stands ready to enforce the proposition "You mustn't *say* that" is only quantitatively different from the monopoly of the means of violence which Weber and Nietzsche saw as supporting the modern state. Against *such* restraints Nietzsche wishes to encourage as much doubt as possible. "We moderns are all opponents of Descartes and struggle against his *easy* doubt. One must doubt better than Des-cartes." [10] Under any question left unasked, Nietzsche identifies a conscious or unconscious moral prejudice. There is a point, he notes in *Beyond Good and Evil*, when the philosopher's conviction finally appears on stage: *adventavit asinus*. If Descartes doubted too easily, something kept him from continuing his process. He was presuppos-ing something, and that kept his doubt from being as "good" as it might have been.

Such presuppositions or convictions are precisely the un-questioned statements. They are matters about which one literally has no questions to ask; as I indicated before, the "value of truth" has been felt in Western moral science to be such a matter. [11] Such questions must remain unexamined and with no form of discourse appropriate to them; any query about them will automatically trans-form them into the first category of statements. To ask a question of something presupposes a stance which, at least for the duration of the question, is "outside" that which is being questioned. It implies, in other words, that one is conscious of that which one is question-ing. Hence that which is questioned is no longer a "presupposition" and is certainly not "beyond discussion."

To be beyond discussion designates then for Nietzsche that system of unconditioned predicates which make a thought or form of life possible. Such predicates function, in Wittgenstein's words, as "hard-ened channels" which make other propositions possible. Since they are taken for granted, they must appear as real; we must take them as real, since we cannot conceive of questioning them. For instance, as Collingwood observes, Anselm's argument for the existence of God proves "not that, because our idea of the existence of God is an idea of that greater than which nothing can be thought, therefore God exists, but that because our idea of God is an idea of that greater than which nothing can be thought, we stand committed to belief in

God's existence." [12] There was a time when the evidence available was such that belief in God could be deduced from other unquestion*ed* statements. Belief in God could therefore be made an "unquestion*able*" proposition. Or again, if it is perfectly obvious that the earth is the center of the universe, one could make certain calculations designed to render compatible that unquestioned presupposition and the observed movements of the planets. Ptolemy did it very well, better in fact than Copernicus in his more "accurate" system. [13]

It should be immediately apparent from these examples and Nietzsche's discussion that nothing remains *necessarily* unquestioned or even beyond the effect of being questioned. There are, for Nietzsche, no necessary and permanent characteristics of a so-called human condition. His view of the world permits the possibility of humans "agreeing" on what is true at any given historical period. However by making the link between unquestioned statements and moral statements essentially psychological (or, as Nietzsche says in *Beyond Good and Evil*, "psycho-physical"), the investigation and disclosure of the basic presuppositions current at any particular time will only be impeded by the people involved having unconscious reasons which ensure the sanctity of the presuppositions. Academic philosophy is thus for Nietzsche a "personal confession of its originator and a kind of involuntary and unperceived memoir." [14] In fact, one can move easily from here to the notion that the practical moral systems of a culture or country are also such confessions, that is, are the manifestations of some set of unquestioned presuppositions. These presuppositions form what I have been calling, following Wittgenstein, a "form of life."

If this is admitted, one then must see that the relation between unquestioned and unquestionable presuppositions changes over time. It is not quite correct to refer to this relationship as "historical." Nietzsche argues as early as *The Use and Disadvantage of History for Life* that life itself requires that some presuppositions be "unquestioned": "This is a universal law: a living thing can be healthy and strong and productive only inside a horizon. If it is unable to draw a horizon around itself, and too selfish to loose its view in another's, it will come to an untimely end." [15] Nietzsche continues on to indicate that human life characteristically reposes on a forgotten past. If one cannot forget, such that all is eternally present, then action and life itself become impossible, for all choices appear equally invalid. I shall return to this in greater detail below, but the "unhistorical," as Nietzsche refers to that which is forgotten, makes human life itself possible. When, later in the essay, he refers to the "historical sickness" which afflicts modern men, his point is the same as the one developed above about nihilism. Nihilism is the historical sickness with which men are incapable of forgetting enough so that a life-giving horizon may be drawn around them. Wittgenstein noted this whole relationship very well: "The mythology may shift back into a state of flux, the river bed of thoughts may shift. But I distinguish between the movement of the waters on the river bed, and the shift of the bed itself, though there is not a sharp division of one from the other."[16] To which one must add that if one could no longer distinguish the "waters" and the "bed," then thought itself would lack a foundation. Such is Nietzsche's concern, even if it was not Wittgenstein's.

The Unmasking Imperative

In *Ecce Homo*, Nietzsche self-consciously proclaims himself a "turning point in history." The change he would make is world-shattering, on the level of that Socrates or Christ made. No matter how one takes such an announcement in terms of Nietzsche as a person, it is also important in terms of implications for his conception of history. Nietzsche sees himself as the first to be able, or the first to dare, to ask the questions that removed certain propositions from the realm of the unquestioned. As I noted in the first chapter, Nietzsche's contribution does not consist of having solved problems in a new manner, but rather of having come up with new questions. It is now apparent that he conceives of these questions as primarily destructive in character. They do not open up new vistas for us to explore, but rather force *into* the world of consciousness those matters that previously had been, so to speak, inaccessible. He is "dynamite" since he blows up that which had appeared to be stable and permanent. By forcing men to give an account of themselves, he will show them that their lives rest not only on illusions, but on dangerous illusions.

Moral propositions can thus move into a realm where their only defense is no longer their inaccessibility, but only that protection afforded by the possibility of being unquestion*able*. To remain unquestion*able*, a proposition must be protected by force if necessary. By finding questions for the previously pre-supposed, Nietzsche must encourage "political" defenses of morality. He makes it increasingly difficult to defend a particular morality (e.g., the values of "civilized Europe") by anything other than the potentially violent self-conscious enforcement of a choice. The change might be phrased like this. At one time, one simply assumed the existence of God; it was part of life. As God was thrown into the arena of discourse (Nietzsche sees Schopenhauer as the first "uncompromising atheist"), it became increasingly necessary to persuade, educate, force, threaten with guilt, seduce, both others and oneself, that there be a God. However, once the questions exist, they will be asked. In a manner analogous to psychiatry, men like Nietzsche will "strive for the forbidden,"[17] to bring to light that which had previously been hidden. Nietzsche is then a "destiny" in his own eyes since he thinks he is forcing the European world into an attempted defense of its basic moral presuppositions, a defense all the more painful and dangerous in that it has no chance of success. By unmasking all those presuppositions that make a certain form of life coherent and possible, he will force a defense that will necessarily be explicitly moral and political; Nietzsche is too Mephistophelian not to realize that eventually all these defenses will, in their turn, prove to be hollow and indefensible idols.[18]

Nietzsche also claims that he is the first to have *dared* such questions, that he is a fusion of Tiresias and Oedipus. The revelation of that from which European man is sprung will be dangerous. Nietzsche accepts this as true, and proceeds to force himself to ask the questions. For Nietzsche, neither the diplomacy of Tiresias, nor the blindness of Oedipus can be maintained: that the combination is tragic may simply be the problem.[19]

To pursue one's origins is also to pursue one's ancestry. Thus the name Nietzsche gives to his unmasking enterprise is *genealogy*. It is in fact a search for parents, for an understanding of the soil from which one springs, and in which one still lives. This is not voyeurism of a *pudenda origo*,[20] but rather the investigation of the logic of a particular line of development of any coherent structure — one might say of a family. For instance, the conceptualization of light rays as particles will direct and focus research in certain directions; all of these directions will be constantly characterized by this presupposition or conceptualization. Similarly, Nietzsche is interested in investigating how and why, for example, the belief in God shapes the moral, political, and logical life of a culture. "Slave morality" should not therefore be construed as a form of society dominated by "slaves"; rather it is a structure that, if accepted, serves as the basis for the corresponding systems of society and culture. What Nietzsche has in mind and what he hopes to reveal through the genealogical method is something quite analogous to what Marx thought he had discovered when he proclaimed "all history to be the history of class struggle." Neither Marx, nor Nietzsche, is saying that history is "determined" by the class struggle, or by slave morality. They are saying that it is *characterized* by it. [21] Such a structure continues to inform those systems built on it. Thus, when one has understood what Nietzsche means by slave morality, one has not understood what a given society is like, any more than when one has comprehended the nature of the capitalist mode of production one has understood anything about France. To anticipate a bit, the concern with genealogy is a concern to discover those structures that continually inform a form of life. For instance, Nietzsche is fascinated by Greece, not because of a yearning for a long-lost perfect society, but rather because Greece lies in thought, politics, art, and morality at the origin or genesis of much of contemporary European society.

The Concept of Genealogy

Genealogy is the centerpiece of Nietzsche's destructive enterprise: the first task is to lay bare and unmask. In *Schopenhauer as Educator*, he advocates "denying and destroying [which is] precisely a result of a mighty longing for healing and salvation. . . . All existence [*Dasein*] that can be denied deserves to be denied; and to be truthful means to believe in an existence that in no ways could be denied. . . ." [22] "All existence that can be denied deserves to be denied" — the aim here, as before, is to uncover with the full knowledge that the light of consciousness will ultimately destroy. Unless we eliminate our parents, so to speak, we will always be of the same family. Such a chthonian imperative is termed genealogy, and is thus radically opposed to a dialectical approach. In Chapter VIII, I shall investigate Nietzsche's judgment on the structures of the dialectical more fully. Suffice it to note here the key difference. In a dialectical understanding, the destruction of a particular form of life (e.g., Hegel's absolute freedom, Marx's feudalism) is in fact the end of a *stage*: it is accomplished by that which forms the germ of its replacement. Thesis and antithesis lead on to synthesis; self-consciousness and alienation lead toward the absolute. Thus the process that causes the destruction of a certain stage is the guarantor of the replacement. For such an understanding, destruction is only achieved by the concomitant creation of the new. Thus, bourgeois society grows out of, destroys, and replaces feudal society. Hegel's word, combining all of these, was *Aufhebung*.

In a genealogical understanding, there is almost no automatic logic to the evolution of a set of events, certainly no *Aufhebung*. [23] For Nietzsche, there is nothing in the evolution of bourgeois society which makes it necessary that such a society be at some point replaced by a qualitatively different system. Since, for Nietzsche, the structure of presuppositions which forms the basis of any culture has no external or natural validity, it cannot lead to a qualitatively different situation. Apparent change will therefore only be change in appearances; the foundations remain the same. A biological analogy — Nietzsche is to use them more and more, and not just as analogy — makes the point. No matter how hard he tries, Nietzsche remains the son of his parents. Despite all efforts to the contrary — he details them in *Ecce Homo* — he is forced to deal with his genealogy and cannot become Wagner, Schopenhauer, or even, as he once somewhat pathetically insisted, a Polish nobleman. [24] Without pursuing Nietzsche's relations to his own past in any greater detail, it should be apparent that the past presents itself much more as a problem in the genealogical perspective than in the dialectical. For dialectics, what was living in feudalism becomes bourgeois capitalism. The rest, destined for the "ash heap of history," no longer affects us. For a genealogist, or a psychologist for that matter, we are never rid of the past merely by the process of getting older. Any such transfiguring change will have to be of a very different kind.

This recognition explains one of the key shifts in Nietzsche's approach to problems. Early in his life he had had the hope that some sort of educational regeneration would be possible for Germany and Europe. [25] This is the period of *Schopenhauer as Educator*, the series of public lectures *On the Future of Our Educational Institutions*, the attack on the philistine educational system that had spawned and approved David Strauss. That he had had such a hope as a teacher is interesting about him as a person; that he came to perceive his hope as impossible and left the University is significant. What Nietzsche comes to see in the course of his investigations is that illness he diagnosed — the development and triumph of nihilism in Western culture — goes far beyond a temporary aberration. It will not be possible to simply *tell* people what is wrong, for the very *manner in which they understand* the world will not permit them to understand the problems at hand. The problem thus lies deeper than simply bad conclusions in the realm of a faulty and dangerous understanding.

In his understanding of the past, Nietzsche will then have to go far beyond recounting the history of the historical logic or the evolution of, for example, morality or consciousness. No matter how good or complete the account of what has happened, unless a change in the manner of understanding is provoked, the account will remain merely a museum. Hegel had in fact already performed this task admirably. [26] There are perhaps no more perfect exhibitions of the monuments of thought than the *Philosophy of History*, the *History of Philosophy* and the *Phenomenology of Mind*.

In the second of the *Untimely Considerations*, Nietzsche accuses Hegel of spreading the "historical sickness which afflicts Western man." This essay, *The Use and Disadvantage of History for Life*, is the beginning of Nietzsche's explicit analysis of the relation of the past to the present. For him, the process of history is, if nothing else, at least the manner by which our past affects our present. This relation, identified by Nietzsche later in his life as the *Grundproblem*, [27] is unveiled through genealogy and in the pursuit of developing questions that bring to light the particular past resonating in our particular present. In a normal Hegelian historical analysis, the present must appear as inevitable as the past; the future likewise, after it happens. In such a perspective, men will be tempted to conclude, in the words of Nietzsche's later accusation against Hegel, that "everything that passes away deserves to pass away." Such a quietistic attitude toward history and one's past is considered by Nietzsche to be an implicit gospel of defeat, despair, or pious faith that men must, in any case, adapt themselves to history.[28] Nietzsche wants, rather, to develop through genealogy an analysis of historical and social configurations analogous to that by which psychoanalysis helps men see their own past, or in which theology sought to reveal the original nature of humans. This method "serves life"; it does not merely justify what is in terms of what was.

In *The Use and Disadvantage of History for Life*, Nietzsche identifies three manners in which history can be beneficial or noxious to life. The genealogical method is to a great degree a combination of all three. It is first of all "monumental" history. This type seeks to provide men with models of grandeur through a depiction of great men, events, and periods of the past. To some degree Nietzsche's portraits of Greek antiquity or Napoleon are cases in point. Such a history is most different from Hegel's in that it is built from the lives of men: individuals are preeminent. Being thus built on specifics rather than on process, it is most useful for educational purposes, because it deals with exemplary cases rather than with ordinary ones. As would be expected from the discussion of education above, Nietzsche uses this approach more in the early part of his career than in the later, though the Greeks persist throughout as a monumental example.

Secondly, history may be "antiquarian" in that it seeks to recreate and preserve some of the elements that made some earlier cultures so healthy. Here again, the function is to a considerable degree educational. Antiquarian history is probably the result of the transformation of monumental history due to a desire to protect the society from idle tale-tellers and charlatans. To keep men from making mistakes, for instance of confusing Gyges and Orpheus, the truly extraordinary had to become part of a tradition that could be used to inculcate the proper forms of reverence. Nietzsche passes over antiquarian history rapidly, probably because he feels that an age already so imbued with the historical sense has no need of more appreciation of historical pasts.

Lastly, and most importantly in our times, such history can be "critical." Nietzsche spends most of the essay discussing this method. Whereas the first two approaches had served to preserve various elements from the past, this one raises the past as a problem. "Man must have, and from time to time use, the strength to break up and dissolve a past, in order to be able to live: he does this by bringing it before the bar of judgment, interrogating it remorselessly, and finally condemning it. Every past, however, is worthy of being condemned, for human affairs are always such that it is in them that human strengths and weaknesses become powerful." [29]

The aim of this third enterprise is not the reduction of a moral system to its turpid source, but rather the investigation of the particular form of life from which the system springs. A moral system then constitutes for Nietzsche an organized attempt to legitimize a particular structure of behavior. It is analogous to what we might call ideology today, a defense of the ultimate validity of a temporary and restricted system of action. In uncovering a moral system Nietzsche seeks to reveal what precisely is being justified. His enterprise is much like an attempt to understand the composition of the soil from which a plant grew by means of a minute dissection of the plant. "Before," says Nietzsche, "one said of every morality: 'By their fruits shall you know them.' I say of each: 'It is a fruit, by which I recognize the ground from which it grew.' " "Our ideas, our values," he writes in the preface to On the Genealogy of Morals, "our yeas and nays, our ifs and buts grow out of us with the necessity with which a tree bears fruit — related and each with an affinity to each, and evidence of one will, one health, one soil, one sun." [30]

The attempt to uncover the genealogical "kernel" of a country or a form of life is not new with Nietzsche, nor did it end with him. It is already in embryo in Montesquieu's investigations into the "spirit" of the laws, and in Rousseau's discourses on the "nature" of things rather than on historical facts "which could be or not be." It is a very close cousin to the principe that Tocqueville sought to discover in America in order to educate a France he saw as about to undergo her version of historical democratization. After Nietzsche, the method is more closely identified with the use of "ideal types" that Max Weber developed from immersion in historical data to allow him to render critical and scientific judgment about the phenomena of his time.

All of these approaches share certain problems. Inevitably the formulation of a coherent picture of the principe of Greek experience, or indeed of modern experience, will imply a principle of selection. Nietzsche will leave out much in his portrayal of Greece, seeking, as William Arrowsmith notes of him, "a unified field theory" by which to understand and judge the chaos of present-day

Europe. [31] A unified field theory, it should be noted, is a set of equations that can be expanded through laws of transformations to generate any conceivable state of affairs. When Nietzsche rhetorically queries "How can something develop out of its opposite?" and proceeds to show that the play of opposites is merely surface, he is doing no less than does Lévi-Strauss some years later: the demonstration of the fundamental unity of phenomena sprung from "one soil, one sun."

In *The Birth of Tragedy from the Spirit of Music*, Nietzsche attempts precisely such a reconstruction of the origins of Greek tragedy. The model he develops was to show European culture how far it had fallen from the heights of Attic Greece, which would thus place the potential effects of Wagner's new *Gesamtkunstwerk*, the new "truly international culture of the modern Aeschylus," in the best possible relief. A considerable portion of the impetus behind the writing of *The Birth of Tragedy* stems from the quarrels and hopes that Nietzsche had for his own world. The picture he elaborates of Greece must bring these out while remaining true to what Greece was and is for us. Consideration of the controversy surrounding the publication of Nietzsche's first major work can thus serve as a defense and illustration of the uses of genealogy.

As a first substantial public contribution in what was supposed to be classical philology, the work of the young Nietzsche produced an uproar. This is the man about whom Ritschl, the foremost philologist of the preceding generation, had publicly declared "he will be able to do anything he wants to"; at the unheard-of age of twenty-five Nietzsche had been appointed to the Basel chair of classical philology; that such a rising light in the German academic world would produce such a strange and unorthodox work engendered first shock and then a furious counterattack. With a vitriolic learned pamphlet, *Zukunftsphilologie*? ("Philology of the Future?"), another rising young philologist, Ulrich von Wilamowitz-Möllendorf, led the attack on the reputation of the young Nietzsche. By and large, in the eyes of Nietzsche's academic contemporaries, the effort succeeded. The bulk of Wilamowitz's accusation was that Nietzsche's method of argument rested on little or no evidence whatsoever, and was in fact demonstrably false at certain points. To Nietzsche's arguments for the antiquity of Homer, Wilamowitz countered with the best philological evidence of the day; in rebuttal of the main claim that the

apparent serenity of Greek art masks a dark underworld, Wilamowitz called upon the authority of Winckelmann. That the Greece of
"sweetness and light" is precisely that which Nietzsche is contesting,
mattered little in face of the overwhelming deference then paid to
Winckelmann. [32]

Nietzsche, his vision of Greece, and his hopes for German philology were left defeated. Despite the best efforts of his friends to reply
to the attack, he was, as he wrote Rohde, "scientifically dead." [33]
Nietzsche's analysis, however, was much closer to the picture of
Greece that has come to be accepted in modern times. Since the
work of E. R. Dodds in *The Greeks and the Irrational*, we are forced
to admit that the Goethe-Winckelmann vision of the Greece of
"sweetness and light" is basically misleading and ultimately untenable. This is rightly considered to be very small help in support of
Nietzsche. Even if we agree with Arrowsmith, as I think we must,
that "time and recent scholarship have ... vindicated not Wilamowitz, but Nietzsche, the man who 'arrogantly' dared defy the schol-
arly consensus of the time for the simple reason that it did not make
literary or cultural sense to him," [34] the problem of the method is
not resolved. How was it that Nietzsche came by an accurate understanding of the nature of Greek culture?

To assert, as one is tempted to, whether friendly or hostile to
Nietzsche, that his results were flashes of poetic insight, or brilliant
intuition, misses, I think, the real thrust and importance of his
position. The fundamental intention of Nietzsche's work must be to
recover and make manifest these underlying presuppositions which
were the foundations of the coherence of Greek culture. It is apparent, for instance, that he does not intend a historical portrait of
Greece shortly after the Cleisthenian reforms. In another context,
speaking of Meyerbeer's opera, he will argue that "it is *now* a matter
of *indifference*" that the founders of opera were revolting against the
Church, and that "it is *enough* to have perceived" that they were in
fact engaged in sub rosa glorification of natural man. Again and again
he will refer to what he *"had* to emphasize," as if his vision of Greece
placed him under some sort of aesthetic compulsion. [35]

Such phrases reflect the picture that Nietzsche is trying to make
available. It rests on a particular understanding of history and historical questioning: the best way to approach the past is through "what
is most powerful in the present." This phrase, taken from the essay

on *The Use and Disadvantage of History for Life*, anticipates the "exceptionally significant and fascinating question" that Nietzsche sets up as a riddle in the 1886 Preface to *The Birth of Tragedy*. This question — "What is dionysian?" — will, in answer, provide the context for a whole set of more immediate questions, including finally those of the nature and limitations of science, the relation of science and morality and their influence on each other.

Without detailing the answer at this point — I leave such considerations to a later chapter — *The Birth of Tragedy* appears now as an investigation into the unquestioned premises of Greek culture, and, by a long extension, into the premises of our own culture. Nietzsche does not *deny* the Greece of Goethe and Winckelmann. He sees it as a scrim which will become transparent to those who can see the light behind. Wilamowitz would not, or did not; and, like so many others, he took the book to be attempting a portrait of the empirical reality that was Greece. However, without being opposed to or contradicting that reality, Nietzsche does not seek to reconstruct what "actually" went on. For instance, in his discussion of the revolution wrought by the Kantian and Schopenhauerian epistemologies, Nietzsche "ventures" a suggestion that they mark the inauguration of a "tragic culture." He is not saying that this happened, but that it *makes sense* to look at Kant and Schopenhauer in this manner. Indeed the whole of the *Birth* goes along these lines: elements of profound cultural importance force themselves on *our* perceptions; *we* perceive them more or less well behind the "veil of Maia," or behind "politics," behind all those terms that Nietzsche gathers together under the general rubric of apollonian. [36] We are then forced into an examination of the grounding of Greek culture, of the hitherto unquestioned underworld which, to fall into a Kantian idiom, "made Greece possible."

The procedure known as genealogy may then properly be seen as derivative of Kant. In the *Critique of Pure Reason*, Kant had sought to show the limits to which reason could attain and which in fact were reason, and had proceeded from there to demonstrate how the world had to be for "knowledge of nature to be possible." Nietzsche's procedure is much the same, with the initial difference that he is not investigating the physical world ("How is knowledge of nature possible?"), but rather a historical one ("How are the Greeks possible?"). Both of them, however, must rely on an answer that allows us to make sense of what is before our eyes. As Wittgenstein notes in the *Investigations*: "Our investigation is not directed toward phenomena, but, as one might say toward the 'possibilities of phenomena.' " [37] The concepts dionysian, apollonian, Socratism, and so forth are not attempts to describe what was going on in Greece, but what made what was going on possible: they allow men to *make* sense out of Greece.

The use of "genealogy" is thus an approach similar in some respects to those of Rousseau and Lévi-Strauss. Much as in *The Discourse on the Origins of Inequality* before him, and with structural anthropologists after him, Nietzsche is in pursuit of "a single structural scheme existing and operating in different temporal and spatial contexts." [38] There are important differences, though, and one should not exaggerate this link. Both Lévi-Strauss and Rousseau believe that inherent in the human experience are those structures of perception which, if they can be approached in an unmediated fashion, will permit the formulation of a universally valid understanding. Thus Lévi-Strauss accurately characterizes his approach as "Kantianism without a transcendental subject." This places him much closer to Wagner than to Nietzsche — assuming the determination of such spatial relations to be meaningful. Lévi-Strauss recognizes this explicitly with the "prelude" to *Le cru et le cuit*, where Wagner is pronounced the "first structural anthropologist." Lévi-Strauss, Wagner, Rousseau all think that societies (forms of life, *Gesamtkunstwerke*) are bound together by a scheme that is universally valid and thus independent of both its subject and its object. Such a resolutely anti-phenomenological attitude is rejected by Nietzsche as ahistorical. It presupposes that "inner experience" can be an appropriate presentation of the world. Nietzsche calls this "a lack of philology" and notes that "to be able to read off a text *as text*, without mixing in an interpretation, is the latest form [of this doctrine of] 'inner experience,' perhaps one hardly possible. . . ." [39] For Nietzsche there are no permanent forms of human experience.

I have suggested that as a method, genealogy has a close ancestor in Kant's critical method. The link to Kant also evokes another set of epistemological cousins to genealogy. The so-called "Neo-Kantians" of the early twentieth century quite self-consciously sought to apply the Kantian techniques to historical and social questions. They were aware of their affinity with Nietzsche's approach. Georg Simmel in fact went so far as to write a book on *Schopenhauer und Nietzsche*. Once again, though, the positions are not really quite the same. With the possible exception of Max Weber, no one of them was as conscious as Nietzsche of the fact that the questions one asks of history must correspond to the historical position of the questioner. We ask questions about capitalism because we find it important to us; Nietzsche asks questions about the Greeks because he sees such an understanding as essential to the crisis of contemporary Europe. Simmel and the others sought answers to questions such as "How is society possible?" and hoped to find a universal set of preconditions; they presuppose that human society in the end rests permanently on certain structural relations, and that bringing them out into the open will not alter that fact. Nietzsche, as I argued above, thinks that societies dwell in the metaphors men take to be true since they have been so "worn out" that they no longer appear as human creations. To reveal them as creations is thus for Nietzsche to force a recognition that, like the rest of human handiwork, they benefit from no permanent validity. This process must be destructive of particular illusions; the universal answers on which the neo-Kantians sought to found their sociology are not.

Nietzsche's picture, for instance, of slave and master morality or of Greek politics should not less be construed as a description of what happened in fifth-century Athens than should Hobbes's picture of the state of nature be seen as an attempt at a faithful reconstruction of some dim anthropological reality. Nietzsche is trying to give *us* (modern men, not abstract entities) a context of meaning that informs us of Greece. A number of such presentations are obviously possible; the important thing to retain is that these are and must be artifacts, assembled and ventured with a governing intention. They do not provide us with new information about Greece or morality (this would be an "empirical" approach) but rather *make appear to us as information that which had previously been hidden*. A light is placed behind the veil, and that which had been seen as solid is now revealed as "mere appearance." [40] Indeed, there could even be "a kind of historical writing that had no drop of common fact in it and yet could be claimed to be called in the highest degree objective." [41]

This construction of origins serves the purpose of forcing on the reader the recognition that he or she may be actualizing and living out a particular set of origins. "Greek antiquity," for instance, "is a means to understand ourselves, to set the time right and thereby to overcome." [42] "Slave morality" is in all men, and all actions tend to manifest it; [43] this must be exposed. What Nietzsche wants to do is impress the consciousness upon Europe that it is slipping toward a passive nihilism. He finds that he has for this "A hammer: to conjure up a frightful decision, to confront Europe with the *consequences* of 'willing' its own will to destruction." [44]

The aim of Nietzsche's analysis is twofold. First, it seeks to show that there are no prior correct starting points for questioning; hence, there can be no foundation for historical truth. The most that such an endeavor can accomplish is the exposure of errors and prejudices made in the past; the preliminary steps of a genealogical investigation destroy the supposed validity of the necessarily erroneous bases on which it was assumed that the validity of a particular form of life rested. [45] Before any steps away from nihilism can be taken, one must first escape the error that there is a stopping point which can be found and occupied by means of investigation; truth does not rest *on* anything. [46] "One would have to *know* what *being* [*Sein*] is in order to *decide* whether this or that is real (e.g., the 'facts of consciousness'); in the same way that *certainty* is, what *knowledge* is and the like. — But since we do *not* know this, a critique of the faculty of knowledge is useless. How should such a tool be able to criticize itself when it can only use *itself* for a critique? It cannot even define itself." [47]

Secondly, the revelation that there is no final foundation stone for truth is at the same time an exposure of the particular error that has been at the kernel of a particular existence. If, as for Nietzsche, the investigation is of our morality, then what is finally revealed to us is what we are. More precisely, what is revealed is what we have been all along, even if we pretended we didn't know it. It is a sign of the profound anti-romantic accomplishment of Nietzsche's work that nowhere does he assume we can uncover anything that is not human-all-too-human. To bring mankind back to itself may be a historically necessary operation; there is no reason to suppose that the image it comes to know for the first time will be a happy one.

The search for truth is then always destined to end up with precisely the results implied at its starting point. To understand this is necessary to understand who one is; but to understand who one is, is to realize that all circles are, potentially at least, vicious. For

Nietzsche, one does not uncover redemption from the past. Understanding does not necessarily lead to growth; it seems in fact to at least begin in destruction. From this search, Nietzsche discovers the cognitive consequences of the particular tools men use in their search for truth. For Nietzsche, all reason must be practical reason, since there can be no realm of theoretical reason. [48]

If there is no truth in itself, two consequences follow for Nietzsche. Firstly, there are also no permanent facts. A "fact" is shaped by a perspective; if there are no stopping points for the perspectives, so also can there be no permanent facts. Secondly, all acts of the intellect must be creative. They do not simply shape the world we perceive; they also must create the preconditions that allow us to make judgments about cause and effect, truth and consequences. "The intellect is a creative force: for it to be able to decide, to ground [begründen] it must first have created the thought of the unconditional — it believes that which it creates to be true." [49]

Along with the Neo-Kantians, but in a much more radical manner, Nietzsche's position appears as a critique of Kant. Further elucidation of the notion of genealogy and the problem of truth requires turning to Nietzsche's understanding of Kant. Nietzsche's position certainly would have been unavailable without the prior discoveries of the three Critiques. And despite the attacks that Nietzsche makes on Kant, there is no doubt that he was fully cognizant of the immensity of Kant's achievement. There are comments and appreciations from the early days in Basel, where Kant is used approvingly in Nietzsche's lectures on Aristotle's Rhetoric, as well as in The Birth of Tragedy; even in the sour days of Nietzsche's last writings, Kant is one of the few men he still feels must be dealt with. Most characteristic is perhaps the passage in The Gay Science which sounds Kant's "immense note of interrogation" of causality as a key part of the preliminary skirmishes around the value of knowledge. [50]

This appreciation refers to the extraordinary achievements of Kant's Critique of Pure Reason. There he had established the limits of human reason. "Human reason," wrote Kant in a famous passage, "has this particular fate, that in one species of its knowledge, it is burdened with problems, which, by the very nature of reason itself, it is not able to ignore, but which transcending its powers, it is not able to answer." [51] Kant then, as Nietzsche points out, attempts to delineate the realm inside which reason can operate. [52] He depicts certain problems, the antinomies — such as "all events have or have not a cause," "there is or is not free will" — and finds them to be not directly solvable through the application of reason. Nonetheless, for Kant, it is possible to come to a solution in these cases if we do not adopt an empirical approach, looking for an object which would make clear what the case is, but rather, realizing that "the object is only in our brain and cannot be given outside it," we adopt a "critical solution which allows of complete certainty [and] does not consider the question objectively, but in relation to the foundation upon which the question is based." [53] The critique — Kant's tool — is of the same family as the genealogy, and thus far it is apparent that Nietzsche has merely followed Kant in his approach to knowledge. At this point, however, a divergence begins. For Nietzsche, Kant's reasoning proceeds as follows.

a) There are limits to reason as made apparent by the fact that contradictory propositions can be demonstrated as apparently true.
b) There are, however, certain propositions which we believe to be universally true and necessary, though they cannot be demonstrated by reason alone (such as, for every effect there is a cause).
c) Because of (*a*) such universal truths cannot spring from experience.
d) Such universal truths must therefore be derived from some other source of knowledge. Such knowledge comes to make up the synthetic a prioris. [54]

The relation of this knowledge to the practical world was detailed in the *Critique of Practical Reason*. To do so was necessary in order to show some relation between the transcendental world of theoretical reason and the world of practical life. If this link could not be established, the world of theoretical reason would necessarily remain without human importance. In Nietzsche's understanding of Kant, this relationship is developed as follows. Kant demonstrates, to his own apparent satisfaction —

a) That the mind and reason are natural.
b) That the outside world, even though not "objectively" perceivable, is also natural.

c) That reason is architectonic (such was the main conclusion of the first *Critique*).
d) That there is a correspondence between the structures of reason and those of the outside world, and that therefore one can act by analogy.[55]

Kant's view now contains the two following elements: There is a form of knowledge (that of theoretical reason) which is affected neither by the act of knowing, nor by the object that is known by it; secondly, the moral considerations of practical reason, that is, how men know how they should act in a particular case, are only objectively resolved if there can be effectuated a link between this world and the realm of theoretical reason. Without such a link or without the transcendental realm, the purity of the reasonable quality of moral actions is imperiled by the necessary practical limits of reason in the empirical world.[56]

To this, Nietzsche responds by denying that there is an actual realm of theoretical reason, and then by developing the consequences of this denial for the realm of practical reason. Referring to the antinomies he claims: "The *origin* of these antitheses *need not necessarily* go back to a supernatural source of reason: it is sufficient to oppose it to the *real* source of concepts. This derives from the practical sphere, the sphere of utility and has hence the strong faith it inspires (one would *perish* if one did not reason according to this mode of reason); but this is no 'proof' of what it asserts."[57] He finds that the very attempt to evolve a sphere of pure reason is in itself contradictory and a denial of the most basic characteristics of existence in the world. In an exasperated note from the period of *The Dawn of Day* he writes: "To think away the subject — that is to want to represent to oneself a world without a subject: this is a contradiction: to represent without representation!"[58]

Nietzsche finds an analogy between the notion of men having a "faculty" that gives knowledge of the world of synthetic a prioris, and Molière's doctor. Asked why opium produced a sleep, the man paused, and then eloquently responded, "because of its *virtus dormitiva*." In Nietzsche's understanding, Kant arrived at the notion of a synthetic a priori from the supposed consequences of one; this, for Nietzsche, was both to reason in a circle and to commit the metonymic error of identifying an object with its consequences.

Such answers are for Nietzsche premised on false comparisons: they are simply "illogical." [59]

Kant, in Nietzsche's understanding, had asked the wrong question. He inquired as to how synthetic a priori judgments were possible; he rather should have asked why they were *necessary*. And, in any case, when Kant found that he had to invent a whole new faculty to keep the world looking as it did to him, by Nietzsche's relentless unmasking imperative he should have doubted that he was doing anything besides reading his consciousness back into his existence. Consciousness for Nietzsche is, as for Marx, an epiphenomenon of existence, not given in advance. Thus Kant's procedure smacks of what Marx would have called ideology, and which Nietzsche claims is an assertion of "the existence of things about which we are not able to know anything, . . . a piece of naiveté . . . [and] the result of certain needs, namely moral metaphysical ones." [60] And, in an important note dating from the period of the composition of *The Dawn of Day*, Nietzsche writes about Kant that "the origin of the categorical imperative is in no way profound [*nichts Erhebliches*]. . . . Most people . . . prefer an unconditional command to a conditional one: the former permits them to avoid bringing their intellect into play [*den Intellekt aus dem Spiele zu lassen*] and better supports their laziness. . . . Thus one wants the imperative to be categorical: an absolute master must be constructed by the wills of the many who are afraid of themselves and of each other. . . . If one did not have this fear, one would not need such a master." [61]

The "moral metaphysical needs" of Kant appear to be closely related to fear, and especially to a fear of oneself and of others. Nietzsche seems to be saying that as long as one is potentially morally threatened, either actively (by direct oppression) or passively (by the dissolution of values), one will tend to look for an absolute and unfailing bulwark by which to defend himself. In Nietzsche's understanding, then, Kant solved the problem of the vulnerability of the questionable base of knowledge simply by concocting a basis which was, by definition, unquestioned, since men could never know anything directly about it. Nietzsche will not abide, though, with what he perceives as willful ignorance; for him the realm of theoretical reason was a Parzival, a "pure foolery," of a concept.

If Nietzsche's radical critique has validity, it implies that *all* is necessarily mediated by the life and consciousness of the knower:

there can be no "reading of Text as text" because *there is no text, only texts*. There will be no knowledge of a "pure world" — *pace* Rousseau, Kant, and Lévi-Strauss — because for Nietzsche, all truth will have to be truth *for* a form of life. In a passage called "On psychology and theory of knowledge," he writes: "I hold also to the phenomenality of the *inner* world: *everything that becomes known [bewusst] to us* is thoroughly ordered, simplified, schematized, interpreted — the *actual* process of inner perception, the *causal connection* between thoughts, feelings, desires, as that between subject and object absolutely hidden to us — and perhaps purely imagination. The 'apparent *inner* world' is governed by the same forms and procedures as the 'outside world.' " [62] The outside world has no privileged position; it is inevitably shaped and formed by the practical activity of human beings. So much had been known since Hume and Berkeley, indeed, since Plato. But for Nietzsche, not only the "outside," but also the "inside world," that of self-consciousness, is equally unprivileged; it too is shaped, ordered, formed. Thus for Nietzsche the notion of "truth" is and must be phenomenological; it will always have to include the transactions of the "we" who hold to it. And, since it must include the existence of thinking beings who are historical egos, change will be a necessary and constant characteristic of all that is called "true." Theoretical reason still seeks, in Nietzsche's reading of Kant, a realm in which there is no change.

Nietzsche is saying that all knowledge is knowledge by a certain form of life and must then correspond to the particular "horizons," distortions, and simplifications that are made necessary by, and define that form of life. When referring to moral judgments, for instance, it becomes easily apparent why "life" is for Nietzsche "beyond good and evil": since "life" is what evaluates, it cannot apply the standards successfully to itself. (This does not mean that it might not try to. In my considerations of the will to power, I shall attempt to show some of the consequences of so doing.) [63]

It is important to make perfectly clear here that Nietzsche is not somehow suggesting that we have "life," and *then* we have truth. Rather, and much more profoundly, a particular life *is* a particular truth. When he speaks in *The Use and Disadvantage of History* of the necessity of "horizons" without which there is no life, he is explicitly not holding a simplistic relativistic notion that somehow *autre temps, autre moeurs*; rather he is noting a formal and ultimate co-terminism of life and truth. A form of life *is* a truth. Thus change in form of life will be change in truth and vice versa. There is not in Nietzsche the facile relativism which assumes that one can change one's notion of truth at will, "because" it is all "illusion."

He will indeed go as far as he needs to fulfill the logical requirements of the rejection of the sphere of theoretical reason. The restriction of reason to the reason of human beings alone constitutes for Nietzsche an impossibly anthropocentric and limping understanding. [64] If logic and reason are the means by which a particular form of life usefully structures the world for itself they are thus the sources of those simplifications required for survival in the world. Reason is the reason *of* a form of life. It is a mistake to think that it is the "same thing" for two different forms of life. It is also a mistake to think that there is a reason that is not "reason about" — just as later it will be a mistake to think that there is any will that is not a "will to." This totally non-Kantian contention must in fact remain one of the most paradoxical and difficult passages in Nietzsche. There is some support for and very likely some accuracy in Nietzsche's contention. When Michel Foucault reports on old Chinese systems of classification in *Les mots et les choses*, and Wittgenstein asserts the possibility that "one human being can be a complete riddle to another," or when Nietzsche contends there could be a moral system where events are judged by what is accidental to them, and insists in *Ecce Homo* that a book might be so strange that it generates the "acoustic illusion that where nothing is heard, nothing is there," we squirm a bit: this seems nonsense. Indeed it is, Nietzsche would answer, but nonsense for us. He will argue that even sense perceptions (let alone judgments) are "permeated with value judgments. . . . Each individual color is also for us an expression of value (although we seldom admit it, or do so only after a protracted impression of exclusively the same color: e.g., a prisoner in a prison, or a lunatic). Thus insects react to different colors: some like this, some that, e.g., ants. . . ." [65]

The desire to hold on to the world of theoretical reason and the persistence in the belief that reason and logic are simple vehicles for striving after "truth" leads to a *division* of the world into "real" and "apparent." More than anything else this is the focus of Nietzsche's hostility to Kantian epistemology. "This world is apparent; consequently there is a true world; this world is conditioned: consequently there is an unconditioned one; this world is full of contradictions: consequently there is a world free from contradictions; — this world is a world of becoming, consequently there is a world of being." All of these are for Nietzsche "false conclusions," consequent to a "blind trust in reason: that if there *is* A, then its opposite concept B must also *exist*." [66] Nietzsche is concerned to see what lies under such distinctions. Why do men make them? The answer, spelled out in full-length discourses such as *On the Genealogy of Morals*, had already been a constant theme from the days of *Human, All-Too-Human*: men make these distinctions because they *need* to. He writes in a note from 1887: " 'The *real* and *apparent* world' — I have traced this antithesis back to *value* relations. We have projected the conditions of our preservation as *predicates of being* in general [Prädikate des Seins *überhaupt*]. So as to be stable in *our* beliefs if we are to prosper, we have made the 'real' world not one of change and becoming, but one of being [*eine seiende*]." [67] This passage notes, by its italicized opposition of *our* preservation to "being in general," an opposition to all tendencies to universalize, be they truth or even the structures of reason.

From such a fiction, the following particular moral system, for instance, might evolve. If there is suffering from which men can and should be able to escape, there is then the freedom to err and suffer; in this case, however, the "apparent" world in which men suffer is a world conditioned by the "real world." The freedom to err and suffer must also be conditioned. As prisoners of this picture, men are forced to ask what in this world of appearances ("this vale of tears") is so conditioned that they suffer. In other words, they are immediately led to apply moral concepts, to seek a justification for being in this world, when, in fact, for Nietzsche it is this world that creates the moral concepts. Such a doctrine is remarkably close to Marx's notion of fetishism: the creations of men's minds assume an alienated existence independent of those minds and turn around to oppose their forgetful creators. I shall investigate the question of fetishism in the next chapter. What remains important here is Nietzsche's insistence that if one abolishes the distinction of "real" and "apparent," there is left "no shadow of a right . . . to speak . . . of *appearance*. . . . The antithesis of the apparent world and the true world reduces itself to the antithesis 'world' and 'nothing' " [68] I shall investigate this more fully when I consider Nietzsche's understanding of the dionysian. It is clear here, however, that for Nietzsche there is either a *particular* world or else chaos. There is no "life-force" lurking below "appearances."

At this point in the discussion enough has been said to permit a further formulation of what is meant by genealogy. The key is Nietzsche's conception that no other form of reason than practical reason is possible. If we do not have access to a realm of pure reason where concepts are not modified either by the knower or by the known, then inevitably man's life must be constantly in the Cave. The distorting effects of reason had been noted and analyzed by Kant. Kant was, however, tempted, so to speak, by the ideal, and thus led, in Nietzsche's understanding, to posit a realm where such distortions of reason would not occur.

If, as for Nietzsche, an unsullied realm of theoretical reason simply does not exist, science immediately poses itself as a problem. If there is no foundation on which to ultimately rest knowledge, and we continue searching for one, or operating as if there were one, it is easy to get into an endless regression. No stopping point at which knowledge might rest appears, and only exhaustion will provide philosophical rest. In the generation after Nietzsche an answer was proposed by the phenomenologists. While this answer is not the same as Nietzsche's, it nonetheless sheds some light on it. In response to Husserl's call to the "things themselves," an attempt was made to "bracket" these effects of human perception on the perceived. This process, called *epoche*, was an attempt to take away all those simplifying and distorting elements that had turned "things" into "facts." By mentally eliminating the effects of human conception, a true phenomenological knowledge was to be possible. Such knowledge would necessarily have to consist not in explanation, but rather in description, since all attempts at the former would be imposition of human and thus distorting order. As men stop inventing worlds to justify their state, so will the world around them reappear as richer.

Epoche brackets the humanly constitutive element in phenomena to return to "the things themselves"; *genealogy*, as Nietzsche uses it, *brackets the things themselves so as to be left with only the constituting human elements*. This is Kant's enterprise as well, except that the elements he sought and claimed to have found are permanent and universal, whereas Nietzsche's are historical. Genealogy is the analysis of that which makes "things" into facts for us; it no more pursues the empirical than does, for instance, the elaboration of the "mode of production" in Marx or the "general will" in Rousseau. [69] "Slave morality" is for Nietzsche not a description of what "slaves" do, but rather the name of that moral system whose constituting elements color most activities with "slave morality." The "context," so to speak, gives to a particular activity a slavely moral meaning.

The operation works on the presumption that it is possible to make statements about wholes which are different than the sum of all statements that might be made about the parts. One might say, for instance, that all members of a family "have the same face." To the objection that no three of them had the same nose, and no four others the same ears, one might want to say in reply that they are all "put together the same way," such that, despite the empirical differences, the effect is the same. The statement "All the faces in this family are 'put together' in the same way" is not a statement about an empirical reality. It asserts that a particular set of empirical realities share a common form of interrelation among their respective parts. To pick up the analogy with Marx again, it is of course true that the economic systems of France, Germany, the United States, and Great Britain are vastly different one from the other. There is, however, a sense in which it is correct to say that these are all capitalist countries, no matter how different their economic practices may appear.

A genealogical analysis will then reveal that many behavior patterns, which even (and especially) the members of a society might see as very different from each other, are ultimately of the same casting. It can only do this by bringing out what had previously been unquestioned and therefore unobserved. In effect, such an analysis says: "You think that you are different because of these practices; but at a more profound level, which you haven't even recognized as important here, you share the same structures of behavior with the people you think you oppose." For instance, a contemporary adolescent might think that he or she was making manifest an antagonism to society by going to live in a cave on Crete or a commune in Oregon. However, both a hippie and a suburbanite might share the need to resolve an Oedipal complex. That they do so in different and opposed manners would not be to Nietzsche as significant as the fact that their emotional life is ruled by the same "principle." He would then attempt to bring out the fundamental unity between the two apparently opposed persons.

The effect of this is, of course, initially destructive. If one finds out that much of the personality system one has painfully elaborated is simply an elaborate justification for a set of unresolved problems, the realization is likely to precipitate a crisis. That which has been the bounds of one's life vanishes in the realization that there is no force to the barriers one has sturggled so long to erect in self-definition; the self-consciousness produced by genealogical analysis weakens the unquestioned bases that were necessary to a particular form of life. For Nietzsche, this is both a necessary and an acceptable price to pay to get at the problems of the present age. Since he does not believe that the genealogy under which the West presently operates can produce anything except peril, decadence, and an ultimate void of meaning, even "destruction" ("wars such as man has never known") is preferable to continuing the "decline to mediocrity."[70]

The Measure of Things

Nietzsche does not consider the statement that moral worlds are all invented and "mere illusion" to be an argument *against* them. That would imply a "real world" from which to launch such an attack. Rather these "illusory" worlds are necessary; Nietzsche never maintains the romantic position that could throw off all errors a natural and happy man would appear from under the verdigris of civilized morality. As I emphasized before, the moral world is not epiphenomenal to the perceiver, to be cast off or changed like a suit of clothes. It is rather our very flesh: man is not the only measure of all things. Such Protagorean anthropocentrism is as false as the Kantian attempts to discover and design a self-centered system. Such a piece of "naïveté," notes Nietzsche, takes "an anthropocentric idiosyncracy as the *measure of things*, as the standard [*Richtschnur*] for determining 'real' and 'unreal': in short to absolutize a conditionality."[71]

A moral system is then a "system of valuations that are in partial contact [*ein Wesens sich berührt*] with the living conditions of a species."[72] There may be "moral interpretation" of phenomena, but nothing else: certainly no moral phenomena in themselves. The ground from which the moral interpretation is launched must necessarily escape from moral categories, much in the way that Wittgenstein proposes that the Sèvres standard for the meter neither *is*, nor *is not* a meter long. Other measures may apply, but not the meter itself. So also, other categories may apply, but not moral ones.

The consequence of this position is important. There can be, by definition, no perfect coincidence between all that goes into making up a form of life and the moral standards that are applied to it. That they are in "partial contact" is evident. There must be some contact, for no society persists in a moral system totally divorced from its prerequisite for life (e.g., all forms of life making a moral command out of the consumption of liquid petroleum disappear, unless they be bacteria). All this says only that Nietzsche sees as impossible a society in which there would be a perfect correspondence between the moral system and the social practices. The most basic characteristics of a given society are those that form its genealogical root; these characteristics always escape the moral valuations of the culture and are "beyond good and evil." By its very existence, a culture presupposes, for Nietzsche, a standpoint "beyond" morality.

Cultures change and evolve, but Nietzsche lacks the valetudinarian faith of men like Edmund Burke and Michael Oakeshott that one may leave well enough alone and that change should simply happen. What has become evident is that Nietzsche understands "truth" to be a yea-saying (an affirmation, whether conscious or not) of a certain form of life, and therefore, of what is necessary for that form of life to be the case. "Truth" is to some degree always an attempt at self-justification and is therefore always to some degree moral. To "perceive something to be true" is for Nietzsche to "take something to be true; to say yes to something." [73] *Truth* then, as understood by Nietzsche, *is the phenomenon of drawing or accepting the horizons within which one lives.* Making something true consists of making something *unquestioned*, in acknowledging it as a horizon. The processes by which this happens have not been investigated yet. But, for something to become true, it must be affirmed, yea-said to, in such a manner that *it is literally impossible to ask questions of it.* It will then serve as a basis for further truth, truth development, we might call it, and, as discussed before, will return in all that which is grounded on it. In a passage I have already had occasion to mention, but which now appears in correct resonance for the first time, Nietzsche asserts:

This is a universal law: a living thing can be healthy, strong, and productive inside a horizon. If it is unable to draw one around itself, and too selfish to loose its view in another's, it will come to an untimely end. . . . The extreme case would be the man who is condemned to see becoming everywhere. Such a man no longer believes in his own existence; he sees everything fly past in an eternal succession and looses himself in the stream of becoming. At last, the logical disciple of Heraclitus, he will hardly dare raise a finger.[74]

Thus, none of this discussion should be construed as indicating that Nietzsche is somehow "opposed" to truth, or to the concept of truth. He simply realizes as does Wittgenstein that "explanation must come to an end somewhere."[75] This means that that which lies beyond the end of explanation and makes it possible, will be different from that which the explanation is about. They are separated by an epistemological chasm. Nietzsche's notion of "life" is the locus of this difference,[76] and the seemingly impossible attempt to bridge the gap and make something "explained" seem "natural" is the task that occupies much of his life.

This leads to the famous and often misunderstood doctrine of "perspectivism." When Nietzsche says that we should see the world out of "a hundred eyes"[77] he is *not* saying that all truth is "subjective." Nor is he making the simplistic argument of cultural relativism, that one man's heaven is another's hell, and that all are entitled to their beliefs. What one sees and knows is not *subjective*, but rather an *error*. By being an error, it is not thereby *false*. Falsity implies truth. One cannot say that something is false without having some notion of what *would be* truth. Yet this is precisely what Nietzsche is trying to get away from, judging on the basis of what something is *not*. One can say how and why an error is made without being able to say what a "truth" would be. " 'Truth,' " writes Nietzsche, "this, according to my way of thinking, does not describe necessarily the opposite of an error, but in the most fundamental cases only the position [*Stellung*] of different errors vis-à-vis one another. Perhaps one is older than the other, more profound, even ineradicable, insofar as an organic entity [*Wesen*] of our species could not live without it; while other errors do not tyranize over us as necessary conditions of life, but on the contrary when compared to such can be set aside and refuted. . . . An assumption that is irrefutable — Why should it for that reason be '*true*' . . . ?"[78]

In *Beyond Good and Evil*, Nietzsche starts by posing the question of the value of truth. If we accept Nietzsche's description of "truth" as the subterfuge for the maintenance of a certain form of life, then the ultimate task of metaphysics crumbles. The significance of the famous dictum of the "madman in the marketplace" — that "God is dead," that we have killed him and continue yet to live on in his shadow — is a premonition of the disappearance of the most secure source of an ultimate and "real" world. Henceforth, as Yeats wrote a few decades later in "The Second Coming,"

> *Things fall apart; the center cannot hold;*
> *Mere anarchy is loosed upon the world.*

Even Kant is still, for Nietzsche, "in the end an underhanded Christian." Nietzsche finds the life of Western man characterized by a particular structure that over time encourages the destruction of all horizons; thus the onslaught of nihilism. To discover a viable horizon, Nietzsche will first have to trace the full genealogical route. Without understanding the present, [79] a solution to these problems can only be "accidental," as Nietzsche thought it had been with the Greeks and with some "peoples, tribes, and families." [80] Without such understanding, one risks in fact merely perpetuating under far more formal and subtle disguises the structures of nihilism now afflicting the world.

Chapter III

THE EPISTEMOLOGY
OF NIHILISM

"So you are saying that human agreement decides what is true and what is false?" — It is what human beings say that is true and false; and they agree in the language they use. That is no agreement in opinions but in forms of life.

— Ludwig Wittgenstein, *Philosophical Investigations*, par. 241

Nietzsche sees the modern age as frighteningly narrow. The concepts with which men grasp the world are so appallingly strait that humans no longer see themselves, nor the world, nor those around them with any clarity. Nietzsche's task, as he sees it imposed on him, is to destroy those prejudices that keep men from acknowledging their condition. For him, the contemporary world is an incredible and self-protective simplification and impoverishment of experience; not only are men subjects in a world increasingly void of meaning, but they are unable to fully recognize and deal with this fact. Epistemological and moral blinders hide it from their experience.

Yet, thin and mean though human life may be, men will not naturally free themselves from such life. For Nietzsche, such existence as men have known is all that they know. There is literally no place available to go from this world. On this score, Nietzsche is often accused of being merely critical and of failing to "provide an alternative." Though such criticism be misguided, it does contain a germ of truth. For reasons I shall investigate fully, Nietzsche cannot *provide* an alternative way: to do so will merely perpetuate the evil that afflicts this one. He can, however, attempt to unmask and destroy those dangerous illusions that keep men in their present nihilistic existence. Nietzsche gambles, one might say, that the chaos that will result from the destruction of the last epistemological and moral props of the Judeo-Christian world may, if properly executed, make possible a new and transvalued life, no longer human-all-to-human. "I am," he writes toward the end of *Ecce Homo*, "by far the most terrible human being that has existed until now; this does not exclude that I become the most beneficial."

In the previous chapter, I argued that genealogical analysis is Nietzsche's central tool in his destruction of the illusions and prejudices that make nihilism possible. Such an approach, I noted, has many things in common with the approach of phenomenology. Husserl's later cry, *zu den Sachen selbst*, is an exhortation to "bracket" all that is casuistically human and interpretive, in order to arrive at the "things themselves," a world of direct and non-mediated experience. Genealogy, on the other hand, does not seek out and describe the "things" that phenomenology holds to be the world, but rather delineates the *manner* in which the "things" are "made" into "facts." Nietzsche tries to bring out precisely how a particular world is put together and made a world; he shows thereby that that world has not natural necessity. Indeed, for Nietzsche, *no* world has any justification — nor can it, since it must repose on human action.

Men, however, do in fact seek out justification for their world; indeed they seem to require it. I argued above that for Nietzsche all life must be rooted in a particular realm of the unquestioned. A foundation must be taken for granted and questions of such a foundation must not exist. In modern Europe, he finds that fundamental questions are avoided by the elaboration of a distinction between a "real" world and an "apparent" world. The changing world that men perceive is the "apparent" one; it rests on a "real" world that is not directly apprehendable. Men are seduced to this position by what Nietzsche calls the "Circe of the ideal," to whose siren song even Kant had succumbed, though, as Nietzsche notes, he had understood better than all others and had posed as a problem the architectonic effects of human perception. Kant's world of theoretical reason is, finally, a ploy, invented to reconcile that to which Kant had been forced by the craft of his intellect with that which he still wanted, in fact needed, to believe. A moral prejudice for certainty finally controls his epistemology. For Nietzsche, however, "final truth" must necessarily be ideology, the unconscious defense of a self-serving position.

Language and Reality

Men do, however, accept the division of the world into "real" and "apparent" spheres. They (we) continually do make sense of the world in a language that does reflect and use such a distinction and the whole family of concepts that must grammatically accompany it. Language thus provides a good place to investigate the particular epistemology characterizing the contemporary world of nihilism. The genealogical analysis of language plays a central role in Nietzsche's destructive enterprise as indeed it must, for with Rousseau in the *Essay on the Origin of Languages*, and Saussure and Wittgenstein as well as many others, Nietzsche sees language not just as the vehicle of sociality, but in fact as constitutive of a particular society itself.[1]

In the first book of *Human, All-Too-Human*, Nietzsche remarks that the importance of language resides in the fact that men take the concepts and names of things as *aeternae veritates* and that such assurance provides a fulcrum by which men think themselves able to understand and master the world in which they live. Men think that "it is really in language that [they] have knowledge of the world."[2] Survival means that men have some control over the world, and they find a language a point from which the regularities necessary to such control may be elaborated.

Men think then that the language they speak provides them an accurate picture of the world. Nietzsche clearly thinks this to be false, if only because language, as a construct, must inevitably impoverish or simplify the complex manifold of the world. Nietzsche finds absurd the notion that a "knowledge-apparatus" could come to know itself and compares it to a self-consuming stomach.[3] Exposing the errors men may have committed in their language will certainly not clear up whatever problems men may have due to their language. There is no hope in Nietzsche that an accurate vision of the world may be recovered by cleaning out the various distortions language may pose; at the same time, however, Nietzsche certainly does find the distortions present in Western language to be particularly pernicious.

We may then look to language to uncover the particular distortions characterizing our epistemology; we must do so, however, without any expectation of finding a "more accurate" understanding of the world. It is important to realize that though Nietzsche thinks language to be a simplification and distortion of the world, he does not "oppose" it somehow. It is, of course, true that a number of people and schools reacted to the Kantian discovery of the limits of reason and the problem of metaphysics by standing the Konigsberg philosopher on his head. Instead of searching for truth in a transcendental realm, or assuming its pure existence, many thought that truth might be found in that of which one could not speak: in silence, mystery, intuition; in the wisdom of emotion, of blood and the soil and the homeland.[4] Just as men could not speak accurately about the sphere of theoretical reason, so also there would be no words for this "home" world. Instead of the transcendental world, the "home of Being" now became a problem. This position is already identifiable in the early Romantic German tradition, in poets such as Hölderlin, and finds its modern culmination, in my understanding, in the work of Martin Heidegger.[5]

Nietzsche, however, must reject any such tendency. "We believe in reason: this, however, is the philosophy of gray *concepts*. Language is built on the most naïve of prejudices. . . . *We cease to think if we will not do so under linguistic coercion*."[6] Language is "a schema which we may not be rid of," for nothing "underlies" in a realm of "greater" reality. There is nothing else for Nietzsche; hence the pursuit of a somehow undistorted "truth" will necessarily be illusory. (I should note here, though I will return to it at the end of the chapter, that this implies that the whole notion of "distortion" due to "perspective" is a mistaken way of understanding what Nietzsche is saying. If there is no "real world" to distort, then our perceptions are not properly speaking distortions: what could they be distortions of?)

It is, however, entirely possible that a new language might be constructed, if one means by "new" a previously unemployed series of interrelated concepts picturing the world anew. It is apparent from the unpublished notes that Nietzsche had dreams of removing from the language those qualities he saw to be the message and herald of nihilism (e.g., causality). More radically, he seems to have hoped to revolutionize discourse into a new language which would rest on a structurally different grammar. Heidegger, for instance, in his massive two-volume work on Nietzsche, argued from these notes that Nietzsche thought all notions of the transcendental, be they ontological or theological, arose from the subject-object distinction.[7] I leave inquiry as the meaning and feasiblity of such a project until a later chapter. Most importantly, though, Nietzsche is no more opposed to language than he was to "truth." Men rather need to understand what they are doing when they speak of truth, or when they use language; that this understanding is somewhat destructive, Nietzsche expected and accepted.

Finally, it is true that Nietzsche saw the world around him as undergoing a new set of experiences for which it had not yet the words. Given the ultimate unity of language and life which he sees, it follows that since men have as yet no words for what is happening to them, they will also have no knowledge of it. Nietzsche sees himself providing the first attempts at dealing with what he thinks to be the coming experiences of the European and Western worlds over the next two centuries. "Let us imagine," he proposes in *Ecce Homo*, "that a book speaks only of events that lie altogether beyond the possibility of any frequent or even rare experience — that it is the *first* language for a new series of experiences. In that case simply nothing will be heard, but with the acoustic illusion that where nothing is heard, *nothing is there*."[8] If the problem of modern men is that they are, as Nietzsche argued in *The Birth of Tragedy*, "too theoretical," this must mean that they do not live their experiences: they have no words for them, no manner of making them exist for themselves.

To achieve the beginnings of a reintegration first requires breaking the hold language now has on men. The practical disjuncture between words and thoughts is not the result of the simple misuse of words; it is inherent in the natural operation of language. In the early essay "On Words and Music," Nietzsche investigates the analogies between music and speech which had already formed the basis of *The Birth of Tragedy*: "In the multiplicity of languages the fact at once manifexts itself that word and thing do not necessarily coincide with one another, but that the word is a symbol. But what does the word symbolize? Most certainly only conceptions, be they now conscious ones, or, as in the greater number of cases, unconscious; for how could a word symbol correspond to that innermost nature of which we and the world are images? Only as conceptions do we know that kernel. . . ."[9] The language and imagery are still those of Schopenhauer. Nietzsche soon abandons the notion of the "kernel of existence," or, what he calls in preparatory work for *The Birth of Tragedy*, the *Urein*.[10] It is nonetheless possible to extract a number of Nietzsche's views of the architectonic quality of language from this passage.

Language and words themselves do not respond to "reality," but are a set of conceptualizations that make a certain type of survival possible. Language is used "like a spider web to capture what we need to know."[11] And, as we talk about the world, so it must be; an at least partially effective feedback must exist. But the "reality to which they [words] correspond is in fact already a humanly invented reality." Thus, investigation of the structure of language will lay bare part of the genealogy which forms our world. "We are constantly led astray by words and concepts," writes Nietzsche in the section of *Human, All-Too-Human* called "The Wanderer and His Shadow," "and are induced to think of things as other than they are, as separated, indivisible, existing in the absolute. *A philosophical mythology lies hidden in language.*"[12] A "mythology" is the formulation of some particular event such that it appears to acquire universal and absolute sense; our mythology is to be uncovered.

The mythology prevents people from seeing language as a problem in itself, since it continually will tend to present to men the same things as problems. If there were to be a totally new set of experiences, then, as Nietzsche notes above, they would remain unknown; men would not have the words for them. The reverse presumably also follows. If we continue using the words and language we have, there will not be a "totally new" set of experiences; in fact, we will be prevented from recognizing them as such by virtue of our continued use of the same language. We are "caught in a picture" — one might say a family portrait. Recognizing this potentially neurotic repetition with exactly the same term that Wittgenstein was later to make famous, Nietzsche writes: "The strange *family resemblance* of all Indian, German, and Greek philosophizing is explained easily enough. Precisely where there is a kinship of languages, it cannot but occur, due to the common philosophy of grammar — I mean, due to the unconscious domination of and orientation by similar grammatical functions — that everything is prepared from the outset for a similar development and sequence of philosophical systems. . . ." [13] In a sense, the focus on language allows Nietzsche to bring Hegel back to the earth: language provides a set of plebian *Weltgeister* which establish the recurrent and recognizable developmental patterns in the world around us. Without language, without the ability to formulate the world, all would appear as it does to an infant — the play and chaos of an unending river which is never twice the same.

Finally, if there is no agreement among languages as to what constitutes reality, neither is there an extra-linguistic of validity by which to judge a language. Precisely because there is no unity among languages, so also is there no language that might on some scale be rated more "correct" than any other. Such a scale would be like a *Ding an sich* in epistemology; it would imply the existence of a world that affects men and about which they by definition could know nothing. This is again the criticism already leveled at the sphere of theoretical reason. The mind, however, Nietzsche remarks, constantly seeks to persuade itself to the contrary. It is a "mask of dissimulation," and "seeks to celebrate its Saturnalia when there would be a happy union of word and world." [14] The imagery is drawn from Hegel. But, where Hegel believed the union possible in principle and in time, for Nietzsche, once again, the mind is only seeking to persuade itself that the world it knows is the one true world.

The Morality of Language

It should by this time be apparent that Nietzsche ascribes to language a sense at least as broad as does Wittgenstein in the *Investigations*. For both men a language is very much an expressable way of doing things and of going about one's business. It does not mean simply the uttering of words used to describe life; such would imply too great a separation of language from the world, and would repeat the error that Nietzsche understands as the division of the world into real and apparent. A language describes and is (part of) a form of life. It is a fuzzily coherent way of doing things. It is not intended to cover all possibilities; rather it blurs at the edges. Thus "words are acoustical signs for concepts; concepts, however, are more or less definite sign images for often recurring and associated sensations, for groups of sensations. To understand one another, it is not enough that one uses the same words; one also has to use the same words for the same species of internal experiences; *in the end one has to have one's experiences in common [gemein].*" [15] As Wittgenstein said in one of his most memorable aphorisms: "To imagine a language is to imagine a form of life."

Here again Nietzsche refuses a simple nominalism or relativism. As he also argues about morality, and as already seen in the previous chapter, things are not just what men make of them; there can be no such separation between doer and deed. Errors are not due to false or improper creation, but rather reside in the whole form of life, which itself is an error, caused by accepting what we see — what the language presents to us — as "real" or even as "appearance" masking reality. Indeed, men are "caught in error," for the "mistakes" to which their language leads them are mistakes for the whole form of life. "Indeed nothing has yet had a more naïve power of persuasion than the error concerning being [*Sein*] . . . ; every word we say and every sentence we speak is in its favor. . . . 'Reason' in language — Oh! what an old deceptive female! I am afraid that we will not be rid of our belief in God because we still believe in grammar." [16]

The link of the belief in God and the faith in grammar shows that Nietzsche does not hold that belief in God was simply a mistake, or deluded pure foolishness; such Voltairiana is far too easy and superficial a criticism. Nor does he assume that because the belief in God is a "mere illusion," a simple announcement might lift this burden off the shoulders of contemporary man. Rather, he is suggesting that the structure of culture is synergistic; a change in one part of it will necessarily eventually show up in the other parts. Such a perspective would usually be fundamentally conservative — it is identified in Western thought with Edmund Burke — except for the fact that Nietzsche wishes to encourage such change. God is dead: so much has been announced; slowly and inexorably, therefore, for reasons yet unexamined, the structure of language must respond to this news. Men continue, in Nietzsche's angry accusation, to live on in the "shadows of the dead God," still influenced and controlled by the leftover effects of such belief. The gradual approach of the "great noon" signifies for Nietzsche that time when all shadows disappear; he has, for instance, only cold contempt for a writer like George Eliot, who while proclaiming herself an agnostic, still retains fundamentally Christian moral principles. [17] In effect, Nietzsche has taken the statement "God is truth" in a chillingly literal fashion. The long process by which men effectuated the murder of God does not stop with the simple announcement of the death of the divinity in the famous aphorism about the "marketplace" in *The Gay Science*. The death of God is simply a signal point in a long process whose ultimate consequence and conclusion is the destruction of the foundations of truth itself. And, as truth becomes in Nietzsche's understanding increasingly impossible, so also must die all that which depended on it, in particular the language that made it possible and that was a part of it. The language will not survive if that which made it possible perishes: it, too, is one of those "great things" which, in the *Genealogy*, Nietzsche noted "perish of their own accord by an act of self-transcendance [*Selbstaufhebung*] : so the law of life decrees. . . ."[18]

Nietzsche then is not asserting that (the) language must be destroyed. Rather he is attempting to make into a problem what he sees as a historical fact. *We are no longer able to talk about what is happening to us*. Making language questionable, seeing it posed as a problem, is appropriate to and possible in a time when society has been forced into moral behavior patterns which do not admit of expression within the moral logic of the language. [19] For instance, in an example that Nietzsche would have understood perfectly, George Orwell evolved a language, Newspeak, for the world of *1984*. His intention was to develop a form of discourse which rendered morally compatible acts and concepts that in our present understanding are antithetical. The society of Oceania required that Love and Hate, War and Peace no longer be antonyms; it was necessary to claim them both with no feeling of moral contradiction. For that purpose, one had to be able to talk about them. Newspeak was to be the language that filled the necessities of the society: it expressed that which was becoming a sociopolitical fact. That this is in actuality possible should be obvious from a short reflection on the army major who had to "destroy the village in order to save it," or on the high officials who were able to maintain in the face of the publication of previously secret documents on the development of Vietnam War policy that there was no deceit practiced on the American people. For Nietzsche, words do not mean what one *wants* them to mean: they mean what they *have* to mean, if the position and the ideology of the utterer is to be preserved.

For Nietzsche, language is involved in making things the same for people, in their commonality and communality. It is also, therefore, a means of enforcing common behavior on individual men. But what it does is enforce *a* common behavior. Nietzsche is attacking the consequences of the effects of a language on a behavior. There is no reason to assume that he is attacking anything more than the *particular* forms of communality that *this* (particular) language enforces. He did not, after all, attack in the same way the communality that was the Greek polis, nor yet the culture of the *Iliad*. If our language develops in response to our needs, it is for Nietzsche *our* language and *our* needs that must be called before the genealogical bar of judgment.

The problem Nietzsche is analyzing must not then be seen in "language" itself, but rather in the specific community that (our, Western) language enforces. Language still brings men together, but it is the quality of that union which Nietzsche calls into question. More specifically, Nietzsche sees men trying to use language for ends to which it is singularly inappropriate. Language is "properly" suited to the communication of strong feelings, but our language has developed in such a manner that modern men attempt to build a community based on thoughts. As we shall see more extensively below, language now separates men from each other, but denies them the knowledge and concreteness of their divorce. Already in the essay on *Richard Wagner in Bayreuth* Nietzsche writes, "man can no longer make his misery known to others by means of language; thus he cannot really express himself anymore . . . ; language has gradually become a force that drives humanity where it least wishes to go. . . . The results of this inability to communicate is that the creations of common action . . . all bear the stamp of mutual non-comprehension."[20]

That which brings men together now also impedes the consummation of that union. Instead of life, men have in their language merely the accoutrements of a hollow idol. The genealogical investigation of language reveals to Nietzsche those structures that give us our particular way of being together. The dissection is of what has slowly evolved as European society.

The Structure of Language

What needs, then, does this language serve? What sort of beliefs are necessary? What types of activity must seem natural? In Nietzsche's terms, what "philosophical mythology" is perpetuated and propagated through and by our language? That Nietzsche finds the categories men use and formulate the key to the epistemology of contemporary nihilism is hardly open to doubt. He calls them the "basic cause [Ursache] of nihilism," and suggests that men have "measured the worth of the world in categories which were founded on a purely imaginary world."[21]

The first category of epistemology[22] that Nietzsche considers is the "actor-action" distinction. It is also probably the most important.[23] In use, it allows men to separate the "dancer from the dance," the person from (his) activity. Consider what is implied in making the distinction. Person A does action X. Nietzsche sees this division analogous to the distinction of the "real" and the "apparent" world. The action is presumed to be a conditioned part of the actor; the actor acquires a permanence that is not allocated to the action. Judgments can therefore be made about him independently of his activity proper. I shall argue in a later chapter that such judgments are made on imputations to the intentions of the actor. Through them, the actor becomes reified into an entity that has conceptual and potentially moral independence of its acts. He is, so to speak, taken out of the world, and is then dealt with in terms of those idealized categories that the language has so conveniently provided just for such occasions. Thus "popular moralizing divorces strength from the manifestation of strength, as if there were beneath the strong a stratum of indifference able to manifest its strength or not." This reads the actor out of the action — it places the emphasis on the perpetrator of the action and presumes that he might have done otherwise. An actor can thus be seen as morally responsible for his supposed choice, while " *'Der Tater' ist zum Tun bloss hinzugedichtet"* — " 'The actor' is merely a fiction added to the deed." Obvious examples of this practice are sentences such as "The lightning flashed." Such propositions are referred to by Nietzsche as a *Tun-Tun*, a doing-doing. They state the same event twice, once as actor (noun-phrase), once as action (verb-phrase), and presume some meaningful relation between them. One is led to investigate the relationship, and the architecture of tautological air castles begins. For Nietzsche, however, *"Das Tun ist alles"* — "Doing is all."[24]

To Nietzsche, the most important consequence of the actor-action distinction appears to be an overvaluation of consciousness. The actor acquires an ability to separate himself from his acts; in turn, this makes him a self-reflective subject. Consciousness makes man qua subject a prime mover in his own right; it tends to fix a supposed correctness on whatever reflexive conclusions the subject may arrive at. The subject becomes "a unity, a entity,"[25] and the conclusions of consciousness are given an unquestioned status. For Nietzsche, this has two important consequences. In the first place, it makes difficult to take into account the possibility that consciousness, even self-consciousness, might merely be, to use the metaphor that Freud was later to make famous, "the top of the iceberg." The tip of the iceberg is not of significantly different material than that which lies under the water, it is merely more visible to creatures who live above the water. So also, consciousness would not, in Nietzsche's understanding, be qualitatively separable from nonconsciousness; men would simply imagine that since they experience consciousness differently, it is somehow different.

The actor-action distinction also gives an imperative toward ahistoricity. For Nietzsche, the lack of acknowledgment of the historical nature of consciousness is a pervasive "hereditary failure" of philosophers due to their tendency to start with the assumed permanence of contemporary man. "In an involuntary fashion man appears as an *aeterna veritas*. . . ." By unquestioned acceptance of the permanence of the products of reflexive consciousness, philosophers are able to ignore the effects of historical change on the *nature* of the subject. They are led then to see "the last four thousand years as eternal," ignoring that there are "no eternal facts and thus there are no eternal truths."[26] For Nietzsche, the realm of the actor-action distinction is, much like the rest of the world of ideality, an attempt to avoid dealing with the historicity or "giveness" of humanity.

As usual with Nietzsche, the philosophical point leads to a more anthropological one. His investigation and denial of the actor-action distinction leads him not only to reject the epistemology implicit in such a distinction, but to assert that such a distinction is maintained in order to give credence to the opinion that there is such a thing as a permanent "human nature." Nietzsche rejects the notion of a "human nature" outside of history: what we now call "human" is for him but the expression of many years of development and does not carry with it ultimate necessity.

It must be emphasized that Nietzsche is *not* saying that there is no such thing as human nature. Rather he asserts that that which has been called human nature is transitory; the present episode seems to be over two thousand years. [27] In other words, what we had taken as permanent — human nature — is, in Nietzsche's understanding, finally coming to an end. There is probably nothing that will necessarily replace it; what overwhelms in Nietzsche is his consciousness of standing at the dusky end of a long era, with a less and less positive answer to the question "What is living and what is dead in world history?"

There is then finally in Nietzsche an extraordinary modesty about himself and his kind. One tends to overlook this because of titles such as "Why I Am so Wise," "Why I. Write Such Good Books," which organize his autobiography. He is, however, simply refusing to allow man to be the measure of all things. He finds those men wisest whom he praises for "going" under, for recognizing that they are a dying breed. While Nietzsche is nothing if not serious, he does not take *himself* seriously: as the product of over two thousand years of western cluture, he still can accept that he and all he has represented is coming to an end.

In a later chapter I shall investigate further the consequences for the moral sphere of the actor-action distinction. Suffice it to note here, that if this distinction be firmly maintained, the punishment of Oedipus (who was after all not "responsible") becomes incomprehensible; arguments such as "I was only doing my duty" must be accepted as an excuse (i.e., the particular relation of actor to acts was such that the actor cannot be held responsible for them); and the whole question of unconscious motivation for (for example) criminal activity must remain unexamined.

The second epistemological premise which Nietzsche criticizes is free will. In the notes prepared for the drafting of the second volume of *Human, All-Too-Human*, he writes that "speech is the way to the belief in freedom of the will." [28] His reasoning seems to be that to speak of free will, it must be apparent that the action of willing makes a perceptible difference in the outside world. If no change is made, or if the change is random, it would no longer make sense to speak of free will. If, for instance, when a person decided to go home again he found that, for no apparent reason, he sometimes made it and sometimes found himself a quantum leap next door, free will would be a meaningless concept. Free will then depends on the consistency of perception of that portion of the world that is not affected by willing. Since perceptions are predominantly formalized through language into an entity with some permanence, it is, in Nietzsche's understanding, through language that the world is structured such that the operation of the will may be visible. Without language, there would be no "facts"; and without "facts," men would not know what they do. [29]

The escape from a world of a Heraclitean undifferentiated river of existence thus finds its "surest grounds" in "words and concepts." Through the conceptualization inherent in speech, the "raging spring torrent" is transfixed as a frozen river and traversed by bridges. Actions now have results, and willing, consequences, which men are able to describe in terms that other people will understand; the bridges enable humans to ignore the river, as long as it remains more or less frozen. Thus Nietzsche continues on: "The belief in the freedom of the will . . . has in speech its greatest evangelist and prophet." [30]

The doctrine of free will contributes to the evasion originally made possible by the actor-action distinction. Men tend to think, since they "are" free, that no necessary historical or epistemological chains bind them. If one does not *feel* tied down to a certain form of perception, all that is perceived tends to confirm the belief that men are, in fact, free. We do not feel the "border as border" [31] and are led to accept as all of experience that which is delineated by our epistemological prejudices. Even though, as Nietzsche wrote in the second volume of *Human, All-Too-Human*, "each word is a prejudice" and affects spiritual freedom, men *feel* free, since the world they encounter is the one their prejudices have to a considerable degree elaborated. For Nietzsche, men have walled themselves in a world of their own making and told themselves that they are still free. That their consciousness of the borders as barriers has vanished does not detract from the fact that it is not the only possible world. [32]

Freedom of the will becomes a manner of justifying a certain form of life and of asserting the legitimacy of that, and only that, over which this form of life has sway. It is thus a manner of preserving a certain *pattern of domination* and of enforcing a legitimacy for a certain set of horizons, without it ever appearing necessary to seek justification for that enforcement. The doctrine of free will is a cunning method of preserving the credibility of the ego-cogito. In fact, Nietzsche writes, " 'Freedom of the will' — that is the expression of a complex state of delight of the person exercising volition. . . . What happens here is what happens in every well constructed and happy commonwealth: namely, the governing class identifies itself with the success of the commonwealth." [33]

The political reference is a metaphor to explore. In a "happy commonwealth" the questions that would threaten its basis of existence do not get asked; they are shut out beyond the "horizons." They remain outside because the class that defines the commonwealth (in the sense that the *aristoi* defined an aristocracy, and the *demes* a democracy) is identified with that which makes the commonwealth what it is. Just as there is no reason to call the freedom of the will into question when will produces results with the unquestioned clockwork of a propelled billiard ball striking another, so also is there no reason to call into question the defining function of the "governing classes" as long as the commonwealth meets with successes, as long as the will of the governing class leads to results, or as long as the words used to define the world enable us to deal with that world. Should failures become the order of the day, then doubts will arise, horizons will be questioned and grounds will have to be sought. Until then the politics of the situation will be happy. [34]

Nietzsche finds the notion of free will an occasionally useful descriptive fiction. Like all the other epistemological categories considered here, it has no ultimate standing apart from its use. The danger, for Nietzsche, is that men grant a natural and independent validity to it. In asserting this, it must be remembered that if Nietzsche denies free will, he does not thereby affirm that men are "really" *not* free. One cannot reject one side of a dialectical proposition without also rejecting the other: Nietzsche's argument rests on the proposition that men are never so separate from the world as to be in a position — physical or epistemological — to have or not have free will.

Nietzsche criticizes the notion of free will and then investigates what beliefs logically attach themselves to this belief. Most prominent among such beliefs is a third epistemological blight on our understanding. The combination of free will with the notion of the independent subject that arises from the actor-action distinction evolves to the doctrine of causality. Nietzsche writes that "the popular belief in cause and effect is founded on the presupposition that free will is *the cause of every effect*: it is only from this that we derive the feeling of causality." [35] Here again, Nietzsche's criticism focuses not so much on the heuristic value of the concept, but on the presuppositions of seeing the concept as "real." One should not, he writes, wrongly "*reify* 'cause and effect' as the natural scientists do (and whoever, like them, now naturalizes in his thinking), according to the prevailing mechanical doltishness which makes the cause press and push until it 'works'; one should use 'cause' and 'effect' only as pure *concepts*, that is to say, as conventional fictions for the purpose of designation and communication — *not* for interpretation." [36] Were there to be an intellect who could see the flux of events as a continuum, and not as a series of distinguished parts, the concept of cause and effect, indeed, of all conditionality could not exist for him. That one can imagine such a situation, if not actually put oneself into it, indicates for Nietzsche that it would be "ludicrously immodest" to behave as if the only legitimate conclusions were our own. [37] *We* may feel the need to use causality as a concept, but that tells us something about *us*.

Here, too, the distinction is enshrined in and by language. "The separation of the 'doing' from the 'doer,' of happenings from someone who *makes* happen, of the process from something that is not a process but enduring, a *substance* thing, body, soul, etc. . . . the attempt to comprehend happenings [*Geschehen*] as a sort of shifting and place-changing on the part of a being, of something constant: this ancient mythology established the belief in 'cause and effect,' after it had found a firm form in the functions of language and grammar." [38] As always, humans read the "unfamiliar back into the familiar," [39] and derive a feeling of power, comfort, and satisfaction from having understood a new event in terms of the structure that ensures them a particular sway over the world. Kant had spoken of the sense of causality as a "natural" feeling; Nietzsche wants to say that it is a response to needs that are historically specific.

Our language then enforces a particular and historically specific understanding. If, however, the feeling of causality is recognized as neither actual, nor yet natural, but as a fiction and a historical one at that, "much follows," as Nietzsche puts it with a self-conscious pedantry. [40] "Causes" are "super-added" to events; in fact, Nietzsche writes, "a necessary sequence of states does *not* imply a causal relationship between them. . . . *There are neither causes, nor effect.* Linguistically we do not know how to rid ourselves of them. But that does not matter. If I think of the *muscle* apart from its 'effects,' I negate it." [41] To which one might add that if I think of myself as a subject apart from the world, I negate myself.

Nietzsche's move here accepts Hume's analysis of causality, then applies it in a characteristic and strange fashion. Nietzsche explicitly agrees that there is no natural sense of efficient cause, and that habit makes us expect that a certain oft observed occurrence will follow another. That events are made calculable through habit is not a sufficient analysis however; we must seek below that. In critique of Hume, Nietzsche is interested in the source and nature of the habit. A page after the passage cited above he writes: "The calculability of an event does not reside in the fact that a rule is adhered to, or that a necessity is obeyed, or that the rule of causality has been projected by us into every event: it resides in the recurrence of identical cases." The notion of causality is derived then not just from habit, let alone from a sense of causality, as Kant thought, but in fact from historically specific necessities. Men must control the world enough that it appears as a series of classifiable and repeatable events; without the "familiar to hold on to," men are disturbed; with it, they are calmed. And, as seen, language is obviously and necessarily the main vehicle producing the "recurrence of similar cases."

This criticism of causality is directed not so much against the *fact* of causality, as against the *notion*. That causality was not a fact, in the sense that a chair or a mountain were, had been firmly established by Hume. Kant, who had been much concerned with Hume's criticism, had pursued this line and, as Nietzsche sees it, not only had shown that causality was a process of the mind and could not be made to inhere in events themselves, but also had delineated the realm in which causality could provide a useful and heuristic tool. [42] So far, so good. But Nietzsche sees Kant as having attempted to deal with this conclusion by the positing of a *Kausalitäts-Sinn* — another Molièrian faculty. Here he pursues his radical critique of Kant. "One is surprised," he exclaims sardonically, "one is disturbed, one desires something familiar to hold on to — as soon as we are shown something old in something new, we are calmed. The supposed instinct of causality is only a *fear of the unfamiliar* and the attempt to discover something *known* — a search not for causes, but for the familiar." [43]

Again Nietzsche sees that Kant analyzed correctly, but that he was kept from pursuing his analysis to its logical limit by a desire to retain a foundation for what his sense told him to be true. To this effect is discovered the "sense" of causality. Nietzsche's criticism is not against the usefulness of the concept for *Erklärung*, but against the conclusion that since man can *use* the notion of causality, there *must be something* that causes and something that is effected.

Nietzsche tries to show that the notion of subject is the unattended locus of all these problems. In conscious opposition to Descartes, he writes in *Beyond Good and Evil*: "When I analyze the process that is expressed in the sentence 'I think,' I find a whole series of daring assertions that would be difficult, perhaps impossible, to prove: for example, that it is *I* that thinks, . . . that thinking is an operation and an activity on the part of a being who is thought of as a cause, that there is an 'I,' finally, that it is already determined what is to be described as 'thought' — that I *know* what thinking is." [44] Men presume, in other words, to take themselves as permanent and real; and, left unquestioned, this prejudice would imprison man as he is. The first realization permitting the "philosophy of the future" must then be the understanding with which the Preface to the *Genealogy of Morals* begins: "We are unknown to ourselves, we men of knowledge." *By making language a problem, Nietzsche gradually leads himself back to the position where men themselves become the problem*: he calls to the bar the fact that they are human-all-too-human.

Thus even man himself does not provide for Nietzsche a firm rock on which one might ground an accurate epistemology. In an important section of the *Twilight of the Idols* he writes:

People have believed at all times that they knew what a cause is; but whence . . . our faith that we had such knowledge? . . . We believed ourselves to be causal in the act of willing: we thought that here at least we caught causality in the act. Nor did anyone doubt that the antecedents of such an act, its causes, were to be sought in consciousness and would be found there once sought — as "motives": else one would not have been free *for* nor responsible *to* it. Finally who would have denied that thought is caused? that the "I" causes the thought?[45]

Nietzsche denies it, and for him, no explanation is achieved by tracing "effects" back to some mental "cause." The conscious intention of the ego is a familiar fact — and, for that reason, is most unknown to the knower. Here again, Nietzsche has traced the problem back to what I might call psycho-anthropological roots. The soil of the problem is human beings themselves. It is compounded by the fact that men assume they have knowledge of themselves. The paradoxical claim that "we are unknown to ourselves, we men of knowledge" must, in light of the above, be read with the *Genealogy* in part as a rumination on how far men have been removed from themselves, and how great the task of "bringing something home" is to be. It is, however, only through the alienation in which "each is furthest from himself" that men will ever be able to recover themselves. The opposition is again to Kant. No more is metaphysics the "queen of the sciences"; Kant's attempted rejuvenation of that "outcast and forsaken matron" fails. Now, rather, the "path to fundamental problems is psychology."[46] Human beings must deal with *themselves* as the source of the problem. The same metonymic fault noted previously occurs also in the relation of human beings to themselves. Men stamp something an event, take the imprint to be real, then seek on the model of their creation to build the rest of the world, which would follow logically from the initial minting. One traces effects back to conscious intentions, assumes that the reality of self-consciousness is given and true, and assumes thereby to have explained an event. What has been done is far more dangerous: in effect men have read themselves out of the world. By making intention the efficient cause of an event the subject is removed from the deed. But, asks Nietzsche, is not the intention *"the* event itself?"[47]

With this statement we have moved again back from the purely epistemological considerations. Nietzsche would show us that our epistemology, with all its problems, does not rest on a few mistakes which, if properly analyzed, can be cleared up. Our epistemology rests in us; we incarnate it, so to speak. Thus any significant change in epistemology will have to be a change in the sorts of human beings who maintain themselves with this particular epistemology and all of its distinctions between actors and action, causes and effect, and so forth. We shall see later just how radical a change this must be.

Truth and Consequences

Language pulls together and is the world: *this* language, *this* world, *these* men. The ability to give names — to extend the control of language over the world — must then be a masterly trait: it consists of saying what the world is. The reverse proposition will also be accurate: knowledge of the power of language may lead to a prohibition on the use of certain names. The Old Testament prohibits, for instance, mentioning the "terrible name of God." [48] To name is to define and to bring under control, to give the determination of the being of the object in question. The allocation of names creates the world in the image of he who names. Such creations are properly termed *meta-phors* (beyond-carriers). They are artifacts which *carry* an intellectual process *beyond* the mind into the world.

Nietzsche's analysis is remarkably close to that of Marx and Freud. Both Freud and Marx develop the concept of fetishism; for both, a man-made object is endowed by its human creator with a power and right of control. The object becomes a "natural" force, and turns back on its creator. In *Totem and Taboo*, a primal band of brothers kill and devour a sexually dominating father, only to see the cycle of mastership repeated as one of them emerges the new father. They eventually find it necessary to take fatherhood out of the world and render it inaccessibly by a forbidden name. Thus was born God, religion, and civilization. For Marx, men mix their labor with nature in order to make a commodity, then buy and sell the commodity on a market, convinced that it is in the order of things that commodities be bought for a price other than the value of the labor with which they created it. In both cases, that which is a human creation is taken to be something wonderful, inaccessible, and out of man's control.

Nietzsche's word for the result of this process in appropriately *idol*. It is his conviction of their "twilight" that informs the destructive side of his writing. As early as the essay *On Truth and Lie in the*

Extra-Moral Sense (1873), he had begun to work out the process by which idols come to be consecrated. Truth is conceived of as metaphor, and, as Nietzsche notes in *The Gay Science*, "unspeakably more depends *on what things are called*, than on what they are. The reputation, the name and appearance, the importance . . . of a thing — in origin most frequently an error and arbitrariness, thrown over things like a garment, and quite foreign to their essence [*Wesen*] and even to their exterior — have gradually by belief therein and its growth from generation to generation, grown, so to speak, on-to and into a thing and have become its very body." [49] The metaphors which first lie on life like a light cloak become an iron cage; Weber had noted the same about the protestant ethic. That which had enabled men to make the world rich to themselves — since these imagined worlds are *"necessary"* [50] — is gradually "enhanced, transposed, and embellished poetically and rhetorically and . . . after long use seems firm, canonical, and obligatory to a people: truths are illusions about which one has forgotten that this is what they are; metaphors which are worn out and without senuous power; coins which have lost their picture and now matter only as metal, no longer as coins." [51]

This "mythological basis of action" is problematic. Nietzsche believes that the logic of fetishism or idolatry wears the metaphors out and makes the idols hollow. Thus, the exposure of the shabby origin of these values — their *mesquine Herkunft* — makes the universe appear to be without sense. The foundations of the world are revealed to have no more ontological status than anything else. But, the illusions and metaphors made are necessary. Survival requires communication and thus language and consciousness; without them there "would have long ago been nothing more (of mankind)." [52] And, to further complicate matters, while these illusions are necessary, and now have revealed themselves as idols and no longer gods, one would be a "fool" to think "it would be enough here to refer to this origin and this nebulous veil of illusion, in order to annihilate that which virtually passes for the world, namely so-called 'reality.' " [53]

This is the same problem that came up in the previous chapter. It is perfectly true that men live in a world which at one point was to a great degree their making. To say that the world is therefore an "illusion" is accurate, as long as one accepts that without this illusion there would have been no world. For Nietzsche, there is no "real" world underlying this one, no Sleeping Beauty to be awakened by a single epistemological kiss. The world as it appears is an adjusted and simplified world in which practical reason works. We "live in it and this is our proof of its truth." Nietzsche continues on: "Our particular case is interesting enough: we have made a conception in order to live in a world, in order to perceive just enough that we may *endure* it." [54] Of course "our" world makes some sense: we cannot imagine ourselves not making some sense. But this is no proof of anything beyond the fact that men have established working circles of events.

Hence the problem will not simply be to *expose* the fact that men "alone have devised cause, sequences, for each other, relativity [!!], constraint, number, law, freedom, motive, and purpose," and mixed and projected this symbol-world into things as if it existed in itself. Men have to do this, or something like it. But the *particular* language seems to be the problem, now, and for these men. "Suppose," writes Nietzsche, "we have finally reached the conclusion that there is nothing good or evil in itself; but rather that these are qualities of the soul, which lead us to cover with such words things both inside and outside us. We have taken back the predicates from things; or we have at least recollected that we merely lent the things these predicates. Let us be careful that this insight does not cause us to lose the faculty of lending and that at the same time we do not become wealthier and more avaricious." [55] It is not just that men impose reality on events, but what happens after they do. The problem is, as Nietzsche writes in a section called "Only as Creators," that annihilation is only possible through creation. To escape from the prison of this world, all must be made new.

Language and Nihilism

If there is nothing wrong in *general* with dividing the world up into fictitious categories, what then is wrong with the *particular* manner in which men have done it? Nietzsche is certainly not saying that any manner is as good as any other, even though all manners are errors. Suppose even that as Nietzsche says, "We will not be rid of our belief in God until we have abandoned our faith in grammar." Is this necessarily so bad that one should get upset enough to spend other than philosophical time on it? Why should men not be happy to rest uncomfortably in "the shadows of the dead God," since, as Nietzsche continually repeats, there is, in fact, no permanent resting place for "truth?" If Nietzsche is to do more than expose, he must believe that other forms of language and life are possible, and that his exposures of the prejudices of this one might overcome its problems.

The ultimate answer requires an analysis of eternal return. It is possible, however, to give some preliminary indications. Nietzsche finds that men have thought that they always possessed consciousness. Since it has not been a problem for them, they have given themselves very little trouble in its acquisition. In particular, they have not attempted to acquire a given *type* of consciousness, but have merely allowed that which was around to determine theirs, as if it were the only possibility. Thus "it is an entirely new problem just dawning on the human eye and hardly yet plainly recognizable to embody knowledge in ourselves and make it instinctive, a problem which is only seen by those who have grasped the fact that hitherto our errors alone have been embodied in us, and that all our consciousness is relative to errors." [56] Two preliminary indications appear in this statement. First, it seems that the problem that Nietzsche sees facing humanity will be that of "embodying knowledge" and "making it instinctive." He had already argued in the second of the *Untimely Considerations* that humanity's present "nature" had been itself acquired through such an embodiment. How this process is to work will occupy much of Nietzsche's work and thought for the rest of his life.

Secondly, it appears that there is some structure inherent in the ways men have approached the world which leads them to develop a life composed only of errors. [57] Again, in the essay *On the Use and Disadvantage of History for Life*, Nietzsche finds that "our whole being is divided mechanically into an inner and outer side, . . . such that we suffer from the malady of words and have no trust in any feeling not yet stamped with words. . . . This . . . life is sick and must be healed." [58]

The sickness of understanding results from the fact that the present method of approaching knowledge is such that men can never be content, and it is this approach that ultimately makes a satisfying answer impossible. All searches for causes, for subjects, are moral searches in the sense that they attempt to uncover who or what is *responsible* for things being as they are. In its essence a *regressus in infinitum*, [59] "knowledge" is ultimately a moral ideology which men apply the better to survive. All points at which they stop in the search for truth are those that they take (temporarily) as obviously true. The search for a stopping point will thus be ceaseless. If one person or school were to stop philosophizing, another must pick it up.

This search for responsibility is ultimately fueled by a moral imperative; it operates in consciousness; thus consciousness will not be able to refrain from applying the same moral energy to itself. In an important passage dated specifically June 10, 1887, as if he had finally gotten something right, Nietzsche writes:

But among the forces cultivated by morality was *truthfulness*: this eventually turned against morality, discovered its *teleology*, its prejudiced [*interessiert*] perspective, and now the *recognition* of this long incarnate [*eingefleischt*] mendacity that one despairs of getting rid of, works as a stimulant. To nihilism. Now we discover in ourselves needs implanted by a long understanding of morality, which now appear to us as needs for untruth; on the other hand, these needs are those on which the values for which we endure life seem to hang. This antagonism — *not* to esteem what we know and not to be *allowed* any longer to value those lies we would tell ourselves — results in a process of dissolution.[60]

Thus, the desire to found knowledge on truth results in a gradual undermining of that which might serve as a basis for truth. As more and more is unmasked, the flux of the world increases until the river becomes a raging torrent which carries all away. [61] The will to truth will, when applied to itself, question those foundations that made it possible. As Nietzsche wrote in *The Gay Science*, it does not imply that "I will not allow myself to be deceived," but rather, "there is no other alternative, I will not deceive, not even myself." As noted above, "great things perish of their own accord." Here the structure by which men have sought truth has finally turned against and unmasked the system of truth itself. That which erected truth has finally destroyed its own creation.

The will to truth carries a perverse necrophilia. If life is in fact appearance and there is no "truth" to be reached, the defense of the will to truth is the assertion of the ultimate validity of a man-made perspective. There is, in fact, no reason that "truth" should be preferred. To affirm it is then to affirm a moral system, that men should live *like this*. This leads Nietzsche to speculate on the possibility that there might lie in the will to truth a "concealed will toward death." [62] Freud was to say no less in *Civilization and its Discontents*.

What, then, is the epistemology of nihilism? The hidden linguistic imperatives of the categories men now live under force them toward nothingness. Since nihilism is the end stage of such a process, it too must be an ultimate state of morality. Men arrive at it, in Nietzsche's understanding, when *they find both that there is no truth, and that they should continue to seek it.* The will to truth drives men even further into the void, and that they may now recognize it as void is no help. As Nietzsche notes at the very end of the *Genealogy of Morals*, "man would rather will the void, than be void of will." Here, then, is the position the epistemology arrives at: *the present structure of human understanding forces men to continue searching for that which their understanding tells them is not to be found.* This is the epistemology of nihilism.

This is no longer simply the "problem" of metaphysics that Kant has noted, subjected to analysis, and found not to be responsible for itself. Since Nietzsche has refused the succor of the realm of theoretical reason, the problems of truth must be found in practical reason. This latter, now detached from any possible link to a purer world, is a human responsibility: the contradictions are ours, and not just inherent in the relations between the theoretical and practical world. As noted above, for Nietzsche the "faith in the categories of reason is the cause of nihilism." That men continue to believe that the world should be meaningful, though unable to discover anything they might recognize as a satisfactory meaning, is the consequence of their inability to admit that the problem lies in themselves. Nietzsche's dictum that one "cannot endure the world, though one does not want to deny it," [63] becomes a comment not, as it was for Kant, on the structures of reason, but on the human (all-too-human) condition.

The unmasking enterprise which is genealogy is part of the growth of nihilism. The ulcers are finally bleeding, men know they have more than a stomach ache. The analysis of epistemology has shown Nietzsche that the categories of reason men use have progressively removed them from the world. This language has given men only "bloated idols"; and the fetishes and spider webs of ideality no longer refer to a sensuous world. Rilke seized upon this divorce in one of his letters.

Even for our grandparents a "house," a "well," a familiar tower, their very clothes, their coat, were infinitely more, infinitely more intimate; almost everything a vessel in which they found the human and added to the store of the human. Now ... empty indifferent things are pouring across ..., sham things, dummy life ... ; a house [now], ... an apple or a grapevine, ... has nothing in common with the house, the fruit, the grape into which went the hopes and reflections of our forefathers. .... Live things, things live and conscious of us, are running out and can no longer be replaced.[64]

If, as Hegel once remarked, "in the dark, all cows are black," our language has, in Nietzsche's estimation, manifested that darkness. He writes to understand and annihilate it.

Interlude: The Philosopher as Physician
of Language, Nietzsche and Wittgenstein

Throughout this chapter and the previous one it has been possible to illustrate many of Nietzsche's points through citations from the work of Ludwig Wittgenstein. This parallel has been noted before, for both share the concern with the hold that language has on life. Both, too, write in a philosophically unconventional manner. Generally, however, the parallels between them have redounded to the philosophical benefit of Wittgenstein; for instance, in *The Birth of Tragedy*, it is only allowed that Nietzsche had some "insights." Articles drawing this link have generally contented themselves with the "pointing" approach: "See, this looks like this."[65]

It is possible, however, to bring the writers together in such a way that their mutual resonance opens new understanding of each man. Nietzsche, of course, could not have known Wittgenstein. Wittgenstein, on the other hand, had apparently read some Nietzsche; he refers in the *Brown Book* to the doctrine of eternal return. Both writers share a common appreciation for Schopenhauer, whom Wittgenstein once defended against Carnap's depreciation to the astonished Vienna Circle. And, substantively, though a considerable portion of Wittgenstein's work is oriented toward specific problems and questions in the philosophy of language, he quickly found it necessary to move in what I might call a more anthropological direction. That he did so (in the *Philosophical Investigations*) is an indication that the writers share an appreciation that language cannot be understood except in terms of its relation to the human condition. The symmetry in their perspective will reflect my understanding of their common intent: to re-cover the world, so that it be again livable.

Late in the *Investigations*, Wittgenstein writes, "that which is to be accepted — the given one might say — is forms of life." [66] In *On Certainty*, a book on which he was working at the time of his death, he notes: "You must bear in mind that the language game is so to speak something unpredictable. I mean: it is not based on grounds [*ist nicht begründet*]. It is not reasonable (or unreasonable). It stands there — like our life." [67] Assuming the two quotes can be linked, he seems to mean something like this. A form of life, be it our existence, or a game that we play, is in general not subject to justification. By virtue of what it is, it "stands there." The categories "reasonable," "unreasonable," "logical" (predictable"), "illogical," *simply do not apply*. There is no sphere or category of reason which might provide a foundation for them.

The concern is repeated throughout Wittgenstein's life and career. Are there grounds for statements? What is the basis for taking something to be the case? And, during the course of his "philosophical journeys," as he called them, he came to the conclusion that at a certain point justification is exhausted. One has reached "bedrock: the spade is turned." And at such times, one is inclined to simply say: "This is what I do." This passage from *On Certainty* probably consciously echoes Luther before the diet of Worms: "Here I stand, I can do no other."[68] After all explanations and justifications, one is left with the "form of life" – the *Lebensform* – which is not itself subject to justification. It is rather, as Wittgenstein wrote in *On Certainty*, a "world picture" which is "part of a kind of mythology."

For me, Wittgenstein here is looking about in the same manner as did Nietzsche. Any proposition is possible if and only if we acknowledge as given, "real," and unquestioned some foundation for our knowledge. Some unjustified grounds have to be recognized and acknowledged as the basis of our knowledge: in the end, remarks Wittgenstein, "knowing depends on acknowledging." [69] A certain form of life makes (a certain) knowledge possible. The acceptance of a form of life thus "designates the form of the account that we give, the way in which we look at things." [70] He shares with Nietzsche the notion that the grounds of a statement appear as "real," that is, having natural foundation, even though they don't have one "in fact." The grounds "appear to have the form of an empirical proposition," but I can only "discover them subsequently like the axis around which a body rotates. This axis is not fixed in the sense that anything holds it fast, but the movement around it determines its immobility." [71]

As in Nietzsche, the grounds for a proposition are not subject to the rules they establish. In a passage I have mentioned before, Wittgenstein notes: "There is one thing of which one can say neither that it is a meter long, not that it is not a meter long, and that is the standard meter in Paris." [72] If it were to properly be (or not be) a meter long it would have to be long in terms of something else. However, it is not a meter *long*, it is a meter. It simply stands there and different words have to apply to it.

Men tend, however, with what Stanley Cavell has called "a philosophical tic," to want to refer to it as a meter *long*. Why such obstinacy? For Wittgenstein, it is because men want the certainty of a single form. "This word forces itself upon you," writes Wittgenstein in an attempt to bring out the mode of compulsion. "It is just a single form which forces the expression upon us." [73] Thus, for Wittgenstein, we are "held captive" by a particular manner of perceiving, by a "picture," and we "cannot get outside of it, for it lay in our language and language seemed to repeat itself to us inexorably." [74] The nature of the compulsion that language controls us by is seen by Wittgenstein to be one of *repetition*: the same structures and functions keep coming back in everything that we do as we use the language. In the crude analogy I have used before, epistemologically language is like the capitalist mode of production which recurs constantly in capitalist societies, or like slave morality which reappears as the form of moral interaction under any number of empirical cloaks.

Wittgenstein is quite clear, for instance, that our notion of identity seems to be expressed and to exist only in language, "Essence is expressed by grammar." When we call objects by the same words in the same language, we tend to "arbitrarily" take rules as expressing intrinsic necessities. In apparently denying that even logic is something in any sense "sublime," Wittgenstein goes beyond all those apparently intrinsic necessities which in language are "essences," be these versions of Platonic forms, or Kantian transcendental categories. Almost echoing Nietzsche's statements tying the belief in God to the faith in grammar, Wittgenstein sees "theology as grammar." [75]

Language holds us captive in the pictures it draws. We think of them as necessary, but "what looks as if it *had* to exist, is part of the language." [76] Wittgenstein occasionally calls this the "ideal" which, "as we think of it, is unshakable. You can never get outside of it; you must always turn back. There is no outside; outside there is no life air [*Lebensluft*] — whence all this: The idea sits on our nose like a pair of glasses, and we see what we see through them. It never occurs to us to take them off." [77] The language chosen in the initial ironic sequence is revealing and informative. There is no "air" to give us "life" outside the world which is the present construction of our life. This is not a denial that there may be other outsides, and thus, so to speak, other worlds. However, for Wittgenstein as for Nietzsche, from the perspective of a world, in *this* language, there is nothing else. When it occurs to us to take off the glasses which have shaped what we have seen, we have efficiently questioned these premises about which we previously had no thoughts. Glasses, for Wittgenstein, and horizons, for Nietzsche, are necessary; but they are not transcendental.

The danger for Wittgenstein is the danger for Nietzsche. By leaving the glasses on, men understand everything in terms of them. Such is a "main cause of philosophical disease — a one sided diet: one nourishes one's thinking through only one kind of example." [78] By making us focus on only one kind of thing, our language in fact bewitches us, and takes us from the realm of everyday life to the realm of metaphysics. [79] Wittgenstein is then concerned to break the hold a language has on relations with the world. It leads us around by the nose, removing our life-world and replacing it with a "house of cards." Through the "bewitchment of our intelligence," we are given an "urge" to misunderstand; [80] in fact, when we do philosophy, "we are like savages, primitive peoples who hear the expressions of civilized men, put a false interpretation on them and then draw the queerest [*seltsam*] conclusions from it." [81]

This, then, is the famous "fly bottle"; we, then, are the flies whom Wittgenstein would show the way out. For Nietzsche, the fly bottle is a web. Both are devices for catching insects, driven and lured willy-nilly in a direction which, even if they think at all, they seem to have no choice but to follow. Release from the attraction of the fly bottle requires a "discovery . . . that gives philosophy peace, so that it is no longer tormented by questions which bring itself into question. . . ." [82] The old problem of metaphysics, first encountered by

Kant, is seen by Wittgenstein as that which must simply be eliminated.

Metaphysics, in fact philosophy, is for Kant, Nietzsche, and Wittgenstein a species of inquiry which seems to finish self-destructively. The solution that Kant finds is not acceptable to either Nietzsche or Wittgenstein. Kant attempts a reconciliation between the intellect and life; for the two later writers these two seem to contradict each other. I understand giving "philosophy peace" to mean the development of an understanding such that it simply no longer occurs or appears necessary to us to raise the questions that philosophy raises. Our form of life would not require it; such questions have become "un-questioned." To achieve "peace" requires a method that allows men to stop doing philosophy when "they want to," a release from a continuous imperative to continue searching for that which we now know cannot be found. For Wittgenstein, a release from philosophizing. For Nietzsche, an overcoming of nihilism. The parallel of release is established, [83] but it is still not clear what this may mean.

"There is not a philosophical method," Wittgenstein says in a famous passage in the *Investigations*, "though there are methods, like different therapies." Properly conceived, philosophy can be something like a therapy: it will remove disease. There are many diseases, many therapies, but never a magic staff. The analogy, as old as Plato, is of the utmost importance. If the task of philosophy is to liberate us from the "ideals" that keep us captive, and thus free us from the tyranny of an absolute world picture, philosophy is not therefore in the business of providing us with answers, any more than the task of the therapist is to provide us with explanations rather than *cures*. Failing answers, the task of the philosopher is still that of Socrates — to put himself out of business. Nietzsche here also wished the "*overcoming of philosophers*, through *annihilation* of the world of being." [84]

The therapy envisaged abandons the "world of being" in which answers are throught and sought. Instead of providing answers it attempts to bring matters down to earth. This is the depth of meaning of "ordinary language philosophy" [85] as Wittgenstein conceived of it: to show man with complete clarity where he is living. Such therapy is begun, for Wittgenstein as for Nietzsche, by revealing as prejudices those structures of language and perception that had always seemed so real. The most important, writes Wittgenstein, are "hidden because of their simplicity and familiarity. (One is unable to see something because it is always before one's eyes.) The real foundations of his enquiry do not strike a man at all, unless that fact has sometime struck him. — And this means: we fail to be struck by what, once seen, is most striking and powerful." [86]

The task is to show us what we ordinarily do, but in such a manner that it strikes us, or seems even a little queer. This is not a matter simply of explanation; rather, "description alone" must be the task. Wittgenstein takes words and concepts, and shows them to us in a context — a "language game" — which makes it perfectly clear what exactly is meant and said at that particular time by that particular person. At this point we *see* what the word is; the understanding is with absolute clarity; there are no more questions to ask than there are of the answer to a riddle.

The tools of "the language game" make this possible. These are "clear and simple" artifacts in which all the component parts are known and under control. It is wrong to think that Wittgenstein is trying here to construct a pure or universalized language; he is not even attempting to "regularize" language, as some of his detractors or supporters would argue. [87] Rather a language game is "objects of comparison which are meant to throw light on the fact of our language not only by way of similarities, but also of dissimilarities." [88] In this sense, [89] language games are not descriptions of reality, but a set of "thought experiemnts," designed the better to help us see the life world around us. They are "so to speak a measuring rod, not a prejudice [*Vorurteil*] to which reality must correspond." A language game by itself does not explain reality, nor does it describe the world; rather, it re-arranges the world that it may be the better described. "These are, of course," says Wittgenstein, "not empirical problems; they are rather solved by looking at the workings of our language, and that in such a way as to make us recognize those workings: in despite of an urge to misunderstand them. The problems are solved not by the giving of new information, but by arranging what we have always known." [90] As with a jigsaw puzzle, the problem is to see appropriately.

The language game thus strikes me as occupying a position in this manner of doing philosophy analogous to the genealogical investigation of Nietzsche. Both are constructed tools. No pretense is made that they somehow describe the empirical world (which is not to say that they do not make the empirical world available). Both are used to shed light on those portions of men's lives which, from either moral prejudice, or habit, from needs or for self-protection, they do not confront fact to face. Both attempt new illumination of that which appears to men, an illumination such that the objects in question are made present in a new manner.

Finally, and perhaps most importantly, while the historical usefulness of particular language games and particular investigations is supposed, the historical accuracy, in the sense of representing the "facts," is not. Both Nietzsche and Wittgenstein are interested in what makes the facts as they are. Thus, in which might appear otherwise to be a puzzling passage, Wittgenstein can write: "If the formation of concepts can be explained by facts of nature, should we not be interested, not in grammar, but rather in that nature which is the basis of grammar?" Here Wittgenstein has set up a potential socio-historical critique of his manner of investigating the world: if the world generates concepts, "should we not" investigate the world. His answer follows immediately. "Our interest certainly includes the correspondence between concept and very general facts of nature. (Such facts mostly do not strike us because of their very generality.) But our interest does not fall back on these problems of the formation of concepts; we are not doing natural science, nor yet natural history — since we can invent fictitious natural history for our purposes." [91] Thus also will Nietzsche place the argument in *On the Use and Disadvantage of History for Life*. He argues that the historian creates "an artistically, not a historically true picture." "In this sense," he continues, "to think objectively of history is the quiet work of the dramatist: namely to think one thing into another and weave the element into a whole: all with the presumption that the unity of plan *must be put into things*, if it is not already there. . . . There could be a manner of writing history which contained not the slightest drop of common empirical truth and could still claim to be called in the highest degree objective." [92]

The cure — to return to the medical analogy — effectuated by this therapy will be to remove the disease. Here again the analogy is instructive. First, the diagnosis. For Nietzsche, the purpose of the investigations he undertakes is "to understand these truisms from *within* and to translate them into a doctrine for one's own use through personal experience." Only this will give us the "clear vision" which will allow us to see that this life is "sick . . . from many diseases" and must be "healed." [93] For Wittgenstein, philosophy reaches "results" when one or another piece of "disguised nonsense" is uncovered as "plain" or "patent" nonsense, such that one sees "the bumps that the understanding has got by running up its head against the limits of language. These bumps make us see the value of discovery." [94] Once diagnosed, the cure is affected by the removal of the disease: therapy consists not of completing a sequence once begun ("answering a question"), but of eliminating the sequence (by showing "disguised nonsense" as "patent nonsense"). Therefore, for both Nietzsche and Wittgenstein, the problem is to find a form of life in which men no longer incarnate only those errors that make for their destruction. This incarnation was nihilism in Nietzsche, and the prison of the search for the "ideal" in Wittgenstein. A change in incarnation, however, is a transfiguration, a becoming new, an alteration in form of life. In an otherwise perplexing passage in the *Remarks on the Foundations of Mathematics*, Wittgenstein writes: "The sickness of a time is cured by an alteration in the mode of life of human beings, and it was possible for the sickness of philosophical problems to get cured only through a changed mode of thought, not through a medicine invented by an individual." [95] The suggestion in both Wittgenstein and Nietzsche seems to be that if it should prove that the disease is so rooted in the very stuff of human life, then the corresponding therapy will have to be nothing less than to change that "mode of life." What a change in "mode of life" or in what is "human-all-too-human" means is not immediately accessible without an understanding of eternal return.

The language game and the genealogical investigation are analogous and are in the service of a similar purpose: the liberation of men from the unknown chains that bind them prisoner to a particular and destructive manner of viewing the world. They are different in that the genealogy is a potentially far more complex tool because it attempts to give a description that is not only synchronic (of the harmonic structure, one might say if this were a piece of music) but also diachronic (of the line development, to continue musically). Wittgenstein certainly understood the need to do this; many passages in *On Certainty* stand witness. [96] He never finally accomplished it. Conversely, the genealogy in Nietzsche's hands often remains a crude, if powerful instrument. Weber was to take some further steps. It remains an unfinished task, however.

Both men do finally point to an immediate and central problem. If

particular existence can be understood, it can only be understood in language, with the words and grammar, the epistemology, that make up that language. And, since there is no knowledge or recognition of others or of self without an appropriate language, if one understands that language, one also can understand what it is to be a human being who speaks that language. A second point follows on the first: since language is the structure in which a system of interactions is maintained, language is only practical; there cannot be a "pure" language, which would refer to a realm other than itself.[1] For Nietzsche, the necessary impurity of the means by which men understand themselves and others places humans irrevocably and definitely *in* the world. No matter how much one is tempted to escape, no matter how attractive the assurances of the ideal, no matter what tools one seeks out, there will be no escape from the givenness of our particular condition, for there is nowhere to escape to. We have only ourselves, even though our epistemology, Nietzsche argues, leads us to avoid that recognition.

As such, language must become for Nietzsche the embodiment of a particular moral system. As we saw, he refers to the "philosophical mythology" which lies hidden in the deep structure of a language and which is maintained by our desire to see it as real. Men are seduced — the word is appropriately erotic and blind — toward the ideal, to embrace the particular way they act as, in imagined fact, the only way. For Nietzsche, the basis of a language hides a moral system. It controls what is permitted to appear on stage as an actor, and what must seem inappropriate or rude.

Divergences in moral conclusions may therefore reflect not just disagreement, but in fact the conflict of two opposite moral grammars. After a certain point, the translation of the actions one person undertakes into terms comprehensible to another must come to an end. Wittgenstein notes in the *Investigations* that at certain times, one simply has to say "this is what I do." Portions of languages may make contact, and of course, forms of life do interact meaningfully. But as wholes, be these English and Chinese, or the languages of morality and teaching, they are separated. This is only as it must be: they may meet on a bias, so to speak, but were they to be in principle completely commensurable, they would be so in terms of something; this would then become the "real world." While Kant found he could make this move, Nietzsche sees it only a phantom called up to keep a particular world in order.

There seems to be here a direct implication, often accepted by commentators, that Nietzsche is some sort of cultural relativist. *Autre temps, autre moeurs*: we have ours, they have theirs, and that is just the way it is. Such however is not Nietzsche's position. As a preliminary step toward demonstrating this, it is useful and pleasing to clear up a debate current among Nietzsche scholars. I replay it here partly because it helps advance the argument toward the problem of cultural relativism, and partly because it is indicative of the problems of approaching Nietzsche as if he should fit into the great categories of Western thought. In my understanding, the problem under examination here — Did Nietzsche have or have not a coherent doctrine of epistemology? — centers around questions which, if properly viewed, disappear.

Arthur Danto, an American philosopher, has recently argued that all of Nietzsche's ideas can be seen as related to a central epistemological position which he refers to as that of a "semantical nihilist and a non-cognitivist in ethics."[2] Without accepting for himself all of what he sees to be Nietzsche's conclusions, he can conclude that Nietzsche's epistemological ventures do indeed have a coherent and instructive validity in themselves. To reduce Danto's argument, it seems to imply something like this. For Nietzsche, most of what men understand as moral and metaphysical problems are in fact not problems at all, but merely the consequences of confused and self-serving manners of thinking. If they were to clean up the detritus of the ages and speak straight, most moral differences would be shown to rest on other differences. In themselves, they would prove evanescent. The position is curiously like that of an existential Hume; perhaps even Ayer or Weldon in the current philosophical fraternity of modern positivism might admit some kinship with it. "If only people used language as it was intended" becomes a lament, which, if repeated enough, might serve to cleanse the Augean stables of metaphysics.[3] All of this is useful enough; it does point out that epistemological concerns run very deep in Nietzsche; it does presume that the root of many problems we have can best be shown in an examination of language. But it misses the basic point. Language *is* intended. Therefore it cannot be understood apart from an understanding of those who intend it.

The other side of this fence in epistemology is occupied by men sharing the same field as Karl Jaspers. He notes accurately that Nietzsche sees the world to be non-structured and ultimately chaos.

Therefore, he concludes, apparently quite sensibly, Nietzsche must realize that epistemology is impossible. The science of knowledge must require an object; the object is not there, thus the science flees also.[4] This view acquires strong support from Nietzsche's own statements on the subject. If, as he claims in the Preface to *On The Genealogy of Morals*, men of knowledge "*must* be unknown to themselves," this certainly implies that epistemology cannot be pushed beyond a certain point. Such, however (and here Jaspers betrays his traditional and Christian perspective), does not mean that epistemologies are not possible. Some are better and some worse than others, though they will of course be so in terms of something that is neither epistemological rules, nor the accuracy of their description of the "real world." Nietzsche does object to the notion that a "good" epistemology might provide one with a privileged philosophical resting point.

Cultural Relativism and Beyond

The above considerations still seem to move Nietzsche in the direction of relativism. He appears to have linked epistemology firmly to moral practice and to have consequently asserted the ultimate equality of moral systems. A more careful look at his practice reveals however that the conclusion does not necessarily follow. Nietzsche never engages in a comparison of moral practices. It is not useful to him to draw relations of similarity and difference between Western and Buddhist or Hindu moral systems. Such surface comparisons must be necessarily misleading and generally erroneous; they lead only to the obvious conclusion that the overt morality of one culture is occasionally the guilty sin of another. It is conceivable that such comparisons could become as complicated as functionalist anthropology sought to become in the period following Nietzsche's death (and still seeks to be). But the search for the particular content of "leadership functions" in various societies begged the question that Nietzsche knew and posed very well: Where might these "functions" come from? *Whose* functions are they? What needs do they serve? Are they really written in an anthropological book of laws, or are they only an idea; if so, whose? If Nietzsche does not escape from cultural relativism, he will be repeating the same error that he so strongly attacked in Kant. He will have posited an ideal world such that one can continue to arrive at desired conclusions, here a world of "functions."

Nietzsche instead seeks to go below the surface and empirical manifestations of moral systems, while refusing himself the ultimate comfort of a "pure" realm of morality. This is genealogy; Nietzsche is not concerned with moral behavior or the diverse practical manifestations of a supposed categorical imperative, but rather with the genetic origins of morality, the soil it springs out of.[5] "Master morality," for instance, describes for Nietzsche not the moral practices of masters, but the structure of a particular type of action. Hence all descriptions of the empirical aspects of a particular moral system will reveal nothing about that which is constitutive and basic. "Perhaps," writes Nietzsche, "there is no more important proposition for all manner of historiography than this one — which though reached with great difficulties, *must* still *be* reached, that the actual causes of a thing's origin and its subsequent usefulness, its factual incorporation into and organization in a system of purposes, lie worlds apart. . . . No matter how well we understand the *usefulness* of some physiological organ (or a legal institution, an artistic genre, a social custom, a political usage, an artistic or a cultic trait) we still have understood nothing regarding its origin."[6] By breaking back through the empirical manifestations of a particular moral code (the "subsequent usefulness"), Nietzsche's intention is to uncover the origin, while recognizing full well that there is no obvious link between the two. Since, however, the origin lives on in the event, he will by the act of unmasking have discovered what necessities are being served; this will tell him something about the men who have those necessities, something about the form of life in question.

He is thus not "exposing" morality in a crude and simple manner. To claim, as he does in *The Twilight of the Idols*, that "morality belongs to the realm of the psychology of error," where cause and effect are confused, or that truth is confused with "the effects of believing something to be true,"[7] is not to deny that it has served a certain form of life. These may have been "false values," but "one must understand that they had to exist: they are the *results* of causes [*Ursachen*] which have nothing to do with premises [*Gründen*]."[8] For Nietzsche, "false" premises are the only kind of premises there are. Men require the veil of illusion (what Nietzsche refers to as the apollonian) in order to survive and maintain a form of life. *Morality is thus a necessary lie* for humans, without which man never would have evolved a human form but would have remained a beast.

These considerations do move Nietzsche away from the cultural relativists. It is certainly true that, as Zarathustra proclaims, "a tablet hangs over the head of each people," and equally true that morality is "a system of value judgments concerned with the conditions of life of a being."[9] But, to move from here to asserting with La Rochefoucauld that the relative worth of all things is referable back to relative cultures is to commit the Protagorean error on a social, even a world historical level. It does make men, rather than man, the measure of all things, but still ignores the fact that "men" might themselves be the problem. The cultural relativists still remain, after the recognition of these facts, at a level that refuses to deal with morality itself as a problem. Nietzsche does not inquire into the *worth* of a particular morality; he knows that it is valued because it maintains a form of life. He *does inquire* into the worth of a form of life. To come to the "conclusion that no morality is binding, after the truth has dawned . . . that among different peoples moral valuations are necessarily different" is still a "childish folly."[10] It does not push the critique as far as possible.

All such critiques assume the sufficiency of criticism about the often foolish opinions that a people may have about its morality. In fact, however, nothing critical has been said of morality as a concept. The cultural relativist, having reduced matters down to a practice, leaves the question there. Good and evil are left uncriticized as categories. Here I broach the most important part of Nietzsche's attack on morality. If philosophical problems were for Nietzsche not so much solved as dissolved, so also the "solution" here would not be to erect a "good" morality, but rather, similar to the recognition that there can be no "pure" language, to escape from those imperatives that *any* morally structured situation may put upon men. Nietzsche does not deny that there is in fact something properly called morality. But he says over and above this that as long as men and women behave in a manner that can properly be called moral, or as long as there are moral problems and choices, the results of men's actions will turn against themselves. In terms as blunt as possible, *morality is a manner of behaving which is necessary only because of the sort of being that we are*. Like language, it makes the world simpler and less fearsome; like language, it will continue to repeat the world to us and ourselves to the world in what Nietzsche sees as an increasingly vicious circle. If morality poses a *problem*, then, in Nietzsche's understanding, the resolution can only come in a form of life in which it is unnecessary to behave in a manner that is morally structured. (This does not mean behaving *im*morally; that would still imply morality. It means the concepts don't apply.) Hence, Nietzsche not only moves back to the origins in his critique, *but beyond that to a critique of the origins themselves.* To do only the former would have been to avoid a critique of the form of life which requires morality; he is not doing a moral genealogy, but a "genealogy of morals." [11]

The Critique of the Utilitarian

There is a previous attempt to criticize morality as a concept. In his main treatise on the genealogy of morals, Nietzsche feels obliged to start with a tribute to these men, and a criticism of their efforts. What he says about them, the British Utilitarians, is instructive, for it not only reveals Nietzsche's own understanding, but also closely parallels his criticisms of Kantian epistemology. In both he finds the burgeon of a deep understanding which is kept from flowering by the desire to retain a certain form of life. The utilitarians essay — a "very English" attempt — an explanation of the origin of moral values in terms of an elaborate rationalization of a pain-pleasure calculus they believe potentially common to all men. [12] Nietzsche's critique of utilitarianism is complex and varied. He wishes to show what is living in it, what may be salvaged, but also that as a whole it ultimately fails.

Firstly, despite the fact that the utilitarian theory is intended to explain the origin of moral sentiments, it tends rather to cut the other way and describe certain sentiments that utilitarians would call moral. It must be so: since it sees morality as the result of a pain-pleasure calculus, it relies on what men think of the consequences of their actions. Nietzsche here implicitly accepts Kant's argument that the structure of moral action must be universalizable. The problem with utilitarianism is that it is based on the multiplicity of human conclusions as to what is moral (painful-pleasurable); it

must then appear to be simply a complicated version of the Protagorean conclusions. For the utilitarians, a hedonistic calculator is the
measure of all things moral. This is far too superficial for Nietzsche.
In an aphorism in *Dawn of Day* called "Utilitarian," he writes,
"Perception's in moral matters now run so much in all directions
[*kreuz and quer*] that, for these men, one demonstrates a morality
[*eine Moral*] because of its usefulness, while for those, one refutes it
precisely because of that." [13] I interpret this to be an argument
against utilitarianism based on the realization that since the doctrine
admits differing conclusions as to moral practice, it in no ways has
penetrated below the surface of behavior. It is, of course, obvious
that men differ in their moral conclusions, but a position whose logic
immediately admits its own refutation cannot be right. A note from
1887 continues this theme explicitly: "What is called '*useful*' is
completely dependent on the *intention*, the wherefore . . . Thus,
utilitarianism is not a basic teaching [*Grundlage*] but rather one
about *consequences* and absolutely cannot bring any obligation for
all." [14] The task is to criticize the category of moral sentiments; this,
however, as Kant had conclusively shown, is by definition potentially
universal. Whatever the utilitarians are talking about, they have not
yet arrived at this category.

In the above criticism, Nietzsche states that the intention was the
most important determinant of what is useful. As such his criticism is
incomplete, for he knows well that "motives and intentions are
seldom sufficiently clear and simple, and sometimes memory itself
seems clouded by the consequences of the deed, so that one ascribes
deeds to false motives." [15] It is apparent that this realization and the
consequent attempt to unravel morality are also at the bottom of the
critique that Bentham had launched at the moralists of his day. The
hedonistic calculus was an attempt to cut through the vagaries of
memory and to ground morality in human behavior and not in
rationality or natural law. Indeed, along these lines, Nietzsche admits
that utilitarianism is a "plausible mode of thought." Certainly he
admires and approves the attempt to ground moral sentiments in a
clear and this-wordly explanation of psychological bases; but he does
not find the pain-pleasure calculus to be such a clear explanation.
Rather, such a calculus seems to him reflective of a desire to do away
with suffering and "invent happiness." So, while approving of the
attempt, the result at which Benthamites and their more warm-

blooded descendents arrive seems to him at best petty. As reads an aphorism in *Beyond Good and Evil*: "Well-being as you understand it: that is no goal; it seems to us a finish, a state that will soon make man ridiculous and contemptible . . . ." [16]

This pettiness occurs because the utilitarians do not realize that their own expression of preference, their calculus, is only a manifestation of their particular desires. In this case, the desires happen to be those of thoroughly civilized Englishmen. It is not so much the explanation that is faulty; this is held to be "self-consistent and psychologically tenable within its limits." [17] It is rather a historical elaboration of this calculus which Nietzsche attacks as sociologically, historically, and therefore philosophically unsound. The utilitarians think "by nature unhistorically . . . . The key notions . . . [of] 'utility,' 'forgetting,' 'habit,' and in the end 'error,' all underlie an evaluation of which the higher man has hitherto been proud, as if it were a general prerogative of man as such." The utilitarians attempt a debunking of Christianity; it fails, though, because it "looks for the genesis of the notion of good in the wrong place . . . : with those whose good it has proved." [18]

The problem now becomes the reason why the utilitarians arrive at such a petty and contemptible conclusion. The answer is not hard. They have failed to realize that they have taken their empirical moral practices and read them back as causes of moral behavior. In epistemology, this was the "error of confusing cause and effect." Here it is also an anti-historical attitude. The Englishmen have taken their moral system, posited it as a universal and timeless fact, and attempted to explain it in a manner that might prove universally applicable. For Nietzsche, their reasoning seems to go like this: "We, Englishmen, behave in a moral manner; this we know. We must explain this behavior in terms that can apply to other moralities as well without denying the fact that either we or they are behaving morally. The principle of utility explains this." But, for Nietzsche, when the task of debunking the origins of Christian values is supposedly accomplished, instead of a new scale to measure moral worth, the utilitarians only come up with conclusions specifically tied to an English notion of proper behavior. *Sans génie et sans esprit,* these men in the end want "English morality to be recognized as authoritative. . . . They would like . . . to convince themselves that the striving after English happiness . . . is at the same time the true path of virtue." [19] In doing so they have falsely understood themselves as timeless inhabitants of the kingdom of "real" morality.

Nietzsche's most important criticism of the utilitarians, then, is of their critique. They remain, just as did the epistemologists, inextricably bound to the premise they are trying to get away from; they make a criticism of moral sentiments, but never of morality in itself. "Utilitarianism," writes Nietzsche, "criticizes the origin of moral valuations, *but it believes in them.*" [20] This final criticism of utilitarianism is not directed at their approach, but at the consequences of their conclusions. Nietzsche feels that a criticism that leaves the question of moral sentiments on the level of "the good is what makes me feel happy" is characteristic of a time that seeks only to reduce the pain and tension it feels. Nietzsche traces this to the necessity of protecting oneself from the tensions of life in the era of nihilism. Hence, for him, the mode of decision characteristic of utilitarianism "smells of the *populace,* who comprehend only the unpleasant consequences of wrongdoing and thus conclude 'it is *stupid* to do wrong' while they identify the good with the 'useful and pleasant, without further ado." [21] The success of the utilitarian must be based on the wisdom of hindsight; unless the experiences that permit pain-pleasure calculations remain fundamentally unchanged in kind and in number, adequate expectations of the results of a given action will be impossible. Utilitarianism must then restrict the availability of experience and deny the possibility of new experiences.

Explaining the Familiar

The confusion of the English is compounded by their attempt to make the moral sciences over in the image of the natural sciences. In physics, one takes as the object of inquiry the strange and unknown. In the moral sciences, Nietzsche feels that the problem has been shown to be the familiar, that which is so close to our faces that we never see it. The utilitarians assume that the reduction of moral behavior to quanta of pain and pleasure might permit a "scientific calculus." This becomes far too easy a conclusion. Still to be asked, in Nietzsche's relentless imperative, is the question of the significance of *what pain and pleasure are* for a particular form of life. That this latter was, or could be a problem, simply did not occur to them;

after all, do not all men know what pain and pleasure are? For Nietzsche, as later for Freud, the answer is no.

Having made the initial false assumption that one knew what morality consisted of (in this case, what pleasure and pain were), previous moral sciences never became scientific. They remained moral, tied to the original assumptions that they were supposed to be questioning. They did, however, give man a feeling of understanding, in fact of controlling circumstances that had previously seemed mysterious. "Since at bottom it is merely a matter of whishing to be rid of oppressive representations," writes Nietzsche in *The Twilight of the Idols*, "one is not too particular about the means of getting rid of them; the first representation that explains the unknown as familiar feels so good that one takes it for true." [22] In this understanding, previous moral sciences, in fact morality itself, remain attempts at regulating the world. They depend on the presupposition of an absolute yardstick against which one could measure and judge activity.

For Nietzsche, these assumptions, which are necessary for there to be morality at all, lead inevitably to self-contradiction. On the one hand, moral activity requires the assumption of the existence of some standards independent of and external to the individual. Without this, there is only *laissez-aller*. Furthermore, for moral action to be possible, there must also be free individuals who can choose to partake (or not) of such standards. If one did the right naturally, it would be hard to speak of morality; whatever instincts are, they are certainly not spoken of as moral. Moral choice is only possible if the ego is not a priori identified with the moral realm, but must in fact choose to be part of it. Thus the acquisition of moral significance must at least originally take place in opposition to what the ego is. The ego which makes such choices must, however, be valued in and of itself; its significance must be acquired in opposition to that which is a priori "not-ego," which here must be the sphere of moral standards. Thus the contradiction: the ego must be independent to make moral choices, but the only choices that it can make to be moral are ones that deny its independence. For Nietzsche, any moral choice thereby leads to the destruction of that which makes it possible.

Any given morality is characterized by the particular form this contradiction takes in it; in all cases, the moral system must stamp out the drives toward individuality, even though it could not exist without them. To this effect, "a whole sphere of fantastic hypotheses" were created with the specific mission of slandering egotistic instincts. Human self-assertion must itself be branded as evil so that man will fail to hope that he might by his own will attain satisfaction. "In short," writes Nietzsche in a late note, "once man had brought his instincts into contradiction with a purely imaginary world, he ended by despising himself as incapable of performing actions that were good." [23]

Morality becomes effectively a case of what Hegel, in another context, refers to as "bad infinity"; it contradicts itself and yet is at the same time incapable of resolution. To maintain the delicate balance between the obligation to eliminate pure individuality, and the concomitant prerequisite of individuality, a number of devices have slowly developed over the centuries. The most effective device is that men become "calculable, regular, necessary." Since moral obligation consists in the acceptance of certain rules for action, it will obviously be the more vigorous the less danger there is that quirks of unpredictable individual action might suddenly take hold. If through processes not yet examined, men are made more calculable, less moral cement is required for the community and there is less danger of disintegration. By making men predictable, writes Nietzsche in *The Wanderer and His Shadow*, a means is discovered "of preserving the community and beating back its tendency to fall apart." [24]

The more men are made calculable, however, the more calculable they are. Gradually the very stuff of their nature alters, until they *are* effectively "regular and necessary" beings. They come to perceive themselves in this fashion. As this occurs, it becomes increasingly difficult on the level of moral action and imperatives for an individual to conceive of undertaking an action from reasons not those of his particular moral community. As before, morality is necessary for survival; this means at least that it gives the men under its sway reasons for doing something. If, as Nietzsche holds to be the case, there appear no reasons for action outside a moral community, then men are held to morality not only by belief and habit, but also by a fear that, were they not, they might find themselves devoid of reasons for doing anything. Hence, one of the cornerstones of morality is fear — the fear that without morality, life will be void of meaning such that we have no choice but simply to give up. As Stanley Cavell once remarked in a slightly different context, "The answer to the question 'Why should I be more moral?' may well be that you are too cowardly for much of anything else." [25] Morality will not let men go. No matter how empty of meaning life is or how great the atomization and loneliness of the world, the fear that there be nothing at all continues to provide enough moral fabric for the community to remain together.

Such fear has an ally. The moral perspective consists of asking "how much or how little is dangerous to the community, dangerous to equality in an opinion, in a state or affect, in a will, a talent. . . ." [26] If men are constrained by fear, they are also lured by the ever present *hope* of attaining that which the moral world promises. The hope of redemption is the other great servant of morality. In his discussion of the story of Pandora and Epimetheus (the half-witted brother of Prometheus) who let all evils except hope out of the box and into the world, Nietzsche writes: "Zeus did not wish for man to throw away his life . . . even though he suffered so much from other evils; rather he should go on letting himself be tormented again and again. Thus, he gives man hope: this is, in truth, the worst of the evils, for it prolongs the torments of man." [27]

Given this vision of morality, release from it may appear as potential liberation of humankind. It is not surprising that Nietzsche does not propose a "new" morality but rather would wish to *annihilate* morality, since he understands it as a world picture from which we cannot escape. Even when morality has developed into nihilism, it persists as minimalist; and though the enterprise itself is called into question (much, for instance, as some modern art calls art itself into question), it continues to be moral behavior. The structures of hope and fear which Nietzsche sees as supporting moral action must be broken; without this destruction there is no escape from an increasingly formally framed dialectic.

In a line left out of most editions of the *Nachlass*, Nietzsche notes that such destruction is "properly the task of a *Tractatus politicus*." [28] As it is, were men to remember the turbulent origins of their moral sentiments, they would never have done with them, and moral life would not be possible. Thus a "politics of virtue," operating by means of a "faculty of oblivion," has effectively *forced* men to forget where they came from. This faculty, so anticipatory of

Freud's doctrine of repression, operates in a manner reverse to genealogy. It sets up the barriers that keep man's genesis from him. "Man, as in his intellectual habit, has forgotten the original purpose of his so-called right and just affairs. . . . How little moral would the world look without forgetfulness of human dignity." [29] The task of the genealogist requires a political treatise, since morality has been erected, enforced, and required of humanity. If its origin and defense are human, and not "natural," then the attack will come from a human footing, and the clash will be between two competing deities.

The Politics of Morality

A community under challenge fights back to preserve the boundaries that are its morality and definition. Origins must be kept unquestionable; if morality were seen naked and ashamed, the resulting trauma would be insupportable. The required control comes mainly through guilt. In the second essay of *On the Genealogy of Morals*, Nietzsche seeks to locate the origin of this feeling in the contractual relationship of creditor and debtor. (*Schuld* means guilt in German; *die Schulden* are debts). This peculiar, though apparently accurate etymological analysis implies for Nietzsche that guilt is a particular pattern of relations between an individual and his society. One is *schuldig* — guilty — if in debt to the society; one feels a need of repayment. Guilt becomes thus a manner of measuring oneself in terms of relation with the community. The society stands "to its members in that same vital basic relation: that of the creditor to his debtor." [30] A man feels guilt toward his community, he feels bound to it in a manner that no act of his alone can affect; it must be an act that society recognizes. If he "pays his debt to society" — the language is still current — he can then be brought back and readmitted. Without such payment, he stands outside and condemned.

Guilt is then a measuring of ones actions by an external standard — a measurement that leaves one wanting. Nietzsche finds that morality has developed such that the debts progressively incurred are less and less repayable. Men are put in an impossible position; the very fact of being a member of society or a human being is made of humanly irredeemable crime. The greatest development of this dialectic, which Freud calls "civilization and its discontents," is reached in relation to the divinity and the Christian God in particular. He is so powerful, and humans so sinfully in his debt, that repayment is inconceivable. Under such conditions, when the creditor is owed so much, the permanent condition of man becomes guilty indebtedness to an abstract entity. [31]

Against Nietzsche, it might be thought that with the decline of faith in God, the sense of guilt would decline. Far from it: "The time comes when we will have to pay for having been Christians for two thousand years; we are losing the center of gravity that let us live. . . . We are now plunging into the opposite values with the same amount of energy with which we were Christians (*mit dem wir Christen gewesen sind*). . . ." [32] That God is dead does not lighten the burden; in fact, since "we killed him," our guilt is thereby increased. Now men live on in the shadows of the dead God, and his death is merely a warning and portent of what is to come. To "live on in the shadows of the dead God" is to continue to partake of the form and outline of a particular mode of action, here Christian morality, while lacking the substance. Nietzsche understands as well as did Max Weber some years later that two thousand years of continuing moral practice have changed more than just religious beliefs. Those practices have become enmeshed in a grid that pickets men's lives. Hence, important sustaining mechanisms, such as guilt, will continue to operate even among those who consider themselves somehow free of religion. To be part of a genealogy is to have an unescapable fate.

In fact, there is another significant sense in which the death of God makes situation somewhat worse for men. For those who were believers, the operation of guilt had a certain meaning; it reminded them of their humanity, their duties, and the source of their inspiration. For those who live without God, yet continue to act in the forms of Judeo-Christian morality, the forces of guilt that may drive them on now lack all goals, even the imagined ones. In the past "God so loved the world" that He might always take back part of the guilt upon Himself. Nietzsche writes in *On the Genealogy of Morals*: "The creditor [*Gläubiger*] sacrifices himself for his debtor, out of *love* (can one give credit to that?), out of love for his debtor." [33] With the death of God, such Christian morality becomes impossible, and even this marvellous sacrifice loses its redemptive claims. As I shall argue in the next chapter, Christ may have embodied for Nietzsche the highest feasible morality, but now this morality is becoming only

truly possible in the wooded isolation of the hermit whom Zarathustra encounters at the beginning of his journey.

In order to understand where Nietzsche sees the proper focus of
the problem of morality it is useful to investigate the direction taken
by some of his occasional comments on more immediate social
matters. The continuing operation of guilt, for instance, implies
responsibility. A person feels guilty for his situation. He reasons that
he must at some point be at the origin of his present distressing
situation. He must conclude that it is somehow his fault, since to do
otherwise would be to question the legitimacy of the moral bonds of
the community. So, while remaining fully attached to the principles
of the community of which he is and remains a member, he must
conclude that he could and should have done other than he did. [34]
We are back to the error of free will; language and morality have
naturally conspired with each other.

Furthermore, by placing the supposed locus of blame on an act
that the individual must have chosen to undertake, men will tend to
see self-consciousiness as a prerequisite for escaping the self-punishment of guilt. Socrates himself seems to conclude that no man will
do evil knowingly. Presumably, the knowledge required to generate
self-consciousness should make it increasingly possible to avoid
"evil" (guilt-producing) acts; without consciousness there seems to
be no manner in which to escape the flux of mere events. This makes
it possible to distinguish between acts committed consciously and
somehow subject to moral standards, and those "committed" unconsciously, for which we may want to refuse responsibility. Thus we
distinguish premeditated, unpremeditated murder, and manslaughter,
or even irrestistable impulse, all in terms of greater or lesser degrees
of consciousness.

This conclusion, which to us seems so natural, raises problems for
Nietzsche. Along the same lines, we might, for instance, be tempted
to conclude that we are in no way responsible for the "moral content
of our dreams." Yet Nietzsche writes in _Morgenröte_, "nothing is
more yours than your dreams." And fifty years later in a piece on
"Moral Responsibility for the Content of Dreams," Freud queries
arcanely, "who else would be responsible?" [35] The implication that
one can distinguish sharply in moral terms between the unconscious
and the conscious is problematic.

In any case, the psyche is a full part of life, and as much or as little responsibility must be taken for it as for that which is conscious. If Nietzsche attacks the transcendental in Kant, *so also must he attack the notion of an unconscious world which would remain in principle inaccessible* and known only through representation. Nietzsche is not saying that the unconscious and the conscious are one. He is attacking the notion of the unconscious, which later becomes dominant in the thought of Freud, as a shapeless locus of that which is never apprehended directly and is known only through posterior signs. In the genealogical understanding, conscious and unconscious are necessarily linked, and known in the same way; they are part of the same family. A moral standard applied to one will apply to the other. And the unity which they are — "life," in Nietzsche's terms — will stand outside such valuations. Nietzsche's conclusion is not, as was Freud's, that we are *responsible* for our dreams; instead, as he writes in *Morgenröte*, "Oedipus was right, we are not responsible for our dreams, nor for our awake life; . . . no one is responsible for his acts, no one for his life." [36] This is a "conclusion as clear as sunlight," that man cannot be judged by his creations, though he may be found wanting *in* them.

Nietzsche's focus is not on individual responsibility, at least not directly. The image of the heroic overman which is usually associated with popular understandings of Nietzsche is dangerously misleading. Implicit in the above analysis is that there is nothing in the psyche of man which, once released from a romantic Pandora's box, will triumph over the pettiness of this world. The standard notion of the *Übermensch* seems to imply that there is in at least some men a potential untapped reservoir of energy which needs only release. But if there is the sort of union of the conscious and unconscious to which Nietzsche holds, this is simply impossible. We must then look elsewhere for the source of the problem.

I pointed out above that the prevalent notion of moral action legitimates a conceptual separation of the actor from the act. It is necessary for this view to hold that the actor could have acted otherwise. I also argued that Nietzsche thought the conceptual separation to be already a piece of moralizing. These considerations are made specifically clear in Nietzsche's comments on criminality and punishment.

In *The Genealogy of Morals*, Nietzsche draws up an unsystematic list of the different uses of the word punishment. It is designed to be unsystematic and resembles nothing so much as the different lists that Wittgenstein also draws up when he wants to point to the various families a word may belong to. By such an approach Nietzsche is again called attention to the fact that there can be no one definition of the word punishment shared by all its meanings. Words are rather "pockets into which now this, now that, now some more can be put." [37]

It might be logical, for instance, to presuppose that punishment is "supposed to possess the value of awakening the feeling of guilt in the guilty person." [38] Yet such a notion implies of necessity that the criminal had a free choice to go against the society; that the society is supposed to awaken the sense of indebtedness in him – he would so to speak have broken a contract; and that now he has no choice but to expiate his crime. Juridical punishment would then be that which "restores both private honor and the honor of society." [39] That there might be something about a society leading an individual to act as he did and so shaping him that he *had no other choice* but to act in such a manner, and thus could not be in the normal sense considered responsible, could simply never be a question under such a perspective. In the moral view, acts are presumed not to have a part, at least not for the purpose of moral judgment. In the character "The Pale Criminal" in *Zarathustra*, Nietzsche argues that the criminal and the insane should be considered as basically the same type. They should be understood in terms of the society by which they are judged criminal or insane. "Those who become sick today are overcome by that evil that is evil today: they want to hurt with that which hurts them. But there have been other ages and another good and evil."

Nietzsche is advancing here a view of punishment which would seem to be related to the later writings of both Freud and such existential psychiatrists as Karl Menninger, Thomas Szasz, and R. D. Laing. With Freud, he holds it possible that a crime be committed in order to expiate a supposed prior guilt. [40] Nietzsche calls this "madness before the deed": relations to social configurations become such that, in order to alleviate the unexplained guilt one has, one is forced to engage in acts that the society will punish. The society punishes and induces guilt, requires expiation, forces a crime so that expiation is possible, and holds the individual responsible for the whole process.

In terms of the society in question, there should then be no logical difference between "criminals and the insane . . . if we suppose that the current pattern of moral thought is the pattern of spiritual health."[41] Nietzsche is *not* saying here that society is healthy and that the immoral and the insane deserve to be treated alike. He is saying that, in terms of the logic of the moral structure, both fall outside the society for the same reasons. They are therefore essentially part of the same category — those who have been driven to their respective deeds by the society itself. To this effect, he goes on in the passage cited above to point to the possibilities of reforming social practices to remove the supposed necessity of revenge in dealing with antisocial behavior. Were all criminals to be treated as insane, he argues, at least society would escape from the notion that such men were somehow in such a morally autonomous and ahistorical position that men might be held responsible for their actions in society's terms. Nietzsche is quite aware that there are no institutions for this sort of treatment; nevertheless he wonders at "how relieved would be the general sentiment of life, if one could rid oneself of the belief in guilt along with the old instinct of revenge and consider it the refined wish of the happy, along with Christianity, to speak well of one's enemies and to do well to those who have offended us."[42]

There is little doubt that these proposals of Nietzsche for institutional reform are meant as devices to demonstrate how different the moral practices of a society are from their self-conscious moral justifications. Nietzsche is driving at something far more radical than simply psychiatric reformism; he is pointing out that while it might be conceptually possible within the moral logic of a society for guilt to be abolished, this will never happen, for it would endanger the society.[43] Situations and societies employ what have to be termed psycho-political strong-arm tactics to make it impossible for the individual to escape naturally some of the contradictions in which they are placed.

Thus, and this is the most important part of Nietzsche's considerations of morality, *the real question that must be posed is not about the relative health of the individual vis-à-vis the society*. At his most profound level, Nietzsche is *not* concerned to find a way to liberate some supposed masterly moral "blond beast" from the prison of social morality. His investigations into the logic of moral structures do not raise for him the question of *how to get healthy individuals*, but rather drive him to "seek out what no thinker has yet had the daring to measure — *the health of a society.*"[44] Questions of the origins of good and evil should not focus on individuals and individual practices, but rather on the society at hand. And, if individuals start behaving immorally, the cause must be looked for in the society, not in the aberrations of particular individuals. Nietzsche is saying that an unhealthy society will in the end leave the individuals comprising it with no place to turn. This is why Nietzsche's moral investigation is bound in the long run to become a political-ideological investigation: an unhealthy society (which has yet to be examined in detail) will produce individuals who can only be kept in line by the mechanisms that have been described in this chapter. This Nietzschean point is the deep significance, for instance, of the title of R. D. Laing's *The Politics of Experience*; moral experience, especially in this day and age, is ultimately defensible only through means that have to be described as political, for the dominant standards of the society are enforced on individuals.

Nietzsche sees morality in much the same way that he sees epistemology. There is a gradual emptying out of that which is living in morality. In the metaphor Nietzsche uses in *The Birth of Tragedy*, men are left "running up and down the banks" of moral forms, guilty, and without sensuous relation between morality and life. To the degree that they are unable to leave these banks, morality is in fact hostile to life, for contrary to Marx, Nietzsche foresees no automatic dialectical process of escape. Nihilism as a stage of morality is "necessary because our present values have in themselves this logical consequence: because nihilism is the logical conclusion of our great values and ideals — because we must first experience nihilism in order to comprehend what the value of these 'values' was — sometime or another we are in need of new values."[45]

This says in effect that the necessary preconditions for our morality are disappearing. It is increasingly impossible to be meaningfully moral, at least in the manner to which we have been accustomed. Much as truth is becoming impossible and the attempt to maintain it hostile to life, so also with morality. Morality has become an idol, a statue; to be killed by it will most assuredly not be a tragic death.

The nihilistic imperative results from the necessity that morality regularize behavior and establish a system of rewards and punishments both psychic and physical. It enforces the ideology or mythology that keeps people attached to a certain form of life. In doing so, it must set itself up as absolute and unquestioned: it is a metaphor that has escaped its creators. In the central chapter of *The Brothers Karamazov*, Dostoyevsky establishes a similar view. Ivan Karamazov relates to his brothers the parable of the "Grand Inquisitor." Christ has returned to earth, is recognized; people begin to follow him. He is then arrested and taken before the Grand Inquisitor who says to Christ: "Be silent . . . . Thou hast no right to add anything to what thou hadst said of old. Why, then, art thou come to hinder us? . . . Tomorrow I shall condemn thee, and burn thee at the stake as the worst of heretics. And the very people who have today kissed thy feet, tomorrow . . . shall rush to heap up the embers of thy fire . . . . Thou didst proudly and well, like God. But the weak, unruly race of men, are they like God?" The Inquisitor continues: "I have joined the ranks of those who have corrected thy work . . . . I shall burn thee . . . . For if ever anyone deserved our fires, it is thou." [46] To all of this speech Christ stands in mute silence, attempts no reply, nor, Dostoyevsky indicates, has he one. At the end he is led away to his death.

The point is clear: organized morality is and will be different from that intended by its founder — and there is nothing that can be done about it. For Dostoyevsky, there is nothing: Christ does not reply to the Inquisitor, but remains silent, unable to challenge the historicist truth presented to him. [47]

Nietzsche however cannot stop with such pious acquiescence. History may be seen as the process by which the praxis and valuations of great men are made viable. Over and above Dostoyevsky's erotic silence, Nietzsche asks that we distinguish origin and purpose. Dostoyevsky had seen the historical reification of moral practice as an inevitable consequence of all forms of moral teaching. Nietzsche seeks however to also investigate this supposed necessity; it is inevitable? If so, why? Is it conceivable that a moral teaching might leave behind something other than its own idol? To these questions I must now turn, in an investigation of the immoralist, the "great man" who is responsible for setting moral practices in motion.

Chapter V

WHO IS DIONYSIAN?
THE PROBLEM OF THE
IMMORALIST

*It is modest of the nightingale not to require anyone to
listen to it; but it is also proud of the nightingale not to
care whether anyone listens to it or not.*

— Søren Kierkegaard, *On the Difference between a Genius
and an Apostle*

In two months I shall be the foremost name in Europe.

— Nietzsche to Overbeck, Christmas, 1888

In the Preface to *The Genealogy of Morals*,
Nietzsche reminds his reader that, prior to the present form of
morality, there existed an "older and more primitive species of
morality" which he calls the "morality of mores." This pattern was
characterized by the nonreflective adherence to the customs or ethos
of a particular society. Manifestly, this stage has come to an end and
has been replaced by the present moral system, in which intentions
of actors and self-consciousness assume a far greater importance.
Nietzsche sees, however, the present moral system also as a stage,
itself drawing to a close. This is not merely historical happenstance.
He understands the structure of the contemporary moral system to

contain a fatal dialectic: it must finish by destroying itself. As such the position is no different from that of Karl Marx, who saw bourgeois civilization creating the conditions of its own destruction. Contrary to Marx, Nietzsche saw no logic inherent in the process of self-destruction which guaranteed the change from the period of the "morality of mores" to the present stage, and no logic that might ensure that the end of this stage correspond with the beginning of a new one. For Marx, the world of proletarian socialism was the death of the bourgeois world that had spawned it; for Nietzsche, there is no reason to assume that the end of Christian morality might be anything but frustration.

To understand why this is so, it is useful to look at the historical shift from the stage of the morality of mores to the "moral" stage. Nietzsche places this in a period roughly between the fifth century B.C. and the third century A.D., and further specifies the world-historical characters of Socrates and Christ as responsible for the direction that moral developments took. The modern world is the legatee of their calling. No doubt, too, he sees himself in the same world-historical position, and wishes to transfigure the world with another new and terrifying transvaluation of all values.

Christ and Socrates are, however, more than just the names attached to a stage in world history. This had been their importance for Hegel; for Nietzsche they are important also as men. It is certainly significant to examine the historical changes that occur as the result of these men, but it is even more so to investigate their particular characteristics as human beings. For Nietzsche any investigation of their accomplishments will also be an investigation of their personalities. I shall leave the history to a future chapter and concentrate here on the men. If it can be shown that in certain important aspects their personality is flawed, Nietzsche wants to point out those flaws that he finds responsible for the development of the moral practices they formulated.

It is certainly true, and Nietzsche will insist on this again and again, that Socrates and Christ broke with their times. They did not simply formulate necessary developments of world history; they were considered criminals in the eyes of their society. Whereas Hegel might say that their "criminality" is simply appearance, due to their progressive nature, Nietzsche wants to say that they did *in fact* make a break in their times. Unfortunately, for different reasons, they make what he sees as the wrong break: their immoralism itself is flawed. It is not enough just to be a lawbreaker.

The Problem of the Immoralist

A person is immoral only in relation to some system recognized as moral. If a man pushes questions so far as to break through the moral horizons of a culture, so as to land outside the arena of accepted practice, he becomes, by definition, a criminal and outcast. Conversely, the society must seek to preserve its moral foundations, and thus develops processes, some of which were examined in the previous chapter, to keep or bring people back in line. Nonetheless, moral perspectives must have a beginning; they are often associated with the name of a founder and with a break in previously accepted moral practices. Moral revolution, the "transvaluation of all values" of which Nietzsche speaks, must need break the boundaries of the society that nurtures it. To be a moral revolutionary, one must, by one's creation, be a destroyer. Nietzsche considers those who have accomplished such revaluations the key figures in the genealogy of morality. They are the fathers; their seed gives an initial and never abandoned direction to subsequent developments.

There is little doubt that this perspective has some historical accuracy. Nietzsche accepts as true the accusation of the Athenian Assembly that Socrates was a corrupter of youth and a destroyer of faith in the gods. On the surface such an accusation might seem strange. The fourth century was a period of turmoil and skepticism and it would appear that few educated Athenians retained a Homeric attitude toward Olympus. This is not to say, however, that they *disbelieved* in the gods. The accusation against Socrates shows the significance that the Assembly found in the gods; it was still politically necessary to keep the realm of the gods unquestionable. The six centuries since Homer had no doubt removed this realm from the unquestioned and obviously true, but it was still possible — or so the Assembly thought — to defend them politically by eliminating those forces that threatened the moral basis of the state.

Christ also, Nietzsche argues, must be understood as presenting a *political* threat to the moral structure of Jewish society. Though Nietzsche often links many of Jesus' teachings with Judaism, there can be no doubt that he saw a tremendous opposition between the Jewish *state* and what Christ did and said. Nietzsche writes: "This holy anarchist, who called the lower classes, the sufferers and 'sinners' into opposition against the 'ruling order' with a language that today would have gotten him sent to Siberia — this man was a political criminal, insofar as political crimes were still possible under those conditions. This brought him to the cross . . . ."[1]

Small wonder then that Nietzsche should have fought so fiercely — I am tempted to say valiantly — with both Socrates and Christ. They broke the moral bonds of their times and effectively forced a reorientation of future history in their own and perhaps idolatrous images. Nietzsche is fascinated with their achievement and, without doubt, wishes for similar success for himself. In a letter to his sister, never sent perhaps because he did not want to make definite the break between them, he writes: "For what I have to do is *terrible*, in any sense of the word. I do not challenge individuals — I am challenging humanity as a whole with my terrible accusation; . . . there attaches to my name a quantity of doom that is beyond telling. . . ."[2]

If Nietzsche is to accomplish his projected revaluation of all values for this coming age, it will be necessary to overcome the legacies of both Christ and Socrates. He *has* to fight with these men; the battle must be joined. For Nietzsche, the time is only now becoming right such that transfiguration is once again possible; for the first time in centuries, immorality on a world-historical scale is potentially meaningful. He writes, for instance, in the late eighteen seventies, that "the strength of custom is remarkably weakened and the sentiment of morality so refined and so elevated that we can almost describe it as volatilized."[3] At the end of his life, he finds in his "unmasking of Christian morality . . . a unique event, a real catastrophe, a fatality — *it breaks the history of humanity in two*."[4] Nietzsche finds the contemporary crisis greater than those crises that confronted the world at the end of the Golden Age in Greece and the end of the Hellenic period. His task, if accomplished, will be even more important than Christ's or Socrates'.

The courage required for this moral warfare is great. Christ already had said that one must reject family, kin, and country to stand firmly outside the community. Here, perhaps, is one of the reasons that Nietzsche inveighs so strongly against the "moral tarantulism" of Rousseau.[5] Rousseau, in fact, shares an outrage against the moral developments of his day; he understands also that morality is coterminous with a community and that moral principles do not transcend the group. But he did believe it possible to develop a form of life in which men might be both fully conscious and also moral. For Nietzsche, the fully conscious individual is necessarily an unmasking and questioning voice. He will inevitably come into conflict with the group. Men like Socrates "all take a new route and suffer the highest disapproval from all the representatives of the morality of custom — they take themselves out of the community as immoralists, and are, in the deepest sense of the word, evil."[6] Nietzsche's occasional praise of the "criminal type" stems from this; such men must be rejected by society. Among occasional criminals he includes "scientists, artists, the genius, the free spirit . . ." and concludes that "all innovators of the spirit must for a time bear the pallid and fatal mark of the Chandala [the criminal outcast] on their foreheads, *not* because they are so considered, but because they themselves feel the terrible cleavage that separates them from everything that is customary or reputable."[7]

Christ and Socrates provide Nietzsche with the two most important cases of immoralists in action. He thinks they both make mistakes in their lawbreaking and thus stand at the head of the dissolution now besetting the world. Since his concern is to trace their genealogical relation to present developments, Nietzsche must not deal only with the substance of their revolution. Moral practices have certainly changed since the ones advocated by Christ. Nietzsche is rather concerned with how the previous immoralists speak; it is the structure of their message which will have persisted to the contemporary world; it is the *mode* of the morality Nietzsche is after. He must discover specific qualities about Christ and Socrates as men which made them err. As elsewhere, it is in unspoken and unquestioned necessities that clues to genealogical developments are found.

Socrates: The Problem of the Virtuoso

It is indicative of how far we are from Nietzsche that his views on Socrates should have caused so much controversy. Many of those who happily have given up the title "believer" and have no difficulty proclaiming their agnosticism — though perhaps atheism involves too much commitment — seem to find it difficult to accept the possibility that Nietzsche might have "been against" Socrates. If Socrates is the cornerstone of Western humanism, it would no doubt appear wrong, certainly rash, to reject Man, as well as God and Christianity. Nothing would be left. Thus, many commentators have invested much time in attempts to "rescue" Nietzsche from his own attack, in order to show that he "really" did not mean and/or say all of those highly critical passages. I shall consider one of the most important of these below.

On the other hand, many other commentators[8] have taken the perfectly natural position that since Nietzsche says he does not like Socrates, this means he in fact does not. More dangerously, they have also assumed that it was perfectly clear what "not liking Socrates" means. Nietzsche, for instance, notes at one point that "Socrates stands so close to [him] that [he] almost always fights with him."[9] For some people, Nietzsche is here admitting, perhaps almost in bad faith, that he is is really one with Socrates. Certainly Walter Kaufmann seizes this aphorism as the centerpiece of his defense of a pro-Socratic Nietzsche. Yet, in my reading, the meaning is not at all obvious. It might mean, for instance, that Nietzsche was afraid of not being original (a comment Freud once made about his own relation to Nietzsche); or, that his doctrine appears the same as that of Socrates, but, in fact, is not; or, that the two men have the same doctrine, but for different reasons, and that the reasons are important; or, that unless Nietzsche is thought of as different from Socrates, he will have no effect, or not the effect he desires. One could probably come up with a few more possibilities. The problem is that neither the notion of a pro-Socratic Nietzsche, nor that of an anti-Socratic Nietzsche tells us anything about Nietzsche. These opinions only manifest and confirm the writer's and reader's intentions.

Be all this as it may, and subject to further investigations. The relation is certainly not clear. By Nietzsche's admission, Socrates created many of the standards on which life would rest for the next twenty-three hundred years. [10] He struggled against the decadence he saw in his own times; whether he was successful or not, his effect was enormous. Jaspers claims that Nietzsche was envious of Christ, which may be the case. He surely was envious of the accomplishments of Socrates.

In his major work on Nietzsche, Walter Kaufmann devotes a lengthy chapter to the demonstration of his contention that Nietzsche was really an admirer of Socrates. His antagonists are men like Richard Oehler, who had devoted a lengthy book to the contention that Nietzsche didn't like Socrates. Since many of the men who wrote as Oehler did had at best ambiguous relations with the Nazis, one suspects that what motivated them was the desire to find in Nietzsche an intellectual ancestor for the new Germany who was a break with the Judeo-Christian humanist heritage. Kaufmann, then, is trying to effectuate the reverse operation, to bring Nietzsche back into the fold of the tradition of Western thought.

No doubt Oehler's one-sided views are misguided, perhaps even obviously wrong. It is worthwhile, however, to devote some time here to a consideration of Walter Kaufmann's view. His is the major understanding in English and the direction that he takes seems to me characteristic of a whole generation of Nietzschean scholarship. Summarily, it consists of attempting to see Nietzsche as another mountain peak in the range of Western thought. Socrates, Shakespeare, Goethe, Hegel, Nietzsche: at the risk of exaggeration, it seems to me that Kaufmann is determined to find a manner to resolve his sympathy for Socrates, for Nietzsche, and presumably for his own opinions. While the presumption that these men *must* all have something in common might be criticized with the same methodological objections that Nietzsche made to Kant, the nature of Kaufmann's contention strikes me as important enough to warrant substantive investigation.

It is difficult to figure out exactly what Kaufmann's conclusions about Nietzsche and Socrates are, once one gets past the perfectly correct notion that Nietzsche does not simplistically reject Socrates. Kaufmann argues that Nietzsche distinguishes between "(1) the men he admires; (2) the ideas for which they stand; (3) their followers." [11] It is not clear that these distinctions are Nietzschean in spirit. In any case, Kaufmann holds that Nietzsche not only likes Socrates the man, but also Socrates the teacher. For Kaufmann, then, the first two points constitute a sort of ambiguous monumental history; Socrates' life and words stand as potential instruction to the contemporary world.

The problem with this appreciation is its neglect of the genealogy of the matter. It is probably a priori wrong to try to compare what

Nietzsche said with what Plato-Socrates said in the dialogue. A genealogical appreciation of Socrates must take into account Socrates' relation to our time; he cannot be seen as simply another lofty peak. Hence, Kaufmann's occasional comparison of what Nietzsche says (or seems to say) with what Socrates said (or seemed to say) implies that the historical Socrates can somehow be lifted bodily into dialogue with Nietzsche. But Nietzsche cannot separate Socrates the man from what Socrates became, since the genealogical kernel is the same in each. [12] The genealogical understanding is not the historical.

The culmination of Kaufmann's argument revolves around an apparent identification of the manifestation of Dionysos described in the commentary on *Beyond Good and Evil* in *Ecce Homo* with the Dionysos mentioned in the next to the last passage of *Beyond* with, finally, a reference to Socrates in *The Gay Science* as the pied piper (*Rattenfänger*) of Athens. In the passage from *Beyond Good and Evil*, Nietzsche proclaims himself as the "last follower and initiate" of a *Versucher-Gott* (god of experiences and temptation), called Dionysos, who revealed to him much that is "secret, new, strange, wonderful, and uncanny." It is to this god that his "first fruits" were offered. [13] Kaufmann claims that this god is in fact Socrates and notes that "since Nietzsche fell pitifully short of Socrates' serenely mature humanity . . . his very admiration invites comparison with the mad drunken Alcibiades . . . who could not resist the fascination and charm of Socrates." [14]

Kaufmann's conclusion poses two problems, that of textual evidence, and that of the meaning of being a disciple of Dionysos, who apparently appears in any number of manifestations. On the first question, the textual evidence appears contrary to Kaufmann's conclusion. His main piece of evidence is the implied identity between the "pied piper" of *The Gay Science* and the god who "caught" Nietzsche in the passage from *Beyond Good and Evil*. The problem with Kaufmann's view is that in the 1886 Preface to *The Birth of Tragedy*, the *Rattenfänger* is identified as Wagner, a man with "dragon killer's bravado and a rat catcher's tricks." The dragon reappears in the first chapter of *Zarathustra* as the embodiment of both Hegel and Wagner and represents an intermediate stage between Christian morality and the destructive aspects of Zarathustra. [15]

Wagner is a likely candidate. Nietzsche had first expected and then hoped that Wagner might become the new Aeschylus who would return the Dionysian to German culture. Nietzsche also finds himself reluctant to praise this Dionysos. This might be true for Wagner. Certainly Nietzsche would have had by 1886 (Wagner had died some two and a half years before) some scruples in attributing to him "fine ceremonious titles of luster and merit."

More telling yet is the reference to the offering of the "first fruits": *The Birth of Tragedy* was dedicated to Wagner. Any attempts to link Nietzsche's first public work to Socrates seems a misguided endeavor. Finally, at the end of the passage in *Beyond Good and Evil*, Nietzsche reports a conversation he has had with this manifestation of Dionysos. The Nietzsche who is talking appears to be young, for he is still surprised by the desirability of evil. During the course of the conversation, Dionysos turns to Ariadne, whom he loves. Nietzsche was to identify Wagner's wife as Ariadne to the point of sending her a postcard shortly after the onset of his insanity, "Ariadne — I love you."[16] (That the postcard is signed Dionysos complicates Nietzsche's subsequent identification of himself, but not his identification in 1886 of this particular manifestation of Dionysos.)

It is important to be clear here about just what has been established. It does not appear that the manifestation of Dionysos to whom Nietzsche refers can be Socrates; it appears that it must be Wagner. This establishes little about Wagner, still less about Socrates. About Wagner we can only deduce that Nietzsche thought he saw something there which seduced him to his later career. It is not clear exactly what that was. About Socrates we can only find that the rejection of the Socrates-Dionysos correlation points strongly in the direction that Socrates is not Dionysian, a conclusion that Nietzsche had first seemed to advance in *The Birth of Tragedy*.

The question becomes one of what the reasons are for Kaufmann's contention. Kaufmann is misled, I think because he neglects the genealogical understanding of the Greek. As noted, he tends to see Socrates in a line of philosophers and wise men which runs from Socrates to Shakespeare, and then on to Goethe, Hegel, and Nietzsche. (This mythography can be explored at length by consulting Kaufmann's *From Shakespeare to Existentialism*.) Much as Nietzsche advances opinions that Kaufmann finds somewhat violent and eccentric versions of his own, so then must Socrates become a serene and controlled version of Nietzsche.

Kaufmann ignores Nietzsche's unwillingness to separate a man from what he does. His understanding of the relation between Nietzsche and Socrates presumes that the separation of actor from his actions and the consequences of his actions is possible. For Nietzsche, on the other hand, as I have tried to demonstrate, we are all, so to speak, potentially world historical; we already incarnate our dreams and our descendants. Kaufmann's judgment is a-historical; it removes Socrates from what became of his acts. For Nietzsche, contrary to Dostoyevsky or Kaufmann, the Grand Inquisitor and Christ are ultimately of the same family, as are Socrates, and say, Kant.

Socrates lived and spoke in an age of social disintegration. Athens was in imminent moral crisis in the period following the Persian Wars; the victory had been too great and the triumph was bursting the bounds of the society. In this situation, Socrates, in Nietzsche's understanding, is trying to recover a foundation for morality. Socrates no longer thinks "unconsciousness" (*Unbewusstheit*) sufficient or even possible in the turbulence of the times. He thus appears to demand that morality now be grounded in self-conscious reason. And, by requiring a self-conscious explanation of behavior from his interlocutors, he in effect pulls the moral practices out of the soils in which they grew and examines them for their survival capacity. He found it necessary to ground morality in something other than the soil of tradition, from which Greek moral practices had grown. Moral practices were made independent of the environment from which they had sprung and for which they had constituted a necessary and useful buffer. Nietzsche writes: "Socrates' reaction . . . *in praxi* . . . means that moral judgments have been torn from the conditionality in which they grew and where alone they had meaning . . . ."[17]

Nietzsche recognizes full well the dangerous position that Greece was in by the end of the fourth century. Socrates offers a fascinating picture to an Athens already vastly changed from the idealized virtue of the Cleisthenian period. Here was a man who presents a new and verbal erotic variation on the wrestling meet as a redemption to a decaying Athens. "Degeneration was quietly developing everywhere: old Athens was coming to an end. And Socrates understood that all the world needed him. . . ."[18] Nietzsche sketches a world for Socrates to counter, a Greece full of both psychic and political potential tyrants, of ascetic passions and an increasingly universal distress. This is the beginning of what Gilbert Murray, in a famous phrase, saw as a "failure of nerve."

To this extent, Socrates sees as already in himself all the new instincts that are being unleashed in Athens and Greece. His answer to this onslaught is to fight back. In the *Apology*, as Nietzsche notes, Socrates finds that he acts for rational reasons and that his instincts — his *daemon* — only dissuade him. He has mastered his cave of passions; indeed, it is made quite clear by the end of the *Symposium* that he has not only mastered them, but has also had full knowledge of them.

In Nietzsche's analysis, Socrates becomes, by the control he has developed over his passions, the first "philosopher of life." For all previous philosophers "life served thinking and knowing," that is, "life" was logically prior and not susceptible to radical improvement by means of philosophy. For Socrates, on the other hand, philosophy should serve life, for "virtue is teachable." Thus, a new and better life, more subject to the controls that the mind might erect, becomes possible. For Socrates, such philosophy is, in fact, the only hope for a society threatened, as is Greece, with moral chaos. In Nietzsche's view, by according philosophy and thought a privileged status, Socrates takes the first important step down the road which eventually results in the erection of the ideal worlds of God, Nature, absolute a priori's, and so forth.

Socrates may not have made this move entirely willingly. Nietzsche sees him confronted with a situation in Greek culture in which no alternative other than rational self-control appeared possible or present. "The fanaticism with which all Greek reflection throws itself upon rationality betrays a desperate situation; there was danger, but there was but one choice: either to perish or to be absurdly rational." [19] But Socrates makes the choice, and such absurd rationality is required precisely because of the desperateness of the situation. Reason, the tip of the psychic iceberg, was all that was recognized.

For Nietzsche, in choosing to fight *against*, Socrates reveals the first flaw in his character: by his attempt to negate what is happening he merely persists in reasserting the dynamics that make possible the Athenian moral and political crisis. "It is self-deception" writes Nietzsche, "for a philosopher and moralist to believe that they escape decadence when they fight against it. This lies beyond their wills, and, though they do not recognize it, one finds that later they were the most powerful contributors to violence." [20] In the Prologue to *Zarathustra*, much praise is devoted to those who "go under," that is, who do not struggle dialectically against that which is sweeping over them.

Socrates is then a dialectician, not only in his thought, but also in his life. To this effect, he denies the grounds of presently held beliefs and seeks new justification for them. He engages in verbal agon's with any and all. Inevitably, or so Plato would like it to appear to us, he wins. [21] It is the *fact* of his victory, not immediately the nature of it, which is first of all problematic to Nietzsche. Nietzsche argues that the practice of ostracism was used among the Greeks to ensure that no man emerged who was so superior to others as to be the single best man. Should one emerge, he would prevent the agon from continuing, and thus stand outside the community of interaction which made the agon possible. I will examine the precise political significance of the agon in a later chapter; here it is important to see into what position it puts Socrates. If he keeps winning his rationality contest, he is in effect in the position of a new and victorious Thrasymachus. In the *Republic*, this blustering but likable hothead argues at length for the proposition that justice is what the strong say it is — a version of "to the victor belongs the spoils." Almost the entire first book is taken up with his exchange with Socrates. By the end, Socrates has won Thrasymachus "blushes," becomes ashamed of what he is saying, and "gives up." Socrates has not *convinced* Thrasymachus, but has in effect silenced him. This may say something about courage. It also places Socrates in a strange position. He has in effect gone Thrasymachus one better: through his more powerful logic, he has decided *how* the discussion of justice will now proceed. Thrasymachus, in the end a far more moral person than Socrates (he can still be ashamed), has been literally conquered.

Socrates raises the discussion from a political to a philosophical level. But, for Nietzsche, he has disguised the "politics of virtue" implicit in his victory. In fact, Socrates is in danger of becoming a new Thrasymachus. Nietzsche finds that "the agonal instinct compelled these born dialecticians to glorify their *personal ability* as the *highest quality. . . .*"[22]

In dialectics, the danger comes with the victory; "nothing is easier to expunge than the effect of a dialectician."[23] Socrates is thus caught in a bind. If he keeps the fruit of his victory, he neither is convincing, nor has he established anything that will serve as a basis to counter the decadence; if he refrains from fighting, the Greek situation will surely get worse. He is in danger of becoming the best man. As the Greeks understood, this undermined the foundations of the City.

The answer, of course, comes in effective self-banishment. Socrates the philosopher-politician-erotic ostracizes Socrates the victor, not "to roister in Thessaly" as he argues against Crito, but rather to the skies. By accepting, in fact by *demanding* punishment from Athens, and by refusing the open gate to flee to another polis, Socrates raises himself and his principle of logic to the ultimate. Plato was seduced into formulating this as the Doctrine of the Forms; the ideal that governs man becomes nothing more or less than Socrates *in nuce*.[24] It is not surprising that the case of Socrates bothers Nietzsche: the man creates an inaccessible world and then appears to inhabit it. It is as if Socrates had been driven to assert a world (which would eventually find its final formulation in Kant) that was just as unearthly as Cloud-Cuckoo Land and then, just as in Aristophanes' *The Clouds*, had in fact taken up residence there.

What then does Socrates' immoralism consist of? There is no doubt that he seeks to break the hold of decadence over Greek society. And yet he does *not* loosen this strangling grip; Nietzsche says again and again that Socrates *contributes* to the decadence. To adequately explain the nature of the image of Socrates' immoralism, it is necessary to briefly introduce here two of Nietzsche's rare semi-technical terms. In *The Birth of Tragedy*, he elaborates a famous distinction between the apollonian and the dionysian. While I shall only later develop these concepts in depth, for the present purposes the following explanation can suffice.

For a treatise on the origin of Greek tragedy, the *Birth* has an absurdly exciting plot. Nietzsche sees art as an attempt by the artist to express his individuality by imposing form on nature. To the degree that an art is dominated "by the laws of plasticity," it is "apollonian." To the degree that it lacks this quality, it is "dionysian." Apollo is associated with form, Dionysos with flux.

Music is the most dionysian of the arts, because it is practically pure expression of will, requiring little or no external form to exist, and disappearing with its performance. In Schopenhauer's terms, music becomes a copy of the will itself. Classic Aeschylean drama,

Nietzsche argues, is an art form that constitutes an apollonian manifestation of music; thus there is a birth of tragedy from the spirit of
music. "The dionysian chorus ... again and again newly discharges
itself in an Apollonian image world [*Bilderwelt*]. ... [Tragedy] is
the apollonian materialization [*Versinnlichung*] of dionysian perceptions and effects [*Erkenntnisse und Wirkungen*]. ..." Tragedy combines an apollonian story with dionysian effects and music — Greek
heroes always speak more superficially than they behave [25] — and is
definitely successful monumental history. It portrays man in all the
depth of which he is capable.

Now comes Euripides. In the next chapter, I will give a more
detailed consideration of the Euripidean revolution in relation to its
social manifestations. Here I only briefly describe his role in the
exposition of the plot of *The Birth of Tragedy*. Nietzsche claims that
Euripides is the first man to make tragedy consciously; he is the first
person to explicitly attempt by means of his art to "deliver a
message" to his audience. In Aeschylean drama, the audience was
drawn in to the drama; with Euripides, the drama goes out to the
audience. Euripides thus writes tragedy rationally. The effect of the
drama is no longer grounded in the unconscious [*Unbewusst*], which
had been the case in Old Attic drama. This new approach to the
world is specifically linked by Nietzsche with Socrates. The reversal
of consciousness and instinct is the foundation of a new hierarchy of
morality. "Whereas," Nietzsche writes in *The Birth of Tragedy*, "in
all productive men the instinct is precisely the creative-affirmative
power, and the consciousness [*Bewusstsein*] operates in a critical and
dissuasive way, in Socrates the instinct becomes critical, and consciousness the creator. ... [Here] the logical nature is, by a hyper-
trophy, developed as excessively as is instinctive wisdom in the
mystic." [26]

By starting with reason, Socrates and Euripides deny the audience
and the polis access to the myths that had served as the unconscious
backdrop to the forms of everyday life. "Even the state," writes
Nietzsche, "knows no more powerful unwritten laws than the mythical foundation that guarantees its connection with religion and its
growth from mythical foundations." When the dissolution of tragedy
is thus effectuated, man is left with only the forms of his activity.
With the dissolution of the union of the two deities of tragedy, *only*
rational dialectic advocated by Socrates remains; to this "there

correspond[s] a degeneration and transformation of the Greek people." [27] By these terms Socrates has asserted a *purely apollonian* form. Enshrined in the inaccessible heaven of the Forms Nietzsche sees the *virtus dialecticus*, that which would have to be true, if dialectics were the proper and valid way of proceeding with the description of the world. Instead, a method was enshrined and, no matter what Socrates may have hoped for, content becomes unimportant. If dialectics can lead to truth then the question of whether or not truth is conditioned might be ignored. Only the method is important. In a passage cited before, Nietzsche accuses Socrates of ignoring the *Bedingtheit* of morality; he has done it by replacing the conditionality of a people with a *form* of knowledge.

For Nietzsche, the great failing of Socrates is not his immoral innovation, but the *manner* in which he was immoral. When he broke the horizons of the law he did so in favor of an *ultima ratio* that was himself, writ *in aeternas*. And, knowing himself a rationalist out of defense against decadence, he thus enshrined both the decadence and his revolt against it at the same time. With this, the "enormous driving wheel of logical Socratism" is set in motion; it eventually leads to "the present age, the result of the Socratism that is bent on the destruction of myth." [28] Socrates attracts on the grounds of his great insight; he fails on account of his intention, to *teach* other men the road to virtue. He knows the cave of appetites, and has mastered them all. His success, however, is due to an "absurd" attachment to reason. [29] And, thus attached to Apollo, he taught others to be. He succeeds only too well: as men lost knowledge of the cave of the instincts, they grew accustomed to the blinding daylight of rationality, to the point that they could no longer see in the dark.

What, then, is important to Nietzsche about Socrates is his skill. He is the first of those "life virtuosos" who desperately and unsuccessfully try to keep Greece from slipping further into decadence. Implicit in the notion that virtue can be taught is the fact of virtuosity. Socrates can do anything, make anything seem correct and true. If the proper method is observed, he will, as in Aristophanes' savage attack, legitimate even the turning of son against father, which, for a society to whom the fate of Oedipus is a main mythological pillar, is destructive even more to the city than to the family. With the proper method and form of argument, anyone else might potentially do the same, even foreigners and men with no attachment to the particulars of the polis.

Nietzsche writes that Socrates' "dialectical skills, so well developed, have no kernel." His approach consists in "denying everything." [30] The "kernel" is what the genealogical method seeks to recover; it is what characterizes a particular family. In the case of Socrates, that the kernel is "nothing" is particularly disastrous, for to operate and essay morality under a Socratic cloak means to perpetuate that kernel of nothingness, and Socrates' case was "in the end but the extreme one, only the most obvious of what was beginning to become a comman distress." [31] The nihilism of the modern age is traced back, in Nietzsche's analysis, to the overweaned and ubiquitous negation of the apollonian Socrates.

Christ: Morality as Foolishness

Socrates, as virtuoso, denies everything. In ancient times, however, the pre-Socratic philosophers had had the excellence to live freely "without thereby becoming *fools* or *virtuosos*." [32] In a parody of the Eucharist in the chapter in *Zarathustra* entitled "The Ass Festival," Nietzsche finds the "higher men" bowing down to the ass who continually brays 1-A (*ja*, Yes) to everything they say. This unselectively affirming animal, who had already appeared as the uncomplaining beast of burden in the first chapter of *Zarathustra*, accepts all. He is praised by one of the guests at the festival with the poem *Nur Narr? Nur Dichter!* (Only Fool? Only Poet!). [33] Christ, symbolized here by Nietzsche as the beast of burden who bears all, is the *Narr* — the other side of the fool-virtuoso opposition, which the great Greek pre-Socratics had successfully avoided. [34]

It is generally thought that no matter what his ambivalence about Socrates, Nietzsche was definitely anti-Christ. Yet upon examination, this judgment must be eschewed, for Nietzsche reveals himself at least as ambivalent about Jesus as he was about the Greek. There is a distinct note of admiring jealousy as well as despair at what the man set in motion. Christ is the "noblest man," who wanted "to take the notion of judgment and punishment out of the world." He was the "destroyer of the law. . . ." [35] The list goes on and on. Care must then be exercised in the first instance to distinguish what Jesus did and said, from what Christianity became. *The Antichrist* is in fact filled with this distinction, to the degree that it might easily have been called *The Antichristian*; indeed, the German title permits such a delightful ambiguity. The distinction is analytic, though. One must also remember that Christ is the ultimate origin of what Christianity became and that he can never be separated from it.

"To love man *for God's sake* — this has so far been the most noble and remote feeling attained among men. . . . Let him remain to us for all time holy and venerable as the man who has flown the highest and gone astray the most beautifully." [36] The man in question is Christ. Why, however, is Jesus' the "most noble feeling?" For Nietzsche, Christ takes morality to the point beyond which it cannot go. Jesus' *life* — which he commands his disciples to emulate — lies already beyond good and evil, outside moral categories as must the life of any lawbreaker. "Jesus said to his Jews: the law was for servants; love God as I have loved him, as his son. What are morals to us sons of God?" [37] By such love for the world, Christ stands outside moral categories.

On this first level, it is possible to split apart what Jesus lived with what Christianity became. For Nietzsche, the villain is St. Paul. Whereas Christ had taught a "new praxis," Paul feels the necessity of emphasizing "guilt and sin." Paul, in fact, erects "in a grand style precisely that which Christ had annihilated through his life." For Nietzsche, it would be an abuse of history to identify such types of decay and unhappiness as "the Christian Church, the Christian faith, and Christian life, with that holy name." "What did Christ deny?" concludes Nietzsche; "all that is called Christian." [38] Nietzsche lays a continuing emphasis on the differences between the life that Christ lived and the requisites of the faith that evolved to allow people to become epigones of this "most noble" life. Nietzsche sees in Christ's life a unity of god and man, much in the manner that in the mind of the Greeks, the Homeric heroes were close to their God. If one looks only at Christ, one sees "no concept of guilt or punishment"; in fact, "any distance holding apart God and man is abolished." Precisely because the promises of the evangels are unconditional and available universally, the emphasis is not laid on performance in accord with certain standards, but on the practical existence of a person. "Blessedness is never promised; it is not tied to any conditions. . . . The deep instinct for how one must *live* . . .: this alone is the psychological reality of 'redemption.'" It is, says Nietzsche, "a new way of life, *not* a new faith." [39]

However, the distinction of master and epigones does not resolve the question; it cannot be settled in so tasteful and Shavian a manner. To do so well be to equate Nietzsche's views with those of Dostoyevsky, who does not hold Christ responsible for the Grand Inquisitor, but rather sees in Christ's silence merely the recognition of the nature of historical processes. Dostoyevsky seems to share with Hegel the notion that the very fact itself of entering world history results in a necessary perversion and formalization of teaching. For Nietzsche, *the manner by which teaching becomes reified into doctrine has something to do with the nature of the teaching,* with its genealogy. In the case of Christ, as was also true with Socrates, the "kernel" becomes the personality of the man himself. Thus Nietzsche wants to say that traits particular to Christ are responsible for what happened to the evangel as it got into the hands of Paul and later the Church. Somewhere in the genius of Christ's character must be a flaw that doomed even this "most noble life." There is almost a note of despair when Nietzsche first writes that Jesus opposes a "life in truth to ordinary life" and that he combats the "over-inflated importance of the person," and then wonders how Jesus can "want to make it eternal. . . ." [40]

Christ went *wrong*: He started an error of world-historical proportions, the end result of which men are still living out. Yet he did so as a lawbreaker, as a man trying to overthrow the dominant moral horizons of his time. As noted in the beginning of this chapter, Nietzsche considers Jesus to have been a political criminal. Early in 1888, he writes even more strongly: "Jesus denies Church, state, society, art, knowledge, culture, civilization." [41] This is to say that Jesus attacks by means of his life all structures and forms of organization. By demanding a life beyond and outside the law, he effectively *makes impossible any of the organized forms of moral life*, and he does so in a universal and nonselective fashion.

The life of Christ is anti-form; a holy life shatters conventions. The preliminary consequence is to make Christianity (in the sense of *imitatio Christi*) possible only as a most private and individual form of life. In the beginning of *Zarathustra*, the herald of eternal return meets a hermit who has not yet heard that God is dead. Nietzsche indicates that the old man lives a good and possible life. Zarathustra thus does not inform him of the death of God, but hurries on so as to leave the man his solitude and virtue. The lesson is clear. *Imitatio Christi* is possible but only in isolation; it does not permit a common moral horizon. "There was only one Christian," says Nietzsche, "and he died on the cross." [42].

The very imperative toward privacy presents Christ with a problem. He loved everyone, unconditionally; such a great unselfish affirmation destroys all horizons that might give some permanence to his teaching. He cannot be satisfied with the flux consequent to his praxis. No one could. The universality of his love leads to the search for some kind of permanence, or redemption. Christ's life will only have significance and justification if in fact all people love him. Unless he makes it necessary for all people to love him, he will disintegrate, since, as a person, he requires and depends on this universal love.

Christ thus *needs* love, and by this need slips inevitably toward morality. He is driven to invert and advocate permanent values, rather than simple praxis. In a very important section of *Beyond Good and Evil*, Nietzsche argues: "It is possible that underneath the holy disguise and fable of Jesus' life there lies concealed one of the most painful cases of martyrdom of *knowledge about love*, the martyrdom of the most innocent and desirous heart which could be sated by no human love, which demanded love and to be loved and nothing else, with hardness, with insanity, with frightful outbreaks against those who denied him love; the story of a man insatiable and unsatiated in love, who had to invent hell in order to send there those who did not want to love him, and who at the end, having grown knowledgeable about human love, had to invent a God who is all love, all ability to love. . . . Who so feels, who knows this about love, seeks death." Nietzsche sets off the next sentence: "But why pursue such painful matters? Assuming, of course, that one does not have to." [43]

Christ's need for love drives him to invent an imaginary world, a world of the ideal where redemption is for all. If all can be loved, all will be loved; there will be no reason to exclude anyone or anything. The implication of a world in which there are no boundaries or horizons − the love is for all unconditionally and uncritically − is, in Nietzsche's understanding, a disappearance of all criteria that permitted man to determine what was real. And, as already pointed out, in a world without horizons or criteria, there will be no rank, no way to tell one person from another. [44] The democratization inherent in universal love makes it impossible to tell who is like whom.

The form of authority implicit in Christ's universal love is the equality of all before a universal Father, who, in turn, has an inexhaustible love for all his children. "All men are equal before the Father" can be maintained as long as there is a Father. In this context, the "death of God" acquires an added significance as the moment when the last horizon of authority, perhaps the most tenuous and abstract of all in Nietzsche's eyes, finally disappears, leaving men with no means of recognizing who might be in the same moral world as themselves.

Until the death of God, there is, however, significance to the evangels and the "redeemer type." The "glad tidings" of the evangels totally annihilate the distance between God and man. *All is blessed.* Salvation is thus not promised — it is simply a given fact. A Christian can only be a Christian, then, if he leads a "Christian life," not because he might *profess* something. Men are known by their fruits, not their words, and thus known only in their life. Thus, for Nietzsche, a true Christian "makes no distinctions," and "does not grow angry with anyone." [45] Like Christ, a true Christian in Nietzsche's sense is not really moral. His life does not *conform* to certain moral laws; he *is* those laws, what some monastic orders call appropriately a "living rule." The gospels can be seen as "means of seduction by *means* of morality." [46] The assurance of salvation means that as long as one is alive the sign of a Christian lies not in conformity to certain propositions, but in his life. Morality as such is promised, a reward necessarily consequent to such a life.

In Nietzsche's understanding, the Christian is "seduced" by morality, by being promised the rewards of moral behavior, namely redemption, before the fact. He is then expected to live a life that is Christian in spirit. Since the redeemer "accepts all," [47] external behavior becomes unimportant and gives way to an emphasis overwhelmingly placed on "inner reality." [48] This is why the old man in *Zarathustra* can, in his isolation, live as a Christian. Nietzsche writes that even though there "are no Christians at all" any more, "genuine, original Christianity is possible at all times," but only as a private way of life. [49] In this context, it is worth noting that the old hermit does not talk with anyone, but rather "sings" with the birds; speech would make privacy impossible, unless the other be as gentle as Zarathustra.

Such original Christianity, however, has no way to deal with historical question. It is successful only in private. But, when confronted with the social world, the distortions that Nietzsche attributes to St. Paul become the only possible organizing tools. In practice, this requires that the emphasis no longer be placed on the practical life of Christ, but rather on rules and moral principles. With this change, Christianity is thrust up into the clouds and is removed from the earth. A Christian existence now must be centered in a mental construct, in an imagined "beyond." [50]

The effect is the same as that of Socrates' insistence on form. From an entirely opposite direction, the "kernel" of such a life is also nothing. The emphasis on the privacy of the individual destroys the foundations of that which made a common life, and thus culture, possible. In a passage from *Antichrist*, Nietzsche is quite specific about the consequences of Christianity for communality.

When one places life's center of gravity not in life, but in the "beyond" — in nothingness — one has deprived life of its center of gravity altogether. The great lie of personal immortality destroys all reason, all that is natural in the instincts — everything in the instincts that is beneficial, preserving of life, or guarantor of the future, now arouses mistrust. To live so that there is no longer any *sense* in living, *that* now becomes the "sense" of life. . . . Why communal sense [*Gemeinsinn*], why further gratitude for descendants and ancestors, why cooperate, why trust, why promote any common welfare? Just as many "temptations," just as many distractions from the "right path" — "*one* thing is needed."[51]

If, during this development, we kill God, as Nietzsche says, then the horizons fly apart and nothing is left. For Nietzsche, God was a guarantor of meaning in this world and is tantamount to final unselective affirmation of everything. In the "fulfillment of the teachings of Christ," as Nietzsche says, "we understand everything, we experience everything, we no longer retain any hostile feelings . . . . 'Everything is good': it costs us pain to say no. We suffer if we should happen to be so unintelligent as to take a stand against anything. . . ."[52] The death of God makes even this universal affirmation impossible — men arrive again at nihilism and want to act even though they know it to be ultimately pointless and impossible.

If Socrates had denied too much, Jesus denies too little. His attempt at universal affirmation is seen by Nietzsche as a refusal to accept horizons for life, and to accept the fact that horizons mean choice and saying *No* to something. (Nietzsche speaks of having rediscovered "the path to a Yes and a No.") The drive for universal-ity implicit in different ways in both Socrates and Christ, is in both ultimately the drive for death, for the very basis of life is selectivity. At this point they fail; both Christ and Socrates understand this and require death for themselves. Indeed, their very success is founded on their death. "The two greatest judicial murders in world history are, with circumlocution, concealed, and well concealed suicides. In both cases they wanted to die, in both they let the sword be plunged into their breast by the hand of human injustice." [53]

Socrates' last words in the *Crito* are, "Oh Crito, I owe a cock to Asclepius." Asclepius is the god of medicine; for Nietzsche, this is an explicit avowal by Socrates that life is a long sickness. The cock is a thank-offering to the god for having finally been cured of the sickness of life — by death. [54] Even at the end, Socrates could not say "yes" to life; his revenge has cost humanity dearly.

Christ, on the other hand, provided an unselective "Yes" to everything. No matter what respect Nietzsche has for Jesus' life, he must conclude that, in the end, Christ, too, sought to *justify* his life. It was to become "the road to a holy mode of existence." [55] Unable finally to escape from his own time, he merely posed a new historical problem; never did he succeed in dealing with history in such a way as not to remain time's fool. "In Jesus' death upon the cross," writes Jaspers in a direct paraphrase from a passage in the *Nachlass*, "he [Nietzsche] saw an expression of declining life, an indictment of life." [56]

Both Socrates and Christ attain, in fact need, the transcendental formulation. The desire for permanence is, however, always seen by Nietzsche as the opposite of life and the denial of the central characteristic of men on this earth: change and mortality. That their success in developing a "permanent" world comes to dominate so thoroughly much of Western life and thought is no evidence for their correctness. Camus phrased this point very well:

The intensity of a perception did not mean . . . that it is universal: the error of a whole period of history has been to enunciate, or suppose already enunciated, general rules of action founded on emotions of despair whose inevitable course, in that they are emotions, is continually to succeed themselves. Great suffering and great happiness may be found at the beginning of any process of reasoning. But it is impossible to discover or sustain them through the central process. . . . The mirror with its fixed stance must be broken and we are perforce caught up in an irresistible movement by which the absurd succeeds itself. [57]

Both immoralists succumb to the effects of history. In history, they are both anti-life because they are unable to avoid the temptations of escaping the change and flux that is life. Christ and Socrates both set in motion a process whose long-term effect becomes that of a deadening superficiality. "This is an age," proclaims Kierkegaard, "without passion: it leaves everything as it is, but cunningly empties it of significance. Instead of culminating in a rebellion, it reduces the outward reality of all relationships to a reflective tension which leaves everything standing but makes the whole of life ambiguous." [58] For Nietzsche, the flaws in the transvaluation of Socrates and Christ stand at the genealogical source of such emptiness.

Dionysos: Preliminary Considerations

Both Socrates and Christ commit a fatal mistake; they seek to make, in fact need to make, their teachings permanent. By this very desire they cast the dice of their own destruction. Inevitably, in time, the logic they set in motion plays itself out: the will to permanence reveals itself as a disguised will to death. To avoid such world-historical sickness as his destiny, Nietzsche elaborates the figure of Dionysos, an "arbitrary choice" of name, as he states in the 1886 preface to *The Birth of Tragedy*. While this is not yet the place to be concerned with a detailed examination of the meaning of the Dionysian and its complex evolution in Nietzsche's life and thought, it is important here to do the same for Dionysos as was done for Socrates and Christ. I am concerned now, then, with the *personality* of Dionysos. I hope to bring out here how he lives and talks, but not yet what he says.

Descriptions of Dionysos by Nietzsche are not particularly helpful. There are the famous references to the "Socrates who is a musician" and to the "Roman Caesar with the soul of Christ," which excite more than they inform. Nietzsche had in fact also once hoped that Wagner would play the Aeschylus to a new Dionysos who was to rejuvenate German culture. In any case, the renewed God must speak and act in such a manner as to forestall the dangers examined in Socrates and Christ.

In *The Twilight of the Idols*, Nietzsche compares Dionysos to an aphorism, as a particular combination of specificity and generality in a superficiality fraught with deep meaning. The aphorism is the "form of eternity,"[59] an instructive formulation for the aphorism is the natural mode of speech of Dionysos. To more fully set it off, I will briefly examine the modes of discourse appropriate to the two other world-historical immoralists considered in this chapter.

Nietzsche argues that Christ, as "redeemer," seeks to effectuate a purely internal change. It is possible to live a Christlike life alone in the wilderness. Indeed, Nietzsche sees this eventually as the only remaining possibility for such a life. The change wrought then is interior; externally, one suffers all. "If I understand anything about this great symbolist," writes Nietzsche in *The Antichrist*, "it is that he *took only inner realities as realities, as 'truths.'*"[60] In this vision, everything else, the entire external world, becomes only "occasions for parables." The parable is surely the appropriate form of discourse for this sort of teaching. The outer world appears only as signs; the analysis is of the internal world. In Nietzsche, reading a parable (such as that of the talents, which were either invested or hidden) may change the character of the person involved. It does not set up a new relationship between individuals, but, with Christianity, implies the "abolition of society."[61]

Such a form of discourse is unacceptable to Nietzsche for two reasons. In the first place, it presumes that significant changes in an individual can be purely private. This implies however that there is an inner world, precisely the notion that Nietzsche spends so much time combating. Secondly, by its emphasis on privacy, it presumes that changes in persons can come about independently of changes in the world of which they are a part. The great weight Nietzsche lays on the interaction between individuals and their world would thus be contradicted by a form of discourse which presumes that one might go directly to the "spirit."

Nietzsche rejects the parable because of its sole emphasis on the internal in man. He also rejects the mode of discourse appropriate to the Socratic man, that of the dialectic. As seen above, to lead to activity, the dialectic requires ultimate transcendental sanctification. The world of the Forms with which Plato enshrined the results of the dialogues requires a separation of that which is said from he who says it. In Nietzsche's reading, Socrates had sought to develop a form of discourse in which the results were "objective," but the ultimate effect is the same as with Christ. In the latter the results are purely internal; in the former, they are external. But, in both cases, a dividing line is drawn where for Nietzsche none should exist, between the speaker and the spoken. *This is not to say that Nietzsche makes "truth" dependent on the sayer: if the distinction between speaker and spoken is denied, then the judgment of one is also a judgment of the other.* Nietzsche is quite willing to say that Socrates and Christ have no right to the form of the conclusions they ultimately came to. In both cases, it is their need that forces them to it, and need will never be the basis of a rank order.

Instead of Socrates or Christ, Nietzsche calls upon Dionysos. [62] It is under the sign of this deity that Nietzsche should like to write, and in resonance with this principle that Nietzsche hopes to effectuate his revaluation of all values. Dionysian speech is aphoristic. Nietzsche writes that he would like to say in ten sentences what others have said, and also not said, in many volumes. It is thus, I believe, wrong to assume that Nietzsche's use of the aphorism is merely a stylistic device or, worse, an indication that he was unable to formulate a coherent argument. Nietzsche devotes considerable time to the demonstration that to talk in a certain way means to be able to say only certain things, and not others. At first glance, an aphorism may appear meaningful, or superficial, or trivially true, or simply nonsense. There is thus an automatic selectivity of interest; those who feel they have been touched and moved will listen. Those who do not react, will not react; in a certain sense the aphorism is not *meant* for them.

"Whoever writes in blood and aphorisms wants not to be read, but to be learned by heart." To understand an aphorism, Nietzsche says, one must take it inside, incarnate it, so to speak, and ruminate on it, "something for which one has almost to be a cow, and certainly not a modern man." [63] One reads an aphorism. If it seems truistic, or patently false, or non-sensical, it is abandoned and forgotten, jogging perhaps only thoughts as to the foolishness of men who would consider such a statement meaningful. Or one is touched by it and responds, something is stirred. It is only at this point that exegesis does, and can, begin. In an important sense, then, an aphorism is the "pure fool" of discourse, being only simple appearance. Yet the attempt to find it out will stir up the fermentation on which it rests, much in the way that Oedipus brings himself to light. The aphorism presents itself as an answer for which we know not the question. [64]

In trying to recover its meaningfulness, one is forced to construct the question for it, and rediscover the world in which it makes sense. I read, for instance, in *Beyond Good and Evil*: "Jesus said to his Jews: 'The law is for servants — love God as I do, as his son! What do we sons of God have to do with morality!' "[65] Because of all sorts of things buried in myself and because of the particular way I am put together as a person, I respond to this citation in a distant yet definite fashion. At this point, if I want to have rest from this aphorism, I am forced to construct exactly what world makes this statement possible, and thus to find out what particular world I respond to. It is both a task in re-covery of the underground of the aphorism and un-covery (to coin a word) of myself.

As such the activity admits of formal categorical thought only with difficulty. Since one is trying to re-construct and re-cover a landscape that makes the aphorism the case, what is necessary is contextualization and not conceptualization. The aphorism is not "out there" waiting to be assimilated into the mind's preexistent categories. It has already broken in, and like the Furies, must be dealt with.

Nietzsche refers, for instance, to the whole third essay of *The Genealogy of Morals* as such an exegetical attempt. There is a slow start, a lot of rumination, "a roll of distant thunderheads." The prose becomes more vigorous and radical, until the end is a challenge to be heard. Like a hero in a Greek tragedy, the aphorism only reveals its depth if troubled. It wants to make people (those who will, those who can) break contact with their present world and break through to the world that makes the aphorism real.

Aphorism readers are thus forced to participate in the creations that make their world real — without this the aphorism does not exist at all. If sufficiently chewed over, it is absorbed deeper than the point of simple acquiesence, until it is "perfectly true," unquestioned and available for life. Attempting to explain it to another person, that is, to place it in mutually understood categories, may be very difficult. The best that can be done is to help another person trace his own journey to that understanding. Thus, for instance, *Thus Spoke Zarathustra* must be approached as precisely such a philosophical journey of the spirit, not merely as a collection of sayings. It is one tremendous aphorism which rehearses the attempt to make manifest in Zarathustra's life the effects of the doctrine of eternal return.

As a form of philosophical discourse, the aphorism puts language to work. One is struck by an aphorism. One attempts to figure out the logic of the movement. Wittgenstein had characterized standard philosophical language as "being on holiday," as "a disengaged gear, spinning and merely giving the appearance of working." Wittgenstein did not "want to spare his readers the trouble of thinking." Nietzsche "despises reading idlers." [66] Both men try, through their mode of writing, to prevent such lassitude.

An aphorism demands and creates an actively participating audience. It is the clue for Nietzsche's understanding of what makes the Greeks so great. Dionysos is "the genius of the heart, . . . the experimenter-tempter God, and born pied piper of consciences, . . . who does not say a word or cast a glance in which there is no consideration or ulterior enticement; whose mastery includes the knowledge of how to seem — not what he is, but what is to those who follow him one more constraint to press ever closer to him in order to follow him ever more inwardly and thoroughly. . . ." [67] What Nietzsche looks for in Dionysos is an understanding of the world which is also an understanding of the self. At the beginning, such an attempt gives the sense of being lost, of not having categories to clutch at. Exegesis aims at complete clarity: the aphorism will no longer be a mystery, but rather simply a description of the world that has become. Still, at first one must refuse oneself the comfort of usual categories in order to experiment with the aphorism. Dionysos calls not for argumentation, as might a dialectician, not for inner light, as does an evangelist, but for creation, the building of a world in which the aphorism will not present itself as a problem.

Chapter VI

WHAT IS DIONYSIAN?
NIETZSCHE AND THE
GREEKS

*Let us look to America, not in order to make a servile
copy of the institutions she has established, but to gain a
clearer view of the policy that would be best for us; let
us look there less to find examples than instruction; let
us borrow from her principles, rather than the details of
her laws.*

Alexis de Tocqueville, *Democracy in America,*
1848 preface

*If we are to be Europeans,. . . the question which looms
before us is "What were the Greeks?"*

— Bruno Snell, *The Discovery of the Mind*

What fascinates Nietzsche about the Greeks, so
that he returns to them again and again? Throughout his life he
ruminates on them. They are monumental intellectual and cultural
ancestors to be admired, dissected, equaled, perhaps surpassed. And,
at all times, the Greeks are a *problem* for Nietzsche: they call
modern times into question and make it impossible to suppose that
contemporary civilization is inevitably coasting along toward a neces-

[135

sary mediocrity. Nietzsche was, of course, neither the first nor the only person to be awestruck by classical civilization. The nineteenth century saw many men who initially dreamed their dreams on the bed of classical studies. In England, an attempt was made to develop the university societies of Oxford and Cambridge in the same intellectual and, indeed, political role for Great Britian that men imagined the leisured class in Athens had played in the polis.

Such retrospective adulation and emulation must be distinguished from Nietzsche's outlook. No matter how admiring his posture, Nietzsche never advocates "returning" to the Greeks, nor making modern society over in their image. Neither does he, as still do some contemporary political philosophers, hold up the Greeks as a model for imitation, on the expectation that one day, perhaps, contemporary politics will once again be able to return to the fare that made Greece great.[1] Nietzsche is a genealogist: he has too real a sense of the weight of history to think that twenty-three hundred years have produced (merely) a cultural verdigris that might be removed by some arduous intellectual polishing. In his notes for *We Philologists*, one of the projected thirteen *Untimely Considerations*, Nietzsche is quite specific about this point. "It is a task: to show it impossible to bring back Greece and thus also Christianity and the earlier foundations of our society and our politics."[2]

If the past is not available to be brought back, why then should Nietzsche study the Greeks? There is a twofold answer. First, the Greeks lie at the genealogical origin of much that becomes Western thought, art, politics, and culture. The genealogical principle holds that the character of the family informs and shapes each generation; the Greeks have, so to speak, a certain ancestral status in the European family. Hence, since Nietzsche is attempting to delineate the genealogical elements that have led Europe to the disastrous situation he now sees it confronting, an investigation of the family ancestry may reveal those defects and strengths of character which have evolved down to the present. Along these lines, then, it is wrong to see Nietzsche's interest in Greece as the result of only his admiration. He rather is investigating the earlier civilization much in the manner one might consult the blueprint of a house one is interested in radically remodeling. It is important to know how the edifice is put together, which portions of it will crumble after particular supports are taken away, which walls might remain standing. Nietzsche's concern with Greece is filtered through his concern with the present.

There is, however, another element in Nietzsche's considerations of things Greek. He sees modern times as a situation analogous to the period when Greek civilization first began to carve itself out of the chaos of nonexistence. There was a time when Greece formed and defined itself *as Greek*. As the culture came to have an existence,

there were periods in which the Greeks were in similar danger of finding themselves, as we are, . . . being overwhelmed by the past and the foreign. . . . They gradually learned *to organize the chaos*, so that they, through the delphic teachings, reflected on themselves, that is upon their real needs, and let the illusory needs fall. Thus, they retook possession of themselves and did not long remain the burdened heirs and epigones of the whole Orient; they became themselves, and through difficult struggles with themselves, through the practical council of the oracle, the happiest enrichers and increasers of the inherited treasure and the ancestors and models of all subsequent cultured peoples.[3]

This passage, from *The Use and Disadvantage of History for Life*, seems to indicate that the Greeks here provide for Nietzsche a model of an attempt at extricating oneself from indeterminacy into the form and shape of a culture. It is not what the Greeks *did* that should provide a model for modern man, but rather what the *nature* of their achievement was. Nietzsche would learn from them what it means to define oneself into a culture, what the pitfalls are, what the consequences of good and bad choices might be. Not what the Greeks did, but the way they did it may provide useful lessons for the present.

Understanding Nietzsche's approach is complicated by the fact that he appears to have explicitly moved to it only in the years immediately following the writing of *The Birth of Tragedy*. In that work, he is concerned with the self-definition of Greek culture and its birth out of the "Asiatic chaos." But he also sees Greek culture providing a model for the rejuvenation of German culture. Wagner is to play the part of the new Aeschylus. He will incorporate into the *Gesamtkunstwerk* the principle of cultural health which Nietzsche had uncovered in the Greeks, and together the two of them will set the stage on which to begin the overcoming of the decadence they both see besetting Europe. *The Birth of Tragedy*, it seems, is ambiguous as to the precise nature of the model that the Greeks provide. The book admits the understanding that the Greeks teach us a particular manner of overcoming the chaos that is not-culture. But many passages and, more generally, the tone, signal that Nietzsche here understands them to do more than that. In this vein, he will write in the Preface to the never completed *Philosophy in the Tragic Age of the Greeks* that his book is meant to be "the beginning of a recovery and recreation of those lives so as to allow the polyphony of Greek culture to at last resound again."[4] And yet, barely a year later, the notion of "recovery" is gone: "To get *past* Hellenism by means of deeds: that would be our task. But to do that we first have to know what it was!"[5]

At this point in his life (1870-1873), Nietzsche seems to hold to an unresolved position. Some texts indicate that man can learn a *substantive* manner of resolving contemporary problems by studying the Greeks. Others, and these rapidly root out the former, indicate that the Greeks can provide an example of the process by which a culture comes to define itself, and that it is the understanding of the conquering of a manner of living and thinking which casts "light on our culture and our development," and thereby becomes "a means to understand ourselves, to set our time right, and thus to conquer [*überwinden*]."[6] It is the fact that the Greeks succeeded (at least for a while) which Nietzsche finds instructive; the substance of their success is of a different importance. To return to the metaphor employed above, Nietzsche wishes most of all to find from the Greeks the secret of how to make blueprints. If he learns this about Greece, he will in the process also have understood something about the particular edifice that becomes European culture. As the classical scholar, William Arrowsmith, puts it in a commentary on Nietzsche's texts about the classics: "Nietzsche saw the job of the classical scholar to be to construct something like a general field theory which could unify the crucial and complex creatures of Hellenic experience. . . ."[7]

Nietzsche therefore sets himself a task dangerously double. On the one hand, since Greece managed for a certain period to "retain possession of herself," he will try to show the immense gulf that separates that achievement from the failure of what passes for "our contemporary 'culture.' "[8] On the other hand, there is also no doubt that Greece slowly and over much time evolved into this "culture"; hence, as the "soil" for the present decadence, it must be analyzed so that it can be surpassed. The lesson is twofold: how to build a building, and what sort of building not to build.

Nietzsche calls the particular genius of the Greek cultural edifice the "dionysian" and asserts that "the Greeks will remain totally incomprehensible for us as long as we have no answer to the question 'What is dionysian?' "[9] I understand this question to refer to the manner in which the Greeks effectuate their "self-conquest"; the answer to this question is an answer about how the Greeks went about becoming Greeks. Bound up in this name, given almost at random, is the secret of what made a people who they were. Under the apparent calm of Greek art, Nietzsche locates a wild and uncontrolled psychic backdrop which the Greeks, for their own protection, cover with a hard-won apollonian scrim. The *sophrosyne* and balance which Goethe and Winckelmann extol, and which Wilamowitz counterposes to Nietzsche's understanding of the tragic world, is seen by Nietzsche not as the essence of Greek art, but as the result of a victory on the part of the Greeks over an uncategorized "Asiatic chaos." In fact, the Greeks are dangerously "prone to every bit of excess, to hubris in behavior and art alike,"[10] but manage to so shape themselves and their passions, that they appear "simple and sincere in their thinking and living."[11]

It would seem that the "chaos" from which the Greeks separated themselves is a general chaos. It lies under any world of culture which must itself be seen as having conquered this realm of limitless nondefinition. The greeks became the Greeks through an act of self-creation, but since the act is human and in history, their culture is constantly threatened with a return to chaos. Thus, for Nietzsche, where there is culture, there is also always the danger that the culture might not renew itself and might disintegrate from its pose and definition into that which simply is not. As an "act of conquest" over the chaos that lies before self-definition, in order to be itself Greek culture requires a constant assertion of power over the immoderation and wildness that lies behind and underneath. Nietzsche does not extol this chaos, but he does recognize that its continued presence is a necessary concomitant to culture.

"Greece," after all, is for Nietzsche a particular coherent manner of living and perceiving; it is, as he repeatedly points out, a "style." As such, it is necessarily an evolved pattern, not natural, but rather an artifact. Like any creation, it is subject to changes potentially so destructive of its integrity as to make it impossible to maintain itself. Hence, the apollonian "illusion" that makes Greek culture possible must constantly interact with the chaotic underworld; Greece is the result of a constant achieving, willing, fighting, and battling. Though the victories won give the appearance of permanence, Nietzsche sees this only an illusion comparable to that which one might have of the stability of the axis of a spinning sphere: it seems at rest only because of the movement around it, and a particular disturbance can cause wild fluctuations. (Even this metaphor is potentially misleading, since it seems to imply a continuous structural element, in this case the surface of the sphere. For Nietzsche, though, Greece changes from Homer to Aeschylus; in terms of the metaphor, one would have to think of a slow metamorphosis from a polyhedron to a sphere.)

What, then, is the meaning of the "dionysian"? It is common to associate Dionysos with frenzied, wild activity, perhaps of a definite sexual hue. An obvious ancestor might seem the figure of Dionysos in Euripides' *The Bacchae*. Yet nothing can be more misleading. In *The Birth of Tragedy* Nietzsche defines the dionysian quite carefully. It means having knowledge that all form is man-given, and that there are no limits or categories, knowable or unknowable, in "nature." The prototype of the dionysian man is, in Nietzsche's account, Hamlet. Nietzsche writes in *The Birth of Tragedy*: "For the rapture of the dionysian state, with its annihilation of the ordinary bounds and limits of existence, contains, while it lasts, a *lethargic* element in which all personal experience of the past becomes immersed. This chasm of oblivion separates the worlds of everyday and of dionysian reality. But, as soon as this everyday reality reenters consciousness, it is experienced as such, with nausea; an ascetic will-negating mood is the fruit of these states. In this sense, the dionysian man resembles Hamlet: both have truly looked once into the nature of things, they have gained *knowledge* and it nauseates them to act, for their action could not change anything in the eternal nature of things; they feel it is ridiculous that they should be asked to set right a world that is out of joint. Knowledge kills action; action requires the veils of illusion: that is the doctrine of Hamlet — and not that cheap knowledge of Jack the Dreamer who reflects too much and from an excess of possibilities does not get around to action. Not reflection, no; true knowledge, an insight into the horrible truth, outweighs any motive for action, both in Hamlet and in the dionysian man."[12]

The passage is important. "Dionysian" appears to be identified not with the chaos, but rather with *knowledge* ("true knowledge") of the chaos and of the artifice of human life and importance. In other words, the dionysian man is a man who knows that the illusion that has been conquered and won and that provides the form and definition of the particular culture is, in fact, merely an illusion. He sees into the fact the the culture — any culture — has no justification, except that created by virtue of its existence. In a sense then, it is accurate to say the "dionysian" replaces the sphere of theoretical reason which Nietzsche had been so intent on eliminating from that which one might accept from Kant. This is what Nietzsche calls in *The Birth of Tragedy* "artist's metaphysics" and is, in its preliminary form, a kind of specialized metaphysics designed to replace those that Kant had left to the world. In Nietzsche's understanding, the justification for Greece must be in the *fact* of its existence, and not because it might share certain of the categories of reason ("synthetic a priois").

Already in this early writing, Nietzsche poses problems that occupy him for much of the rest of his life. Life and action require illusion; the chaos has to be left behind for order. However, dionysian knowledge tells man that there is no justification in the "nature of things" for any particular order; by itself, then, "nature" is a plain of inaction, a dark midnight of a world that permits no categories or action. If, however, the form of the present world is out of joint, a new world will only be possible if modern men, like the Greeks, pass through the chaos-world, that is, develop dionysian knowledge. But to do so seems to take from men precisely those abilities that are required for transfiguration of the present. This, it appears, is what Nietzsche understood by the dionysian in his considerations of things Greek. It is important to be quite clear that the above description is of what Dionysos *does*; it is not a description of the psychology of the dionysian. Nor has any question as yet been raised or answered as to what the time-consciousness of the dionysian state is, how it sees itself, what sort of creation it may make possible. All that I have asserted thus far, is that at the very least, *"dionysian" has to mean knowledge of the chaos out of which culture can be created and won.*

I shall save a developed consideration of the psychology and physiology of the dionysian state until the last chapter. But this preliminary indication already permits a substantial reinterpretation of the relation of the dionysian and the apollonian. I see it as wrong to understand their primary relationship as simply antagonistic-dialectical. [13] Their relation is, rather, properly and possibly genealogical. In tragic art at least, Dionysos and Apollo complete each other. Through their interaction, the artist defines the world in forms (Apollo) which are themselves informed by the knowledge of the particular manner in which one has separated oneself out from the chaotic underworld. [14] Apollo is thus the god who makes a living Dionysos possible, he is the fulfillment that provides the continual rejuvenation of culture which Aeschylus sought to portray in his drama. The interaction of the two deities is not a sort of dialectic for which tragedy is the *Aufhebung*: a much more appropriate metaphor would be to see Dionysos as a light source and Apollo as a lens, which serves to color and focus. In fact, as Nietzsche says, the very appearance of the suffering Dionysos (in the form of Oedipus, Prometheus, etc.) is only made possible through the intervention of Apollo. [15] As noted before, the Aeschylean hero is like an aphorism: he is the particular and specific embodiment (apollonian) of the general style of the definition of a particular culture (dionysian). [16]

I have been talking, as does Nietzsche occasionally, as if there were a real separation between what one might call the "principle" of a particular culture (dionysian) and the manifestations in which it is embodied (apollonian). A word of warning is necessary here. While this distinction might be true on some analytic level, in terms of the reality of the situation it makes no actual sense to Nietzsche. Apollo and Dionysos are, in the best of Greek tragedy, perfectly linked, and the triumph of one is the fulfillment of the other. By extension, the form of a particular life or culture is ultimately tied to the manner in which it comes to exist vis-à-vis the chaos that lies below all form and meaning. In tragedy, we find a *particular* Dionysos and a *particular* Apollo: the triumph of Aeschylus is to have understood what in Greece *was* dionysian and what might be apollonian.

These considerations shed light on Nietzsche's enthusiasm for Wagner's *Gesamtkunstwerk*. Wagner was to have been, in Nietzsche's early estimation, a new Aeschylus, because his work unified music with words and actions in a manner not even Beethoven had been able to achieve. His opera was the life of the German Dionysos. Later, or, perhaps more accurately, when Nietzsche came to understand Wagner better, [17] Wagner began to write music such that Apollo and Dionysos no longer worked as one. In Nietzsche's judgment, he begins to make his form (text, action) call up his music.

Hence the bulk of Nietzsche's attack in *The Case of Wagner* centers around protestations about Wagner's *music*, not his librettos. "Wagner's music," writes Nietzsche, "is never true." This has, so to speak, Hegelianizing consequences for Wagner: the mind moves before the world, much as the *Geist* in Hegel has a certain priority to its embodiment. (Nietzsche will in fact link Wagner specifically with Hegel.) Now Wagner separates form and meaning and tries to seek "music for the discoveries he had watching drama." [18] When Wagner begins to write music to make effects, his "epistemology" is no longer dionysian. He is no longer embodying whatever dionysian knowledge he might have; rather, he is looking for tools with which to convey it. For Nietzsche this leads to theatricality, and Wagner becomes merely an actor (albeit a great one).

The question "What is dionysian?" then assumes a particular importance in modern times. If, as the inheritors of Socratism, men spend their time, in Nietzsche's words, "running up and down the banks of the river of existence" without ever daring to jump in, their problem is a lack of dionysian knowledge. They do not know why they do what they do and they have lost all knowledge of the underworld over which they once set themselves as victors. They are thus unable to free the culture from its present discontents. The investigation of the Greeks will be for Nietzsche not a study of the phenomenon of their art and culture, but rather of *that which makes such art necessary*. Nietzsche feels he can provide an example of a particular victory which a particular people won and in which they were themselves. The knowledge of the dionysian which is gained from such an investigation may serve as an example of what will be necessary for contemporary man to undergo.

Hence, Nietzsche does not ask "What is apollonian?" at this point – that is no problem. One cannot understand culture as a victory, as the creation of oneself, without understanding the particular nature of that victory. In the 1886 "Attempt at a self-critique," which Nietzsche adds as a new Preface to a new edition of *The Birth of Tragedy*, he argues that what is enduring about his first work is not the notion of an aesthetic justification of the world (though many people continue to take this as Nietzsche's last word on the world), but rather the analysis of *Wissenschaft*, that is, of the epistemology of investigation implicit in the search for the relationship between Apollo and Dionysos. As he says in 1888:

In the end, I concern myself to discover only *why* precisely Greek apollonianism had to grow out of a dionysian underground: the dionysian Greek found it necessary to become apollonian; this means: to break his will to the monstrous, the complicated, the unknown, the horrible on a will to measure, to simplicity, . . . to rule and concept. The immoderation, wildness, the Asiatic lies at the roots of the Greek nature: his courage comes from his fight with his Asiaticism: beauty was not given to them, any more than was logic, or the naturalness of morality — it is conquered, willed, battled for — it is victory.[19]

The simple achievement of a "victory," however, is not the end of the problem. The combination of Dionysos and Apollo which is effectuated must not be so rigid as to make change impossible. Here once the genealogy is established, a certain ongoing dialectical renewal of the relationship is necessary. In the period extending roughly from Homer to Socrates, Nietzsche finds that the Greeks manage this repeated rebirth and have what he refers to as a "healthy" culture. Before proceeding to the examination of the various renewals that were realized, I must make the notion of "health" somewhat more specific. Despite the Darwinian overtones, Nietzsche has something other than purely physiological characteristics in mind. The "health" of a culture may be measured, in his estimation, by the degree to which that culture does not set itself insoluble tasks. As was pointed out before, tasks demanding to be performed though they do not permit accomplishment are the keystone of nihilism. Any culture may require its members to act in certain ways. These ways are what is meant by being a member of that culture, they are the sign and symbol of the victory over chaos which that culture is. The culture also gives its members the strength and abilities to carry out, or attempt to carry out, these particular tasks. For instance, if a culture is patterned such that men earn their living individually, rather than, say, communally, the culture will be healthy only to the degree that it provides its members with the psychic and physical wherewithal to do so. Should it not, its members are what psychiatrists call in a double bind — that which calls them to perform a task also makes that performance impossible.

A particular pattern or arrangement may thus work for a given time. Homer's accomplishment, as we shall see, was to have given birth to a world that was still informative to men living four hundred years later in Athens. But changes always accrue, whether external (natural forces) or internal (the logical development of a particular form of life), and, if the culture is not able to meet the problems of transformation, it will necessarily release its particular pose and definition. The "Asiatic chaos" to which Nietzsche repeatedly refers appears to be the threat of that which is *barbaros*, which is not *"in Greek,"* and thus threatens the culture that calls itself Greece. In *The Birth of Tragedy*, Nietzsche refers to the position of the Greeks, "placed between India and Rome and pushed toward a seductive choice," who, nevertheless, "succeeded in inventing a third form in classical purity...." [20] The clear implication is that the long set of transformations which the Greeks played out in the period from Homer to Socrates still constitutes the family of what we call Greece. In the end, of course, these transformations all fail. And, after the heroic world of Homer, the political-scientific realms of the pre-Socratics, the dramatic rites of the old Attic stage, Greece is left with the dialectical cunning of Euripides and his admittedly *new* gods, with only the sardonic conservative laughter of Aristophanes lurking in the background as a reminder of the older Dionysos.

The World of Homer

One of the main unspoken contentions of *The Birth of Tragedy*, which draws the direct brunt of Wilamowitz' attack, is the notion that Homer was ancient in origin. That Nietzsche's intuition was correct has been demonstrated by subsequent studies. [21] It was an important point in Nietzsche's overall thesis, since the greater the antiquity, the closer Homer would have been historically to the chaos that was not Greece. If Homer comes at the very beginning of that which men came to see as Greek he is, as an "artist-meta-physician," thereby the source of much of what it means to be Greek. The creations that are the *Iliad* and the *Odyssey* thus become truly extraordinary phenomena: *they serve to define what it means to be Greek.* To a society barely emerging out of barbarity, Homer gives so overwhelming a form and definition that his view of the world continues to dominate for the next several centuries. Aeschylus himself will refer to his own works as "slices from Homer's mighty dinners." In Nietzsche's appreciation of Homer the important thing to retain is that, contrary to what one might have expected, he sees Homer throughout as an apollonian. He writes that "the Homeric 'naïveté' can only be understood as the complete victory of apollonian illusion." [22] Dionysos is the reality that gives necessity to Homer's song.

While it is not yet clear what Nietzsche finds the substance of the Homeric illusion to be, there is no doubt that the effect of such a victory is to enable men to attempt emulation of the heroes and the gods, and thus, without their knowing it, to enable a "natural process to be accomplished." Homer's achievement is so overwhelming that he makes possible the operation of a society without it ever becoming necessary for the men within it to become conscious of what the society is. As I shall point out in more detail below, strictly speaking, no one in the Homeric world is faced with the problem of ethical choice; the society is defined enough that the problem of "what to do when" is not raised.

What, then, is for Nietzsche the nature of this Homeric "reckless health, instinctual security and confidence in the future"? [23] The first striking thing in the epics is that no one can be said to reason about moral alternatives. In the modern sense of the term (implying a firm personality structure which selects between alternatives presenting themselves to it as a whole), there is no ratiocination about what is right or wrong in a particular situation or in general; nor is it ever indicated that such categories of reason are lacking. [24]

Conflicts do occur; indeed, for Homer they are the basis of the Greek spirit. But they occur between men, who, for Homer, are individuals not generally separable from their own special, defining characteristics. Ajax is strong, Odysseus clever; the conflicts that arise, arise between them, never between ideas. There is no realm of ideas to which intelligence and reasoning might be applied. Even Nestor, who is wise, gains his authority not through intelligence, but rather through experience. [25] General categories, or the "truth of celestial matters" which was to be so lampooned in a rearguard action by Aristophanes, are not the ethos of the epics. There is no general structure of categories to which reason might be applied, and which might be seen as independent of the actual people involved. Nor can this be a problem. Such a use of reasoning would imply a structure, the structure would require a framework, the framework is common and shared world view. [26] In the *Iliad*, however, the basis of interaction is the agon, the conflict of men; the heroes have nothing of importance to figure out.

Homer's achievement consists in founding a society based on the agon, He achieves a magnificent thing. Nietzsche writes that he "liberated the Greeks from Asiatic pomp and gloom and . . . attained clarity in architecture in both the large and the small. . . . Simplicity, flexibility, and sobriety were not lightly given to this people; they were wrestled for. The danger of a relapse into Asia always hovered over the Greeks. . . ." And Nietzsche goes on to explain what the *content* of that liberation was. The Greeks recognized man and *so structured their society* as to allow it outlets that were not destructive to man. The Greeks "allow to the evil [*Bösen*], the dubious, the animal, as well as to the barbarian, the pre-Greek, the Asiatic which still lived in the depths of the Greek consciousness a moderate outflow, and did not strive for its total annihilation." [27] This was the achievement of Homer and it was reflected in the structure of Greek society. Homer is glorious because of his naïveté; he can be "child-like" because he is so close to the world that he is weaving into a pattern. It must always be remembered that Homer's achievement is the complete victory of apollonian illusion. He created a model of gods and heroes which had a signal function: the real role of the Homeric epic is to ennoble. [28]

This conception of nobility will depend on and be limited by the gods on whom it is modeled. In *The Greeks and the Irrational*, Eric R. Dodds draws a distinction between the Homeric "shame culture" and the (at first) Asiatic "guilt culture." [29] In the Homeric world, the gods are only feared and imitated as more powerful human models would be. There is certainly no conception of higher justice or divine retribution. Men act in such a way as not to be shamed before their colleagues. Achilles thus rejects Odysseus and the others who are trying to persuade him to enter combat. He has proud reasons for refusing:

> Fate is the same for the man who holds back
>   the same if he fights hard.
> We are all held in a single honor, the brave
>   with the weaklings . . . .
> Nothing is won for me . . . in forever
>   setting my heart to battle.[30]

In other words there is no reason to fight, if there is no reward. This, when taken with the Homeric view of the relation of man to the gods, makes for a limited sense of nobility. Nietzsche remarks: "The Greeks neither saw the Homeric gods as lords [*Herrn*] nor saw themselves as servants [*Knechte*] as did the Jews. They saw only the mirror image of the most perfect example of their caste, that is, an ideal, not as the opposite of their own being. . . . Man thinks nobly of himself when he gives himself such gods and puts himself in a relation such as that of a higher to a lesser noble. . . ." [31]

The lesser form of nobility is restricted, however, to those who are already noble by the accepted standards of the nobility. It offers no creative possibilities. Either a hero does what is his to do and live or die, or else he is constrained by public expectation. In both cases, though, his self-definition remains limited by the society in which he exists. Non-societal expectations — even friendship — are simply excluded from the heroic ethos. And, in some moments, this proves very destructive. Hector, for instance, is unable to rise above the expectations — one might almost say the social pressure — of the Trojans and, though never a natural warrior, is constrained to leave the haven of Troy and fight Achilles, thus precipitating the downfall of Troy.

Such a conception makes impossible any signally new creation. The Greek heroic ethic remains fatally tied to the social configurations laid down in Homer. Change eventually becomes a problem. For this reason, the Homeric Greeks are identified in Nietzsche's writings only with the second stage of the metamorphoses of the spirit, the level of "I will." They do not reach the level of the new creator, the self-affirming child. [32] Nietzsche does not think (though many of his commentators do, apparently) the aim of man to be modeled on the Homeric "master" races. In the end, neither the heroic, nor the concomitant master morality remain possible.

Nietzsche elaborates on these considerations in a passage from the *Genealogy of Morals*. He has just finished an attack on the Christian notion of God.

Of itself, the conception of gods need not convince us that such a belief will result in morbid imaginings. . . . there are *nobler* ways of creating divine imaginations than the kind of self-crucifixion and self-punishment in which Europe has excelled in the last centuries. . . . [The] *Greek gods* reflected nobler and prouder [*selbstherrlicher*] men, in whom the *animal* in man felt itself made divine, and did *not* tear itself apart nor rage inwardly. For a very long time the Greeks used their gods precisely to keep "bad consciousness" at a distance from theirselves [*Leibe*] in order to keep the freedom of their soul [*Seele*] happy. . . . But one

hears and sees here at the same time that the Olympic spectator and judge is far
from holding a grudge against them or thinking evil [*böse*] of them therefore.
"How *foolish* they are": this he thinks of the misdeeds of mortals. . . . Foolishness is not sin. . . . [Delusion] by a god was a typically Greek solution. It was
the office of the gods to justify up to a certain point all the ways of man — *they
serve as founts of evil* [*Böse*]: in those days they did not take the punishment
upon them, but what is nobler, the guilt.[33]

As apollonian creations of the dream-artist Homer, the Greek gods
keep the early Greek world from all tendencies that might lead to a
breaking of the moral horizons of the culture. Crimes and wrongdoing — moral transgressions — need not be ascribed to a noble
Greek. If he commits an egregious error (it can hardly be called a
"sin"), the fault is a god's. Thus, throughout the *Iliad*, on the notable
occasions when a hero fails in his endeavor, it is never his responsibility. The superior power of a hostile god accounts for the failure to
finish off an enemy. In this understanding, it is impossible to call a
hero to moral judgment for his acts. Since the individual is always to
the best of his ability doing what comes naturally, there can be no
question of his making a wrong moral choice.

The great achievement of Homer is to protect the Greeks from a
pre-Homeric world, a "life over which rule only the children of night,
conflict, lust, deceit, old age, and death."[34] The Homeric poems
portray *precisely the envy, jealousy, and ambition that keep men
from falling back into the chaos of "Asiaticism."* But the great
danger is that Homer achieves this so fully that he also becomes the
most powerful curb on the development of the Greek spirit. He also
makes Greece more and more "shallow," because no matter how
attacked, he is always the victor.[35] Nietzsche writes then that the
"greatest fact in Greek culture remains that Homer so early became
Panhellenic. All mental freedom the Greeks attained is due to this
fact. At the same time it was fatal to the Greek culture through the
same process, for Homer weakened as much as he centralized, and
relaxed the serious drives for independence. . . . All great spiritual
powers have both a liberating and oppressing effect. . . ."[36]

Homer's dominance allows the Greeks to express their "personality" in an immediate and unreflective fashion; the principle of the
agon which he enshrines allows a social order that can support the
frequent cruelty and excess this might entail. All the drives and
desires and lust for war are recognized by the Greeks as human and it
is on them that the institutional structure is built. The wisdom of

their institutions lies then for Nietzsche in their *nonmoral* structure, in the lack of a real distinction between good and evil. "This is the root of all the freedom [*Freisinnigkeit*] of antiquity; one sought for the forces of instinct and nature a measured discharge, not annihilation and denial. . . ." [37] Eventually this structure will reappear, transformed, in the polis.

The danger Homer presents to the Greeks comes from the universality of his triumph. The world of the hero is a world that neither recognizes nor needs the intellect, nor, indeed, the instincts. Since what to do and what men know are not problems in the Homeric context, the vision of the epics has trouble changing when both the intellect and the instincts become problems. Homer does not feel it necessary to be concerned with origins. For Nietzsche, it is a sign of his "reckless self-confidence" and incredible artistic success that we can land in the middle of a situation in the *Iliad* and not feel the need to know from what it stemmed.

This is already not the case for his near contemporary, Hesiod. Hesiod is concerned explicitly with the birth of the world order, specifically of the gods in the *Theogony*, and of the races of men in *Works and Days*. He sees the world emerging out of chaos, which to him means simply that "preexistent state of affairs out of which the world order came into being." [38] Nietzsche pays very little attention to Hesiod, whom he may have read as a folk poet justifying frugality and industry. The few comments he does make, however, are interesting and come in the context of seeing him as the agonistic opponent of Homer. His most concentrated attempt to evaluate Hesiod comes in the lecture "Homer's Contest," written in 1872, while Nietzsche was still teaching at Basel.

According to legend, Homer did actually engage in a contest with Hesiod. Traditionally, King Panedes awarded the prize to Hesiod, despite the love of the crowd for Homer, for Hesiod sang of industry, peace, and good strife, whereas Homer sang only of war and bloodshed. Nietzsche sees as a significant fact that Hesiod had been forced to look back into the pre-Homeric world. He reads in the opening of the *Theogony* a world of "night and terror," and sees "an imagination accustomed to the horrible." "What kind of earthly existence," he asks, "do these revolting theogonic myths reflect? Let us imagine the atmosphere of Hesiod's poem, already hard to breath, made still denser and darker. . . . In this brooding atmosphere combat is salvation; the cruelty of victory is the pinnacle of life's jubilation."[39] In Nietzsche's reading, Hesiod reveals this dark world of the "children of the night" in the *Theogony*, and, in *Works and Days*, establishes a principle by which men can keep from falling into the chthonic horrors of the first world. This appears as "good *eris*," good strife, and is contrasted with bad *eris*.

Nietzsche finds that this distinction saves Greece from the wave of mystery cults spreading over it after the social consolidation that follows from the acceptance of the expiation of paternal murder.

The names of Orpheus, Musaeus, and their cults reveal the consequences to which the uninterrupted spectacle of a world of struggle and cruelty was pressing: toward a disgust with existence, toward the conception of this existence as a punishment and penance, toward the belief of the unity of existence and punishment. But it is precisely these consequences that are specifically Hellenic. . . . The Hellenic genius was ready with still another answer to the question, "What is a life of struggle and victory for?" and it gave that answer throughout the whole breadth of Greek history.[40]

This answer was the distinction between bad and good strife. The former leads to "hostile fights of annihilation" and is characteristic of conflict between "powers that should never fight, [such as] men and gods." Good *eris*, though, is strife between men, and leads them to quicken their activity to excel each other. Its consequences are found in the practice of ostracism, which ensured that no one might become so dominant as to destroy further competition.[41]

In Nietzsche's reading, Hesiod retains the agonistic principle as the basis of culture, and, in his contest with Homer, manages to establish an agon that is purely human and no longer tied only to the immortal gods. By emphasizing the human nature of the agon, Hesiod opens the contest up to potentially much richer variations.

Homer had not been writing myth; the epics appear as if there were no possible separation between a mythical and "real" world. In Hesiod, however, the task of bringing the agon more into the world of men requires an implicit separation of the world of the gods from that of humans; indeed, each subject pretty much has a book of its own. Hesiod opens the door for an independent evaluation of the world of the gods. The time was not long wanting for men to fill that gap. It falls to the first philosophers, who we call now the pre-Socratics and whom Nietzsche sees as the philosophers of the "tragic age," to call the world of the gods into question as mythology. They seek, writes Nietzsche, "a more brilliant sun. . . . Myth to them was not pure enough, not brilliant enough. They found this light in their knowledge, in that which each of them calls his 'truth.' "[42]

To see the world of the gods as myth is new; but the pre-Socratics are not for Nietzsche an alternative to Homer. They continue to solve the problem of origins and the nature of that from which men, and thus especially Greeks, spring. In this sense, they do not constitute a radical break from Hesiod. There is no doubt, however, that the air they breathe is much different.

The Pre-Socratics

About the time men began to think it necessary to write down the Homeric poems, there arose, first in Ionia and then elsewhere in the Greek world, men now seen as the first intellectuals and philosophers. These are the pre-Socratics, or as Nietzsche sometimes calls them, the "pre-Platonics," the philosophers of the "tragic age of the Greeks." The Homeric answer is failing, precisely because it is beginning to appear as an answer, and because it has never satisfactorily resolved the problem of origins. Hesiod had given some tentative answers to this latter problem. It is to these accounts of origins, now perceived as mythological, that the attention of the pre-Socratics turns. "One can represent these men," writes Nietzsche in the fragments *Science and Wisdom in Conflict*, "as those who experienced Greek appetite and custom as anathema and a barrier: thus they are self-liberators (struggle of Heraclitus against Homer and Hesiod, of Pythagoras against secularization, of all against myth)."[43]

The appearance of these men in history is truly extraordinary, for, even accepting the changes in Hesiod, Homer had lain immense burdens on the possibilities of creative thought. For the Greeks, before philosophy, "man was the truth and the core of all things; everything else was but semblance and the play of illusion. For this reason, they found it unbelievably difficult to comprehend concepts as such. . . ."[44] Thales and those who follow after him attempt to deal with the problems arising as soon as men move outside the realm of the morality of shame and custom. For Nietzsche, the problem the pre-Socratic philosophers face is to preserve the agonistic basis of Greek life and solve the problem of origins at the same time; as such, they are attempting to resolve the problems of the relation of knowledge of the world with a form of life. In their attempt to provide other than mythological account of origins, they are forced to provide a humanly accessible understanding of the world; in their effort to break the hold that shame-morality has upon men, they seek to ground knowledge of the world not in the relation of the gods to forces on this earth, but in categories and "empirical" concepts; they thus open the pathway to science. Whether it be "water" for Thales, the *nous* for Anaxagoras, "Being" for Parmenides, or "Becoming" for Heraclitus, the attempt is the same: to break through the "disguise and masquerade" by which the world had previously been justified. [45]

To an extent, then, all of the pre-Socratics are, as Nietzsche calls them, "genuine statesmen." [46] In addition to whatever specific political roles they might have played — some did and others did not — they seek to ground Greek understanding in an unshakable form; they are thus both destroyers of old forms and erectors of new. Above all, they seek a way to relate human perceptions and activity (individuality) to an overarching structure (commonality).

Overall understanding of Nietzsche's opinions on the pre-Socratics is difficult. As a group of men, Nietzsche loves them all; as protagonists of philosophical doctrine, his preference for Heraclitus over Parmenides is not hard to observe. There does exist a large fragment *Philosophy in the Tragic Age of the Greeks*, and many notes for its continuation. [47] In this work, he is concerned to "tell the story — simplified — of certain philosophers . . . to emphasize only that point of their systems which constitutes a slice of personality and hence belongs to that incontrovertible, nondebatable evidence . . . which is forever irrefutable." [48] All of this presents problems. Despite Nietzsche's claim that he is depicting the "personality" of each of the men, he appears at a number of points to have made mistakes in judgment (which I shall attempt to note in passing). To a certain extent these can be considered incidental to his task, which is to show each of the philosophers engaging in an agon with the others, and all of them forming the Greek contingent against that which is not Greek. "Philosophical systems are wholly true for their founders only. For all subsequent philosophers they usually represent one great mistake. . . . On the other hand, whoever rejoices in great human beings will also rejoice in philosophical systems, even if they be completely erroneous. They always have one incontrovertible point: personal mood, color."[49] Nietzsche first focuses on the manner in which the philosophers confronted each other.

Nietzsche is concerned to show that as a group they manifest what philosophy can be to a healthy culture and thus serve to set off Greece from the rest of the world. "It has been pointed out assiduously, to be sure, how much the Greeks were able to find and learn abroad in the Orient, and it is doubtless true that they picked up much there. . . . As to the general idea, we should not mind it, if only its exponents did not burden us with their conclusion that philosophy was thus merely imported into Greece rather than having grown and developed there in a soil nature and native to it." Understanding these men will permit, in Nietzsche's view, an understanding of what the Greeks genuinely were, for "the philosopher's mission when he lives in a genuine culture (which is characterized by unity of style) cannot be properly derived from our own circumstances and experiences, for we have no genuine culture. Only a culture such as the Greek can answer our questions as to the task of the philosopher, and only it can, I repeat, justify philosophy at all, because it alone knows and can demonstrate why and how the philosopher is not a chance wanderer. . . ." Greece was such a culture. By understanding these men, Nietzsche will understand Greece and philosophy.

Thales is the first, and he barely emerges from the mythological background against which he is set; his importance lies only in his intention. In claiming everything to be water, he is making no mere proclamation, but is exposing previous myth as the mask of a primal unity, which for him happens to be water.[50] That he may not have been right is much less important than his attempt to focus attention on questions of origin; the new ontological orientation lays the foundation for all subsequent metaphysics. As had Hesiod, Thales moves beyond mere empiricism to seek a grounding for his propositions about the world. He is not only allegorical; he is attempting a statement about the world, and thus also lays the foundation of science. Finally, and most important, he breeches a basic problem: if in the end all is one ("water"), how are men to account for the diversities and differences they observe about them? Thales seeks an understanding of this world firmly in this world. That he does so in an ultimately unfruitful way is of less importance to Nietzsche than the decisive break with the prior nonscientific world view.

Thales tries, albeit in a confused and preliminary manner, to show the fundamental unity of all things. Anaximander accepts this from Thales and sees it clearly enough to pose two additional questions. If all is one, then how can men explain change? And since human beings change, what is their relation to the one? He retains the notion of primal unity and concludes that it must be literally indefinite; were it to have categories, these, too, would pass away. Since as the original unity it is eternal, it can be designated "by human speech only as a negative, as something to which the existent world of coming-to-be can give no predicate." Nietzsche sees this as a functional "equal to the Kantian *Ding an sich*." [51]

The source of all that comes to be is forever removed from human knowledge. The more one seeks to fathom it, the darker the night becomes. Human life then can never understand itself; the only way the human world of the many and of becoming can ever be reconciled with the primal *Urein* is through death.

With Anaximander, philosophy formulates the problems that are to occupy it for the next several thousand years. The attempt to understand the world in philosophical and scientific terms leads to the creation of an "indefinite," necessary to solve the problems of relating man to his moral existence. Nonetheless, for Nietzsche, Anaximander draws the important conclusion that all that has come to be is merely an "illegitimate emancipation" from the indefinite and thus will pass away, having in itself only definite characteristics which will perforce change. In this realization, Anaximander becomes the first man to raise the question of the value of existence.

Since, for Anaximander, all that has come to be has only illegitimate existence, he is forced to conclude that this world is worthless and, in fact, merely an expiation for the sin of having come into being. Heraclitus next illustrates this dreary scene with a "divine stroke of lightning." While retaining from Anaximander the notion that this world offers nothing permanent, he simply denies that there is a world of the "indefinite" from which all that is transitory has sprung and to which it, in expiation for its existence, will return. This leads him to a second and bolder negation: he denies the notion of being altogether. If men see things as definite, permanent and given, it is merely the fault of their sense perceptions. Men will use names that endow permanence, yet what they call a stream once, and do so again, has not the same waters.

Seeing all as impermanent has the effect of an "earthquake." All confidence in the familiar grounds of life vanishes and one is reduced to the immediate and obvious. All that can be certain is that things come to be and they pass away. Guilt, moral standards, injustice, suffering are all consequent to the human eye, which invents entities and endows them with rest. By denying being, Heraclitus is able to retain the view of Anaximander that this world is a world of suffering where morality has sport. But, at the same time, he can see that it is the world of humans and as evanescent as humans are. The disappearance of Being as such puts the world back together with man.

The principle of motion and change must then be based on the unity of coming to be and passing away. At any moment there are two forces struggling with each other in an agon that is both cosmic and specific. "Qualities wrestle with one another, in accordance with inviolable laws and standards *that are immanent in the struggle*. These things in whose definiteness and endurance narrow human minds, like animal minds, believe, have no real existence." "They are," says Nietzsche, "but the flash and spark of drawn swords, the quick radiance of victory in the struggle of opposites." [52]

This is possibly the most important aspect of Heraclitus. By realizing that with the constant agon that makes the world what it is, the laws and standards are immanent in the struggle, Heraclitus draws attention to the essential innocence of becoming as a whole. In the understanding of Heraclitus, the world is a game "of the child Zeus," or of "fire with itself." The world cannot be referred to some external moral standard by which it can be judged. Instead, all revelation is in the world; the world contains literally everything man needs to seek about himself. [53]

Nietzsche certainly feels great affinity with Heraclitus here, yet this is not his final position. At the end of his life he proclaims that only Heraclitus comes close to an inkling of the doctrine of eternal return. The problem with Heraclitus' view, however, is that it is almost impossible to maintain. It is easily turned into an "invitation to every passerby to *plaudite amici*": the universal tragic acceptance of the innocence of becoming is not feasible over a long run or among men. "Perhaps," writes Nietzsche, "in some remote sanctum, among idols, surrounded by a serene sublime architecture, such a creature might seem more comprehensible." Some form is necessary as the apollonian counter to the dionysian earthquake of playful innocence.

The counter — exaggerated and archetypal as the portraits of all these men are — is Parmenides. Heraclitus had never formulated exactly what "coming to be" was. Indeed he could not, for that would have already pointed at something beyond mere and simple becoming. Paramenides is lead to effectuate an understanding in very specific human terms. He argues that for it to be possible for things to come to be, there has to be both the realm of the existent and the realm of that which does not exist. To show how these two seemingly contradictory realms come together (since as opposites they should seemingly flee each other), "Parmenides appeals to a *qualitas occulta*, to the mystic tendency of opposites to attract and unite, and he symbolizes the opposition in the name of Aphrodite. . . . Desire unites the contradictory and mutually repellent elements: the result is coming to be. When desire is satiated, hatred and inner opposition drive the existent and nonexistent apart once more."

With this conclusion, Parmenides has only made a preliminary step. He must now ask himself where the existent comes from. If there is anything at all (which there certainly seems to be), it cannot have come out of the nonexistent, for this would be a contradiction in terms. It must then have come out of itself; this means however that the existent must be one and eternal. Everything that was and will be, is already, according to Parmenides. Men, however, claim to have new experiences; hence their perceptions must be illusions. With this relentless conclusion, Parmenides is led to cast suspicion on men's senses, which can yield but illusion, and to value the power of thinking which reveals their illusions to them. By this move, the mind is divided into two separate capacities. The experience of phenomena, even of one's self, are conceits. Men know this because they have an organ, the mind, which permits them to reach into the essence of the existence without being sullied by experience. Any conclusions to which one might properly attach the name of "truth" cannot have anything to do with phenomena, since this would make them by definition illusions. For Parmenides, the "truth shall live," as Nietzsche notes, "only in the palest, most abstracted generalities, in the empty husks of the most indefinite terms, as though in a house of cobwebs."

For Nietzsche, Parmenides realizes that truth as an in-itself cannot have anything to do with phenomena, since these are by definition sorrowful and illusory. His teaching is extended by disciples such as Zeno to the concept of motion also. [54] The Eleatics demonstrate that even motion itself must be an illusion since, for Achilles to catch up with the proverbial tortoise, he would have to traverse an infinity of spaces in a finite moment of time. Thus, if he does seem to catch the tortoise, it must be merely an illusion. One might think, notes Nietzsche here, that instead of abandoning the world of phenomena, Parmenides and Zeno might give up on the world of the mind. They do not, however, for they have assumed that the best and decisive criteria as to the constitution of being and nonbeing are found in the human capacity to think. This prejudice leads to the assertion which Nietzsche finds the greatest of their mistakes, albeit a necessary one if the whole philosophical edifice is to be saved. They must assert the unity of knowing and being, despite the fact that such knowledge and being are bloodless and void of humanity.

Parmenides and his followers seek a solution to the philosophical problems of the relation between human beings and the world in this reduction of the sensuous content of their understanding. Even with this eviscerated and pale world, however, there remain unresolved questions. The next philosopher in Nietzsche's gallery is Anaxagoras, who raises two objections to the Parmenidean world. For Parmenides and the Eleatics, "being" had to be motionless. They had been driven to effectuate an identity of being and thought. To this it can be objected, *ad hominem*, as Nietzsche puts it, first, that thoughts do succeed each other and that there is motion in the process of thought itself. If such motion has being, then what Parmenides saw true of being must also be true of motion. It, too, must be eternal and indestructible. True being is thus multiple, not unitary; all things that will exist, do exist, and have existed. Change would be the rearrangement of what is due to motion. The second objection is that if the senses provide only illusory impressions, they become problems in and of themselves. They cannot be part of the world of illusion, however, for one cannot speak of them as actively dissembling and distorting. Were they to be active mystifiers, then they must have some standing in the world of being. But, in that case, they would not themselves be illusory, nor would there be a source for the illusion that Parmenides sees besetting the world of the senses. [55]

Anaxagoras makes both of these objections and concludes that the world, in all of its appearances, must be real. Change is merely the mixture of all the simultaneously existing essences in motion. "We have," says Nietzsche, "then the same situation as in a game of dice. The dice are always the same, but falling now this way, now that, they signify different things for us." Anaxagoras is the first man to understand that the world is in fact one, yet that it is one *in* all of its appearances, and that the unity does not lie *behind* it. The call Nietzsche raises to "remain true to the earth" will depend on this understanding of the world.

Since motion tumbles the various essences about into the worlds they make up, truth must then lie not in fixity but rather in motion. The chaos implicit in the manifold essences can only be given shapes if there is motion. Men escape the chaos through motion — this is the Anaxagorean *nous*. The *nous* infuses all that is with concrete existence. A close relative to Hegel's *Geist*, it is the principle in all things which makes them things, an *a-theos ex machina*, as Nietzsche sardonically remarks. In the pell-mell of chaos, a certain type of motion had to be infused into the manifold world in order to start it off on the road to becoming. Taking an image from Anaximander, Anaxagoras calls it a spiral. In the form of "a small turn, and in ever greater orbits, this circular movement spans all available being, by its centrifugal force pulling out all likes to join likes," and so on, and on *ad aeternam*.

But neither the Greeks nor Nietzsche could remain satisfied with this "whirl," as Democritus calls it. The larger it is, the stronger it must become since it carries with it more and more of the universe; and when infinity is reached, the process will necessarily stop. The particular calculus of infinities implicit in Democritus raises insurmountable problems for Anaxagoras. For the motion to reach infinity in space it must have started at an infinitely rapid rate and the first spiral described must have been infinitely small. There is then however no reason not to suppose that there should not have been simply an infinity of infinitely small "whirls" rotating about themselves. These become "atoms" in Democritean physics. And, if there be an infinite number of them, they cannot by themselves produce the whole cosmic dance that is the result of the working out of the *nous*.

Democritus has arrived at the conclusion that the Anaxagorean *nous* cannot be purely natural force. (Nietzsche and Marx were to make the same criticism of the *Weltgeist* in Hegel.) To say that the world acquires shape through the *nous* entails the conclusion that the *nous* was at some point a "creative artist," and that "coming to be . . . [must be understood as] an aesthetic phenomenon." The world of men is created from the free willing of the *nous*, "purposeless, roughly like a child's game and an artist's impulse."

Empedocles breaks sharply with this view. [56] The *nous* was simply too complicated for him and smelled philosophically of the "indefinite" or Anaximander. For Empedocles, motion was the given, not that which had to be explained. He sees only two kinds of motion, toward and away from, which he names love and hate. All that men see in the world is to be understood as the interaction of these two natural forces. The world is and always will be an ongoing agon. There is no need to assume or posit anything more than that. [57]

Nietzsche has run through the pre-Socratics in such a manner as to bring out that which endures of each man. His approach is curiously like that of a Platonic dialogue: each man is interrogated as to what makes him what he is; Nietzsche then retains some and passes the rest on to the next sage. As an end result, Nietzsche retains those points that form an outline of his own attitude toward the world. The final step — eternal return — is of course missing. To sum up what is living for Nietzsche in the pre-Socratics:

1. They attempt a scientific understanding of the world (Thales).
2. They must thereby give an account of change and values (Anaximander).
3. They must perforce then deny any permanence in the phenomenal world (Heraclitus).
4. What men perceive as true and real are but abstractions (Parmenides and the Eleatics).
5. Value can only be found in plurality (Anaxagoras).
6. Value, beauty, and reality must be sought in the world; they are to be understood as the result of different attitudes (Empedocles).

The pre-Socratics make possible a dialogue between philosophy, science, and politics. Their attack on the Homeric and Hesiodic worlds consists mainly in showing that men are bound neither to a mythological or unbreakable view of the world hierarchy, nor to their immediate sense impressions. If such understandings are incorporated into action, different forms of life, efforts at reform, and something other than a pious acceptance of what is, become possible. As mentioned above, many of the philosophers of this tragic age were actually involved in politics. Nietzsche certainly applauds this. But of more basic importance to him is what he refers to as the "political significance [Sinn] of the older Greek philosophers, which is due to their strength of metaphor." [58] The pre-Socratics were all politically significant in that they were attempting to solve the problem of the relations of the individuals and the world by providing a common manner of viewing questions. In the next chapter, I shall examine this contribution and the reasons for its failure in somewhat more detail. Nietzsche does see in these men those who liberated the individual from the limiting horizons of Homeric Greece. After them, for the first time, the shaping and active individual can play a role in the world. The pre-Socratics fail for reasons both philosophical and political, but they had made possible the use of the intellect in determining the relation of the individual to the world around him. Whereas Homer had achieved this in a nonreflective manner, the scientific orientation of the pre-Socratics forced the development of consciousness and explanation and, for the first time, made choice possible.

In Nietzsche's understanding, the attempt of the pre-Socratics provides the means that make tragedy possible. He writes that these men "felt the Greek air and morality as confinement: thus they are self-liberators. . . . [They are] the forerunners of a reformation of the Greeks, but not that of Socrates. . . . One set of occurrences carried all this reformation spirit: The development of tragedy." [59] The thought of the pre-Socratics makes it possible to artistically develop paradigmatic situations by which one might consciously educate and remind a people of its foundations and grounding. Homer had achieved this, but not in a conscious fashion; after all, he had not had the past history of being Greek to deal with. In drama as it develops in the Golden Age, tragedy will play the same instructive role to the polis that the Gods did to the heroes, with the politically all important difference that consciousness and intellect may now have a role.

The World of Aeschylus

In Homer, the underworld was not a problem. The heroes were

terrified of it when threatened; in more normal circumstances, they were uninterested. The sway of the illusion Homer wrought was so great that in the epics the Greeks could appear in childlike naïveté in war and play. Not so in Aeschylus. Here the dionysian rises as night, barely held off in the forms and conventions that make a play. There exist some records of the behavior of Attic audiences during the performance of tragedies. By all accounts, as we shall investigage, the effect was tremendous.

To assert, however, that Aeschylus merely revives the underworld is to misread his purpose. As Eric R. Dodds writes in a very Nietzschean vein: "Aeschylus does not have to revive the world of the daemons: it is the world into which he is born. And his purpose is not to lead his countrymen back into that world, but on the contrary to lead them into and out of it." [60] Aeschylus, as Nietzsche knew, was not simply engaged in writing good and intriguing tragedies. His plays bring back under the Greek roof the soil from which his people had sprung, and do so in such a way that the Greek spirit is renewed. As such, it was a dangerous task that Aeschylus set himself, especially since he had not the awareness to protect himself from the disapproval of the crowd. Nietzsche notes that he was accused of profaning the mysteries by representing them on stage. [61] But, despite the dangers of blasphemy, his drama provided for his contemporaries a powerful and vital dynamic arena in which to relate their contemporaneous experience and contront it with the basis of their culture. For Nietzsche, this is the proper contribution of tragedy to the health of the state. [62] The aim of tragedy is to give the audience an experience of the ongoing and formative foundations of what makes them a people. The confrontation and melding of stage and audience provide an ever renewing experience by which the culture can change and yet continue as it is.

Thus the specific plots of the plays are not important. If old Attic tragedy is the most mature literature in the West, it is so because Aeschylus managed to find a vehicle for effectively presenting genealogical truths to his audience without winnowing them through a gin of exclusively present times. If the *story* had become important, Apollo would have dominated and the effect would have been lost. Every Greek knew the myths: it is the manner in which they related to them, their style as an audience during the dramatic presentation, that becomes important.

To understand how the plays worked such a renewal, a detailed consideration of the precise relation of audience to and the performance of old Attic tragedy must be undertaken. The tradition is quite clear in that in the oldest tragedies, the chorus plays a primordial role and is the main dionysian protagonist. The earliest extant Aeschylean plays, such as *The Suppliant Maidens*, have a very reduced heroic lead who functions mainly as the spokesman for the chorus. Later, the chorus coexists with heroes; the tradition still clearly reveals, though, that this is a development, and that originally, "tragedy arose from the tragic chorus." [63] In both cases, the nature of the chorus is to comment upon the action; appropriate to its dionysian nature it *knows*, but does not *do* anything. The Aeschylean play moves forward not by the action of the characters, who, as Nietzsche says, "stutter and err," but rather by the illumination of their actions in the choral odes and epodes.

Since the plot is known in advance, the resolution is not in question, nor is the action of the characters itself of interest. The world of the dramatic representation may, in Nietzsche's understanding, depict a situation familar from the world beyond the theater, but it in no way attempts to comment on it. It is left to comedy (and later to Euripides) to use the stage to talk about what went on outside the arena. Whatever effect the Aeschylean play has it must have by making its audience part of the resolution of the play, rather than by providing them with tools and recipes they might use in the world. In Aeschylus, it is only *in* the play that the conscience is caught.

Given this background, Nietzsche lays great stress on the importance of the physical situation of the audience at whom these seemingly superficial plays are directed. In the eighth chapter of *The Birth of Tragedy*, he combines a description of the nature of the audience with a description of its physical relationship to the stage. "A public of spectators as we know it was unknown to the Greeks: in their theaters, the terraced structure of the concentric arcs of the spectator place [*Zuschauerraumes*] made it possible for everyone actually to *overlook* the whole world of culture around him and imagine in satiated (*gesättigt*) contemplation that he was a chorist." The German word for "overlook" is *übersehen*. Both languages permit the double meaning, intended by Nietzsche, of "survey" and "fail to see." I interpret this passage to mean that the audience, "in satiated contemplation," had before it, during the time it was in the "spectator place," only that which was on stage. (I apologize for the lack of grace in "the concentric arcs of the spectator place"; the standard translation has solved the problem by leaving it out. It does seem, though, to imply an important opposition to the "whole world of culture.") As spectators, the audience knows first that everything occurring on stage has an awful necessity and that there is nothing that can be done about the process. The spectator will not therefore "run up on stage and free the god from his torments." The chorus he beholds is of dionysian and satyric ancestry, a "chorus of natural beings who live ineradicably, as it were, behind all civilization and remain eternally the same, despite the changes of generations and the history of nations." [64] The spectators apprehend the dionysian chorus (which "does not act"), and in "rapt contemplation" know that there is nothing that can be done about the action on the stage. In effect, the spectators are in a dionysian state, since they have knowledge and cannot act.

The relations between the audience and the drama being performed are not reciprocal. The actors on stage are in the presence of the audience; the audience sees them. The reverse however is not true. The audience is not in the presence of the actors. The players on stage do not see the audience and there is no way in which the audience can, as audience, compel the action on stage to acknowledge it. The audience is, as was just noted, in a dionysian state; so, however, is the chorus. The correspondence of psychic and physical structures allows the audience (who can relate to the stage only in a manner that cannot be reciprocal) to be swept up into the stage through the medium of the chorus. This flow must go one way. Thus Nietzsche writes: "The proceeding [*Prozess*] of the tragic chorus is the *dramatic* protophenomenon: to see oneself [as embodied in the chorus —TBS] transformed before one's very eyes [as spectator — TBS] and to begin to act as if one had actually entered into another body, another character. . . . And this phenomenon is encountered epidemically: a whole throng experiences this magic transformation."[65]

At the high point of the drama, the godhead Dionysos himself appears as necessary *illusion*. This is "the apollonian complement of [the audience-chorus] state"; by it, the tragedy can assume a unified, perfect, and repeating vision. The spectator can see himself as the chorus, which in turn sees Dionysos; the god is an illusion and apollonian, but it is the illusion characteristic of the state the chorus is in. Thus, there is a unification of Apollo and Dionysos in a perfect image. The audience is wholly in the world of the play and, through the perfect illusion, finds the dramatic world whole and perfect; it is no accident that Dionysos is dismembered and reborn. The spectators never have to *consider*, as audience, the question of origins. Instead, the play solves that question through a circular "illusion" that constantly informs the audiences. The origins are always sensuously there: through these operations they become a foundation for the audience.

Aeschylus confronts the problems of values in situations where the old horizons no longer appear to hold, or have, at best, ambiguous reference. The end of the *Oresteia* portrays a situation in which a potentially threatening individualism, which Orestes feels obliged to embody, is redirected into a renewed moral community. Sins there are punished on this earth, and the resolution is generally viewed as social in nature; the drives the Furies represent must also be integrated into Athens. In *The Persians*, the Danaides must also be admitted as part of the legitimate past: Argos cannot by an act of will deny what it has been. Presumably in the lost *Prometheus Unbound*, the reborn Titan would have come back down from his rock.

Nietzsche refers to the function of myth as that of a "noble deception" and would seem to suggest with these words something analogous to the Platonic conception of the "noble lie," which formed the public basis of the state in the *Republic*. It protects the Greeks against too close contact with the real foundation of their culture; Nietzsche finds that the Greeks fear the "extraordinary strength of their dionysian and political instincts," and sees in tragedy the politically happy combination of myth and music which permitted a healthy culture to live. In what he calls "only a preliminary expression of these difficult ideas [which] . . . are immediately intelligible only to few," Nietzsche writes: "Between the universal validity of its music and the listener, receptive in his dionysian state, tragedy places a sublime metaphor [*Gleichnis*], the myth, and awakes in the spectator the illusion, as though the music were only the highest means [*Darstellungsmittel*] toward the animation [*Belebung*] of the plastic world of the myth." [66] The world of illusion created by the tragedy serves as the continuing and repetitive basis for the renewal of the state. This permits the reconciliation of the dark knowledge "into the true nature of things" with the "uniformly vigorous effusion of the simplest political feeling." Nietzsche then argues, in a passage shortly before the one cited above, that the illusion generated by the tragic arts made it possible for Greece to avoid the pure politicization of Rome and the "ecstatic" evaluations of Indian Buddhism. "Placed between India and Rome, and pushed toward a seductive choice, the Greeks succeeded in inventing a third form, in classical purity." A form of association was found such that each individual could express himself fully. This required that they live inside the same horizon of illusion; for the agonistic conflict, which makes greatness possible, to continue, the interaction generated by the illusions of tragedy were prerequisite.

One might object that all of this sounds very "un-Nietzschean." Such talk of moral communities and rejuvenation of culture clashes with the resonances of "free spirit" and "Prinz Vogelfrei." But what has been made of Nietzsche is not always what Nietzsche is. Aeschylus, much as Socrates and Christ, stands outside his community; he was even accused of profaning the mysteries. He is successful, or almost so, in a way that Christ and Socrates were not, because he managed to recover horizons for the world where virtuous action remained possible. Such tragic art is a form of domination;[67] it makes the world appear worth living in. The genius, Nietzsche says, while speaking of tragic artists, has "the power to hang a new net of illusion around the world."[68]

A second main theme which emerges from Nietzsche's appreciation of Aeschylus is the full recognition of the nature of human responsibility. No longer is the fact that a god made one do something an excuse. Whereas in the early play *Seven Against Thebes* Eteocles had been able to argue in a Homeric fashion that it was "the god that drove the matter on," later Aeschylus requires his characters to take upon themselves the guilt for what they were blindly obliged to do.

Thus, Orestes in *The Eumenides* says:

> I plead guilty
> . . . .
> Apollo shares the responsibility:
> He counterspurred my heart. . . .

This is my case. Where my fate
falls, I shall accept.[69]

Much like Heraclitus before him, Aeschylus is saying that character is destiny.[70] There can be no separation, *no matter what the
outcome*, of a person and his acts. If the jury decides against Orestes,
he is fated guilty, he *is* guilty.

For Nietzsche, the virtue of Aeschylus lies in the quality of his art.
The *Oresteia*, after all, is at one very important level the depiction of
two conflicting principles of law seeking allegiance from the Athenians. The narrow decision of the jury in favor of Orestes and
"young laws" justifies a new form of legitimacy. Henceforth, it is at
least conceivable in Athens that the requirements of the polis may
necessitate the death of mothers. This was no easy argument to a
society that had barely made the transition from the dominance of
the cult of the Great Mother to some form of patriarchy. That
Aeschylus succeeds in grounding his justification of the new system
in a world that could still call upon the authority of both Homer and
the oldest myths is no mean feat. To the degree that he is convincing,
the Greek state will live through the painful social and psychological
transitions it undergoes.

His success, of course, is neither complete, nor lasting. For reasons
having partly to do with his art, but more with the unyielding
historical situation which Athens confronts, Aeschylus begins to
appear to his public as the man of Athens' noble past, rather than of
the present. A sympathetic portrait has come down in the comedies
of Aristophanes. (I shall consider Nietzsche's analysis of his failure
more closely in the following chapter.) In Athens, new dramatists
rapidly claimed the allegiance of the Greek audiences. Foremost
among these are Sophocles and Euripides. It is to them that I now
turn.

Nietzsche gives very short consideration to Sophocles and, accordingly, I shall also. Nietzsche seems to think of Sophocles as a great
author who could speak most strongly to Athens only in the short
period that constitutes a lull before the storm of the Peloponnesian
War. In some ways, Sophocles attempts to finish the task of Aeschylus. In the earlier playwright, the problem is to deal with the continuing onslaught of the new; what the gods want is not known and
constitutes the problem to be solved. In Sophocles, on the other

hand, the gods pose no new and significant problems. Rather, having accepted the Olympian revolution implicit in the concerns of Aeschylus, the problem in the writings of Sophocles becomes the lack of knowledge that men have of themselves. There are no competing deities in *Oedipus the King*. The task is the nature of self-knowledge in the new social situation represented by the monarchy of paternal descent. Oedipus is the son of his father, despite himself; he still must understand this. [71]

Nietzsche is concerned with the problems of change. He can thus pass over Sophocles as representing an unfortunately temporary respite from the ferocity of Greek politics. He considers him mainly in the notes preparatory to the writing of *The Birth of Tragedy*; as opposed to the two other great dramatists, Sophocles is hardly mentioned thereafter.

The key figure for Nietzsche is, of course, Euripides. With Aristophanes in *The Frogs*, Nietzsche sees Euripides as the important opposition to Aeschylus; and again as with Aristophanes, he finds in favor of the older writer. At first glance though, it might seem strange for Nietzsche to dislike Euripides. [72] The Euripidean view of the universe certainly has no more obvious order than that of Nietzsche. There are no higher truths; the behavior of the gods is only slightly more ignoble than that of mortals. Such a reading, however, presupposes that Nietzsche's quarrel with Euripides is primarily with his doctrine. It is my contention that this is misleading. As with Wagner, whose music Nietzsche finds "never true," so with Euripides, whose art must be called into question. No less than Aeschylus does Euripides seek to educate and instruct his audience, it is the manner by which he seeks to do this that Nietzsche would condemn.

Euripides writes in a time of social disintegration; old standards are falling away, no new ones have yet arisen to take their place. If Athens has solved the problems of political organization inherent in becoming a polis, it is not coping very well with the problems inherent in the resultant individualism. No one has described this general situation better than Thucydides.

When troubles had once begun in the cities, those who followed carried the revolutionary spirit further and further and determined to outdo the report of all who had preceded them in the ingenuity of their enterprises and the atrocities of their revenges. The meaning of words no longer had the same relation to things, but was changed by them as they thought proper. . . . Frantic energy was held to be the true quality of a man. . . . The seal of good faith was not divine law, but fellowship in crime.[73]

According to legend, Euripides was born on the day of the battle of Salamis. This, the signal victory of the Greeks over the Persians, marks for Nietzsche the beginning of the end of the Greece that Aeschylus seeks to preserve. "The Persian Wars," he writes, "are the national disaster. . . . The danger was too great and the victory too overwhelming."[74] Most specifically, the wars bring out in the Athenians the desire to dominate the rest of Greece, both politically and culturally. Thucydides details the resultant chaotic individualism, and the plays of Euripides in their own way are as much attempts as are those of Aeschylus to bring some new pose and definition to the changing world. As William Arrowsmith has noted: "There is a new spirit of divisiveness abroad in the Hellenic world: appearance and reality, nature and tradition move steadily apart under the destructive pressure of war and its attendant miseries. . . . It is my belief that the theater of Euripides is a radical and revolutionary attempt to record, analyze and assess that reality in relation to the new view of human nature which the crisis revealed."[75]

At the source of this attempt lies Euripides' different treatment of the relation of audience and spectator. In Aeschylus, the medium of the dionysian chorus of capric satyrs is the vehicle by which the audience is brought on stage and bound up into the myth. Euripides does quite otherwise. In the eleventh chapter of *The Birth of Tragedy*, Nietzsche repeats the accusation against Euripides already common in Athens: "Euripides brought the spectator on stage. . . . Through him the everyday man forced his way from the spectators' seats onto the stage. . . . The spectator now actually saw and heard his double on the Euripidean stage, and rejoiced that he could talk so well." As a poet, Euripides feels superior to the masses he brings on stage. And, since these masses oppose each other, evaluation of the play as a whole becomes difficult. To fully understand the consequences of this it is necessary to look somewhat more deeply into the mechanics of this drama.

The driving force in Euripides does not seem to be a person or hero after the manner of *Prometheus Bound*. Rather, one sees the working out of impersonal forces, to which the characters really have a peripheral relationship. [76] In a real sense, there are hardly characters at all. In the end, the plays are about ideas, and the conflict of persons or social forces is replaced by the conflict of the ideas. The crime and the downfall of each person — it is hard to find a central character — comes from their respective denial of what each of the other characters symbolizes. Thus in *Hippolytus*, Phaedra symbolizes Aphrodite; she carries this trait to excess and is countered by her son, who is matronized by Artemis. Each of these "inverted cripples," as Nietzsche called them in *Zarathustra*, embodies a necessary, if human — all-too-human — trait. They all come out, then, on a roughly equal basis. As Arrowsmith puts it, "the characters are no longer people but specifications of the shaping ideas of the play." [77] The resolutions of the plays are of dialectical character rather than genealogical; they require the traditional *deus ex machina* to bring a halt to the proceedings. If, as Wittgenstein put it, men are unable to cease philosophizing when they want to, so also Euripidean drama can never resolve naturally. It has no other ending than the mechanical.

This structure and these characters are hardly appropriate to the creation of great cathartic heroes. Here, I must differ from the understanding of Arrowsmith, who sees the Euripidean universe merely as *devoid* of order. Euripides is concerned with redemption from the *blind* order of the universe. For instance, in *Hippolytus*, Artemis announces at the end:

> Your sin is great. Yet even you
> may find pardon for what you have done.
> For it was Aphrodite who to satisfy
> Her resentment willed that all
> This should happen; and there is an
> Order [*moira*] in the world that no one should seek to
> Frustrate another's purpose. . . . You did not know
> The truth. . . This frees you from the deepest guilt.

Euripides becomes a Schopenhauer of the intellect. Virtue lies in resigned acceptance, in the pessimism of weakness. In *Iphigenia in Tauris*, Thoas is considered wise when he proclaims at the end:

> To hear a God's command and disobey is madness. . . .
> No honor comes of measuring strength with the Gods.

It is immediately apparent that this is not exactly a Promethean conception of virtue.

Euripides wants to address the same social problems with which Sophocles and Aeschylus had dealt. In Aeschylus, the problem of value choices in a changing historical and social situation is resolved by the reintegration of the spectators into a mythic framework making possible a rejuvenated and vital understanding of their actions. The problem of meaning and social change is also addressed in the first chorus strophe of *Hippolytus*

> When I remember that the Gods take thought
> for human life, often in the hours of grief
> to me this faith has brought
> comfort and heart's relief.
>
> Yet though deep in my hope perception lies
> wistful, *experience grows and faith recedes;*
> Men's fortunes fall and rise
> Not answering to their deeds.
>
> Change follows change; *fate purposeless and blind*
> Uproots us from familiar soil.

Several points appear important.
1. Intellect is destructive of old tradition.
2. There is no justice in the relation of act and reward.
3. The workings of change make old habits impossible — *volens nolens.*

Thus the situation forming the plot of the play — the fatal and unnatural love of Phaedra for her son, her suicide, Theseus' curse and Hippolytus' death — is ascribed to no one's ultimate responsibility before or after the fact. Hippolytus' "tragic flaw" is at the most priggishness. However, whereas the Sophoclean and Aeschylean hero takes upon himself the guilt accruing to him through the faults of his ancestors, the Euripidean hero is not finally culpable. Indeed, it would be difficult to make a tragic hero out of Hippolytus willing his own priggishness. All the principals are thus excused from all guilt in the proceedings. The play is brought to an end, as always in Euripides, by the *deus ex machina*, in this case Artemis. She absolves Hippolytus and his father, together they forgive Phaedra, Hippolytus dies (assisted by the chorus), and all praise his nobility.

What causes Hippolytus' downfall is not *hubris*; even less it is a curse inherited from his ancestors for which he had to shoulder responsibility. It is, rather, a very commonplace fault. All in all the message of *Hippolytus* seems to be, firstly, that there is no escape from external fate and, secondly, that mortals can best meet this by circumspection and prudence. Thus, Theseus is admonished for giving "no room to question of the slow scrutiny of time."

Nietzsche does not leave the matter here. He asks himself *why* Euripides feels obliged to structure his plays around one dimensional characters embodying the various emotions and ideas that exist in the public, to show the dangers of their interaction and, finally, to counsel prudence and the recognition of the fallibility of one's countrymen, with a cautious pessimism about the general state of the world. "Fate" is "purposeless and blind"; it is because of this blind order that men are relieved from ultimate responsibility. As noted before, in Nietzsche's view, Euripides as poet feels superior to those he puts on stage; how then can he refuse the Aeschylean form of resolution?

Euripides sees the problem, which he presents as the incommensurability of human desires and ideas due to a lack of prudence and definition. Nietzsche argues that Euripides had, of course, been to representations of old Attic drama and had

sat in the theater, and striven to recognize in the masterpieces of his great predecessors, as in paintings that have become dark, feature after feature, line after line. And here he had experienced something that should not surprise anyone initiated into the deeper secrets of Aeschylean tragedy. He had observed something incommensurable in every feature and line, a certain deceptive distinctness and at the same time an enigmatic depth, indeed an infinitude of background. . . . A similar twilight shrouded the structure of the drama, especially the significance of the chorus. And how dubious the solution of the ethical problems remained to him! How questionable the treatment of myths! How unequal the distribution of good and bad fortune! Even in the language of the older tragedy there was much he found offensive, or at least enigmatic; especially he found too much pomp for simple affairs, too many tropes and monstrous expressions to suit the plainness of the characters. So he sat in the theater, pondering uneasily, and as a spectator he confessed to himself that *he did not understand his great predecessors.*[78]

The plain message of this imagination is that Euripides is too critical to permit himself to accept older drama. For Euripides, to do the right in this historical situation requires knowledge; Nietzsche attributes to him the sentiment that "since Aeschylus created unconsciously, he created wrongly." Hence, none of Euripides' plays can *embody* the principles of right; instead, these come self-consciously from the playwright. Euripidean drama becomes "naturalistic": it provides intelligible comments on social practices in order to educate the audience.

At this point, Nietzsche notes that one must go below the simple notion that Euripides puts the masses on stage and makes them speak beautifully. If that were true, the public should embrace Euripides as their ideologist. Instead, notes Nietzsche, he suffers many failures. For the only voices he accepts as legitimizing his enterprise are not those of the public, but of himself as critical intellect, and of Socrates. Neither of these spectators has any esteem for tragedy as it had been practiced — they are both too critical — and this necessitates a radical structuring of the dramatic conception.

Euripides, along with Socrates, is concerned to educate the Athenian public. Nietzsche sees him "in torment" from his lack of comprehension of the older drama. So instead of relying on the audience to put the meaning of the play together for itself through reliance on "a noble artistry which . . . masks the necessary elements and makes it appear accidental," Euripides announces in his prologues (usually given by an unimpeachable source, such as a god) exactly what is going to happen. In Aeschylus, the spectator had to make something real for himself; the play was so structured as to make that possible. In Euripides, the spectator is faced with an intellectual task and no longer a dramatic one. It is, as Arrowsmith remarks, a "theater of ideas." Nietzsche sees the poet as "an echo of his own conscious knowledge."

For Nietzsche, this constitutes the bond between Euripides and Socrates. [79] Both men feel obliged to rely on their conscious reason for the effect they are seeking to reach. They both wish to didactically teach something *to* their audiences. Neither man, as ideal spectator, can accept the illusion that had completed the dionysian-apollonian unity in Aeschylean drama. To them Dionysos was simply unintelligible. As Nietzsche says, Euripides, then, has "abandoned Dionysos," and thus Apollo abandons him. He often treats the same myths as do the earlier dramatists; but he renders the underworld which gave those myths power inaccessible by his determination to make the problems intelligible, and thus substitutes "naturalistic effects." "Now," writes Nietzsche, "the virtuous hero must be a dialectician; now there must be a necessary visible connection between virtue and knowledge, faith and morality; now the transcendental justice of Aeschylus is degraded into the superficial and insolent principle of 'poetic justice' with its customary *deus ex machina*." [80]

This criticism of Euripides-Socrates raises an important point. Nietzsche would argue that some forms of acceptance or understanding, what I have called the unquestioned, simply *do not admit of being didactically taught*. Either they are presented in such a way that they penetrate below conscious assessing, or else they are simply unmeaningful. As Stanley Cavell has remarked in relation to the style and purpose of Wittgenstein's *Philosophical Investigations*: "Either the suggestion penetrates past assessment and becomes part of the sensibility from which the assessment proceeds, or it is philosophically useless." [81] In trying to tell Athens what he feels it should know about itself, Euripides is precisely in the same position Nietzsche as Zarathustra is in at the beginning of *Thus Spoke Zarathustra*. They both have a good grasp of the problem — Euripides of Athens, and Zarathustra of the crowd in the marketplace of the town called The Piebald Cow. But they are both talking *at* their audience. Zarathustra finds that he is obliged to reject this approach, for there "are not yet ears" for what he has to say. It is simply not possible to tell his audience what he wants them to know. Euripides however persists; Nietzsche's understanding of his last play, the *Bacchae*, in which Dionysos seems to return, presents a Euripides already expressing fear and anxiety over the social consequences of his earlier plays. The fault that Nietzsche finds with Euripides and Socrates is that they attempt to teach virtue, or at least a method by which virtue can be attained. He sees them roughly in the position of a (bad) psychiatrist who when confronted with a severely neurotic patient would say "Here is what you are going to do today." The patient might follow the instructions of the doctor on that day, and indeed for many days; but unless at one point he can make a jump to being able to figure out for and by himself what he should do, one would hesitate to call him cured. Teaching, it would seem, is an activity that can only meet with success when there is already a community of experience. One can't teach or tell someone something unless the other person would be in a position to ask for that particular thing. Unless there were a preexistent community (of the unquestioned), telling something to someone, or trying to teach him virtue, is likely to be an expedition on the wrong path. [82]

Euripides can never reach his aim. What, however, is the effect of *attempting* to teach virtue? In an early manuscript, Nietzsche develops this problem in terms of the structure of tragedy. In older Attic drama, there had originally been no dialogue. As can still be seen to a great extent in a play like *Seven Against Thebes*, there is no dialectic or combat of ideas. "In the exchange between the hero and the leader of the chorus, the dialectical struggle was impossible because of the subordination of one to the other. However, as soon as two equal principal characters confronted each other, there grew up, in accordance with deep Hellenic drives, the contest [*Wettkampf*] and in fact the contest with word and argument [*mit Wort und Grund*]...."[83] The net result is to create a tension in the spectator and to deny the educational unity that the older tragedy seeks to effect in the hero. There is a "dualism of style, here the power of music, there that of the dialectic," and the gradual triumph of the latter. Much as he was later to describe the triumph of the slave morality over that of the master, Nietzsche argues that this is mainly due to a new appreciation of the role of the intellect. Virtue becomes knowable through thought, that is, *it can be taught*. In one powerful and marvelous sentence Nietzsche compressed the whole relation of tragedy and Euripides-Socratism. *"Wenn Tugend Wissen ist, so muss der tugendhafte Held Dialektiker sein."* "If virtue is knowledge, then the virtuous hero must be a dialectician."[84]

Nietzsche's key accusation against the new conception is that it changes the basis of virtue. Virtue can now be taught and is thus democratically accessible to all comers; it is no longer appropriate or relative to an individual or class, but universally available. Being universal, it is forced to become abstract and acquires the false aura of not being subject to historical change. In a fragment that was to be part of the section on Socrates in *Philosophy in the Tragic Age of the Greeks*, Nietzsche states: "Socratic philosophy is absolutely practical.... *It is for all and popular: for it holds virtue to be teachable.*"[85]

Virtue is removed from the realm of the *ethische Instinkte* whose air Heraclitus and Aeschylus had breathed, and is made an abstract goal to be reached. Nietzsche's hostility to this should not thereby be interpreted as a preference for blind instinct and anti-intellectualism. Rather, for Nietzsche, as for Wittgenstein, the justification of the realm of moral values is not something that can be done on its own terms. A person cannot be convinced by rules without accepting the whole world of discourse in which the rules and teaching operate. To use Wittgensteinian terminology: *the language-game of moral ground-ing does not contain that of didactic teaching*. For Nietzsche, no matter what their intention, Socrates and Euripides remove values from the immediacy of experience, absolutize them, and tend to endow conclusions with validity independently of the social and historical situations giving rise to them.

In Nietzsche's understanding, Socratic teaching gives some order to the world and makes doing the good dependent on the lessons one may learn from those who teach virtue. In his attempt to bring order to the political and moral chaos that was Greece at that time, Socrates finds it necessary to establish a science of ethics; to the degree that he succeeds, the preservation of the tragic, let alone of the heroic world, becomes impossible. Tragedy, after all, depends, as does much of the ethos of the *Iliad*, on the fact that intentions often turn out to be irrelevant to the moral problems that are confronted. In Homer or Aeschylus there is no obvious, point by point relation between the choices an individual makes, and the outcome to which he submits. The action is the unfolding of a person's character, and character, as Aeschylus remarks, is destiny. If, as with Euripides, one tries to make choices on the basis of the accurate knowledge of the prudential consequences of one's actions, heroics and the tragic are impossible — impossible to this extent, Sheldon Wolin has pointed out, that in the early Christian world (which Nietzsche sees as the first extension of Socratism), the notions of the Second Coming and the Last Judgment become the final straws on the back of an already over-burdened heroic world. [86] The results of the work of Euripides and Socrates seem to make necessary that one think that responsi-bility comes only through intellectual awareness; if so, one must develop a method of making men aware enough to be responsible. For Nietzsche, this becomes the optimistic doctrine that men can, through dint of persevering with the right (intellectual) tools, shape the world in their own image. [87] If, however, the problem rather lies, as Nietzsche thinks it does, with men themselves, then Socratism in no way provides a manner by which to change men such that they will not simply replay their own genealogical problems, in their attempt to control the world.

The above considerations establish that Nietzsche's criticism of

Socrates and Euripides centers around what he believes to be their contention that the intellect and learned moral skills can be a sufficient counter to the chaos then buffeting Athens. The tool they center on is the dialectical method as enshrined in the dialogues and embodied in the characters in Euripides' plays. It makes virtue at least appear teachable; through it, they hope, Athens may be set on the path to some sort of health. Yet Nietzsche contends, as we have already seen in Chapter IV, that the dialectical method necessarily affirms not only the proposed remedy, but also the decadence of its proponent. Nothing is ever really accomplished.

I might leave Nietzsche's appreciation of Socrates here: it looks much like the image that has come down to us in *The Clouds*. Nietzsche's choice would appear to be much like that of Aristophanes in *The Frogs*: in favor of Aeschylus and the recovery of the old gods. A problem remains, though. The criticisms that Nietzsche launches against Socrates (and at this point we may ignore the problematic relation to Euripides) are very close to those that Socrates himself makes of Protagoras. As already seen, Nietzsche rejects the position of Protagoras as narrow and overly anthropocentric. Socrates, Nietzsche also says, is so close to him "that only for to recognize it, I am almost constantly engaged in struggle with him." [88] This famous citation, already examined in part above, can now be unpacked some more. What is Nietzsche's relation to Socrates which he has to fight at every turn?

A brief examination of the dialogue *Protagoras* is instructive, for, appropriately enough, it deals with the possibilities of teaching virtue, and presents some of Socrates' conclusions about the claim that it is possible, and thus also about the responsibilities and nature of teaching. After an early awakening, Socrates is drawn by a youthful enthusiast to the house of Callias, a sort of Athenian Fulbright Fund, which maintains open house, bed, and board for visiting sophists. There is an initial encounter with Hippias, a man who believes that "custom is the tyrant of mankind," and is peremptorily dismissed as a man who utters words the consequences of which he does not know. Socrates then turns to Protagoras. They agree to a public discussion where only matters of general and popular concern, as opposed to any private secrets and feelings, can come up. Protagoras, much as Euripides, claims that virtue (in this case civic and moral virtue) can be taught. Socrates, surprisingly enough, denies this at first. The argument goes through a long and tortuous set of indirections. But, at last, Socrates argues that virtue in fact consists of doing what is honorable and good, and therefore (as he has shown) also pleasurable. However, as Socrates then rightly observes about his own position, it is something that can be taught. So, he says his position seems to have reversed itself. [89]

The actual conclusion of the dialogue is problematic for it appears inconclusive. Socrates, having noted his apparent self-reversal, states also that they still have not decided what virtue is, even though they have decided to break off. At this point Socrates has not attacked the Epimetheus myth which Protagoras proposed at the beginning of the dialogue. He now states that he still prefers Prometheus to Epimetheus, or at least will in the future make use of him to determine exactly what virtue is. Epimetheus means hindsight; Prometheus, of course, foresight. By this comment, Plato may wish to tell the reader that the kind of virtue Protagoras talks about exists, but that it is the virtue of hindsight, or afterthought. One of the reasons that good men do not always have good sons is that they can only teach them what virtue was in the past, and not how to determine what it is going to be in the future. This virtue of hindsight would be precisely the result of Protagoras' pain-pleasure calculation which in almost all cases can give a guide to action solely on the basis of past experience. It is, in fact, the necessary result of any system, based simply on a method, which accepts present realities as both subject and object of the method. Such a method, when accepted, determines the conclusions that will be reached and limits them sharply to the manipulation of the already existent — in the *Protagoras*, to the opinions of the many. (This, incidentally, may give a clue to Nietzsche protestations against herd morality, for, if anything is wrong with Athens, it is the Athenians.)

The true nature of Socrates' opinion on the question of teaching virtue is obscure in this dialogue. At first, he seems to advocate the position that it cannot be taught; this sharply contrasts with Nietzsche's evaluation of his position. At this point, he attacks Protagoras' view that it can be taught on the grounds that virtue is something that cannot be taught in the manner that a skill can. By the end, though, he appears to have accepted precisely the position that Nietzsche would saddle him with. Any way out of this dilemma is problematic and speculative. A clue is given though, I think, by the fact that on one level it is obviously true that some virtue can be taught in the manner that Protagoras advocates. Knowledge of what gives pain and pleasure is useful knowledge, and is probably some part of the knowledge necessary for virtue. Socrates also treats Protagoras with much more respect than he accords to, say, Hippias, who holds opinions that Socrates does not even consider worth talking about. The fact that Socrates winds up appearing to agree with Protagoras indicates to me that he does not feel it necessary to thoroughly discredit Protagoras in this public place they have so conspicuously been arguing in. No matter what Socrates' position may in reality be, he would then think that Protagoras' position is of some potential usefulness to the city.

If this be so, then Socrates is making a judgment relative to Protagoras and Athens: the social-historical situation of Athens is not such that one need throw away all moral knowledge based on the pain-pleasure calculus, that is, on the past and inherited knowledge.

Can the reader assume this amount of tortuousness in both Socrates and Nietzsche? We are left in a difficult position. One may refuse to admit that Socrates' treatment of this question in the *Protagoras* contains a judgment of the sorts of remedies appropriate — or at least not dangerous — to Athens. Or else, one may accept the view that Nietzsche is simply opposed to Socrates. If the latter view is taken, one can judge Nietzsche either correct or foolish; both conclusions, though, are problematic, since too many texts indicate an ambivalence — both an admiration and an accusation. In each case, the whole question of what it means to try and teach virtue in a *particular historical situation* (and Nietzsche is nothing if not conscious of his place and supposed role in a particular time in history) is not resolved, nor is it apparent why Nietzsche might thereby have felt any attraction to the pale Athenian. Finally, one thereby prejudices Nietzsche's intelligence without searching for an explanation that makes sense of all these elements. To resolve this, I can only suggest that the following seems possible.

Nietzsche rejects for himself the position that Socrates appears to accept at the end of the *Protagoras*. He may do so for one of two reasons. One, he believes it to be Socrates' true and only position. This cannot be refuted directly, but may be viewed as unsatisfactory. I have already given considerations as to Nietzsche's double attitude toward Socrates. Nietzsche also goes beyond what he calls the *niaiserie* of Protagoras[90] in much the same way that Plato does with the same philosopher in the *Theatetus*. For instance, attacking the notion of human-centered perception as the determinant of truth, Plato wonders why "Protagoras did not begin his book on truth with the declaration that a pig or a dog-faced baboon or some other strange monster which has sensation is the measure of all things." [91] Nietzsche, when speaking of the physiological demands for the preservation of a certain type of life, indicates that such judgements may be a foolishness which "is precisely necessary for the preservation of beings such as we are — assuming, of course, that not just man is the measure of all things." [92] It is of course true that Socrates-Plato and Nietzsche go in very different directions with this condemnation, but they both reject the Protagorean premise.

There is a second possibility. Nietzsche may judge wrong Socrates' assumption that the Protagorean notions were at best inoffensive in Athens for that time. In any case, Nietzsche certainly finds the effect of such a notion disastrous in the time in which Nietzsche lives. It might be objected that one could always find another understanding of Socrates; Nietzsche would retort that *the Socrates of the end of the* Protagoras *is the effect of the teachings of Socrates* whether or not Socrates would have admitted to it; after all, if character is destiny, destiny is also character. The utilitarian approach apparently advocated in public by Socrates (and recognized as the basis of some sort of primitive virtue) assumes the presence of social conditions that would, at least, not make it destructive. Such conditions might be, say, those of upper-middle-class Englishmen. As we saw in Chapter IV, it is not surprising that in the early nineteenth century they do persuade themselves of the truthfulness of a utilitarian approach. But this choice presupposes a viable ongoing public world in which men can continue to interact with reasonable expectation of not harming themselves through choices made on the basis of knowledge of the past. If, however, it should no longer be possible to choose in such social situations because of modern developments (themselves the result of those premises and choices), then this form of "virtue" becomes dangerous. If the Athenian situation was as bad as Thucydides describes it, the virtue based on pain-pleasure calculations will merely further the selfish and private individualism already rampant in the cities. The same would apply to modern times. Socrates then at the very least made a mistake in his evaluation of the Athenian world. For Nietzsche, the laws that Socrates upheld in the *Crito* by refusing to escape the hemlock benefited *only Socrates*; in terms of Athens, Nietzsche thinks they should have been broken and that Socrates should have escaped. From the perspective of the end of the nineteenth century, Socrates holds it still possible to propose a teaching that would ensure a certain form of behavior, while never calling into question its basic premises. Socrates believes that men might do one thing and yet achieve another; in this case, they might act on the basis of pain-pleasure calculations and yet further the moral foundations of the state. The fact that Socrates was required to choose the dialectic for this task guaranteed, however, that he set in motion those processes that led eventually to nihilism. After more than two millennia, those processes have taken their toll. To work at all, they require the continuing existence of a social and public realm that can be fostered by private behavior based on the Protagorean criteria, *The foundation of Nietzsche's criticism of Socrates is then that such a public world no longer exists*, and thus cannot be preserved through actions that rested on fundamentally wrong premises.

All is now private: this is Nietzsche's conclusion about modern times. All is done purely with reference to *self* — and without horizons. This is the nihilism of modern times, a nihilism made possible by Socrates, and which now makes Socrates impossible. For this reason, there is no going back. If Nietzsche's command is to become who you are, the necessary implication is that one also is what one has become. Such judgments are at the basis of Nietzsche's occasionally almost pathetic protestations in *Ecce Homo*. He is desperately afraid of being misunderstood precisely because the abolition of the distinction of public and private virtue which this age requires, renders possible the dangerous and democratized development of his doctrine. Nietzsche can see for himself no alternative; if he is to speak it must be in the most private of terms. Thus *Zarathustra* is "a book for all and a book for none." There are no criteria that one might have to meet before hearing it. (In Socrates there were. Only those who could, would penetrate to the deeper levels of the dialogue, but there was no danger in remaining, as does Protagoras, fairly near the surface.) But if Nietzsche speaks in the most private of terms, anyone who hears him will be able to think that he has understood him. The uses that can ensue are known.

Socrates' *private* knowledge may well have been correct for Nietzsche. So much could only be established in a lengthy examination of the dialogues. But the public form that was its expression takes social and historical precedence and finally destroys the private content. One cannot simply talk as if there were a viable public realm. To do so would be to deny the intervening years of history; to stand at the end of a historical process is not the same as to stand at the beginning.

The New Komos

Nietzsche's attitude toward Socrates then appears to be much the same as that of Aristophanes.[93] No matter what their agreement in private — and one might remember here that in the *Symposium* Aristophanes' speech is the only one not refuted by Socrates — Aristophanes holds publically that the style of argumentation Socrates introduces has socially disruptive consequences and fails to weld a disintegrating culture back into a whole. Aristophanes' preference for the old style was already marked in *The Clouds*. There he shows how "unjust argument" — which is what Socrates teaches — does, in fact, in all cases triumph over "just argument" by forcing the latter to adopt its point of view. And, in *The Knights*, the Euripidean Sausage-Seller wins by providing Demos with the comforts of everyday life and then rejuvenates him by boiling him in a large sausage kettle. The parody is ferocious and the point clear; such a Dionysos is hardly what Athens needs. Finally, in *The Frogs*, Aeschylus wins the poetry competition to see which dramatist has the most claim to the right to attempt to heal Athens. The contest is exceedingly close, but Dionysos, who first came to the underworld lured by his great love for Euripides, chooses the older playwright, because *persuasion*, always Euripides' forte, must lose to more basic considerations of life and death.[94] Nietzsche, too, despite his attraction to Socrates, is compelled to choose with Aristophanes. Their position rests on the fundamental political judgment that the social consequences of the approach of Euripides-Socrates to the problems of Athens, and by extension for Nietzsche, of Socratism for the present age, present flaws so great as to be not only unworkable but also self-destructive. Socrates and Euripides presuppose, in Nietzsche's understanding of them, that a healthy state can be founded on and by self-conscious men pursuing rationality in all their affairs. Nietzsche, as I read him, sees this not only as a task without rest, but worse, as an enterprise which, over time, generates the conditions of its own failure. The oldest Attic comedy and tragedy both end with a *komos* or marriage in which a unity, a new beginning and grounding, is established. [95] An end to what comes before is marked; a renewed path can be pursued. The logic of Socratism, however, is the constant pursuit of a goal that could never be satisfied. This starts the journey of the Western world to nihilism; to repeat it today is merely to further the process.

The old foundation of the Greek culture and state had been mythological rather than rational. As Nietzsche writes in *The Birth of Tragedy*, "the Greeks had felt involuntarily impelled to relate all of their experiences immediately to their myths. . . . Thus even the immediate present had to appear to them right away *sub specie aeterni* and in a certain sense as timeless." [96] The last part of this quotation explains what Nietzsche means by "mythological." The myths are *constantly* present in pre-Socratic Greek culture. They inform all actions and enable the Greeks to press upon their acts "the stamp of the eternal." Nietzsche judges the acceptance of myths — be it in a culture or a person — as fundamentally analogous to the ability to accept the dramatic presentation as real. If the spectator-citizen insists on "strict psychological causality" (as in fact Socrates had done), then the myth will not retain its power over him. Thus, Nietzsche writes toward the end of *The Birth of Tragedy*:

without myth every culture loses the healthy natural power of creativity; only a horizon defined by myths completes and unifies a whole cultural movement. Myth alone saves all the powers of the imagination and of the apollonian dream from their aimless wanderings. The images of myth have to be the unnoticed omnipresent demonic guardians under whose care the young soul grows, under whose sign man can interpret his life and struggles. Even the state knows no more powerful unwritten laws than the mythical foundations that guarantee its connection with religion and its growth from mythological notions.[97]

It is important to note here that despite the romantic rhetoric, Nietzsche is making fundamentally the same epistemological point that he makes in his discussions of language or of the audience-theater relationship. *The myth is a consciously held illusion, held as such, and about which one has no questions.* To so hold an illusion allows the *foundations* of the time and culture to escape from the effects of the historical process, and become "eternal." The choice of word is significant. Eternal does not mean infinite in time, it means *always present.* It does not mean stretching backward and forward in time over an infinitely long path, but now and always. Thus, the mythological stamp put on the horizons of a culture keeps them from changing. This does not hold the culture itself static, but makes it able to be changed only in terms of those horizons — if the proper artist is around. A resort to a comparison with Marx is helpful. A capitalist society, no matter how much it changes, is still a capitalist society because the capitalist pattern of interaction (mode of production) remains. (That Marx finds succor and help in history is not relevant here. It merely means he uses a form of automation that Nietzsche, correctly I believe, rejects.) As long as Greek society is characterized by the illusion of those myths and can use them as criteria for understanding, the culture remains of the same "style." This is why the great danger that Euripides presents arises from his destruction of "illusion," and the consequent impossibility of a continuing and recurring acceptance of the myths in a naïve and affirming manner.

Old Attic tragedy provides for Nietzsche the best example of the crafting of this acceptance. By successfully combining the natural and instinctual elements that had been so attractive in the Homeric world with the developed intellect that marks the tradition of the pre-Socratics, it joins instinct and consciousness in an artistic fusion the more astonishing for its success in recovering the myths for the polis. Euripides splits this union in favor of critical self-consciousness. (He worships, as Aristophanes points out, "gods of another metal, . . . his own stamp, newly struck.") By this fission, the ever present mythological basis of the polis fades in the chaos of the period of the Peloponnesian War. The ultimate consequence of his rationalism forces all men to be their own playwright, so to speak, since few accept anymore an unquestioned cosmic order. I shall detail the consequences of the growth of this individualism in the next chapter.

Thus, in the end, "we must overcome even the Greeks." [98] The teaching of eternal return, itself a new world of "conscious innocence," is given but little direction from Greek experience. For the present age, the problem becomes one of dealing with the historical consequences and development of a society and an ethos founded on self-conscious rationalism. Since men have lived through twenty-four hundred years of such a society it is, for Nietzsche, impossible to deny that experience; somehow it too must be acknowledged and dealt with. Before approaching this task, there is much to do. The end of Greek culture was the beginning of Europe. I shall relate and contrast the two. Only this may allow an understanding of what Nietzsche means by the human-all-too-human, and what doing away with it might signify.

Chapter VII

PARABLES OF THE SHEPHERD AND THE HERD: NIETZSCHE AND POLITICS

The new development for our age cannot be political for politics is a dialectical relation between the individual and the community in the representative individual; but in our times the individual is in the process of becoming far too reflective to be able to be satisfied with merely being represented.

— Søren Kierkegaard, *Journals*

The destiny of our times manifests itself in political terms.

— Thomas Mann, *Nietzsche in the Light of Our Experience*

. . . Conditions such as no utopians have ever imagined will become possible.

— Friedrich Nietzsche, *Nachlass*

Perhaps no opinion about Nietzsche has been so readily accepted as the claim that he was "anti-political."[1] Throughout this book, however, I have claimed that Nietzsche's understanding of contemporary times goes in fact in a "political" direction. He thinks that the structures holding society and life together – what I have called the unquestioned – have slowly broken down over the evolution of the West to such an extent that they are now only maintained by various moral, epistemological, and political strong-arm techniques. If they are to be replaced with new foundations, they will have to be shattered. This task, which Nietzsche sets for himself, can only be accomplished by breaking that which still holds culture together. Nietzsche is willing to risk all on the desperate gamble that, with proper preparation (this is why he writes), a transvaluation may be accomplished, once the genealogical chains of the past are definitely shattered. As such, the enterprise might be thought to be political; through volition and domination it seeks to replace one form of existence by another.

On the face of it, this opinion has suffered a bad fate in the hands of Nietzsche commentators. Walter Kaufmann thinks Nietzsche to be everything except political. Martin Heidegger views Nietzsche's accomplishments as setting the stage for the end of Western thought; in his eyes, Nietzsche's accomplishment lies fundamentally in the realm of ideas, not in the realm of life. The general prevalence of such judgments is probably due to the controversies generated by the abuse the Nazis made of Nietzsche's thought. They read him so thoroughly (and so inaccurately) as a foundation for their politics that most more recent commentators, desirous of being sympathetic to Nietzsche, have gone the other way and simply ignored any political dimensions his thought might have.

This is encouraged because the location of his political thinking is not precisely identifiable from chapter titles and book names. There are a few generally unknown but important writings dealing specifically with political questions. Central among these is the early essay, *The Greek State*. There are also pieces of major works which deal with present-day political situations in a manner analogous to that with which Nietzsche deals with problems of morality, language, and the like. These are found in short sections of *Human, All-Too-Human* ("A Look at the State"), in several chapters in *Zarathustra*, and in *Beyond Good and Evil* ("Peoples and Fatherlands," "The Natural History of Morals"). There is secondly, and most importantly, his analysis of the source and nature – the genealogy – of the present crisis of civilization. Nietzsche deals with this most specifically in *The Genealogy of Morals* and in the "We Scholars" section of

Beyond Good and Evil. Finally, there are his political prescriptions and analyses of the future which are found most particularly in "Why I Am a Destiny" in *Ecce Homo*, in "What Is Noble" in *Beyond Good and Evil*, and in much of the vast and disparate material composing the *Nachlass*.

Part of the *Nachlass* was made (by Nietzsche's executors) into the book known as *The Will to Power*. To prevent misunderstandings, a few things should be noted. Due to a modern tendency to see the word "power" as designating "political power," there is a natural temptation to read *The Will to Power* as Nietzsche's description of the world he was trying to build. Suffice it to note here that since he repeatedly claimed "all life is will to power," the notion is at least so catholic as to make its application only to any particular state of affairs — past, present, or future — overly restrictive.

There is also a temptation to view the book as somehow sequential to *Thus Spoke Zarathustra* and therefore as a more "definite" statement of Nietzsche's thoughts. In fact, of course, it comprises aphorisms drawn from his notebooks of the last decade of his life. Whatever the book can communicate as a whole is therefore necessarily comrade to the rest of his writings. An interpretation of all or even a part of Nietzsche's work resting mainly on a differentiation of *The Will to Power* from the rest of his work must be considered wrong.

What, however, were Nietzsche's opinions about politics?[2] There is no central text to which one might turn for a summary. Nietzsche's comments are as chaotic as the world they describe, though they do fall into two distinct categories: one dealing with the Greeks, the other with contemporary Europe. Nor is this accidental. If Nietzsche finds himself the "last of the anti-political Germans," he also knew and admired the pre-Socratic philosophers as "genuine statesmen"; if he counseled would-be philosophers to stay out of politics entirely in Bismarck's Germany, he also recognized as monumental historical models both ancient Greece and Renaissance Italy — hardly periods devoid of politics.

In times of philosophical statesmen such as Heraclitus and Empedocles, Nietzsche finds a unity of philosophy and politics. In modern times this union is dissolved; in the present, Nietzsche finds no "genuine philosophers" who are also "commanders and legislators."[3] The most profound level of Nietzsche's political thought cannot then be concerned with the erection of systems in the manner of classical political theory. There can be no Nietzschean *Contrat Social*, because the unit of philosophy and politics (the "dominating philosophy") which would correspond to it does not (yet) exist. Nietzsche rather will be concerned to investigate the reasons why it is no longer possible to live a political-philosophical form of life. Thus he will be only incidentally concerned with specific political happenings of his time. Such ignorance of them is willful. On the surface, it would appear ridiculous to consider Wagner a more important political figure than Bismarck; this valuation follows logically, though, as I shall attempt to demonstrate, from the deduction that since there is no active governing principle of philosophical authority, present-day political *happenings* are at the most unimportant.

On a deeper level, as the first essay in the *Genealogy* makes clear, moral systems and politics are codetermined. Since the very existence of moral categories depended on the desire to assert power over another group of people — and under slave morality to *control* and render them predictable — all morality is fundamentally a form of politics. It is possible to understand Nietzsche's fulminations against modern politics in the same light as those against morality: given the nihilistic nature of modern valuation systems, all attempts at asserting values, whether in morality or politics, must, of necessity, encourage the onslaught of nihilism. A short reflection of the consequences of the modern mixture of morality and politics and the ensuing ideological conflicts should give one pause before condemning Nietzsche's attack on morality. He is saying that the fact which makes modern politics so dangerous is precisely that morality and politics are of necessity tied. As André Malraux has recently pointed out, Nietzsche understood far better than anyone else that the twentieth century would be the century of great ideological wars.

The Uses of History

It is not accurate to say that Nietzsche's vision of things Greek is essential to his understanding of the present. This puts the historical cart before the horse. As has to be true in any genealogical analysis, it is his view of things modern which is important for his understanding of things Greek. Thus, to answer Nietzsche's account of Greece in the period from the Cleisthenian reforms to the Peloponnesian War with the comment that this is simply "not how it was," misses the point; Nietzsche holds his analysis of things Greek justified and correct insofar as it depicts what is important in the development of that period for contemporary times. The question Nietzsche asks of Greece is not precisely "What happened?" but rather, "What is living of that time?"

In a preliminary fashion, for instance, there is a more familiar approach in the portrait that Max Weber draws of Benjamin Franklin in the *Protestant Ethic and the Spirit of Capitalism*. For Weber, Franklin becomes the type of the early protestant and capitalist. He is constantly deferring gratification, always worrying about consequences, incapable of living in the present. To such an etching, a historian might object that Franklin had, after all, thirteen illegitimate children, and was, while in Paris at least, a notorious lecher and *bon vivant*. Such hardly constitutes ascetic behavior. True, of course. But that Franklin had uncounted bastardy or was attracted to the *belles dames* of Paris is *not* of significance to those who are interested in understanding capitalism. If capitalism is, as Max Weber thought it to be, a central fact of all our existence now, then the facts about Franklin just referred to constitute part of what Marx once designated the "ash heap of history." As Weber with Franklin, so also Nietzsche with the Greeks. If one wishes to quarrel with what Weber found important to see in Franklin, one would also have to quarrel with his interpretation of the significance of capitalism. Assuming that Nietzsche has done his work properly, if one wishes to quarrel with his understanding of the Greeks, one will have to first attack his analysis of the present.

From his analysis of things Greek, Nietzsche extracts what William Arrowsmith refers to as a "unified field theory," by which to judge the chaos of present-day Europe. Hannah Arendt has repeatedly urged upon her readers the notion that politics have changed since Greek times.[4] The perception is also Nietzsche's and, as such, not in itself particularly interesting. But what is generally not noted in her analysis is also that which is at the basis of the usual accusation that Nietzsche is anti-political. Both judgments fail to see that both her and Nietzsche's positions hold that something essential has been *lost* in the experience of politics from the times of the Greeks to the present. It is not just that politics have changed; for Nietzsche, as for

Arendt, life in the polis was characterized by traits which have to a large extent disappeared from modern life. Both writers wish to set off this sense of loss. Nietzsche is concerned then to attack the *manner* in which the Greek experience has been assimilated into the Western political tradition and Western culture. This assimilation is shaped by many things, in part by simple historical accident, in part by elements already specific to the tradition in the Golden Age, in part by the very process itself. All of these Nietzsche seeks to identify, the better to teach contemporary Europe the nature and direction of its loss. For this, no simple history, no matter how technically perfect, will ever be of use to any modern political philosopher. It would simply reproduce the story, and will not "move on to action."[5]

Nietzsche is not just holding up the Greeks as an example to modern times. Such a path seems to me to be the one chosen by Hannah Arendt, Leo Strauss, Eric Voegelin, and occasionally Sheldon Wolin.[6] Their approach is to some degree to keep alive the historical intellectual tradition in as much purity as possible. Strauss and Voegelin go back to the Greeks to get a "pure" approach to the problems of politics. Hannah Arendt finds lessons for the modern experience of the disintegration of authority. She envisages to some degree the same conditions arising again when authority disappears (immediately after the act of revolution for instance), as existed during Greek times. Nietzsche, on the other hand, does not hope to find real conditions in modern life which might correspond to those existing at the times of the Greeks; the burden of the history we bear is far too great for this to be possible. Rather, he hopes to create a bar of critical judgment: we will at least learn what we have to take into account. The tradition — glorious as it may be and certainly Nietzsche knew it as well or better than any of us — simply will no longer suffice. Twenty-four hundred years of experience have made it simply impossible to return to "purity."[7]

If this be true, one may well ask why the Greeks, rather than the Persians, or Egyptians, or Goths? The answer here is determined by the nature of Nietzsche's inquiry. If our understanding is ever to help us to proceed out of the situation we find ourselves in, it is necessary to return to the origin of *European* politics, the Greek polis. As the parent to most of the Western ways of thinking and speaking about things political it has a particular genealogical purity. Thus it is of particular importance since the coming age is to be that of "great politics," concerned with Europe, and eventually the world as a whole. Greece is of particular genealogical relevance for this new development since it relates to that which is properly European, not that which is French, Italian, German, etc. If Nietzsche were seeking to understand something about German politics, Greece would be of far less use to him; but if one is to be European, "What were the Greeks?" must be answered. He is not interested in Greece except as it speaks to Europe.

Finally, instead of stressing the similarities, potential, actual, or imagined, between this world and that of the Greeks, Nietzsche is concerned to show the differences, the lack of relation between our present world and politics and those of Attic Greece.[8] Throughout his life Nietzsche learned from, fought with, and expounded the Greeks. But to think that they provide historical lessons for modern practice is to mistake a historical lesson for the genealogical. No more than Tocqueville thought that America was a pattern France might follow, does Nietzsche think Greece was one modern Europe should emulate.

The Genealogy of Greek Politics: The Polis and the Importance of Political Space

As one of the first to see through the nation of a Greece of "sweetness and light" to that of a dark and masked underworld, Nietzsche understands things Greek to contain an affirmation both of the serenity and also of that which is terrible. In no fashion will Nietzsche ever downplay the violent and awful aspects of Greek politics: he thinks that the power and strength of the civilization rested to some considerable degree on this violence.

Nietzsche's vision of the healthy and violent politics of the polis cannot be comprehended without an understanding of the arena in which they took place. For him, Greek politics is an activity engaged in by those who are liberated from the world of private necessity.[9] Political men thus are not under a constraint to use politics for their own private ends. In fact, since they have escaped from the realm of necessity, they are under very few constraints of prudence. Except for certain unconscious preconditions (to be dealt with below), political men are basically free to express their non-necessary drives and ambitions in an arena with other people doing the same.

They did so, I mentioned above, *in* an arena. The particular relation of the political Greek to his polis is of prime importance. This relation forms the "horizon" that Nietzsche notes in an early essay as prerequisite for life and culture. "This is a universal law: a living thing can only be healthy and strong and productive inside a horizon. If it is unable to draw a horizon around itself, and too selfish to lose its own view in another's, it will come to an untimely end. Cheerfulness, a good conscience, belief in the future, the joyful deed — all depend in the individual, as in a people, on there being a line that sets off the surveyable [*Übersehbar*], the clear from the unilluminated and dark."[10] As Hannah Arendt has pointed out, the polis ... is not the city state in its physical location; it is the organization of the people as it arises out of acting and speaking together for this purpose. No matter where they happen to be ... action and space create ... the space of appearance in the widest sense of the word, namely the place where I can appear to others as they appear to me, where men exist not merely like other living and inanimate things, but make their appearance explicit."[11]

Nietzsche brings out the particular relationship that the Greek has to his city. The citizen existed *in* the city-state but not *for it*, an experience repeated in healthy aristocracies where, for Nietzsche, the "essential characteristic ... [is] that it experiences itself *not* as a function (whether of monarchy or commonwealth) but as their meaning and highest justification. ... [The] fundamental faith simply has to be that society must not exist for society's sake, but only as the foundation and scaffolding on which a choice type of being is able to raise itself to its higher task. ..."[12]

For such an unquestioned and unquestioning stance to be possible, the language and mode of thought has to be highly integrated with the social institution of polis. Without sharing J. P. Vernant's attempt to minimize the difference between pre-Socratic and Socratic thought, Nietzsche would agree that "the birth of the polis and of philosophy are so tightly linked that rational thought must appear from its origins to be solidary with the social and mental structures that are proper to the Greek city. ..." Aristotle, in defining man as "a political animal," underlined that which separates Greek reason from that of today, and accordingly Vernant continues: "if homo sapiens is . . . a homo politicus, it is that reason itself is essentially political." [13] In the polis, therefore, there arises an extraordinary preeminence of speech over all other instruments of power. It remains the "daughter of the city" until, in Nietzsche's eyes, the actions and teaching of Socrates loosen the organic relation.

This autochthonian relation of language and politics marks for Nietzsche the extraordinary distance that separates modern man from the Greek. The very characteristic of a "strong" group of men is their ability to name things for their own life. In such a use of language as a political instrument — albeit nonreflectively — Nietzsche sees the strength of this society. [14]

In the best of Greek times, the state is thus the arena where people compete, both physically as in the games, and, more importantly, publically through argument. Politics never is a tool that one uses to compete, nor is language (or, more properly, rhetoric) a skill that one learns from someone else *in order* to win battles. As we have seen, according to Nietzsche, Socrates "holds virtue to be teachable." [15] The basis of Nietzsche's whole attack against Socrates and Euripides is that they make language (and virtue) into something which can be learned and taught by almost anyone.

The pre-Socratic conception exemplifies a "healthy" relation between men and politics. Nietzsche sees the state as an apollonian scrim on which dangerous dionysian understandings are transvalued into culture or, as shall be gone into below, exteriorized into warfare. For Nietzsche, then, the most important Greek political institution will be the agon — contest — in which the chaos lurking in desire for domination and in domination itself is refracted in a healthy manner, such that political stability and continuity — the prerequisite for culture — be ensured. [16] In the ongoing agon, no one person can become the best and thus be able to determine by himself the categories of conflict. It is in this light that one should understand the passage laudatory of Plato in the early essay, *Homer's Contest*, where Nietzsche has Plato compare his achievements favorable to the best that others have done only to disavow them; thus also Nietzsche's curious approval of ostracism: by preventing the best man from emerging, it helps the health of the state. As we saw in Chapter VI, for Nietzsche Socrates destroys the agon.

For Nietzsche, the Greeks are "a priori 'political men in themselves' and . . . history knows no second example of such a frightful unleasing of political instincts. . . . This bloody jealousy of city to city, of party to party, the murderous greed of each little state. . . . Whither does the naive barbarism of the Greek state point? What is its excuse before the tribunal? by the hand it leads a flowering woman, Greek society." [17] What is important about and makes possible the occasionally awful political exuberance of the Greeks is this: the Greek state and politics does not exist for itself, the state is not its own justification. It is, rather, the arena in which people compete and out of which higher culture and individuals emerge. It is a delicate situation and will persist as long as no contestant is able (has the language and epistemological position) to identify himself with the whole arena. If someone could look down on the arena, he would be in a commanding position. He can, so to speak, *make* the categories and thus will enjoy a different relation of consciousness to them than do the other players. As long as the genealogical parentage of the state is hidden behind what Nietzsche refers to as the "veil of Isis," culture will flourish. *The role of strong politics for Nietzsche is thus to hide from consciousness the genealogical foundations of the state.*

The Institutionalization of Political Space

Along with the need for strong politics at the foundation of the state goes a requirement for continuity. Indeed, this is only natural; no matter how firm the foundations, without duration no culture can evolve. Nietzsche lays heavy stress on this necessity, to the point in fact of insisting that fathers without sons be denied full civic rights. "In the natural *bellum omnes contra omnes* society [*Gesellschaft*] cannot strike root on a scale larger than and beyond the reach of the family. . . ." Instead of the constant struggle necessary for survival in pre-political times, the state (at least the Greek state) concentrates outbursts so that, if perhaps more violent, they allow "in the pauses . . . for society, under the effect of that war now turned inward and compressed . . . [to grow] and flourish, so that when there come warmer days, the shining blossoms of genius may show forth." [18] In Nietzsche's understanding, if the state is to be healthy, it must fundamentally and always be a communal institution, *eine Organismus*. It is *not* a simple collection of strong individuals, as

Julius Binder argues;[19] no individual must feel himself outside of the polis and capable of using it to his own ends. He may have other ends — the "culture" Nietzsche wants is a form of psychological health — but inside the political space of the state, politics *happen*, they are not *used*.

Such a happy situation was maintained precariously throughout a period of Greek history by men who were artists, philosophers, and statesmen; as we have seen, the pre-Socratics and the early tragedians are of the same cloth for Nietzsche. Nietzsche understands the *Oresteia* as a dramatic trilogy about social and political problems of changes in moral consciousness. The cycle of plays ends with an integration of the two conflicting moral and epistemological views in a society that retains the integration necessary for communal health. In another instance mentioned by Nietzsche, Thales, recognizing the dangerous disintegrative potentialities in the proliferation of the polis, attempts a cultural unification of Greece by means of a political confederation.[20] His failure, as will be shown below, was of capital importance. In any case, this delicate ongoing *Aufhebung* can only be maintained through the efforts of men like Thales and Empedocles — "genuine statesmen," as Nietzsche calls them.

Without this continuing artistic effort, however, a number of antagonistic contradictions implicit in the notion of continuity take over. Like all organized political power, the polis wants to maintain social and political configurations as they are. Such *stasis* is hostile to the ongoing development of *Bildung*. In plays like the *Oresteia* and *Seven Against Thebes*, Aeschylus resolves this problem. But, without the continual rebirth that the *lauter Staatsmänner* provide, the state, as the apollonian element of the culture,[21] constantly attempts to assert dominance over the dionysian progenitor it is supposed to refract into culture. To the degree that the state succeeds, it selects a number of affects "through which the regularity of performance would be guaranteed. . . ."

The apollonian characteristics of the state constitute a denial of the necessity of change. More immediately, the state attempts to develop principles whereby some men in the state will begin to find agreeable that which is in fact disagreeable. The state generates then what we might today call a "false consciousness," "that one should like to do disagreeable things."[22] In fact, Nietzsche writes that the necessity for continuity gives rise to a class structure; there develop two classes, one of "compulsory labor and one of free labor." The organized power relationship between the two is "the strongest typical relation after the pattern of which other relationships are unconsciously formed." As this relationship becomes the central focus of the state, problems immediately arise. [23]

There occurs rapidly a transformation structurally parallel and analogous to those diagnosed in *The Genealogy of Morals*. The lower classes should have no reason to love the state. However, in relation to the ruling class, they are weak and suffer, and so seek justification for what has happened to them. To accomplish this they begin to identify with the force which is hostile to them. "Just as if a magic will emanate from them [the conquerors], the weaker forces attached themselves with mysterious speed, changing wonderfully under the influence of the sudden swelling of that power-avalanche under the charm of that creative kernel. . . ." [24]

Such an attachment is the very basis of *ressentiment*. The lack of a dominating will on the part of the weak leads them to tie themselves psychically to the strong. Psychologically, this compensation is at the source of the genealogy of slave morality; socially, it has important consequences. Such a development in the state allows an evasion of responsibility by those who identify in this negative fashion. In slave morality, men behave not as individuals but as parts; so also through the division of labor, the state now makes men do things contrary to their nature. The "huge machinery of the state quells the individual, so that he declines responsibility for that which he does. . . . Everything that a man does in service of the state he does against his own nature." [25] The necessary organization of a state makes people different "by the division of responsibility, of command and execution through the intervention of the virtues of obedience, duty, patriotism [*Vaterlandesliebes*] . . . ." The state represents on a social level epistemological changes characterized by the separation of will from action, of cause from effect, and so forth. [26]

Social organization and the state in particular thus generate in many people the behavior associated with slave morality. As time progresses, this tends to affect all the people. Social organization is for Nietzsche consonant with morality and makes possible and acceptable severe distinctions of power in society.

The Division of Labor and the
Direction of Ressentiment

The division of labor is the main tool that the institutionalized state uses to ensure that its members act as parts and not as complete human beings. It is "the principle of barbarians. . . . There are not divisible entities in an organism." Under the impact of the division of labor, the political space of the agora which made the agon possible rapidly begins to disintegrate.

The individual person is encouraged to be personally irresponsible for his actions. Like a Euripidean character, he can blame his actions on powers outside of himself. He can now act *for* the state activity since the political world is becoming a mechanism distinguishable from the individuals who compose it. (He can, of course, also *not* act for the state — the existence of the choice implied in the consciousness of "for" is the problem.) "Everything he learns in service of the state," says Nietzsche, "is obtained through the division of labor." [27]

Through the division of labor the state fosters "imperfect but more useful individuals." For the first time, individuals can be considered in terms of their utility. It will be a short step to a consideration of the state itself as a source of useful power. In a division of labor society, Nietzsche writes, men are "inverse cripples" — one part of their skills becomes so magnified that, in their essence, they become that part. The portion of their being that is not being "used" by the society is so alienated that, in Nietzsche's image, one needs a "magnifying glass" to vindicate the humanity of these "human beings who are nothing but a big eye, or a big mouth, or anything that is big." [28]

In the midst of such structural changes in the Greek state, there intervenes a set of historical events which speed up the development of the division of labor and the slavely moral state. The agonistic development of culture is premised on the basis that no one person or state was in fact the "best." Foremost in this practice of politics is, as noted above, the encompassing political space that prevents people from standing outside the political myth and using the state to their own private ends. Nietzsche sees the victory the Athenians win in the Persian wars as the source of a most important change in orientation. The wars appear as a *daemon ex machina*, and put an end to Greek political conflict. [29] The danger to the very existence and definition of the state is so great and the Athenian victory so complete that Athens becomes convinced that political strength and predominance is the only thing they can rely on to maintain their supremacy and security. Out of the victory over the Persians, Athens develops a new attitude toward politics. In the fragments *Wissenschaft und Weisheit in Kämpfe*, Nietzsche writes: "the spiritual domination of Athens hindered all reformation. One must think back to the period when this domination was not present: it was not necessary; it came first on the heels of the victory over the Persians, that is when it became a matter of physical power." After this, even Aeschylus is too late to work anything but a holding action, and other reforming attempts such as those of Empedocles are kept from fruition by the development of Socratic epistemology. When all of this becomes firmly established, it brings about "the foul theory that one could only attend to culture when armed to the teeth and wearing boxing gloves." Even Thucydides, Nietzsche notes sorrowfully, exhibits this trait by his belief that without the state men will tear each other apart. [30]

This combination of natural development and historical accident moves politics away from being an activity that gives rise to a healthy polis to being an end in itself. Such objectification — parallel to and manifest in the Socratic revolution in epistemology — is a general disaster for all of Greek culture. The predominance of Athens is so total, that no external enemies remain on whom to fashion the aggressions that the inner contradiction of the state releases. Much as Freud was to point out later, when external object cathexis is impossible, libidinal aggression is turned inward and results in neuroses and psychoses. [31]

It is most important to keep in mind here a general point about Nietzsche. The evolution of the Greek polis (or any entity) follows a certain ontological pattern, but is by no means inevitable from its very beginning. At a key moment, the Persian wars give a different impetus and qualitatively change the structural foundations of the Greek world. The importance of the specific historical occurrence shows that Nietzsche, contrary to Hegel, thinks that concrete human action can be of prime importance in the course of human events. If such a realization opens a door of historical possibilities, it also withdraws from the historical process any notion of a dialectical logic leading inevitably to a different social condition. If things are to become different, then men will have to do it themselves (whatever that implies is, of course, not clear).

The disastrous objectification of the state has far-reaching consequences for later political and social evolution. As the state becomes transformed from the *arena* of power into the instrument of power, a new kind of men arise to make use of this tool. Armed with Socratic abstractions and self-consciousness, they stand essentially outside the moral horizon of the community. Since most people who remain in the community necessarily forget the origin of their moral sentiments and get caught up in the inertia of their unexamined beliefs, those who possess self-consciousness can begin to manipulate the state for their own private ends and will identify with it only insofar as it serves and corresponds to their own instincts. "In considering the political world of the Hellenes, *I will not hide those developments of the present which I fear dangerous atrophies of the political sphere.* If there should exist men who through birth, as it were, should be placed outside the cultural [*Volks*] and state instinct . . . then such men will find their ultimate political aim to be the most peaceful coexistence possible of large communities, in which they will be permitted their own purpose without resistance." [32] Such men tend to *destroy* politics. It is clear that Nietzsche finds fault in them. In modern times, for instance, Nietzsche might admire Bismarck early in his life when he still thought an educational rejuvenation of German culture possible, but he rapidly comes to perceive Bismarck as a new Alcibiades. His appreciation for Bismarck and Alcibiades is for their *skill*; never does he indicate that they had any role comparable to those reserved for the great Greek tragedians and the potentiality of Panhellenic culture. This is why Wagner and his new "international culture" is, despite his lapses into nationalism, a more important figure for Nietzsche. Much like Thucydides, Nietzsche thinks both Pericles and Cleon had many faults as leaders, but truly responsible for the downfall of Athens is the stateless man, Alcibiades, who *uses* the state to his own end. [33]

For the state to be used, it has to be made calculable. To risk its destruction in war would be dangerous. Thus, in modern times, the promulgation of the doctrines of the "liberal optimistic" viewpoint have tended to take the antagonistic quality out of war. The conscious competitive war is replaced with the mass movement, particularly susceptible to ideological manipulation. [34] When this development combines with the lack of responsibility also engendered by such a state, the dangers become tremendous. Contrary to those who see in modern times the happy development of the autonomous individual, Nietzsche finds modern man to be not a "personality, but merely an isolate [*Einzeln*]. He represents all atoms against the communality. . . . He instinctively sets himself up with other atoms; what he fights, he fights not as a personality but as the representative of atoms against the whole." Already in *Schopenhauer as Educator*, Nietzsche notes that we "live in a period of atomistic chaos." [35]

As with all slave morality, the trend toward fragmentation is fostered by the desire to become like the strong. Such a person, though, is "weak and [an] extremely vulnerable piece of vanity and demands that everyone should be made equal: that everyone should only stand *inter pares*. . . ." [36] This might possibly allow some petty vanities to be assuaged — in a civilized age almost everyone has some modicum of talent — but the basis of culture must necessarily perish. For everyone to become equal means to Nietzsche for everyone to become individualistically oriented toward his private gains, and thus in the totality of his being to be equally subject to the realm of necessity. Both of these are incompatible with the root of the agonistic prerequisite for culture and politics.

The consequence of the long development of the slavely moral state is quite clear for Nietzsche. There is a progressive *lessening* of politics. "The democratic movement is *not only a form of the decay of political organization*, but a form of the decay, namely the diminution, of man, making him mediocre and lowering his value." [37] This is not the position of a man who is "against" politics, but rather of one who is against the human consequences of what we *now* call politics.

The progressive evolution of the Greek political experience can be summed up as follows.

1. Culture depends on the existence of strong and agonistic politics.
2. Such politics depend on the existence of the state.
3. The state progressively tends to depend on slave morality for its existence.
4. The combination of slave morality and politics inevitably leads to a democratization of relations between classes and a decline of the agon.

5. The maintenance of institutions thus requires the growth of individualism.
6. Democratization and individualism make culture possible.
7. This tends to further erode the possibility of strong politics.
8. The outcome is thus characterized by the *absence* of politics and of the public sense.

Such a sketch is an outline of the grandeur and decline of Athens. It is also meant, of course, to be a general sketch of any political relationship; as genealogy, it contains lessons for any limited time span. From his examination of the Greek state, Nietzsche has developed a position which will allow him to examine the genealogy of modern politics also.

Modern Politics: Its Genealogical Prospects

No point has been made more often than that Nietzsche has no coherent doctrine of modern politics. By this is generally meant that he provides no political program, no comprehensive political analysis. Yet, for Nietzsche, this is as it should be. As I mentioned above, like the politics of his day, Nietzsche's political opinions are in fragments. This as we now see must be so; there is simply for Nietzsche no coherent way to talk about politics of his day because — in genealogical perspective — the politics tend to be incoherent. Phenomenological description must remain atomistic, because of the absence of any unifying arena in which politics occur and out of which new men and culture might arise. The one attempt Nietzsche makes at providing a unified perspective *explicitly* on politics is probably the long section "On Peoples and Fatherlands" in *Beyond Good and Evil*. And yet this, to our confusion, is essentially a discussion of music. For a modern man the reason remains obscure, even if a note from the period of *The Birth of Tragedy from the Spirit of Music* reminds us that "modern men hold themselves toward music in the way that the Greeks did toward their symbolic myths." Nonetheless, it is possible to work out *how* modern political phenomena manifest the genealogy that the Greeks formed and passed on.

Nationalism, the Ascetic Priest of Politics

The above developments describe a change in the relationship of the individual to the state. In a long section of *Human, All-Too-Human* entitled "Religion and Government," Nietzsche analyzes this change. As long as religion and politics are joined in the symbiotic unity typical of the polis, religion provides "an attitude of tranquillity, and temporizing and confidence" during the inevitable crises that arose. Its antiquarian function ensures the continuity of the polis. Such a religion, however, inevitably has an authoritarian and hierarchical basis and survives only with difficulty when equalitarian ideals spread. "When the state is no longer allowed to draw any use from religion or the people think too diversely on religious matters for the government to be able to adopt a consistent and uniform procedure with respect to them — the way out of the difficulty will necessarily present itself to treat religion as a private affair and leave it to the responsibility of each individual conscience and custom." [38] The development of individualism breaks up the original unity of the polis.

Christianity encourages this separation with the concept of "render unto Caesar" and is destructive of the unity of society. An immense number of sects are generated, which culminate in the hostility of the religious, and the overattachment of the irreligious, to the state. Nietzsche refers to "primitive religion as the abolition of the state. . . ." [38] No matter who wins in these struggles, be it the religious through a form of more or less enlightened despotism, or the irreligious through education and schools, it makes, in the end, little difference. Reverence for the state is destroyed, "the utilitarian attitude is encouraged." Scrawled on the back of an envelope he received from Overbeck in March, 1878, Nietzsche notes that "the decay of the religion is also the decay of the state." [40]

The separation of the this-worldly state from the other-worldly religion that Christianity fosters is thus one of the main aspects of the Christian religion that Nietzsche rejects. He puns on their relation by linking *Christ und Anarchist* (Christian and anarchist). For Nietzsche, Christianity is explicitly a possible life, but only "as the most private form of existence: it presupposes a narrow, remote, completely *unpolitical* society. . . ." The impossibility in the present day and age of combining Christianity and any public sense is underlined most strikingly in *Zarathustra*. The first person Zarathustra meets is a pious hermit. Zarathustra does not tell him that God is dead.[41] The social message is clear; as with Socratism, implicit in Christianity and its liberal offshoots are elements that make society and the public weal impossible. Its epistemology endlessly destroys the horizons that make all culture and life possible.

This is Nietzsche in a very Burkean mode. Since illusion is necessary to all culture, if the Apollonian scrim is torn aside, all is lost. Almost echoing Burke's notion of the "politic-well-wrought-veil" Nietzsche argues that "if religion disappears the state will inevitably loose its old veil of Isis and will no longer arouse veneration." Continuity, the necessary prerequisite for a strong culture, becomes impossible since people shy away from tasks that are not privately rewarding in the utilitarian sense.[42]

The disintegration of the public and political continues on. Men arise who stand psychically outside the state, which, in turn, becomes merely the "ruling arm" of this class of people — mainly financiers, according to Nietzsche. "In the end — one can say it with certainty — the doubting of all government and the insight into the useless and harassing nature of those short-winded struggles [between religion and the state] must drive men to an entirely new resolution, to the abrogation of the concept of the state and the abolition of the contrast 'public and private.' Private concerns gradually absorb the business of the state."[43] In Nietzsche's analysis, then, the public disappears, and strong politics is no longer possible.

Though such a development constitutes the decay of the state, it leads an individual no more than does slave morality lead him to total annihilation. The decaying state resists disintegration through *nationalism*, which Nietzsche sees essentially as a reactionary movement since, as the characteristic form of modern politics, "this arrogant conceit" focuses the interests of the individual on entities that prevent (much as Bismarck comes to) the cultural unity of Europe. The gradual development in Europe of a "supranational and nomadic type of man" possessing great powers of adaption — the "evolving European" — receives great setbacks due to nationalism. In the end, though, this attempt will have exactly the same ironic reversal as socialism and anarchism; it will continue to encourage the festering modern state, and prevent man's attention from focusing on that which now unites men, the fact that they are *European*.

Nietzsche is not saying so much that nations and/or modern political entities are in themselves evil, but that they now consist of evil sets of perceptions about the processes that are going on in the world. Nationalism allows people to avoid coming to terms for awhile with the gradual disintegration of meaning — what Nietzsche formulated in the aphorism of the "death of God." It provides an artificial and "overly modest" meaning for life. It is thereby *an epistemological disaster* logically analogous to the "innocent" and "guilty means" that the ascetic priest uses to maintain moral life for the individual and to the pity that keeps Zarathustra from eternal return. The nationalistic state wants to be all, but provides only a very low-level form of association. [44]

Thus, in *Zarathustra*, the nationalistic state is the "new idol," the "coldest of cold monsters" because it *follows* and is, in fact, made possible and encouraged by the death of God. "The monster . . . detects you too, you vanquishers of the old God. . . . Your weariness serves the old idol." [45] Previously nihilism triumphs in the name of a slavely moral religiosity; now it triumphs under the banner of man.

Nietzsche sees as dangerously false the supposition dear to Kant and nineteenth-century liberals that once republicanism is freed from the fetters of feudal religiosity, healthy states will spring forth. In unmasking them, his intention is to point out exactly how little the psychological foundations of the state have changed in the last millennia. The transition to democratic rule merely encourages — to some degree even speeds up — processes that were already ontologically implied in the foundations of contemporary politics.

With the death of God, all falls into the decay of the modern state. For now, "accepting the belief that God has passed away, to the question 'Who commands?' my answer is, 'The herd commands.' " The state is the "*coldest* of the cold monsters" because there is no creating will behind it, no public arena except the shadow of a dead God; no value framework can be provided. "Coldly it tells lies too; and this lie crawls out of its mouth: 'I, the state, am the people.' That is a lie! It was creators that created people and hung a faith and a love over them: thus they served life. It is annihilators who set traps for the many and call them 'state.' " Through such reification, the state is the "slow suicide of life." [46]

Ultimately, for Nietzsche, the modern state fails in that, by democratization and nationalism, it drains the potential sources from which creation of new values could come. Thus, for instance, of justice: "The 'state' as administrator of justice is a piece of cowardice because the great man by whom standards can be set is missing." [47] There is no ruling class. At the most there is a *shepherd* — a person whose total identity emanates from the herd that he leads. The creative "class" of today has, in Nietzsche's understanding, disappeared beneath the relentless logic of concomitant moral and epistemological genealogical developments.

Such an ongoing democratization of social relationships implies a society where "everyone feels he has a right to every problem" and where "everyone may sit in judgment on everyone else." Such a situation is a denial of that political space that Nietzsche feels necessary to strong politics. In Greece, only certain people could sit in judgment on others — those who had access to the same agora. Men with other political moralities had no commensurable rights. Thus for Nietzsche, justice demands that "what is fair for one cannot by any means — for that reason alone — also be fair for others." [48] If everyone can judge anyone, there is no order or rank, no definition of alike and different, neither friends nor enemies, no agon and consequently no culture.

One might object, as does Henri Lefebvre, that socialism is a modern reaction against the individualizing tendency of the slave morality state. [49] Nietzsche, however, considers this possibility. As the relation of individuals to each other becomes more and more atomistic — as the sense of the "*public*" diminishes — rationalistic comparisons between people arise. This is the birth of the notion of equal rights, a notion that develops naturally and appropriately in a society operating on such premises. In *The Gay Science*, Nietzsche notes that "the commonest man feels that nobility is not to be improvised and that it is his part to honor it as the fruit of an extended culture. But the absence of superior presence, and the notorious vulgarity of manufacturers with red, fat hands, brings up the thought to him that it is only chance and fortune that has elevated the one above the other; well then, he reasons to himself, let us in our turn tempt fortune and chance. Let us in our turn throw the dice — and socialism commences." [50]

It is important to note three things about this analysis of socialism. Firstly, though Nietzsche thinks of socialism as in part a *reaction* to the over-atomization of society, he does *not* think of it as something qualitatively *different*. Socialism is merely the logical continuation of political developments characteristic of any society and of the western world in general since the Peloponnesian War. He notes: "Socialism . . . grasps that, to attain anything one must organize oneself to a collective action, to a 'power.' " But what it desires is not "society as the purpose [*Zweck*] of the isolate [Einzeln], but rather society as the *means of making possible many isolates* — this is the instinct of socialists about which they frequently deceive themselves. . . ."[51] Socialism is the logical continuation of slave morality. All attempts, such as socialism, to cure the ills of society by reforming institutions are bound to fail, for they will be subject to the same genealogical ontology.

Secondly, it is a mistake to think that what Nietzsche is calling for is merely some aristocracy of noble producers. In the notes for *Human, All-Too-Human* he observes: "When a lower worker says to a rich manufacturer 'you do not deserve your happiness' he is right; however, his conclusions from that are false. No one deserves his happiness, no one his unhappiness."[52] In other words, in modern societies, all attempts at moral valuation are simply ideological falsifications designed to justify a self-serving position.

It is inconceivable for Nietzsche, that there be a group of men with power, such as capitalists, who would ever be entitled to their position. They must share in the decadence that characterizes the whole.[53] Nietzsche does not want to place "noble" men at the head of *this* system.

Lastly, Nietzsche sees contradictory elements in socialism. It is progressive in the sense that it furthers and hastens the tendencies toward leveling which must be accomplished before significant change might become possible. (A Marxist would say that one must "sharpen the contradictions.") Socialism thus "maintains [*unterhalt*] men and brings to the lower classes a sort of practical-philosophical language. Thus far it is a source of strength of the spirit [*Kraftquelle des Geistes*]."[54]

Despite this progressive tendency, there is also a reactionary strand in socialism. In the modern democratic state, Nietzsche sees, as did Tocqueville and Saint-Simon, a concentration of power patterned on that of despotism and increased exponentially by the concomitant social-atomizing tendency. Socialism is the "fantastic younger brother of the decrepit despotism which it wants to bury; its efforts are thus in the deepest sense reactionary. It demands a fullness of state power, such as only despotism has had. . . . It wants the caesaristic power-state of this century, for it . . . wishes to be its successor. . . ." [55]

Generally, two points stand out in Nietzsche's analysis of contemporary politics. *Firstly, the modern state represents the concretization only of slave morality.* "Where are the masters for whom [today's] slaves work?" One must not always expect the simultaneous appearance of the two complementary classes of society. The modern state manifests the disbelief in the possibility of great men, and "at the bottom we are all herd and mob." [56] *Secondly, the nature of modern nationalism is to keep political life at a very low level.* The "innocent means" which the ascetic priests have at their disposal probably correspond to elections, national holidays, etc. The "guilty means" — the "orgies of feeling" — we will examine below under "great politics."

To assert that Nietzsche attacks politics is to miss the key point. *This is not a specifically anti-political doctrine.* Nietzsche is the last of "the anti-political Germans," because he is opposed to what *Germans* call "politics." Germany manifests in its politics the same sickness it manifests in the rest of its society. Nietzsche sees the main characteristic of the modern situation as a nationalistic state in which people have little or no political relationship to the power concretized in the state. Most developments — even socialism — tend to further this power.

The Politics of Entr-acte

Nationalism is, as pointed out before, essentially a resisting force. It does not want to return to something atavistic, but wants to stabilize the onrushing nihilism. "Owing to the pathological estrangement which the insanity of nationalism has induced, and still induces, among the peoples of Europe; owing also to the shortsighted and quick-handed politicians who are at the top today with the help of this insanity . . . owing to all this and much more that today simply cannot be said, the most unequivocal portents are now overlooked, or arbitrarily and mendaciously interpreted — *that Europe wants to become one.*" [57] For Nietzsche, the increased cultural, commercial,

and nomadic (with decreases in landholding) contacts between peoples should lead to the ultimate destruction of nationalities; at
present, however, nationalism causes the isolation of countries from
each other. This is what Nietzsche calls a *künstliche Nationalismus* —
an artificial nationalism, artificial and temporary because it works
counter to those forces that he sees unifying Europe, such as democratization. It requires "artifice, lying, force to maintain its repu-
tations." [58]

It is temporary precisely because it is artificial. Its existence will
depend on the continuing presence of the artificers — the commercial
and social classes in whose interest such a situation is maintained. On
this topic, Nietzsche engages in an almost "Marxian" analysis of the
basis of balance of power politics such as Europe knew in the middle
of the last century. As in Greece, there evolve men without state
instinct (possibly parodies of Alcibiades) as well as a system of large
equipoised states. Nietzsche discusses this in what might appear an
atypical fashion. Behind this development, he sees "truly international homeless hermits," who, due to their lack of "state instinct,"
abuse politics as an apparatus for their own enrichment.

If therefore I designate as the most *dangerous characteristic of the political
present* the application of revolutionary thought to the service of a *selfish
stateless* gold-aristocracy; if I conceive of the enormous dissemination of liberal
optimism as the result of modern financial affairs fallen into strange hands, and
if I imagine *all evils of social conditions together with the necessary decay of the
arts to have either germinated from that root* or grown together along with it,
one will have to pardon my occasionally chanting a paean on war.[59]

It is obvious that Nietzsche is disturbed by the existence of men who
have no loyalty to any group or rank order. Such men would seem to
represent the ultimate logical development of the position that
Socrates occupied vis-à-vis Athenian society. But they cannot propose a morality of any kind; they are only ultimate nihilistic epigones of the great Athenian.

It does not appear that Nietzsche ever followed up such considerations, though he is saying something important. Nationalism seems to
be a direct result of social democratization. He sees a situation in
which people whose loyalty is only to money manipulate such
nationalistic feeling for their own ends. Such men have no political,
only economic loyalty. This is, in fact, pretty much the situation

that Lenin diagnosed in *Imperialism: The Highest Stage of Capitalism*. Contrary to Lenin, Nietzsche does not think that finance capitalism and its concomitant nationalism is the *source* of the great wars of the twentieth century. They are rather a restraining force in themselves. Great wars have at their origin something else; this is the problem of great politics.

Great Politics

For Nietzsche, war is a possible solution to the problems engendered by the brake of nationalism. Just as Greece had its wars, so must Europe now recover in the form of "great politics" those antagonisms that might permit a cultural rebirth. "Nationalism, this *névrose nationale* with which Europe is sick, this perpetuation of European political particularism [*Kleinstaaterei*], of small politics [has] deprived Europe of its meaning, of its reasons — [has] driven it into a dead-end street. Does anyone beside me know the way out of this dead-end street . . .?" [60]

The way out is a daring gamble: great politics. Only this might lead to conditions permitting a cultural rebirth. Like most other things for Nietzsche, due to its genealogical structure, great politics begins by making things worse, before it might make them different. On one level, then, great politics means international politics. This reinforces the nationalism characteristic of the modern state and binds people, especially strong creative people, to the state; it thereby furthers the progress of nihilism. For instance, Nietzsche fears that even the youth of nations will be drawn into the vortex of such politics, with as a most dangerous consequence not the cost or the "public hecatombs," but that "the political growth of a nation almost necessarily entails an intellectual impoverishment and lassitude, a diminished capacity for the performance of work which requires great concentration and specialization." [61]

On this level, the balance of power, which Nietzsche sees profiting the stateless men, will be upset. Specifically identified is the "blood and iron" politics of Bismarck. In Nietzsche's view, Bismarck is trying to prevent the spread of individualism — much as Wagner comes to do in *Parzival*. The judgment of Thomas Schieder is only a little too harsh, perhaps prompted by the fact that monographs must make points: "Bismarck is in one word all that against which Nietzsche flung his lightning, which he hated and which he wanted to expose as decadent."[62] Nevertheless, for Nietzsche, there is little doubt that in terms of his international system, Bismarck is fighting a rearguard action, which while temporarily preventing unity from coming about, will ultimately favor it. The system must finally dissolve in "the great spectacle in a hundred acts reserved for the next two centuries in Europe — the most terrible, the most questionable, and perhaps the most hopeful of all spectacles. . . ." The curtain has already risen on Europe, *but in an uneven way*, for some nations are "ahead" of others. "The sickness of the will is spread unevenly over Europe; it appears most strongly and most manifold where culture has been at home the longest . . . in France. . . . In Russia . . . the strength to will has long been accumulating and stored up; there the will — uncertain whether to be a will to negate or a will to affirm — is waiting to be discharged."[63]

Nietzsche's argument is not in favor of individualism per se; rather, a final transformation away from petty politics will only be possible when all nations in Europe have reached the same far stage of atomistic individualism. It is "the next century," Nietzsche writes, which will "bring the fight for the dominion of the earth, — the compulsion to great politics."[64] Just as with morality, this transforming political change comes about through the search for justification. "The leveling process of European man is the great process which should not be checked: one should even accelerate it. . . . The leveled species requires, as soon as it is attained, *justification*. . . ."[65] Nationalism and such developments impede the need for justification by trying to maintain politics at a very low level.

On the other hand, conscious of the need for a new "politic well wrought veil," Nietzsche also thinks that the struggle for the dominion of the earth must come about at the right time — when a group of new men exists who can put it back together again. Since they will have to attempt "a fundamental artistic and conscious breeding" of the new type of men,[66] the attempts on the part of socialists to rush to the final revolution are particularly dangerous. They want to "set one's hand to the plow when no one can show us yet the seeds that are afterwards to be sown on broken soil."[67] What is needed *first* is "a higher species of men which thanks to their preponderance of will, knowledge, riches, and influence will use the democratic Europe as their most suitable and supple instrument to take the destiny of the world in their hands and work on 'men' as artists. Enough; time is come for us to transform all our views on politics." [68]

Nietzsche seems to feel a danger in men engaging in the "guilty means" of great politics without philosophers to rebuild the arena; if so the situation would only wind up in a worse state. The ascetic priest triumphs in morality only because all other values were lacking; a similar triumph in the social-political sphere by nationalistic and ideological tendencies can possibly spell a common disaster. Each nationalistic state, inevitably beset with the anxiety due to inwardly turned aggressive tendencies, will tend to feel the other states responsible for its discontents. The elimination of the other will then seem to be all that is keeping the world from being peaceful. This is the fallacy that Nietzsche wished to expose when speaking of "liberal optimistic" doctrines; it follows for nationalistic states also. [69]

It is ideological war, a last desperate attempt to link modern slave-morality politics and religion in a now disastrous union, that frightens Nietzsche. It is not only inevitable, but men are desperately unprepared for it. "When truth enters into a fight with the lies of the millennia, we shall have upheavals, a convulsion of earthquakes, a moving of valleys and mountains, the like of which has never been dreamed of. The concept of politics will have entirely been merged with a war of and for minds [Geisterkrieg]; all power structures of the old society will have been exploded — all of them are based on lies: there will be wars, the like of which have never been yet on earth." [70]

If men engage in the "guilty means" of great politics without philosophers to redraw the horizons, for Nietzsche the situation will wind up being worse. "All attempts made to escape nihilism without transvaluing all previous values only makes the matter worse; it brings about its opposite." [71] This seems to be Nietzsche's second understanding of great politics. It presents both more possibilities and more dangers. Though it can be an attempt to redefine horizons and to escape from the nihilism that pervades the culture more and more, Nietzsche fears that it will produce only what Hermann Rausching, already a disillusioned ex-Nazi in 1939, calls "The Revolution of Nihilism." Revolution does not imply for Nietzsche, as it did for Marx, transvaluation.

In the end, this is one of the main points of Nietzsche's argument against the moral point of view. In slave morality cultures, one must inevitably judge and take one's standard in comparison with other peoples. Thus two cultures or politics claiming different moralities will inevitably conflict with each other. The conception of international politics as the Hobbesian war of all against all acquires progressive truth as history moves on; only in modern times, Nietzsche realizes, has the disappearance of political space between cultures begun to manifest itself in its barbaric fullness.

Nietzsche sees the coming period of great wars engendered by nihilism (not by nationalism) as "good" only under one circumstance, if it make possible new forms of life. If it comes without the overdetermination of "new men," all will be in vain. This in turn implies something about political consciousness. The problem with modern political men is that the realms of their consciousness have expanded so far and so abstractly that politics is no longer a public matter: it is no longer the subject of a common consciousness. As long as men continue to have this kind of problem with consciousness, they are not going to be able to draw the veil of illusion which allowed for great culture over others, let alone over themselves. Hannah Arendt once wrote that "to look upon politics from the realm of truth . . . means to take one's stand outside the political realm." [72] One must only add that if truth has destroyed itself, the political realm must fall away also.

Philosophical truth concerns man in his singularity and is apolitical by nature. On the other hand, politics is necessary for higher culture. Therefore what men need are new artist-philosophers, a new Aeschylus, for it is not possible to solve the problems of consciousness on the social level. For Nietzsche, this is true by definition, as we have seen. If someone could *das Sein neu gründen*, to use Heidegger's phrase, and overcome the problems of self-conscious slave morality, the foundations for a new culture might be possible. The "solution" as described here looks somewhat like *Die Meistersinger* without the juvenile self-doubts of Walter, or the occasionally rather tired cynicism of Sachs. Nietzsche notes a danger in that the age of ideological politics will simply go on, more and more destructively, and there will be no *creative* destruction. This can be no dialectical "negation of a negation" — such produces only priests and nationalism. They are parasites on decadents.

Politics: Midnight and Midday

Nietzsche wishes to launch Europe on an experiment; he finds it necessary to precipitate an inevitable, but perhaps fatal, contest for the domination of the earth which may, *just* may, have as its consequences the emergence of a new order of rank and a new culture. He holds that unless the wars that are *necessarily* going to be fought in the twentieth century are fought to bring about this new world, nothing, or anything, may happen. The wars will be fought anyhow: the new "veil of Isis" requires philosophy and philosophers and they do not seem to be forthcoming. (The doctrine of eternal return is designed, though, in Nietzsche's view, to make philosophy possible once more.)

For Nietzsche, almost anything may be possible; the increasing disintegration of society itself creates the preconditions that make new worlds conceivable. Two factors appear especially prominent. [73] Through their mastery of the world men are increasingly able to produce the conditions under which they affect the world. Though Nietzsche does not see this as an unmixed blessing as Hegel did at the end of the *Phenomenology*, he does see it as a new characteristic of modern times. Secondly, the change occurs in a situation in which society is no longer perceived as its own justification. Men and women can require something else.

The required transvaluation is to be achieved by means of the doctrine of eternal return. As I understand it, this notion, the most obscure and difficult in all of Nietzsche's writing, is intended to make possible the sort of arena that ensured the politics of Attic Greece, and there constituted the soil for what Nietzsche sees as still having been the most mature culture of the West. The full exposition of this teaching must still await the last chapter. However, Hannah Arendt in her major work, *The Human Condition*, undertakes an exposition of what she believes to be "eternal recurrence," and a consideration of her notion can provide some preliminary ground-clearing for a more complete treatment. The difference between what she means by eternal return and what Nietzsche means are of great use in the determination of Nietzsche's final position on politics.

In Arendt's view, the cyclical nature of certain political processes manifests itself in their "eternal recurrence" at certain moments in the development of any system of relations. For instance, when authority disintegrates — as just before revolution — men reassert a fraternal political bond, which she believes can best be understood by looking to Greek thought for a description. Similarly the present "failure of nerve" in the United States may very well generate a reassertion of the Tocquevillean *principe* which forms the country.

This is not the time or place to criticize this view at length. Rather, I simply want to point out that it is very different from that of Nietzsche. He simply does not believe that under the growing chaos there is anything eternal that might repeat itself. The crisis extends — this is why it is so profound and its consequences are so potentially radical — to the "infrastructure" itself. In fact, it springs from the nature of the infrastructure. There is literally nothing in the configuration of modern events which might, by recurrence, generate health.

For Nietzsche, a society that develops not as its rationale and that therefore does not permit of a nihilistic self-consciousness, must come from, or at least be coequal with, the appearance of men who do not share the ontological problems of the present men and their society. It appears, then, that those commentators who have chosen to ignore Nietzsche's lengthy passages about "breeding" and "race" are ignoring what Nietzsche himself regarded as a central portion of his thought. No positive social doctrine can come out of Nietzsche without such an appreciation. As long as men remain "human-all-too-human," nothing new will be possible.

Nietzsche feels that whatever is done will have to be done over a much longer period than before. As shown above, the increasing democratization of people's relationships makes this possible. "Each natural process of the cultivation of mankind . . . which until now was operating slowly and unguidedly could be taken in hand by men; . . . *whole portions of the earth can dedicate* themselves to conscious experiments." [74] Interestingly enough, this means that Nietzsche thinks the possibilities of guided social change to be far greater in advanced industrial societies — providing only that there are the men to undertake them. Societies less along the path toward democratization — or perhaps escaping from the Western flow altogether — will be less subject to such conscious experimentation.

Only two possible examples come to mind in the present: China and Cuba. Neither of them are, however, as much developed along the path to atomistic individualism as many others. They do both have self-conscious rulers and are dedicated to the very Nietzschean proposition of creating "new men." (One might look below the surface nonsense of the "creative application of the thought of Mao Tse Tung" to understand the Great Proletarian Cultural Revolution as an epistemo-ontological revolution designed to induce in the Chinese people the attitude that nature can be mastered through abstract thought, rather than — as in the Confucian mode — bent before like a reed. What the ultimate outcome of this will be is hard to say. The problem is far more difficult in advanced industrial societies which are in many ways just coming out of the organizational period that China and Cuba are entering. Nevertheless the possibility in these countries should raise similar questions about those in more technological ones.)

For Nietzsche, finally, man had much the same situation in politics as in morality. Contemporary developments of the political have made it more abstract and removed from the life of the individual; this has also happened with morality by the death of God. That which had been a sensuous force is now but a hollow shell, which, however, is kept from breaking in and out of its own logic. In morality, the preserver is the ascetic priest; in politics, it is nationalism. These residues are now all that is important in governing man's life. The ascetic ideal is, in its totalitarian logic, the *only* ideal that governs men's lives. Nationalism is a similar residue in politics and is also the *only* form of politics; it totally shapes the political life of man. Worst, it prevents new genius — true philosophers — from emerging.

Men are confronted with a startling paradox. In the quote selected for the epigraph to this chapter, Kierkegaard points out that in the future, what will be important for the individual cannot be politics, "for politics is a dialectical relation between the individual and the community in the representative individual; but in our times the individual is in the process of becoming far too reflective to be able to be satisfied with merely being represented." Yet, at the same time, as Mann puts it, "The destiny of our times manifests itself in political terms." It is as if the two parts of the Aeschylean assertion that character *is* destiny have been separated by modern political developments. Those forces which shape a man's character no longer have any relation to his destiny. The democratization and atomization involved in the modern political form of nationalism mean that men's lives get shaped by abstract forces to which they can only react. Since this effectively dominates their lives, true creativity, such as was possible with the strong personal sensuous political life of the Greeks, is impossible.

Never has politics been so important; but never has it been so remote. For Nietzsche, in opposition to Marx, the solution to this dilemma must *first* be individual, and only then social. Societies no longer have their own revolutions out of their own logic; now history and the dialectic lead only downward.

Chapter VIII

THE WILL TO POWER

A people without history
Is not redeemed from time, for history is a pattern
Of timeless moments.

— T. S. Eliot, *Little Gidding* V

We are what we pretend to be; therefore we must be
careful about what we pretend.

— Kurt Vonnegut, Jr., *Mother Night*

The will to power and eternal return tradi-
tionally represent the greatest stumbling blocks in any interpretation
of Nietzsche. Separately, they are obscure enough; but their relation
to each other leaves most commentators in the embarrassed position
of having to make a choice. If the will to power is seen as the most
central and important part of Nietzsche, the reader tends to come up
with an image of Nietzsche favoring strong individuals who assert
themselves almost ruthlessly on an unstructured moral and human
environment. Certainly, this is the picture that was common in
Europe in the 1920's and still subsists today, in altered form, in
American understandings. If, on the other hand, eternal return be-

comes the main motif, it is possible to read into Nietzsche a vision of the cosmos which, though absurd, still contains the basis of order. Such notions are generally retained today by commentators who wish to see Nietzsche as attempting to replace the dead God with a new principle of value. This view gives a far more "religious" Nietzsche.

The origin of this divergence is not hard to discover, for both schools share an understanding of a contradiction between the will to power with its apparently definite implications of linearity, and the doctrine of eternal return with seemingly equally definite implications of circularity. If the man of the will to power is constantly to "overcome" himself (accepting for the moment that one understands what this means, and that Nietzsche actually says it), how might this be reconciled with the notion that the man of eternal return comes back "always the same" (accepting again, as even more surprisingly most commentators do, that one knows what this means and that Nietzsche actually said it, too). In this apparent dilemma, interpreters tend to take which side they want, most American writers showing a very Anglo-Saxon predilection for the bright individualism of the will to power, and most continental writers joyfully embracing the dark fatalism of eternal return.[1]

I intend to show that there is no problem in accepting both the will to power and eternal return. It is not a matter of reconciling them, for, properly understood, they are not in conflict. Indeed it would be surprising for them to be so, since nowhere in Nietzsche's writings, either published or unpublished, does he give the slightest hint that he saw their relationship to be problematic.

I shall begin with the will to power, but a few preparatory warnings are necessary. When reading Nietzsche, one must always pay close attention to any inherited preconceptions. A certain amount of self-conscious naïveté is probably safe, for, if Nietzsche is in fact doing something new, as he repeatedly claims, it is then dangerous to approach his words and work with old ideas and concepts. For instance, as we have seen, very few people, even among those who would claim some considerable acquaintance with Nietzsche, have managed to see what is plainly said, that Hamlet is the "prototype of the dionysian man." This is without doubt due to the tendency to see "dionysian" in somewhat wild, sexual, and uncontrolled hues, denoting orgies, debauchery, and what have you. Yet as we have seen, this is certainly not Hamlet. Similarly, in the case of the "will to power," we may be tempted to naturally attribute plus signs to the notion of "will," without ever investigating if Nietzsche did the same. Or again, many commentators accept the definition of eternal return as that "which comes back always the same," as if it were obvious what this mean. But, as has been seen in previous chapters, the hermeneutic promise of Nietzsche is that he is never obvious, if only because his readers are unable to look and see what he says.

A second warning: to take Nietzsche seriously, it is especially necessary here to assume, for a while at least, that he might make some overall sense. He is too aware of the possibility that men will misread him, or think that he has nothing to say,[2] for us not at least to credit him with the possibility that even his "big concepts," such as the will to power and eternal return, might be, as he claims they are, the central focuses of his doctrine. To accept the possibility that Nietzsche does make sense overall and that even his strangest notions have to be taken seriously requires also that we admit, at least in a preliminary fashion, his own hierarchy of his concepts. Thus, in considering the will to power, it is worth remembering that Nietzsche explicitly makes eternal return the centerpiece of his work.[3] Thus, any interpretation, such as Heidegger's or Kaufmann's, which tends to make the will to power the fulcrum in Nietzsche's philosophical achievement, must necessarily go against Nietzsche's own under-standing of himself. This is not to say that Nietzsche could not have been mistaken about himself; to suggest as much, however, already raises a whole new set of questions.

A last reminder deals with the temptation to assume that the book entitled *The Will to Power* is in fact a book about the will to power. I have discussed this to some degree already, but it is worth repeating here that this book is the compilation of various sections of Nietz-sche's notebooks of the period 1880-1888, selected and arranged by his editors. Not only does the term "will to power" not appear until 1885,[4] but any sense that the arrangement of these selections makes, and any resonances they seem to acquire by being beside each other on paper are to be radically distrusted. At best, the book serves an indexing function.

The Will and the Problem of the Past

All of this raises a problem for an understanding of the will to power and will raise a similar one for eternal return. Nietzsche never wrote a systematic scrutiny of the question, as he did for instance of morality in *On the Genealogy of Morals*. Interpretation is thus difficult.

To meet this problem, it is necessary here and in my final chapter to change my approach somewhat. Until now, I have been able to draw from all of Nietzsche's works and have attempted to puzzle together material to give an understanding of the coherent thrust of Nietzsche's thought. With the will to power and eternal return this proves impossible. Most of the references to these doctrines are in the unpublished material that Nietzsche was trying to shape into a major philosophical opus, at the end of his life. It is dangerous to work only from a set of citations about which we can have at best only an intuitive feeling of their respective importance. Hence, I have elected to first explicate in detail those portions of the published work that deal with the subject material of these two chapters. If this task is done well, it should then permit at least the outlines of a picture into which other material can be fitted.

The main published consideration of the will to power comes in the chapter "On Redemption" in *Zarathustra*. A detailed exegesis should cast some light on the complexity of Nietzsche's understanding of the will to power and, in addition, throw some light on how difficult a serious reading of Nietzsche can be; as is often the case, it is nearly impossible to understand the significance of Nietzsche's writing without working through it. As with an aphorism, there is nothing one can *do* with a chapter in *Zarathustra*; it is not a ready-made tool. The parts only acquire the full dramatic meaning when they are understood in the manner in which they unfold.

The chapter "On Redemption" opens with a temptation scene. Zarathustra has crossed over "the great bridge" and is surrounded by cripples and beggars. A hunchback begs him to cure each in this multitude of his respective ailment. The episode is a development of the first major scene in the book which also involved masses of people. In the "Prelude," Zarathustra had come to a town and attempted to preach to a crowd, already assembled to watch the performance of a tightrope walker. The multitude had laughed at him. Now, the deformities of the mass, which were once simply internal, have acquired physical manifestation; they are more and more obvious. Zarathustra, too, has learned more: he has crossed over the great bridge symbolizing man, and is moving away from the role of preacher or shepherd of the human-all-too-human. He will no longer attempt to prove to these men that he is to be believed in; mere belief will not be enough, a change in their nature is required. He replies then to the hunchback with a piece of folk wisdom to the effect that such minor deformities as these men have at least give them a self-definition which one should not take away. ("When one takes away the hump from the hunchback, one takes away his spirit. . . .") Indeed, after this chapter, Zarathustra will talk to no one for the rest of Book Three. In Book Four he only speaks to his fool, and then to the higher men. The temptations to make the world in his own image have disappeared.

But there is a greater problem. Worse, far worse than these men are those whom Zarathustra says he used to encounter, Euripidean characters, who have so developed one part of their personality that everything else has fallen away. He found huge ears supported by a tiny stalk, which upon microscopic investigation turned out to be the rest of the man. Such people Nietzsche calls "inverse cripples," the result, one might say, of a tyrannical division of labor such that the society has forced them to exaggerate one portion of their physical anatomy in its service. These men are the parodistic end products of the effects of the division of labor examined in the previous chapter.

The strange and surrealistic introduction to the chapter marks two things. First, Zarathustra is no longer interested in directly teaching masses of people. As in Nietzsche's accusation against Socrates, public education, even for those who want it, will simply not do. What Zarathustra has to say cannot be understood, there is no common experience between Zarathustra and his audience on this matter. The reason for this is the second important point of this introduction. One will never free people through education, even people who are willing to learn, since one cannot therewith free them from their pasts and their genealogy. It is the "now and the past" which Zarathustra finds unendurable, and which he "could not support" unless he also finds a different future to be possible.

We are thus launched headlong into the problems of dealing with one's genealogy and with one's past; if this were simply psychiatry, I would say that Nietzsche is trying to figure out how to deal with the effect of deep, ongoing structures of neurosis and psychosis. Zarathustra is tempted to redeem the world in his own image, but he refuses to take this burden upon himself. Looking back to the three "metamorphoses of the spirit" in the introductory chapter to the first book of *Zarathustra*, we find it apparent that Zarathustra is shifting from the stage of the beast of burden who bears all, to the stage of the willing lion who destroys. Indeed the discussion now shifts to the question and notion of the will.

This, then, is a discussion of only the second or willing stage of the spirit. Zarathustra is not the overman, at least not here; rather he is, as he says, "a cripple at the bridge." The important recognition that he is a John the Baptist figure or, as Heidegger says, a *Fuersprecher*,[5] shows that he is still preparing the way for eternal return. In the previous chapter ("The Soothsayer") he had already refused a dream interpretation that made him into the overman; now, here, to make clear why he cannot yet be anything but a "herald," he enters into a long discussion of the will and willing. This will show that, as a dominant activity, willing is only characteristic of the second state of the spirit, and that, *as long as men make it the center of their activity*, they will not enter into the final "child" state. "The lion must become a child," as Zarathustra says in the first speech; "the will itself to be overcome," he remarks in a note from the middle 1880's, signifying that as long as one has to overcome and conquer the outside world, one feels constraint and has thus not acquired the new nature of the overman. "All feelings of freedom," the note continues, are "no longer to be conceived of in opposition to constraint."[6]

Such considerations are of genealogical import. Nietzsche now believes that a new form of life, radically different from that of the inverse cripples, will only be possible if the basis of the old form has been destroyed. This precisely is the link to the following discussion of the past. If men are to be *redeemed* from what they are, they must be redeemed *from* their past. "Redemption" seems to imply that the past would be abolished, or made not to matter any more. Such is the usual religious view. Nietzsche writes: "To redeem the past and to recreate all 'it was' into 'thus I willed it,' that was *first* called redemption to me."[7]

One must proceed very slowly and with circumspection here. It is not clear yet exactly what Nietzsche thinks about redemption as a manner of dealing with the past. It is clear that redemption at least makes the past into a problem. If men are not to be time's fool, they must do more than simply acknowledge the past (which Hegel, after all, had done brilliantly); they must aim, as Nietzsche says at the end of the chapter, "higher than reconciliation." Redemption might be, or so he thinks at first, "recreating all 'it was' into 'thus I willed it' "; however, he goes on to say: "The will itself is still a prisoner . . .; it cannot will backwards, it cannot break time, and the covetousness of time." As I read this, it indicates that willing is not a process that itself can lead to redemption, since the latter involves breaking the hold of the past, and the will is fatally tied to the movement of time. The will is part of a configuration that has had a past. It cannot break that past without destroying itself, and, since implicit in it are elements of the past by which it came to be, it can never break the past. Should it attempt to, it will merely perpetuate the past; "it cannot will backwards."

The attempt to deal directly with the past, to try to annihilate it, is dangerous. If a person or society cannot live with its own nature, the attempt to voice and focus displeasure and anger results in destructive frustration. Nietzsche continues on: "The will, the liberator took to hurting; and on all who can suffer he wreaks revenge for his inability to go backward. This, indeed this alone, is what revenge is: the will's ill will against time and its 'it was.' " If the will is turned against the world, it will attempt to destroy boundaries; if turned inward, in an attempt to deny the reality of those boundaries in terms of which one is (who one is) instead of potentially healthy eristic combat, one gets "revenge." In both cases, though, the will is destructive. "I will" is always for Nietzsche a negation of what is; this characteristic presumably is also in some way true of the will to power.

If turned inward, the will produces the phenomenon of "revenge"; the implications are important for Nietzsche. If one seeks revenge for something, in this case, for the harm the past has done to the present, it becomes for Nietzsche, as Heidegger acutely notes, "an attempt to deny time past."[8] Such an attempt, however, can only be premised on the surmise that there is potentially a value to the whole process; that somehow the past should not have done what it did to the present; and that thus we should not be what we are. The attempt to take revenge on the past presumes that one could or should not have acted as one did. Hence, the turning of the will inward also implicitly advocates a certain form of morality. The desire to punish and find redress implies, first of all, a potentially "proper" way to be and behave, and, secondly, an attempt to absolve oneself from what one has become. Taking revenge is an attempt to deny the reality or necessity of one's past, and thus also of one's existence. It becomes a denial of the historicity of a person in favor of a more absolute notion of what that person should be, and thus is cousin to the search for permanence which Nietzsche so often criticizes.

The main focus of the chapter "On Redemption" is the problem that the past poses for significant change in the future. Nietzsche is here concerned to investigate how what men have been affects what they are and, perhaps even more importantly, what they might become. His initial indication is that men desire to be redeemed from the past, and thus also from themselves. Nietzsche pursues his line of inquiry in four capsule summaries of the main attempts previous philosophers have made to deal with the problem of the past. Much as in Hegel's *Phenomenology of Mind*, though specific individuals are not mentioned by name, it is not hard to pick out who is meant. All of these men represent positions that Nietzsche is at some pains to reject.

First come Hegel and Anaximander. Nietzsche writes: "Because there is suffering in those who will, inasmuch as they cannot will backward, willing itself and all life is supposed to be — a punishment. And now cloud upon cloud rolled over the spirit, until eventually madness preached 'Everything passes away; therefore everything deserves to pass away. . . . Thus preached madness.' " Hegel, like Anaximander, attempts to solve the problem of transitoriness by locating value precisely in the phenomenon of change. Such a solution really avoids dealing with the problem; as with all dialectical solutions, it presumes a priori that movement is in itself a good and redeeming thing. Anaximander and Hegel are willing to accept the past as a whole on the grounds that whatever was in it was part of human history and that since history was eventually leading to a unity of actuality and potentiality, all of the past must be seen as good. The universal affirmation of the past sees value in the whole process; it constitutes saying Yes to all that has been. For Nietzsche, from such a perspective one must say that whatever discontents are suffered are merely temporary and not world historical. Contrary to this, Nietzsche sees the whole of Western civilization suffering from certain basic and radical defects of an original character, much in the way Freud did.

The second view is the as-if fatalism of Kant and Anaxagoras, which Nietzsche renders: "Things are morally ordered according to justice and punishment. Alas where is redemption from the flux of things and from the punishment called existence?" Nietzsche also sees madness in positing an unknowable world which is nevertheless fraught with the characteristics of that which is valued. There is again no a priori reason to assume the existence of a morally structured universe which allows us to justify and condemn this one. Anaxagoras and Kant find an escape from the problem of time in asserting it to be a necessary product of the mind. There is, however, especially in Kant's view, an unknowable but apprehendable world of theoretical reason to which the concepts of human existence might correspond. It is in this world that Kant finds his "redemption." For Nietzsche, however, nothing is gained by what he sees as the invention of an imaginary world which has the categories necessary to do away with the problems of this one. The solution is just too pat: the problems of the self-conscious knower are suddenly solved by the discovery of a world not subject to self-consciousness.

It is important to be quite clear that both Hegel and Kant approach the problem of the past in manners that Nietzsche feels must be rejected as the voice of "madness." Nietzsche now passes to a third conception of time and redemption. "Can there be redemption if there is eternal justice? Alas, the stone 'it was' cannot be rolled; so must all punishments be eternal. Thus preached madness." This is the cosmic fatalism of Schopenhauer. He conceives of joy as a release which, if effected, is automatically aimed at a negative state. The doctrine is destructive in both its effect *and* its ultimate aim. Schopenhauer then teaches that there is no possibility of creation. Nothingness is all that could be willed. And, indeed, Nietzsche concedes that men may act as if Schopenhauer were right; they may "will the void, rather than be void of will."[9] But, for Nietzsche, this constrained perspective is not the only one possible. The ascetic ideal, which is the originator of this notion, triumphs only because there is no opposition.

This theme is picked up again in *Zarathustra* when Nietzsche speaks of a new tablet "recently found hanging in the marketplace" where it is proclaimed that "wisdom makes weary, worthwhile is nothing; you shall not desire." [10] Since willing is destructive, if willing is, as Schopenhauer thought, the only alternative to representation, it can only lead to nothingness. In this perspective, there is no choice except annihilation or chaos: in both cases, the world is held to be unalterable in its fundamentals. In Nietzsche's terms, Schopenhauer conceives of the world as a "monstrous man," whose actions are manifest and whose nature is totally unalterable. For Nietzsche, this is simply the result of Schopenhauer taking his own psyche as ultimate and general. This is not totally inaccurate, but it is not necessary. For, Nietzsche notes sardonically, one is not forced to say that "the world is Schopenhauer writ large. . . ." [11]

As Jean Granier remarks, Schopenhauer's conception of the will remains "fatally aporetic," [12] self-contradictory in that it remains tied to "the old thing in itself" and to the phenomenon. Schopenhauer, in Nietzsche's understanding, commits a basic error in not seeing that "desiring (the 'will') is only a manner of *knowing* and nothing else." [13] What Schopenhauer has done is replace the transcendental world of Kant with an empty world of nothingness; but the structure of the approach is not thereby changed. That the ultimate reference of one's actions be nothingness (as a transcendental quality) rather than the realm of theoretical reason may depress men; it does not mean that they approach problems differently. If Schopenhauer's doctrine leads inevitably toward nothingness, it does not follow that willing nothingness will release men from an epistemology that drives them constantly *toward* an ever vanishing goal. When Nietzsche proclaims that man would rather "will the void, than be void of will" he is making an anti-Schopenhauerian statement. He is suggesting that the state that Schopenhauer thought to be the logical result of his investigations (being "void of will") is simply not attainable. *The problem of humankind is therefore not to be approached by willing something new, but by changing the form of life that requires willing.* As an attempt to change the world, willing leads, it seems, to a blind alley. Hence, one would suspect that for Nietzsche, the forms of life which might require willing will have to be changed. The "lion" will have to *become* a "child."

Even in the ultimate development of Western morality — nihilism — men persist through their will in giving form to a repeated development of the structures in which they already exist. Will may be destructive of content, but not necessarily of form; and, in some conditions, such as those of morality, it merely perpetuates the intentionality of the willer.

Nietzsche is thus able to say that a pure act — that is, an act leading to no consciously or unconsciously unintended results — can only be an "unconscious one"; in fact, "all perfect acts are unconscious and *no longer willed*."[14] He does not imply by this, however, that *just any* "unconscious" will do. As we shall see in the final chapter, Nietzsche believes that there are many differently structured forms of the "unconscious": the problem is to discover how to acquire one that is not nihilistic. In any case, the next capsule in "On Redemption" appropriately concerns Wagner, who, in his libretti and music, wrestles at length with the thorny problem of the relation of conscious and unconscious acts. Nietzsche has him say: "No deed can be annihilated: how could it be undone by punishment, this is the eternal in the punishment called existence [*Dasein*] — that existence also again must be deed and guilt. It happens then that *the will at last redeems itself and will becomes non-will.* . . . But, my brothers, you know this fable of madness." Wagner recognizes that self-consciousness (knowing what you will) poses a problem for redemption. It is on his solution to this problem that Nietzsche ultimately breaks with Wagner. Wagner's answer is then worth developing at some length, for it casts light on what particularly offends Nietzsche.

In *Lohengrin*, the hero explicitly enjoins Elsa from seeking to know who he is. *Das sollst du mich nicht fragen* — "That you must not ask me" — is the motif most repeated in libretto and music. When the fatal question of consciousness is asked, all comes to an end, and the would-be redeemer must sail back to the "distant land, named Monsalvat." To depend on the restraint of humans will clearly not work.

In *Die Meistersinger von Nürnberg,*[15] Wagner attempts to solve the problems of the young untutored genius Walter von Soltzing. Walter wants to attain happiness in the form of marriage to Eva; to do this he must obtain admission into the Meister Guild. Since his first song lacks all rudiments of form — even though sung from the heart — he is rejected by the guild. It is obvious that Wagner and the benevolent cobbler Sachs feel that this new artist, if properly tutored, would vastly enhance the quality of the Guild. Thus we are confronted with a problem analogous to that of Greek tragedy. Sachs must solve the old with the new, such that the city of Nürnberg be renewed and rejuvenated. Sachs achieves this integration by teaching Walter some of the rudiments of form and manipulating the social net of illusion in such a fashion that the young artist finds fulfillment and the society is renewed. In the famous *Wahn* monologue at the beginning of Act III, Sachs self-consciously sets himself this task:

> Now let us see
> How Hans Sachs works
> To cunningly guide illusion
> So to do a noble work. . . .
>
> Thus it is with such affairs:
> They rarely work of themselves
> And never without illusion.

The *Meistersinger* solution — for Sachs weaves his finery well — holds that one need not overcome the past in order to be redeemed. If there is someone in the position of a Sachs, all may, in the end, work out. This, however, manages well enough to end the opera, but it does not solve the problem of "redemption of the redeemer." Even Wagner recognizes the artificiality of this solution when, just as Sachs places the chain of acceptance into the Meister Guild over the head of the young Walter, the new Meistersinger exclaims:

> Not *Meister!* No! I would be blessed without Meisterhood.

Art here remains the basic pattern of redemption for Wagner, but the degree of self-consciousness required for successful manipulation is such that the attained result is always seen as problematic. In the opera, Walter is immediately hushed by Sachs (for one thing, the production has been going for five hours), and the problem is postponed with an expression of confidence in German art. But the point is clear: to know what you are doing somehow threatens the "naturalness" of the results. Walter instinctively wants to be blessed, but without having to be taught. In other words, he wants to be redeemed from the past simply by not having it and by not having to deal with it. As with Nietzsche, the option of direct didactic teaching is rejected, but, in Wagner's understanding, self-consciousness must also be abolished.

These problems are taken up in the Ring tetralogy. In order to save the world from the domination of the power of the ring, Wotan has to break his own laws. The whole situation can only be redeemed from this disaster-provoking act by the actions of a man who is not subject to the past. Siegfried, who, as Anna Russell has savagely pointed out, is "very brave and very strong, and very handsome, and very stupid" is the redemptive hero. He is of unnatural birth, never knows his father, and constantly loses memory of what little experience he has by imbibing magic draughts. Yet he is, as Wotan tells Fricka in the first scene of the second act of *Die Walküre*,

> . . . a man
> Who, free from godly protection
> Is free from the laws of the gods.
> Only such can accomplish the deed
> Which though gods would perform it
> No god dare perform it for himself.

Instead of actively manipulating the web, as does Sachs in *Die Meistersinger*, Wotan must enforce forbearance on the part of all other gods. Since this counteracts Brunhilde's natural and active love for Siegfried, the solution achieved also suffers from artificiality and self-consciousness. Wagner does not advance far beyond the dilemmas of *Meistersinger*.

It is not until *Parzival*, the opera occasioning the final and public break between Nietzsche and Wagner, that one finds Wagner's ultimate solution. Here, at last, the opera explicitly ends with "redemption for the redeemer." Parzival is the "pure fool," an unconscious bumbling artist who finds the Grail and redeems everything and everyone because he does not know who he is, where he comes from, or what he is doing. Even the erotic kiss from Kundry is transformed into an affirmation of the chastity of innocence.

This is simply unacceptable to Nietzsche. That the solution to the problems of the world should depend on the sudden appearance of a man who has remained totally outside the world and that his unthinking action should allow the world's redemption as well as his own was sociologically too implausible. In the early Wagner, at least, some active hope had been offered in the notion of an artistic redemption. Nietzsche now sees this too as mistaken. But the Wagner of *Parzival* is simply unbearable. Nietzsche caustically suggests that what is required after Wagner's last opera is "redemption *from* the redeemer." [16]

In the end, Wagner is merely non-rigorous Schopenhauer. [17] The notion that the will itself has to be redeemed implies that existence itself is a crime which must be expiated, for from which one must be rescued. *The search for redemption*, in the sense of finding a way to escape from the past, *is then precisely what Nietzsche moves away from* in his capsule summaries of Kant, Hegel, Schopenhauer, and Wagner.

So far, Nietzsche has considered the answers of three other philosophers, as well as that of an artist. In a real sense, these represent the positions he encounters during his years of schooling. Determined as he is to "become who he is," he feels obliged to move away from these positions and these men. During the period of *Human, All-Too-Human*, when the necessity of breaking with Wagner becomes evident to him, he notes:

When I celebrated Schopenhauer as my educator, I had forgotten that already, for quite awhile, none of his dogmas had escaped my misgivings; I was not bothered, though, by how often I had written "badly proved" or "indemonstrable" or "overstated" under his sentences. I was only thankful for the great impact which Schopenhauer, free and bold before the world [*die Dinge*], in confrontation with the world, had exercised upon me for a decade. When, later, on a festive occasion, I brought my veneration to Richard Wagner, once again I had forgotten that for me his only music was shrunk to some one hundred measures taken here and there, . . . and . . . that I had forgotten what I knew about Wagner in respect to the truth.[18]

In *Ecce Homo*, Nietzsche insists in an almost pathetic fashion that one may legitimately substitute his name for those of Wagner and Schopenhauer throughout the *Untimely Considerations* without fundamentally changing the impact. Such a rejection of what had appeared to him, at least for awhile, as authority leads to the final capsule in this chapter "On Redemption." The last rejected alternative solution to the problem of the relation of the will and the past is the one that he himself advanced (or appeared to) in *The Birth of Tragedy*. Nietzsche writes: "I led you away from all these fables when I taught you 'the will is a creator.' All 'it was' is a fragment, a riddle, a dreadful accident — until the creative will says to it 'But thus I willed it.' . . . But has the will spoken thus? And when will that happen?" *The Birth of Tragedy* points in the right direction, but it does not provide the right answer. The will can only "speak thus" when there is "reconciliation with time," and "something higher than reconciliation," only when the "will is taught to will backward." This last will is the will to power.

What does it mean that the will to power must will "higher than reconciliation?" Interpretation of this whole passage calls for extreme caution; indeed, at this point Zarathustra breaks off his speech and has an exchange with the hunchback, who is upset that Zarathustra has spoken differently to them than to his disciples. Zarathustra retorts that with hunchbacks, one speaks in a "hunchbacked" fashion. His interlocutor does not rest content, though: "Why does Zarathustra speak differently to his students, than to himself?" And, with that, the exchange is cut off; for a long time Zarathustra will engage in no conversation with anyone.

In the midst of these difficulties, Zarathustra seems to be saying that the standard notion of redemption attained through an act of will which comes to terms with, or simply eliminates, the past, is unsatisfactory. The previous attempts, by Hegel, Kant, Schopenhauer, Wagner, and even in *The Birth of Tragedy*, are all deficient in that they either permit an attempt to ignore the weight of the past, or else simply assert the possibility of escaping from it. For Nietzsche, these older conceptions of will are all mistaken; they "do not exist at all," for "instead of grasping the formulation of a single willing into many forms, [in them] one eliminates the character of willing by subtracting from the will its content, its 'Whither?' " [19]

So far, Nietzsche has argued that the past weighs on the living so pervasively that there seems to be no way in which men may be rid of it. Willing merely reaffirms the past. At the end of the chapter "On Redemption," Nietzsche drops a hint that a "will which is the will to power" might possibly be able to will backward and thus overcome the power of time. To determine precisely what this means, it is now necessary to break away from this chapter in *Zarathustra* — continually keeping in mind the topics that a discussion of the will naturally raised here for Nietzsche — in order to turn to some of his late notes. The combination permits, I think, a fairly precise understanding of what Nietzsche means by the will to power, and this, in turn, will allow me to make precise the message of this chapter.

Nietzsche constantly refers to the will to power as something that cannot be satisfied. It requires, he writes, a "whither" in order to be what it is. He sees it as a "forward thrust again and again and becoming master over that which stands in its way." [20] He indicates that the will to power is in constant motion against what it is not; it does not seek any particular state of affairs, but rather control of all that it encounters. [21] Pleasure, pain, and such are seen as superficial manifestations of the drive of life itself which, for Nietzsche, is the attempt to give one's characteristic definition to that which is encountered. Nietzsche proposes, in fact, a sort of eidetic reduction of all that is phenomenal (such as pain and pleasure), so that there remain "no things, but only dynamic quanta, in a relation of tension to all other dynamic quanta: their essence lies in their relation to all other quanta, in their 'working' [*Wirken*] on these. *The will to power not a being [Sein], not a becoming, but rather a pathos is the most elemental fact from which a becoming, a working first emerge.*" [22]

This is not the clearest writing that Nietzsche ever undertook. Nevertheless, an important clue is offered by his reference to the will to power as a *pathos*. In *The Gay Science*, Nietzsche makes the classical distinction of *pathos* and *ethos*, and suggests that as long as men continue in a particular form of life they tend to think of it as *ethos*, that is, as the "only possible and reasonable thing . . . henceforth." A truer understanding, though, would be that life is *pathos*, that it is "not one's lot to have (certain particular) sensations for years." [23] Nietzsche's point appears to be that life is a process always happening, such that particular states of affairs and feelings must be epiphenomenal to something else, here *pathos*, and, in general, to the will to power.

Liddell and Scott's authoritative *Greek Lexicon* offers more clues. *Pathos* can mean "that which happens to a person or a thing," what "one has experienced, good or bad"; it refers sometimes to the "incidents of things." *In no case* does it imply a notion of change or growth, but only the different states a person or a thing may assume. It is thus quite different, for instance, from the notion of *physis* which Heidegger tries to associate with the will to power. *Physis* is a term denoting origin, or the natural form of a person or thing as the result of growth, occasionally even the regular order of nature. [24]

The will to power refers then not to an ontological principle, nor to something that has evolved; "it cannot have become," says Nietzsche.[25] *It is rather the movement itself*, and thus has neither being, nor becoming. It can only be understood in terms of its "whither." Nietzsche is saying that if one looks at a people, in fact at organisms and matter in general,[26] their most basic characteristic is the attempt to incorporate into themselves and define all that they meet. This is their will to power, which must therefore be a matter of constantly giving form, or, more precisely, of giving one's own particular form to that which is encountered. All the forms a thing acquires constitute its *pathos*, its will to power. The various "whithers" are only manifestations which, in their totality, are the will to power of an organism. It is thus correct to proclaim as Nietzsche does in one of his most famous aphorisms, that "all life is 'will to power.' "[27]

Nietzsche's emphases are constantly on the constructing nature of the will to power. Here the English language tends to obscure an important point. In German, "will to power" is *Wille zur Macht*. *Macht* however is related to *machen*, which means "to make," and thus to give form. I suggest then that one must understand the will to power as that which gives the forms which are the *pathos* of any life. Even more simply, in the notion of the will to power is the answer to the never asked question, *What is the apollonian?*

Apollo was the god of form who was required to refract dionysian knowledge. It was he who gave it particular form and thus made a particular culture, society, art, religion, politics, even language possible. Nietzsche uses the notion of the "will to power" in order to assert that any range of forms is possible. Just as Dionysos can be embodied in any number of forms, so also, for example, most Western moral configurations may be seen as partaking of the same genealogy. The dionysian genealogical knowledge is embodied *in* each morality, but in very different ways.

The Inescapability of the Will

With this understanding, significant modifications in the usual view of the will to power become necessary. It is obvious that all forms of life have it, from the most masterly moral, to the most slavish. The will to power is the process of the domination by each of these forms of life. Nietzsche writes: "The will to power *interprets* (— it is a question of interpretation during the building of an organ): it sets limits, defines degrees, differences of power. Mere differences of power could not feel themselves to be such: there must be present something that wants to grow, which interprets by its standard [*auf seinen Wert hin*] any other thing which wants to grow. Equal *in that* — in fact, interpretation is a means to become master of something." [28] The will to power "interprets"; it is, as Nietzsche notes in the second essay of *The Genealogy of Morals*, a "form giving . . . force" [29] and it interprets in terms of something. Most generally, the will to power interprets the "new in the forms of the old." [30]

A living organism tends then to attempt to organize the world around it in its own image and to make it part of the sphere of its domination. I have examined how Nietzsche sees this process at work in language, morality, politics; it should now be apparent why there is no escape from a genealogy. The will to power operates in such a manner that the same forms get repeated, in a compelling cycle. *Even the nihilist wills*, though he perpetuates the void which is the kernel of *his* will to power. [31]

If this understanding be admitted, it should follow that there are potentially a number of different and alternate genealogical principles. Nietzsche has at least two: master morality and slave morality. (There is also that of the overman, which I shall investigate in the next chapter.) This realization however allows a conclusion that was not possible at the end of my analysis of the chapter "On Redemption." It had appeared there that the *will that is the will to power can possibly somehow deal with the past*, and can somehow do so in a manner such that the here and now will no longer suffer from "historical sickness." It is not true, however, that the will to power *necessarily* does this; certainly the will to power of slave morality and the ascetic priest do not liberate men from this malady. Hence, the will to power does not *automatically*, by virtue of its "nature," transform every " 'it was' into 'thus I willed it.' " Zarathustra's conclusion does, however, raise the possibility that if one understands that the will to power operates, and what the nature of the genealogy of present western society is, then *it might be possible to make a past*, for oneself and for others, which would produce a present not subject to the ravages of nihilism. Such a process would be strongly analogous to the achievements of certain forms of psychoanalysis, except that Nietzsche would have the results on biological, social, and historical levels as well as on the individual. In psychoanalysis one first destroys the present, problematic structures of a neurotic personality, and only then constructs that personality that would be healthy. There is a sense in which it is right to say that psychoanalysis seeks to eliminate a portion of a patient's past and replace it with something that does not lead to neurosis. Presumably, if the will did "will backward," the effect would not be to ignore the past, nor to break with it, but, since the willing must be done in the present, to recreate a new past and by making it new, so also make the present new and thus liberate man from what has held him captive. I am suggesting here that "to will backward" in fact means to *change* that which has been the past, not to abandon it, *but to make it other than that which it has been*. The will to power would still be that which creates what is.

This understanding has many points to recommend it. In *On the Use and Disadvantage of History for Life*, Nietzsche speaks of the dangers of critical history. Judging the past, he writes, is

> always a dangerous process, dangerous even for life itself; and the men or times that serve life by judging and denying a past are always dangerous and endangered men and times. For as *we are merely the resultant of previous generations*, we are also the resultant of their errors, passions, and mistakes, indeed of their crimes. It is not possible to completely free oneself from this chain. Though we condemn the errors and hold ourselves to be free of them, we have not laid aside the fact that we spring from them. . . . We arrive at best at a conflict between our *innate, inherited* nature and our knowledge, as well as a struggle of a new strong growth against that which has been from the past cultivated and inherited *[das von alters her Angezogene und Angeborene]; we plant a new form of life [Gewohnung], a new instinct, a second nature which withers the first.* It is an attempt to give oneself *a posteriori a past from which one might have sprung, as against that from which one does spring* — always a dangerous attempt, because it is so difficult to find a limit to the denial of the past, and because the second nature is generally weaker than the first. . . . But here and there the victory is achieved and a special conciliation attained by the combatants, by those who serve life with critical history: to know that this first nature — it, too — was once a second nature and that every conquering second nature becomes a first.[32]

I have cited this passage at some length because, despite its obvious importance, it has generally remained unnoticed. Here, already at the beginning of Nietzsche's career, are the elements that continue to occupy his endeavors. Men have, indeed they inherit, a nature that is the result of the actions and choices of previous generations. This nature is severely flawed, yet men cannot free themselves from it even if they understand that it is flawed. Instead, men must abolish their past, and replace it with a new one, which will give them a new nature. This is an immensely difficult task, but one that must be accomplished. Without a new form and definition, men will always remain entangled in the discontents that are a necessary characteristic of their present nature.

To this extent, the general problem Nietzsche sets himself, in the chapter "On Redemption" as well as elsewhere, is the transfiguration of one form of the will to power — slave morality — into some other form characteristic of the "overman." How this process may come about, how that will that is the will to power will be able to change the past, is still obscure. Perhaps the most useful fashion in which to approach the problem of the transfiguration of this world into that of the overman, which Nietzsche hopes to bring about, is to examine a past transformation of equal intensity and importance. There is in Nietzsche a detailed consideration of the process by which man's present "nature" moved from being a second to a first. This is his analysis of how slave morality replaced master morality. Nietzsche devotes considerable attention, especially in *The Genealogy of Morals*, to the origins of our present moral system. This system, which he calls slave morality, came into existence at some dim point in the past. It replaced master morality, and has come, in Nietzsche's understanding, to totally dominate the contemporary world. I turn now then to his analysis of the shift from master to slave morality.

Masters and Slaves

Much has been said about these two categories in Nietzsche, and little of it is very favorable to the contemporary understanding. Master and slave have somewhat ominous resonance; memories of the Nazis and the racial contexts in which these terms were used by them leads easily to a conclusion that the categories have at best an emotive value, which is most happily distrusted.

This conclusion is, however, hasty, and on the surface of it, surprising. The notions of master and slave have an obvious apparent ancestry in Rousseau and Hegel; at the time Nietzsche is writing, Marx is developing an understanding of history as governed by the interaction of the oppressors and the oppressed. [33] While a detailed consideration of the similarities and differences is not possible here, this is surely distinguished company; and, indeed, it should be, for Nietzsche is trying to deal with the same problem the others are. He must determine how the structure of action of one period comes to be replaced by that of another. When Hegel tries to uncover how one moves from the stage of the Enlightenment to that of absolute freedom and terror; or Marx, the transition from feudalism to capitalism; they, as well as Nietzsche, are trying to explain the transformation of the *pathe* of one period into that of another. The two principles meet, combine, interact, destroy each other, evolve, transform themselves.

The Genealogy of Morals is about the shift from one form of morality (master morality) to another (slave morality). It is a critical genealogical analysis of what Nietzsche believes to have been a development of the history of men's relations with each other. He seeks to show why the change came about, what its nature is, and to depict as its final consequence the development of men — the "last men" — who are no longer capable of generating new values, but merely of justifying their plight.

For Nietzsche, the development of the (moral) nature of the human-all-too-human has, as its result, the "last men." I take the term "last men" absolutely literally: Nietzsche means *last*; after them, no significant evolution is possible. The species has, so to speak, played itself out and can evolve no further. This serves to reemphasize the evolutionary nature of Nietzsche's view of morality. *The Genealogy of Morals* does not contrast master and slave morality; certainly it also does not seek a return to master morality, nor even advocate it. While there is little doubt that Nietzsche finds that men prey on themselves less in master morality, he also realizes, as had Rousseau before him, and Freud after, that it is in slave morality that much of Western culture has evolved. Unless one remembers that Nietzsche's book is designed to express the evolution and change of slave morality, and that the various notions of "bad conscience," "*ressentiment*," "guilt," the "ascetic priest," and so on are signal instances of the *pathos* for the will to power of slave morality, the book will remain as a collection of more or less well linked aphorisms. It is very important not to miss the scope of the book; it encompasses in outline both Freud's metapsychology of the West

(*Civilization and Its Discontents*) and Max Weber's attempt at tracing the evolution of Western rationalism back to the problem of theodicy (*The Social Psychology of World Religions*). [34]

In *Beyond Good and Evil*, Nietzsche gives a short summary of the conclusions he had reached a year earlier in *On the Genealogy of Morals*. "There are master and slave moralities — I add immediately that in all higher and more mixed cultures there also appear attempts at mediation between these two moralities . . . , at times they even occur within a single soul. The moral discrimination of values has originated either among a ruling group whose consciousness of its difference was accompanied by delight, or among slaves and dependents of every degree." [35] Even before any substantive consideration, three methodological points stand out. Firstly, the terms master morality and slave morality can be to some degree called ideal types. While a given historical period may be characterized more by one of them than by the other (much as Weber's "traditional authority" is increasingly a thing of the past), it is possible for them to be mingled, even in a single soul. Hence, as with ideal types, these are ways of looking at the world; they are not meant to correspond to something particular in the world, but rather to express the genealogical characteristics of a particular combination and logic of events. Secondly, a slavely moral individual is defined according to his or her "nature," not according to his behavior. Since these are not primarily sociological categories, and do not refer to empirical social data, there is no reason why someone who occupies the status of a president or king might not be slavely moral. One does not have slave morality in the same manner as one has social-economic status, or even in the manner in which one is a negro or Anglo-Saxon.

Master and slave morality may thus be found in some combination in anyone. There is no doubt, though, that Nietzsche sees the last twenty-three hundred years as increasingly dominated by slave morality. But the mere fact that one might happen to control the destinies of several million people is, in itself, no indication that one is a master. Conversely, a "slave" is not impotent, at least in the sense of lacking a will. What counts, in both cases, is the particular relationship between one's sense of self and one's sense of others.

In the passages in which Nietzsche describes the shift from master to slave morality, [36] a number of important observations stand out. The masters "do not know guilt, responsibility, or consideration";

they are "born organizers." The masters exteriorize their will on the environment around them; they almost, in fact, create it in their own image. The *direction* that their will to power assumes (the "whither?") is from inside out. Nietzsche thus sees their action as fundamentally characteristic of a "state," in which the masters "work" until the "raw material . . . [is] at last . . . formed."

These are obviously not slaves, but, as Nietzsche goes on to say, it is through their actions that slave morality becomes possible.

> They are not they in whom bad conscience develops. . . . But it would not have developed without them, this ugly growth; it would be lacking if their artist violence had not with its hammer blows created a tremendous amount of freedom out of the world, at least out of that which was seen, and had made it, as it were, latent. This instinct of freedom which is forcibly made latent — we understand it already — this instinct of freedom which is pushed back, which has subsided, which is imprisoned within us, and, in the end, which is only let out and discharged against itself — this, and only this is what bad conscience is in its earliest beginnings.[37]

As far as I can tell, Nietzsche is saying that the direction of the will had been turned outward in masters, that the slaves had taken the achievements of the masters and had turned them forcibly inward, thus giving rise to "bad conscience." Important immediately here is that the *direction* of willing seems to be the key difference. It is outward and expended in the masters, inward and "imposing a form upon oneself" in the slaves.

Aside from the matter of direction, to which I will return, Nietzsche also indicates that the practices of masters seem to give rise to the practices of slaves. In this section, master morality is tied to the early imposition of a state upon nomadic tribes by some early group of "blond beasts." It appears as deficient as Siegfried in the use of self-reflective consciousness (which would be turned inward). Indeed, the shift to bad conscience is "an illness, there is no doubt about that, but an illness as a pregnancy is an illness."[38] It seems that, for Nietzsche, the future is to the slaves, as it was in Hegel to the bondsman, and in Marx to the proletariat.

Why the Future Is to the Slaves

Nietzsche writes in *Beyond Good and Evil* that in the case of the master, "when the ruling group determines what is 'good,' the exalted proud states of the soul are experienced as conferring distinction and determining order of rank. . . . The noble type of man experiences itself as determining values; it knows itself to be value-creating." [39] Master morality is sufficient to itself and therefore lacks the sense of a time in which things might conceivably become better. Since such a person *is* his own standard, there can be no question of somehow moving closer to it in the future. Rather, the master seeks to behave in an honorable and unashamed fashion toward those who are his peers and his equals in that they too embody their own "morality." (It would seem that Nietzsche has in mind something like the assemblage of the Greek and Trojan heroes.) Much as in Hegel, there is a reciprocity of relationship. The master, for instance, does not "see the enemy as evil [*böse*]; he can requite [*vergelten*]. In Homer, both the Greeks and the Trojans are good. Not he who does us harm, but he who is contemptible is bad [*schlecht*]." [40] Evil (*böse*) and bad (*schlecht*) are technical terms introduced by Nietzsche to signify a difference in relation between master and slave as to whom they find morally "wrong." The Greek recognizes the Trojan as someone like him, even though this person seeks to kill him. The first recognition is sufficient for master morality.

It is different with the slaves. Nietzsche continues:

Suppose the vitiated, oppressed, suffering, and unfree who are uncertain of themselves and weary, moralize: what will their valuations have in common? Probably a pessimistic suspicion about the whole condition of mankind. . . . Slave morality is essentially a morality of utility. . . . According to slave morality, those who are evil [*böse*] inspire fear; according to master morality, it is precisely those who are good that inspire and wish to inspire fear, while the bad [*schlecht*] man is found contemptible. [41]

When the master had judged those he found contemptible as bad (*schlecht*) he was applying to them the same standard he applied to himself and his peers. It is not that the "bad" men fail to live up to a standard, but rather that they do not have one. The slave, on the other hand, makes his moral judgments on a quite different basis. His initial premise is to set himself off from those who would do him harm, from the evil ones (*bose*). The reciprocity of peers — whether enemies or friends — becomes impossible.

Masters and Slaves: The Fable of the Lamb

How then does the evolution and change of morality take place? What is its *pathos*? The distinction between master and slave morality can be formulated as the distinction between two paradigm statements. Characteristic of the master: "I am good, therefore you are bad." Characteristic of the slave: "You oppress me, are thus evil; I, therefore, am good." The important root of the difference lies in the sort of interhuman relation implied in each case by the word "therefore." In the master's statement, the second part of the sentence is merely negative. There is no comparative element. The master's sense of himself is not dependent on a calculated comparison with the outside. As Nietzsche says: "The bad of noble origin . . . [is] an after-production, a side effect, a contrasting shade. . . ."[42] The premise of the statement is positive and affirmative, as is the sort of man who perpetuates himself through this stance. This is why Nietzsche says that no degeneration can come out of noble soil; none could, for in itself it contains no seeds of corruption.

The slave statement, "You oppress me, are thus evil; I, therefore, am good," is signally different from that of the master. The moral sense of self and the identity of the slave become in effect a negation of a negation, and consist of denying something that affects one from without, and then asserting one's identity as the opposite of that by which one is afflicted. As such, this notion of identity is not structurally different from that which Hegel describes in the *Phenomenology*, where selfhood is arrived at by progressively distinguishing oneself from nature and then from other people. (Hegel, however, thought this to be the only form of knowledge and selfhood.) The ultimate logical expression of this stance is found, as Nietzsche comes to realize, in Schopenhauer. Schopenhauer, like Silenus, thinks that release from the will is the only answer to the problems of suffering. Here, too, identity does not consist of an active component, but is reaction to something outside; action in itself, with its inevitable self-assertive qualities, must then become something evil, since it is identified with that against which one is reacting. The will to power of slave morality must constantly reassert that which gives definition to the slave: the pain he suffers by being in the world. Hence, any attempt to escape that pain will merely result in the reaffirmation of painful structures. As seen in the consideration of nihilism, already in the logic of (slave) moral ethics are those elements that lead to the ultimate triumph of nihilism.

The logic of slave morality leads men on; behind every moral statement lies a myriad of nihilistic imperatives. Nietzsche considers the sentence, "It was my fault."[43] The speaker must accept that morality rests on responsibility, which, in turn, rests first on the belief that matters could not have been otherwise given that I acted the way I did. This implies that my action must be understood as faulty, in terms of some standard that I must inevitably take from outside myself. The assumption, however, that there are moral standards outside of me to which I did not live up, and that my willed actions can be judged by those standards, is an assumption that my "true self" can be premised on that which is "not me." For Nietzsche, in such a perspective, negation is the very premise of the personality.

Furthermore, it would seem that in making such a statement about another person ("It was his fault"), or about oneself ("It was my fault"), one is guilty of treating not only the other person as an object, but also oneself — not, one might say, as one's own peer. Master morality, on the other hand, Nietzsche calls a "hard" morality. It insists that one demand both from oneself and others that one act and judge according to *his* will, and that the escape from self permitted by "It was my fault" simply not be allowed. Only if a person is bad (*schlecht*) can one recognize his insufficiency.[44]

The essays of *On the Genealogy of Morals*, which Nietzsche refers to in his autobiography as "three decisive preliminary studies leading to a revaluation of all values," form the most coherent expression of the steps by which master morality is transmogrified into slave morality. Slave morality itself is the consequence of transvaluation of all values effectuated by Socrates and Christ. This constitutes a useful reminder: slave morality is not just master morality stood on its head, a simple reversal of the sociology of domination. It starts from different premises and arrives at *different*, not reverse, valuations. Nietzsche works out this process in an account of the lamb who became reflective.[45]

It is not surprising that a lamb dislike a bird of prey. After all, for apparently no reason the eagle swoops down every now and then and carries off one of your companions; since they appear to have committed no fault, it is not impossible that one day the eagle may take *you*. The lamb, if he be somewhat of a rationalist, will seek to understand this process and try to stop it. Certainly he feels oppressed by the bird of prey, whom he calls evil; certainly thereby he would want to feel himself as good. However, no matter what protestations the lamb may raise, the bird keeps swooping down.

In effect, the lamb wishes that the eagle would not behave as an eagle. He wants the bird of prey to stop doing what he apparently does simply because he is an eagle. Yet this is problematic, for, as Nietzsche continues in the *Genealogy*, "to demand of strength that it not express itself as strength, that it not be a will to overcome, to cast down, to become master, a thirst after enemies, oppositions, and triumphs is just as absurd as to require strength to express itself as weakness." [46]

The lamb thinks to himself something like this. "I have no reason to carry off lambs, but the eagle must have a reason for doing what he does." This implies that the eagle has the *choice* of carrying off the lamb and that the bird of prey sees the situation as presenting alternatives. If one is somehow *able* to produce an event, then the whole notion of an interior calculus becomes very important. And, "exploiting this belief for his own ends," the lamb will begin to think that the bird of prey may have acted other than as a bird of prey. It should be noted here that the lamb is attempting to account for its own suffering and can only do so by positing some general rule to which both he and the eagle should agree. If the lamb should come up with such a system, then, in terms of the system, the eagle would be evil (since he is not living by the rules), and the lamb would be good (since he is, though he can *do no other*). Such system of beliefs, though, is the product of the fact of his suffering.

The task of the lamb is clear: he must seek to force the eagle to think and reflect upon the sources and natures of his action in terms of a system that will stop him from carrying off lambs. If this can be achieved, the will of the master-eagles will be separable from their actions. The eagle is, however, set up for this process. It is the principle of his "morality" that it not be reflective. As with the Homeric heroes or with Siegfried, reflexive intelligence and knowledge are fatal curses. The slave will then seek to understand the outside world far better; indeed, such intellectual comprehension is, in fact, the very source of his identity. Generally speaking, therefore, intelligence and calculation ("what should one do when . . .") is characteristic of slave morality. The slave, Nietzsche writes, "honors cleverness to a far greater degree," for it is much more essential to him than "the perfect functioning of the regulating unconscious instincts." (I might add a reminder here that Socrates had, in Nietzsche's view, found the "unconscious" — *Unbewusst* — no longer an adequate basis for behavior.) And, in Nietzsche's interpretation, the slave-lamb proceeds to do just that. The masters are cunningly frustrated by the slaves through knavish dialectical tricks. And, when the hitherto unconscious will no longer results in successful action, the masters seek for a reasons, and with that comes their fall into slave morality.

This is a description of the process that Nietzsche sees at work in Socrates. There arise certain problems with unreflective unconscious action; even Homer becomes obsolete due to changes in the world situation. The glory of Aeschylus, in Nietzsche's eyes, is his near success at transforming the Homeric world to fit his times without causing a self-doubting break in the continuity of the polity. [47] Socrates, on the other hand, thinks the "unconscious" to be so inaccessible (Nietzsche indicates that this was true of *him* and Euripides, but was not universal) that reflexive reason is the only resource left. Hence, Socrates constantly seeks to make people explain and justify their opinions and actions. This, however, is the very basis of slave morality: slave morality seeks to make the will to power (that which defines and makes a world) explicit and self-conscious, to force the eagle to think, and in the lamb's terms.

Until this point, I have been considering the process by which slave morality is set in motion, essentially the theme of the first essay of *The Genealogy of Morals*. The consequences of this beginning do not remain static but develop through a relentless internal logic. To this problem Nietzsche devotes much of the second and third essays in the *Genealogy*.

The Paths of Ressentiment

In considering the problems of the will in the chapter "On Redemption" in *Zarathustra*, Nietzsche notes that the attempt to deal with time often leads men to seek revenge on the past. In his consideration of slave morality in the *Genealogy*, Nietzsche links the pursuit of revenge with his notion of *ressentiment*. The term refers to the process of allocating responsibility and blame for the pain one suffers; in *ressentiment*, one takes the outside world seriously as a cause of the pain one suffers, and thereby assumes that if only one could deal with the outside world the pain would be alleviated. For Nietzsche, slave morality begins with "the *ressentiment* of natures that are denied the true reaction, that of deeds, and compensate themselves with an imaginary revenge. While every noble morality develops from a triumphant yes-saying to itself, slave morality says from the outset no to what is 'outside,' what is 'different,' what is 'not itself'; and *this* no is its creative deed. . . . This *need* to direct one's view outward instead of back to oneself is of the essence of *ressentiment*: in order to exist, slave morality always first needs an external hostile world; . . . its action is fundamentally reaction." [48]

Ressentiment, it would seem, occurs when men do not exteriorize their affect into action, or more precisely when the affect does not *necessarily* lead to action. Should *ressentiment* "appear in the noble man," it will, writes Nietzsche, "consummate and exhaust itself in immediate response, and therefore does not poison." The noble nature is able to get rid of what goes on inside, and thus is not permanently affected by reaction. Nietzsche proceeds to give an example of such a nature.

To be incapable of taking one's enemies seriously, one's accidents, even one's misdeeds seriously for very long — that is the sign of strong full natures in whom there is *an excess of the power to form, to mold, to recuperate, and to forget* (a good example of this is Mirabeau, who had *no memory for* insults and vile actions done to him simply because he — forgot). Such a man shakes off with a *single* shrug much vermin that burrows into others; here alone genuine "love of one's enemies" is possible — supposing it to be possible at all on earth. How much reverence has a noble man for his enemies! — and such reverence is a bridge to love.[49]

Except for the word "single," the italics are mine: they serve to signal Nietzsche's notion that for the noble man, the past simply does not present itself as a problem; the will of the noble man is in no way trapped by what he has been. This problem was at the focus in the considerations of redemption at the beginning of this chapter. For Nietzsche, the will to power characteristic of *ressentiment* assimilates experience into the person (makes it his past) in such a way that the man of *ressentiment* is always driven forward, unable to rest with the present. Since the will to power "functions in the assimilation of the new under the form of the old, the already experienced, that which still lives in memory," [50] it is the *manner* in which the new is assimilated which is first important, *not* the specifics that have been assimilated. As Nietzsche notes about the time of *The Dawn of Day*, "it is not . . . the presenting [*das Vorstellen*] of the goal, but rather the performance [*die Vorstellung*] of logical forms . . . in the form of wishing. Thought must give the content." [51] Thought is opposed to will to power, which as *pathos* is the series of instances in which thought is manifest.

The past that will not let a man live in the present is the past of *ressentiment* and of slave morality. It seems to me here that Nietzsche in effect takes the behavior that Weber later diagnosed as characteristic of the Protestant and tries to show that its genealogical kernel is implicit in Western culture far before the time of the Reformation. The character that Weber imputed to Franklin is of a man constantly deferring gratification, always concerned with consequences, drawn by the future and pushed by the past, not toward fulfillment, but always and only onward. This process, which Weber sees as the structure of action of Protestantism, is, for Nietzsche, implicit in the attitude toward the past found in the men of slave morality. The only difference for Nietzsche is that by the time one gets to Protestantism and capitalism, the mnemonic principle has risen into consciousness itself, such that one is not only pushed by the structures of the mind, but actively encourages them. [52]

It is worth noting as an aside here that this account shows immediately why the notion that Nietzsche is a "Darwinian" is wrong. (One might have suspected as much, since Nietzsche is *also* castigated as a Lamarckian!) [53] "Natural selection" is not what Nietzsche is ever talking about; not only does he believe that the mediocre win out instead of the most fit, but also, much more importantly, in a real sense he does not believe that there has been any social "progress" at all. For Nietzsche, the genealogical root of slave morality contains in bud all that it becomes. If the "new is apprehended under the form of old," then it makes little sense to speak of evolution as the survival of the fittest, or even of the mediocre. In this analysis, it is rather the operation of the unactualized internalized will that concerns Nietzsche.

Here Nietzsche's analysis seems to rejoin that of Freud. In *Totem and Taboo*, Freud works out a philosophico-anthropological account of the beginnings of human social existence. By his analysis, after many cycles of fruitlessly killing their father to gain access to women (their mothers), a primal band of brothers decides that, in certain areas of their life, no externalization of hostility and aggression will be allowed. A taboo is placed on such behavior and the figure from whom aggression is deflected back into the psyche of the primitives becomes a totem. From this, for Freud, repressed behavior, religion, society, and civilization itself are born. Nietzsche's account, as I have given it, resembles this, but is far more subtle. He sees a similar process not in some distant pseudo-anthropological past, but at some (admittedly dim) historical epoch, and sees the clash not in terms of tyranny versus self-repression, but in terms of two competing principles of morality and authority. But, for Freud and Nietzsche, the consequences are the same: the victory of *ressentiment* allows for a system of morality based on cleverness, on the rationalism required for teaching about tabooed areas, on a science of ethics, and on a class of people to teach such ethics. Both men understand subsequent civilization to represent the victory of the world of totems and taboos. Slave morality is to *ressentiment* what civilization is to neurosis.

So far, Nietzsche has tried to demonstrate that the existence of master morality necessarily generates conditions in which men are tempted toward *ressentiment*. Master morality always implies an oppressed class, but one that will inevitably win out, since it is more numerous and becomes much cleverer. *Ressentiment* seems to be characteristic of the first stage of slave morality; men who live in it attempt to account for their impotence by blaming the outside world and seeking ways in which to thwart their eternal enemies. Gradually, however, the victory is achieved. Men finally find themselves "enclosed within the walls of society and of peace." [54] They do not find peace through this achievement. To make his point as dramatically as possible, Nietzsche then compares the new situation of the slavely moral man to that of the animals who first came to be amphibians and then land-dwellers.

The situation that faced sea animals when they were compelled to become land animals or perish was the same as that which faced these semi-animals, well adapted to the wilderness, to war, to prowling, to adventure: suddenly all their instincts were disvalued and "suspended." . . . They felt unable to cope with the simplest undertakings; in this new world, they no longer possessed their former guides, their regulating, unconscious, right-leading [*unbewusstsicherführenden*] drives; they were reduced to thinking, concluding, calculating, coordinating cause and effect, . . . to their "consciousness," their weakest and most mistake-making [*Fehlgreifen*] organ.

Nietzsche proceeds to argue that the old instincts do not cease to exist simply because these men, for their own security, now live inside walls, be these political or psychic or, more properly, both. The old instincts can now no longer discharge themselves, and thus seek "subterranean gratification." The old instincts are forced "backward against man himself" by those bulwarks that make up the walls of the city and are required for its continuity, or on the psychic level of the metaphor, by those calculations necessary for slave morality. This turning inward marks the shift from *ressentiment* to the stage of bad conscience. "The man who, from lack of external enemies and resistances and forcibly confined to the oppressive narrowness and punctiliousness of custom, impatiently lacerated, persecuted, gnawed at, assaulted, and maltreated himself . . ., this yearning and desperate prisoner became the inventor of bad conscience." Whereas *ressentiment* had said "it is your fault," bad conscience now must say "it is my fault."

This is a key shift inside slave morality. In the *ressentiment* aspect of slave morality, man is driven by the inability to get rid of the memory of suffering. In the stage of bad conscience, man is driven by himself: for the first time a process is set in motion by which man himself will eventually be called into question. Man now perceives *himself* as the cause of his own suffering; to alleviate this suffering, he must find a way to redeem himself from himself. He begins to say in effect: "I cause my own suffering; to redeem myself, I must punish myself to expiate the fault for which I am suffering." (Nietzsche gives a lengthy account of the various forms of punishment.) From such a dialectical process, Nietzsche sees the development of the concept of original sin (as a "causa prima"), and Schopenhauerian notions of the worthlessness of existence. "The aim," he writes, "is now to turn back the concepts 'guilty' and 'duty' . . . against the 'debtor' . . . (where they spread) until the irredeemable debt gives rise to the conception of irredeemable penance." In the slavely moral perspective, even God does not escape this process, for "God sacrifices himself for the guilt of mankind, God makes payment to himself, God is the only being who can redeem man from that which has become irredeemable for man himself." [55]

In this account of slave morality, Nietzsche is attempting to show that the state of *ressentiment* leads physically and socially to bad conscience, which in turn sets in play dynamics that eventually force man himself into question. If man is seen to be the ultimate source of his own suffering, redemption from oneself can only be effectuated as it is in Christian morality, by the act of God becoming man and freely redeeming himself. There is a very strong clue here to why Nietzsche thinks that the announcement of the *fact* of the "death of God" breaks "history in two." The logic of slave morality had driven men to the point where the divinity was all that was holding the moral fabric together. After His death, men do not suddenly cease behaving along the moral lines to which they are accustomed; but, gradually, the horizon that had given human moral life some coherence becomes a pale husk. This is the "twilight of the idols"; what was once divine and sensuous is now empty and clanging. The end of this process cannot but call man himself into question.

An ultimate questioning of the "human-all-too-human" does not happen either immediately nor even, it would seem, necessarily. Humanity develops a whole set of ideals by which to ward off the awe-ful ultimate question of its own worth. These ideals are the subject of the last essay in the *Genealogy*. Nietzsche certainly thinks that the modern period marks the *end* of a long line of development. He does not think that the end will come of itself; it is too frightening not to be resisted. To more fully understand the nature of man's resistance, it is necessary to make some preliminary remarks about what it means for Nietzsche to speak of humanity coming to an end.

The End of History

The *Genealogy of Morals* and *Zarathustra* form a coherent sequence. Despite the fact that they were written in reverse order, the former is intended to clarify human morality during the genealogy that makes Zarathustra possible. The *Genealogy* ends with the death of God; *Zarathustra* starts with the prophet's encounter with a man who has not yet heard of this great event. With the death of God, the strength and sensuosity of the old genealogy have played out. Men now live — the "last men," Zarathustra calls them — in the "shadows of the dead

God," still under the forms of behavior characteristic of the old order, yet unable to move into a new one. The two worlds of which Matthew Arnold sang, "one dead, the other powerless to be born," are the worlds that Nietzsche sees. The end of the *Genealogy* thunders the news that morality has perished; yet it neither announces a new morality, nor dispels the vacuum left by the death of the old. The new is not yet, if it ever is to be, for the nature of the will which is the will to power of slave morality is, in the end, rather to "will the void, than be void of will."

Nietzsche is, of course, not the only person in the nineteenth century to have had a sense of a great and impending change in human affairs. Hegel had already argued that the course of the dialectic was to ensure the future to the bondsmen; the *Phenomenology of Mind* was designed to portray such historical development as the gradual externalization and rationalization of knowledge.[56] In other words, as men operate in and with the world and interact with each other, for Hegel, the implicit structures of the knowledge — which make knowledge possible — gradually acquire content, and become subject to reason and rationalization. History, from this perspective, is the becoming-explicit-and-conscious of that which is implicit and potential. Once such a process is completely realized, the mode of existence that it manifests — what Hegel calls History — must be replaced by something else, or result in a static state. This is why Hegel can speak of History as the realization of the *Weltgeist*: the world spirit becomes more and more immanent in reality until there is a final unity between being (world-spirit) and becoming (historical process). The realization of reason is thus also for Hegel the rationalization of reality: at the end of the *Phenomenology*, we arrive at a state of absolute knowledge, and Science replaces History as the mode of being.

All of this has many resonances in Nietzsche. He also sees in modern times the gradual cessation of tension between slave morality and historical reality. *The Genealogy of Morals* goes to some pains to describe the progressive unification of the two. But there is an all important difference. Nietzsche sees the unification not as a valid form of life, but as the least valid. His understanding of the principles of valuation implicit in contemporary morality can only lead him to conclude that the unification of the two must, in the end, result in a gradual and progressive affirmation of nothingness, that is, of nihi-

lism. There is an agreement, however, between Nietzsche and Hegel
that the world is no longer going to be moved by the same processes
as before. Change, in this "post historical" period, if it occurs at all,
will have to be from something else, since the tension between being
and becoming is finally more or less resolved.

Marx, too, had found that the future was to the slave: the
proletariat has nothing to lose but its chains, and, in the process of
effectuating a final unification of potentiality and actuality, a whole
world to gain. In the "Introduction to the Critique of Hegel's
Philosophy of Right," Marx notes: "The task of history . . . is to
establish . . . the truth of this world. . . . In the formation of a class
with radical chains . . . which can involve no historical but only
human title, . . . which in a word is the complete loss of man . . .
[there can be achieved] the complete rewinning of man. . . ." [57] The
communist revolution is designed to put an end to the historical
process characterized by the dialectic of master and slave. Marx
shares with Nietzsche and Hegel the sense of a new world coming;
but, with Hegel and against Nietzsche, he believes there is something
inherent in the logic of the present dialectic which will bring about
the new world. For Marx, if the class opposition is carried to its
ultimate extreme such that the slaves are only bound to the masters
in terms of the logical structure of their existence (which for Marx
comes down to the mode of production), then, Marx believes, out of
this will result a new form of life (communism) which is no longer
subject to the structures of the old.

Nietzsche never read Marx — though he did read a number of the
other so-called "left Hegelians" [58] — but his criticisms are not hard to
imagine. They are a combination of the arguments made against
Hegel and Socrates. As Hegel understood, the dialectic is essentially a
willful thing. Its continuing operation depends on the activity of an
essentially mental force, which refuses to remain quiet with any
conclusion. The process moves ever onward, and what was living in
the old becomes transformed into the new. And for Marx, as for
Hegel, and at least superficially for Socrates, this is all there is, or all
that is needed. It follows then that Nietzsche sees Marx's view as
much too narrow. The dialectic of the two classes which forms the
center of Marx's historical analysis exists for Nietzsche, but only
inside slave morality. Both historical sides of the slave-master relationship are, in Nietzsche's eyes, caught up in the same genealogical

situation. [59] It is then a fundamental mistake to wish to see the dominant class in Marx as somehow equivalent to the masters in Nietzsche. Such a judgment neglects the fact that the activity of Nietzsche's masters is *not just the converse of that of slaves* (oppressing rather than oppressed), but is in fact a *different* form of activity. Marx would see all activity as part of the same dialectical process, or else doomed to historical obsolescence. Where he sees unity, Nietzsche sees potential diversity.

For Nietzsche, the world is very different from the vision of either of his great nineteenth-century contemporaries. It is true that for all of them the "slave" figure is the winner in the development of morality and politics. For Nietzsche, however, there never was a real contest. The dialectic does not have a happy result; Nietzsche sees both poles of the process as sharing the same fundamental genealogy. The net effect of this position is to make the world both more hopeful and infinitely more despairing: men are prisoners of their forms of life and change can only come by breaking out of them. The sound and fury of the historical dialectic which so obsesses Hegel and Marx is, for Nietzsche, merely the significance of the slow, unfolding victory of one kind of existence, slave morality, a triumph not by the overthrowing of its adversaries, but simply from lack of opposition. If Weber is right in identifying the rationalization of the world — *die Entzauberung der Welt*, to use his magic phrase — as the dominant characteristic of modern times, a change in form of life will have to be particularly destructive, since the system does not carry the germs of its own demise. Indeed, one might be tempted to ask Nietzsche, with tongue only half in cheek, why, given his analysis, there is something rather than nothing. If men are destined to will the void, then why doesn't it come and why don't they drop through the bottom into a referenceless emptiness. The system does, in fact, perpetuate itself — this is the difference between genealogy and dialectics. In Hegel and Marx's view, the interaction of parts of the system could give rise to fundamentally new configurations and realities. For Nietzsche, the system is the same, even though it be voided of important content in terms of the humans that live by it. Thus, while men are for Nietzsche at the end of history, they are also not about to break through into a new world by and through the logic of their actions alone. "The end of history" means simply that the manner by and through which men have known value and have

"to fight a certain weariness and heaviness grown beyond all proportions." [61] For this, he has two types of means at his disposal,
"innocent" ones and "guilty" ones. Nietzsche is concerned here with
the dialectical tricks that keep men from fully realizing what is
happening in their lives. Nationalism had provided a respite, albeit a
dangerous and artificial one, from the disintegration of meaningful
political life. So also the ascetic priest alleviates temporarily the
disasters of moral life. Nietzsche lists the "innocent" means as
(a) reducing the feeling of life to its lowest point (e.g., yogic trance),
(b) mechanical activity, (c) "petty pleasures," and (d) the formation
of a herd. [62] Such means are referred to as "innocent," because they
are all generally approved by the society that they are keeping
together. In using these diverse means, the ascetic priest is not curing
men of the increasingly "dominating sense of displeasure" – he is no
physician. Rather he is merely alleviating the discontents by providing temporary palliatives.

In the struggle with displeasure – what Freud was later to see as
civilization and its discontents – the ascetic priest also has at his
disposal more effective and interesting means, the "guilty" ones. All
of these involve some kind of "orgy of feeling." The ascetic priest
"presses into his service indiscriminately the whole pack of savage
hounds in man and lets loose now this one, now that, with always
the same end in view: to awaken men from their slow melancholy . . . if only for a time . . . and . . . this kind of cure is, by
modern standards, 'guilty.' " By such "orgies of feelings," I understand Nietzsche to mean the sudden release of an affect in a total and
uncontrolled way. The Greeks had managed to control their dark
side by carefully filtering it through the ministrations of Apollo;
without this veil, the "orgiastic" affects totally take over. This
sudden release – and here we see again why Nietzsche was frightened
of modern politics – must be paid for physically: the atonement is in
guilt. This increases this discomfort, in turn gives rise to "psychic
lightning bolts," until, imprisoned in the chalk circle of their sin,
individual and society slowly go into a *folie circulaire*. [63]

Through these artifices, the ascetic priest seeks to preserve the
ascetic ideal, to protect a certain form of life and to keep it from
crashing through nihilism into nothingness. The ascetic priest is thus
one of the foremost contemporary wielders of the will to power,
even though this springs from "the protective instinct of a degenerat-

ing life." He prescribes "fundamentally an excitement of the strong-est, most life-affirming drive, even if in the most cautious doses, namely, of the *will to power*." [64] This is the reason why, in the genealogical perspective, there will be no significant change in form of life until something new happens: it cannot come in *this* world, nor indeed from men who are human-all-too-human.

By reducing the will to power to the sole role of justifying suffering of theodicy, the world, and "life" itself, are also reduced. The ascetic priest can "tolerate no power . . . on earth . . . which does not first . . . receive a meaning, a right to exist, a value as a tool to the ascetic ideal, as a way and means to its goal." [65] Such an ideal triumphs so completely that there is simply no opposition. Even science, which one might imagine as providing a counter to the onmarching skeleton of Christian morality, is no hope. It, too, for Nietzsche, serves the old world, and "requires in every respect an ideal of value, a value creating power, in the service of which it could believe in itself — it never creates values. Its relation to the ascetic ideal is by no means antagonistic." [66]

One may be tempted to assume that since Nietzsche appears to "approve" of "life," and since the will to power is held to be coterminous with life ("all life is, and is only, will to power"), then the will to power is something on which Nietzsche places a single valuation. His position, in this perspective, would then be something like "the more life the better, but life, nonetheless." This is in part true, but such an interpretation neglects the basic point. It has been the burden of this chapter to demonstrate that *the problem for Nietzsche is not just "life," but rather the nature of the particular life*. The will to power of the ascetic priest is involved in the preservation of the dregs of a life of slave morality. The fact that the will to power is involved does not thereby change Nietzsche's conclu-sion that men must find a way to escape and break out from the will to power of slave morality into something else. It is of no matter that, by the end of the nineteenth century, the ascetic priest may be losing his grip a bit; were his will to be stronger, men would still be subjected to the same genealogical logic.

As long as one wills in a slavely moral way, one is doomed to the *folie circulaire* mentioned above. Nietzsche is trying to force the recognition that master morality and slave morality (and anything else, for instance the "extra moral" existence mentioned in *Dawn*) are not somehow poles at opposite ends of a scale that would be the will to power. Master morality is not equivalent to a strong will to power, nor is slave morality (necessarily) a weak will to power. Both kinds of morality are will to power, but in different ways;[67] this is only the logical conclusion of Nietzsche's notion that the will to power is a *pathos* and not an ontological principle.

Hence, as already seen in the chapter "On Redemption," Zarathustra understands that, with the present triumph of slave morality, *willing is not the way to remove the discontents*. The difficulties Western man is confronted with arise out of the ascetic ideal and the willing of the void. This, in turn, is consequent to the death of God from over abstraction,[68] itself already the necessary result of the will to power of slave morality.

Nietzsche will pose this as Zarathustra's problem. "The psychological problem in the type Zarathustra is that he says No and *does* No to an unheard-of degree, to everything to which one has so far said Yes, and can nevertheless be the opposite of a No-saying spirit; how the spirit who bears the heaviest fate, the fatality of a task, can nevertheless be the lightest and most transcendant [*jenseitigste*]...."[69] Zarathustra's task is to prepare the paths for the overman in the wilderness of the ascetic ideal; it is not just to negate the ascetic ideal, but to provide the affirmation of a new kind of life — no longer human-all-too-human — which, in coming to existence, will annihilate the old form.

This is difficult, as is apparent in Zarathustra's realization that *not just any* affirmation will do. The "higher men" at the end of *Zarathustra* do want to take up the burdens left by the death of God, but they are incapable of an affirmation that is also a negation and can only repeat the Yea-Yuh (I-A, *Ja*) of the ass who brays acceptance at everything.[70] As Zarathustra remarks: "I honor the recalcitrant and choosey tongues and stomachs, who have earned the right to say 'I' and 'Yes' and 'No.' But to chew and digest everything, that is the swine's manner. Always to bray Yea-Yuh — that only the ass has learned and whatever is of his spirit."[71]

The course of the life of Zarathustra as herald of the *Übermensch*, the overman, is to deny even the higher men. This is the meaning of the last chapter in which the lion — symbol of the destructive will — finally comes back to Zarathustra. He is changed now, for he laughs and provides a test for all those who claim to will in a new manner.

The higher men return also, thinking themselves changed, for the previous night they were given an understanding of the midnight song. But, as they reach the cave, the lion roars and they all vanish in an instant. The new will to power, the "laughing lion," has simply canceled their existence. Zarathustra too seems changed, but he goes out into the sun to be about his work. If he has finally become the overman, Nietzsche does not tell us how to recognize it.

A preliminary clue to the meaning of the *new* will to power of the *Übermensch* is given in the short comments Nietzsche makes about an "extra-moral" form of existence, when the value of an action would depend precisely on what is unintentional to it. In *Human, All-Too-Human* he writes: "Everything is necessity — so says the new knowledge. And this knowledge is itself necessity. Everything is innocence and knowledge is the road to insight in this innocence. . . . *A new habit is forming in us*, and in thousands of years will perhaps be powerful enough to give humanity the strength to produce wise, innocent (*consciously innocent*) men as it now produces unwise guilt-conscious men — this latter is the necessary preliminary step, not its opposite." [72] This particular vision and understanding is most difficult to comprehend. Aside from the breath-taking paradox of "consciously innocent," I am struck by Nietzsche's insistence that "knowledge" is a "necessary preliminary step." Presumably this means that there is no chance to return to a state of nonrationality and that what men have learned in slave morality must not be rejected, but rather transfigured. It certainly means that a usual picture of Nietzsche as advocating that men live more "instinctually" is desperately wrong; the implications of the above are that *men do not have "instincts" to live by any more, and that they will first have to develop them.* There is not in Nietzsche that petty romanticism that finds "natural" man under the verdigris of civilization.

If this has any preliminary meaning, it sheds some light on the concept of "conscious innocence." Such a notion may be seen as corresponding to the last transformation of the spirit in the first chapter of *Zarathustra*. The second state, that of the willing destructive lion, is changed into the new child. Nietzsche writes at the beginning of the first book of *Zarathustra*: "But say, my brothers, what can the child do that even the lion could not? Why must the preying lion still become the child? The child is innocence and forgetting, a new beginning, a game, a self-propelled wheel, a first movement, a sacred "Yes." For the game of creation, my brothers, a sacred Yes is needed: the spirit now wills his own will, and he who had been lost to the world now conquers his own world." Within this framework, "consciously innocent" appears to mean that it will have to be possible to attain such a state as that of the child through intended actions, yet with a final result that one go from consciousness not into death, as Schopenhauer and Marsyas had it, but rather into life. Such an enterprise is, I believe, what Nietzsche understood by eternal return. It is now necessary to turn to this, the most difficult and central of all Nietzsche's teachings and doctrines. Without eternal return — *pace* various commentators, for Nietzsche says so himself — the rest of Nietzsche's work is merely a set of more or less brilliant and titillating insights.

Chapter IX

THE DOCTRINE OF ETERNAL RETURN

The sickness of a time is cured by an alteration in the mode of life of human beings, and it was possible for the sickness of philosophical problems to get cured only through a changed mode of thought, not through a medicine invented by an individual.

—Ludwig Wittgenstein, *Remarks on the Foundations of Mathematics*

We are reaching the end of a journey through Nietzsche. I have tried to establish that the nihilism besetting the Western world lies, in Nietzsche's analysis, so deep as to require a change in the very stuff of humanity. *Everything* is in error, *all* will have to be made new. The task of transfiguration seems, however, to be made impossible by Nietzsche's investigations of the will to power. He finds the will to power that which gives form to any existence. Form, however, must be given in terms of what is, and the problem immediately arises as to how beings who are radically flawed, who are human-all-too-human, can in fact transfigure themselves. Must not everything they do suffer from what they are?

Nietzsche seeks an answer to this problem in the doctrine of eternal return. In this concluding chapter, I shall try to explicate this, the most difficult and obscure portion of Nietzsche's thought. Without an understanding of eternal return, I believe, the rest of Nietzsche is very little different from the writings of many other nineteenth- and twentieth-century cultural critics. Without the doctrine of eternal return, it is difficult to take seriously Nietzsche's claims of preparing a new transvaluation of values on the order of those effectuated by Socrates and Christ.

Eternal return presents problems to all commentators. Not only does Nietzsche give even less of an account of it than he does of the will to power, but furthermore, as a concept, it appears to fly in the face of common sense. If Nietzsche seriously intends to suggest that everything always comes back the same, and means by that that the present configuration of the universe will repeat itself and has already repeated itself countless times, one simply doesn't know what to say. Such a notion, even if true, can only have a heuristic significance for the practical life of human beings, since, obviously, they are destined to pass away, only to reappear again and again and again always unchanged. As such, the doctrine hardly seems worth taking seriously, except, perhaps, in the light of offering some new form of moral behavior by which the individual might relate his choices to a universal principle.[1]

Beyond the fact that, interpreted as a cosmic cyclical vision, eternal return doesn't seem to make much sense, there are additional difficulties. Nietzsche claims explicitly in *Ecce Homo* that eternal return forms the "fundamental conception" of *Zarathustra,* and constitutes the "highest formula of affirmation that is attainable"; he links "the philosophy of eternal return" with Dionysos as the sign and indicator of the transvaluation of values which he is seeking to achieve.[2] It would seem, then, that we will attain an accurate interpretation of what Nietzsche means by eternal return only if we can at least show how Nietzsche could have thought eternal return to be a "fundamental conception." It is necessary to note here that there is no a priori reason to see the will to power as somehow leading to eternal return; the analysis in the previous chapter gives no indication that there is a necessary link. In fact, Nietzsche, as far as I have been able to ascertain, with one possible exception always speaks of the two separately.

Nietzsche's method of exposition raises even more problems in this case than it does in that of the will to power. He writes to Gast from Sils Maria on the fourteenth of August, 1881, that "thoughts have arisen such as I have never seen before" and hastens to add that he "will not speak of them, but will keep [his] unshakable peace." His account of a "vision" of eternal return, "six thousand feet above men and time" as he writes in *Ecce Homo*, and his subsequent furtiveness and secrecy in discussing it (mostly with Lou Salomé) are well-known. For whatever reasons, he apparently thought it was something that could not simply be said. In *Zarathustra*, the main exposition of eternal return comes in a chapter that ends with a riddle ("The Vision and the Riddle"); it is probably fair to surmise that this chapter constitutes some sort of account of the vision that he, Nietzsche, had on the plain between Sils and Silvaplana in the Swiss Engadin, and that he still finds the "riddle" to be the only possible means of expounding it. It is certainly true, and he writes Gast to this effect from Sils at the end of August, 1883, that *Zarathustra* is a structured book, each portion of which, in Nietzsche's mind at least, "forms a basis" for the subsequent portion. *Zarathustra*, however, was never completed. There do exist plans for a major book to be entitled "Philosophy of Eternal Return: An Attempt at the Transvaluation of All Values." And, while there are hints as early as the first book of *The Gay Science* of something apparently resembling the notion of eternal return,[3] the doctrine itself is announced only in the second book of *Zarathustra*, dealt with in the third and fourth, and not mentioned again in finished work until *Ecce Homo*. In any case, Nietzsche never actually *says* what eternal return is; the reason seems to be that men, as Zarathustra discovers in his first public appearance, "have not yet the ears" for such a new thought.[4] At the end of *Zarathustra*, the reader has a distinct feeling of dissatisfaction: something has happened to Zarathustra, but Nietzsche does not say what it is.

These preliminary considerations do serve a purpose, though. They give me some clear ground, making it possible to say what eternal return is *not*. If Nietzsche means anything, whatever he means will have to occupy a central, decisive, and coherent place in his thought as a whole. To begin by asserting that "all that is 'great' in Nietzsche no longer is so for our time . . . [and that] Nietzsche is great for us because of his 'little' sociological and social finds"[5] is to prejudge the issue. Similarly, Jaspers, for instance, finds Nietzsche's greatness in that he "moves men's minds"; for Kaufmann, eternal return is "a most dubious doctrine which was to have no influence to speak of," which as a doctrine "transforms a fruitful notion into a rigid crudity."[6] Whatever the validity of these conclusions, they *cannot be* what Nietzsche thought, since none of them would allow the doctrine the central importance Nietzsche ascribed to it. They are, in fact, an intellectual operation which Nietzsche repeatedly criticized: they constitute an "as-if" on which to ground existence. Nietzsche, as we have seen, devotes much time to attacking world views and philosophical stances of which the most important member can only be intuited, or is in principle unknowable. In fact, notions such as the above are a way to avoid taking Nietzsche seriously; they proceed on the assumption that Nietzsche could not have meant anything *real* by eternal return. The doctrine is then judged either fruitful or not, depending on how the commentator approaches it.

I shall proceed here on the assumption that Nietzsche is being perfectly straightforward when he speaks of moving from the human to the over-human and thinks that eternal return can accomplish this. To do this, I shall avoid coming to conclusions about what Nietzsche "must" have meant and rather try to find out if he *could have been* saying anything meaningful, given the other terms of discourse that he sets for himself. An understanding of eternal return which makes no sense of the rest of Nietzsche is probably wrong.

In any case, my considerations above seem to me to eliminate a number of understandings on a purely methodological basis. Danto, Jaspers, Kaufmann, and the others cannot give us an understanding of eternal return which only either makes little sense of or contradicts other important portions of Nietzsche's writing. Having discarded these views, we are still in somewhat of a quandary, for when we turn to the few substantive things Nietzsche did say about eternal return, we find that they are not set out in direct statements, but rather in an exposition in a "vision and a riddle." I shall shortly give some indications why Nietzsche chooses this mode; firstly, I must set out the terms of the riddle.

The chapter "On the Vision and the Riddle" in the third book of *Zarathustra* is full of complex symbols, all of which have general meaning for Nietzsche. Zarathustra is recounting to some sailors his vision of climbing a mountain, while carrying on his back "his archenemy, the spirit of gravity — half dwarf, half mole."[7] This creature represents the inverse of Zarathustra: he is the same person who jumped over the tightrope walker in the first book, a person who seems to overcome the human-all-too-human, but must in fact be carried along by someone else or skip necessary stages of development. Zarathustra finally calls a halt to bearing this burden, and the dwarf jumps off and squats beside him. Despite the dwarf's tenacity, he is not able to bear Zarathustra's "most abysmal thought." This thought is *not,* as the *dwarf* would have it, that time runs in a circle. Such a doctrine would be a caricature of Zarathustra, just as the spirit of gravity will be a caricature of Zarathustra's lightness. The abysmal thought is named "eternal return."

Zarathustra wonders aloud to the dwarf if they have not all been here before, whispering as they are now, under the gateway of moment, with time running in a straight line backward and forward into the past and future. Then, of a sudden, Zarathustra hears a dog howl, feels pity, and everything around him vanishes. A riddle is about to be proposed, that of eternal return.[8] Zarathustra sees a shepherd in whose mouth has bitten fast a large black serpent. He recoils in horror, and cries out to the youth to bite off the head of the serpent. The youth does so, spits it out, and is immediately transformed, apparently made new in the act of biting and expelling. As part of the riddle, Zarathustra asks his audience whom he has seen and what he has seen. This riddle is posed before the shepherd bites the serpent's head off. In appearance, and for some commentators, the presentation of eternal return is broken off at the end of this chapter,[9] but in appearance only. Zarathustra has not yet the "strength and lion's voice" to *summon* eternal return.

In fact, the vision that Zarathustra has had renders him sick and nauseous. By the end of the third book he is no more than convalescent. He is still divided in himself: "Acting as if someone else were still lying in his place who refused to get up . . . Zarathustra . . . spoke these words: 'Up abysmal thought; out of my depth; I am your cock and dawn, sleepy worm . . . and when you are awake you will stay awake eternally. . . .'"[10] Even here Zarathustra is still not strong enough to support his thought. It causes so much nausea that he again falls down senseless and remains thus for seven days — the time of creation. When he awakens, his animals attempt to comfort him by asserting the beauty of a purely cyclical version of eternal return. Zarathustra rebukes them: "Oh you buffoon and barrel organs. . . . Have you already made a hurdy-gurdy song out of this? [11] The animals then refuse to let him proceed with an explanation of the true nature of eternal return; he is still a convalescent and must "cure his soul." The animals can probably assert a cyclical understanding without suffering nausea because, as Nietzsche points out at the beginning of *The Use and Disadvantage of History for Life,* they do not suffer from the "historical malady." The notion can be quite acceptable to them, but for men it is a hurdy-gurdy song, a mechanistic parody of creative art. [12]

This presentation does allow some steps forward. In the first place, whatever eternal return is, *it is not a theory of the cosmos.* The *state of being* of an individual (and of an animal, in the example above) seems to make the difference. The thought has to be "awakened" by Zarathustra, that is, he has to do something or act differently for it to come "out of [his] depth." The shepherd is *transfigured* by his act, and he laughs "as no man has ever laughed before." In a late note, Nietzsche proclaims, "when you incarnate the thought of thoughts in yourself, it will change you." [13] It is wrong, says Nietzsche — in fact, "one must guard against it" — to think of eternal return on the example of the "stars, or the ebb and flow, day and night, seasons. . . ." [14] The focus of most of Nietzsche's comments seems to be human beings, their souls and bodies. Once Zarathustra overcomes the dissociation of himself and that body lying there as if "in his place," his convalescence will be over. He will then "be awake [and] will stay awake eternally." It appears from these texts that we must look upon eternal return at least as the description of a particular manner of existing.

Secondly, the emphasis on what will happen *when* the "thought of thoughts" comes, *casts considerable doubts on the notion that eternal return is the return of everything "always the same."* As long as we mean by "always the same" that everything will come cyclically back and that there is no change, it seems we mean something other than what Nietzsche does. He speaks of eternal return as the "pivot point of history," [15] and of himself as "breaking history in two"; above, as we saw, he explicitly rejects analogies to cyclical notions of time. Indeed, this is hardly surprising. In *Ecce Homo,* he finds his idea of eternal return to be an entirely *new* idea, approached only perhaps by Heraclitus, and discovered "six thousand feet above men and time." It is unlikely that a man well acquainted with Hinduism and an expert on things Greek might have thought cyclicism a *new* idea. Part of the source of this confusion comes from a misunderstanding of the meaning of "eternity." For Nietzsche, eternity does not "become," it has no past and future. [16] It simply *is*: the exterior provided for the scene with the dwarf and the shepherd in the chapter "On the Vision and the Riddle" takes place under the gateway of moment, in stopped time, as it were, for dramatic evidence. When something is eternal, it is with one always. It does not stretch out into infinity, since it is eternally present. [17]

Thirdly, whatever eternal return is, it is concerned with the question of how human beings deal with their past and their history. *The Genealogy of Morals* and the first book of *Zarathustra* establish the fact and the problem of the death of God. The rest of *Zarathustra* is the investigation of the consequences of that problem, both actual and to come. As we saw in the previous chapter, by the end of the second book, in "On Redemption," Nietzsche sets out as a central issue the question of the relation of the past and future to the present. Both memory and the past are now, in Nietzsche's views, problems and weights to men; yet, in his understanding, there can be neither going back nor, a la Hegel or Marx, the hope for a solution from the practical inertia of historical logic. Men cannot, for Nietzsche, *escape* time. It is the effort to remove oneself from history which Nietzsche sees at the root of the various attempts at redemption: Hegel, Kant, Schopenhauer, along with the Christians before them and science after, all maintain the existence of a world of transcendental concept(s) (be this God, theoretical reason, the *Geist*, the laws of physics), as the source for a solution to the problems of earthly being. [18] "Redemption" consists in escaping from this world to that one, or, conversely, having that world take this one over. Given, however, Nietzsche's general hostility to such notions of transcendence and two-worldliness, it is unlikely that he would assert the possibility or desirability of escaping the reality of time.

It then seems that interpreters of Nietzsche who see men as constantly "overcoming" themselves and rising higher and higher in a long succession of overmanliness miss the key point. If the chapter "On Redemption" establishes that man cannot "escape" time, and yet time is a *problem,* then men will have to find a manner of being-in-time so different that it no longer frames a problem. Failing such an existence, one can only adopt the traditional metaphysical stances, or possibly the cynical cyclicism of the dwarf. In the doctrine of eternal return, Nietzsche then tries to evolve an understanding of a human relation to time which is neither a circle, nor a straight line running backward and forward. [19] One might formulate this question as follows. "Evolve a form of life in which the past never presents itself as a problem (one might say, as a source of neurosis or cyclical compulsion) and in which men (as contrary to animals) are nevertheless self-conscious." Nietzsche's vision here is breathtakingly specific and grandiose. He is concerned that his teaching "slowly sink in as to how generations must build and be fruitful on the basis of it — so that finally it becomes a great tree and overshadows the coming humanity. (Two thousand years for Christianity — many thousand for this.)" [20] From this, it appears that Nietzsche is talking about conscious breeding or evolving of life, no longer human-all-too-human, and that this will or can come about because of the teaching of eternal return.

So far, I have not said very much about what eternal return *is;* rather, I have given some indications as to how it might be recognized. If this is a doctrine which cannot yet be taught because there is no audience for it, then saying what it is will do no good. In fact, it might be harmful. "One only understands these things when they have been achieved in practice," writes Nietzsche as early as a note from the seventies. [21] To attempt to say them directly, as Nietzsche is increasingly tempted to do, or, at the end of his life, finds necessary, lays open the possibility of being dangerously misread and misused. [22] ("Above all, do not mistake me," he warns in *Ecce Homo.*) Hence, as a writer, he "dramatizes his ideas," [23] and fashions them in such a way that understanding can only come from having lived through them. *Zarathustra* is a recognition of this on a large scale: its doctrine is presented in "a book for all," the true meaning of which is not available ("a book for none"), which is perhaps why Nietzsche thought that anyone who had truly understood six sentences of *Zarathustra* would have accomplished a great thing. The ideas are "dramatized" in the sense that Nietzsche brings them on stage and sets them to work. Understanding comes by the grasping and acknowledging of the coherence of their interaction. Eternal return is *first* conceived in a manner that makes Zarathustra nauseous. He has only been able to express it to sailors, themselves already *Sucher-Versucher,* in the form of a riddle. Riddles, I have suggested

before, can be characteristic forms of philosophical discourse when
one is attempting to get something across for which nothing other
than *perfect* clarity will suffice. "What is black and white and red all
over?" One is presented with fragments of a world and is asked for
the logic that would make them a picture. After initial confusion, if
the answer is come up with, that is, once the bits are tied together in
a picture, as "an embarrassed zebra" or "a bloody nun," the *problem
no longer exists.* A riddle can't be asked twice, because after the first
time, one has *got* it. However, the answer to a riddle doesn't come
just from the pieces of information provided in the question; the
answer has to be *made.* Once you have it, there is no problem
anymore; but until then, it remains a mystery.

As with riddles, so with Nietzsche on eternal return. Here, though,
the problem is complicated by the fact that the reader does not
know a priori what counts as portions of the answer. This, as
suggested, is partly due to the subject material, but also to what
appears to be Nietzsche's inability to finish anything that contained
creative themes. [24] The reader can only follow out the leads given
and hope to discover the journey they describe.

The Problem of Audience

I have pointed out above that eternal return is not something that
can be taught, and that it seems to require a particular state of being
in order to be able to understand and achieve it (the shepherd is
transformed, Zarathustra is rendered nauseous). To me, this indicates
that eternal return must operate more than just in thought. Since a
particular *type* of person both experiences and understands eternal
return, the doctrine cannot be effected only in the world of ideas. If
there were no way in which the process of individual change might
affect the process of general social change, Nietzsche would be
contributing nothing more than a Hegelianized version of Kant.
Some interpreters have indeed professed to find, in the doctrine of
eternal return, analogies to the Kantian categorical imperative, to
which Nietzsche adds a historical dimension. [25] To escape the judgment that eternal return is nothing more than esoteric Kant, one
must show that what is seemingly merely a form of individual
conception or understanding can have specific and actual human (I
might more properly say "anthropological") consequences. [26]

Zarathustra understands this. "It is not enough to bring a teaching; one must also forcibly alter men, so they adopt it. . . ."[27] Men are not changing, for their relation to the nihilism afflicting Europe is "passive"; they "allow it to happen to them."[28] Should men attempt to directly overcome decadence as such, as Socrates did, they will only bring it back in a cyclical fashion, for no matter what specific historical circumstances may bring, the genealogical root will always be there. There have even, in fact, arisen forces that tend to ensure that the shape of modern morality will always be repeated. Such, for example, is the ascetic priest, who has as his historical mission to be "the predestined savior, shepherd, and advocate of the sick herd."[29] Here the repetition of this form of nihilism maintains life inside the pattern of slave morality, even though this pattern has reached complete logical emptiness. "The ascetic priest," says Nietzsche, "this apparent enemy of life, the deny-er, precisely he is among the great conserving and yes-creating forces of life."[30] The life the ascetic priest preserves is the passive, accepting, nihilistic one. He provides a moral cloak for the *schlecht-weggekommene*, the "badly developed," who can maintain life only through "passion extirpation."[31] Without the ascetic priest, "the oppressed man would perceive that he stands on the same ground as the oppressor and has no individual privilege, no higher rank than the latter. . . Admitting this belief in morality could be destroyed, the badly developed would no longer have any comfort and perish."[32] In other words, unless one can destroy the means by which people keep themselves in their present slavely moral condition, there will be no possibility of escaping it. Nietzsche goes on to indicate that this process will be accomplished through a means of self-destruction. "The *perishing* [Zugrunde-gehen] presents itself as a *self-condemnation* [Sich-zugrunde-richten], as the instinctive selection of that which *must destroy.*"[33] Already in the Prologue to *Zarathustra*, Nietzsche devotes much attention and praise to those men who wish to "go under."[34]

Earlier in the section of the *Nachlass* cited in the previous paragraph, Nietzsche indicates that eternal return may finally break the hold that European nihilism has on men. It appears that if "the unhealthiest men are infected by" eternal return, it will provoke a "*crisis,*" the value of which is that "it *purifies,*" for it will "extirpate everything that is meaningless and aimless."[35] This appears to mean that eternal return, if "infecting" men in the last stage of slave morality, will unroot the nihilism reigning in them. This would be the "completion of nihilism," which the ascetic priest has been holding at bay. And, for Nietzsche, it represents the "period of the catastrophy," which sees the advent of "a teaching which *filters* men...." [36] I read this to mean that eternal return is a manner of taking a stance toward the past, and thus toward oneself, which will eliminate ("filter") those portions of a man and those men (the *schlecht-weggekommene*— those whose "physiology" has become characterized by nihilism) who manifest nihilism. As an analogy, and only an analogy, I might suggest that eternal return would appear to be a manner of dealing with oneself which would eliminate those portions of one's character which formed an ongoing neurosis. (I repeat that this is, so far, only an analogy. Nietzsche's conception is far more complicated, for his language is physiological. And, in any case, it is difficult to understand what it means to get rid of — eliminate — a portion of one "character.")

If this initial characterization of eternal return is accurate, we can begin to understand why Nietzsche thinks his teaching is so significant. As seen above, Nietzsche holds that all previous teachings and philosophical doctrines have merely confounded the error initiated by the attitudes characterizing the historical Socrates. He writes about his own activity in a manner entirely consonant with the notion of "filtering" expressed above. "It has been my good fortune, after thousands of years of error and confusion, to have recovered the path that leads to a Yes *and* a No. I teach the No to all that makes weak — which exhausts. I teach the Yes to all that makes for strength — which stores up strength, which justifies [*rechtfertigt*] the feeling of strength." [37] It appears, then, that eternal return "filters," that it eliminates certain ways of being in the world (nihilism), and that it consists of both a Yes and a No. This means that *eternal return is selective;* only that which is not filtered out by the "yes and no" will return. Presumably, this would eliminate those things (those memories, that portion of the past and its concretion in and as a person) which are not lived "in eternal return." *Eternal return will not then be a sort of universal affirmation;* such would not be selective. For instance, the I-A (*Ja*-Yes) braying of the ass and the higher men in the last book of *Zarathustra* can only be a caricature of the life of eternal return to which the higher men are attempting to rise. [38] Universal affirmation is not selective, for it affirms everything unconditionally and thus remains in the service of nihilism. As a beast of burden (like the camel), the ass carries all on its back. Its "yes" contrasts with the child's dionysiac Yes which negates, because, as an assertion of a new creation, it destroys a previous world. [39]

It is important here to understand on what scale Nietzsche intends his teaching. For two millennia, men have behaved in a slavely moral manner. Nietzsche calls this the human-all-too-human, and investigates the ramifications in all aspects of human behavior. These ramifications delineate a situation where men appear constitutionally incapable of behaving any way except that in which they do. The judgments about the world characteristic of slave morality hold man a prisoner. Nietzsche interrogates himself on this problem: "But if everything is necessary how can I control my affairs?" And he immediately answers: "Thought and belief are of chief importance; all other factors are in addition to this, which is greater than they. You say that nourishment, place, air, society determine and change you. Rather say, your judgments [*Meinungen* — which can have the sense of legal opinions] do it even more, for these determine your nourishment, place, air, society.   When you incarnate the thought of thoughts, you will be transformed." [40] For "transformed," Nietzsche uses the term *verwandeln,* which also carries the notions of transubstantiation and metamorphosis; indeed the three *Verwandlungen* of the spirit in the first chapter of *Zarathustra* are often translated as "metamorphoses." That Nietzsche uses the same word here seems to indicate that he thinks the transformation effectuated by eternal return is on the order of passing from one kind of "spirit" to another.

In saying that eternal return is selective and transforming of the person who is living by it, I assert that Nietzsche understands eternal return to produce in human beings a transformation sufficiently deep and general as to completely change the nature of *all* interactions men have with themselves, with others, and with the world around them. Men are transfigured. By the selective and filtering effect of some activity, men can flush out some or all of what they have been. Nietzsche's language, for instance, often draws on the digestive (he accuses the Germans of "constipation"), and he is occasionally preoccupied with questions of food and nourishment. The concern is probably more than metaphorical, for the imagery is appropriate. If the human problem is the weight of the past on the present, then men must learn *how* to carry and how to get rid of that which is a block. In the imagery of the chapter "On the Vision and the Riddle," the dwarf must jump down off Zarathustra's back. To move from the human-all-too-human to the overman (i.e., to that which is not "human") means to get rid of and transform all the processes by which men have related to the world over the last twenty-four hundred years, in fact to transform men themselves. [41]

As such, eternal return begins to look like Nietzsche's answer to the "problem of metaphysics" which Kant poses at the beginning of the Preface to the *Critique of Pure Reason*. Kant argues there, as is well known, that "human reason . . in one species of its knowledge . . . is burdened by a question which, as prescribed by the very nature of reason itself, it is not able to ignore, but which, as transcending all its powers, it is also not able to answer." [42] As we saw in Chapter III above, Nietzsche calls activity under this dilemma nihilism, and extends the notion to the entire sphere of action of the slavely moral man. If eternal return can do away with "the problem of metaphysics," it will require at least a transformation in what men mean by reasoning and thinking. In the light of eternal return, the answers sought will be different sorts of answers to different questions; it could hardly be otherwise, for if men remain in the form of discourse analyzed by Kant, they will necessarily eventually be led to the dilemma he notes.

It is not surprising, then, that Nietzsche's thought has often been grouped with "irrationalism." Most interpretations following this vein do not have a very deep understanding of Nietzsche; their naïveté, however, has kept them from finding a reading of Nietzsche so sophisticated as to avoid recognition of the fact that Nietzsche really does want to abolish many of those forms of discourse which we identify as the exercise of reason. This is not, of course, to say that they have read Nietzsche correctly. Crane Brinton's book, which falls in the "naïve category," is much less a book than is Kaufmann's *Nietzsche*. It fastens on the obvious, but does not know what to make of it. Kaufmann, on the other hand, tends to disguise the obvious in Nietzsche and not deal with it. Nietzsche does think that the reasoning characteristic of metaphysics leads to nihilism and should be "extirpated." He does not mean, as later positivists did,

that man should simply *turn away* from that form of thinking. [43]
The scope and import of his genealogical investigations is to assert
that all forms of activity are in the same slave "family." Hence, there
is no such thing as simply "giving up" metaphysics as pointless; one
can no more "give up" metaphysics than successfully deny one's
parentage. The problem is more general, to find a form of behavior
which is not subject to the dilemmas apparently inherent in the
present one.

Nietzsche knows that any new "non-metaphysical" world cannot
simply be just created. One must first learn to deal with and eradicate this one. Therefore men must understand — much more profoundly than ever before — the precise nature of this world. All of
Nietzsche's genealogical study is designed to show that moral valuations are the result of illustions, and that illusions are the necessary
and inevitable characteristics of particular action in the river of
existence. The important question is thus about that which underlies
and informs a particular set of actions, for Nietzsche is not so much
concerned to attack the *validity* of moral valuations as the soil in
which they are rooted. The true significance of Nietzsche's thought is
that it destroys not only by unmasking, but also through the provi-
sion of a new ontological setting. Nietzsche in a late fragment gives
eloquent summary to the need to define this new dynamic atti-
tudinal basis. "All goals are annihilated. Men must give themselves
one. It was an error to suppose that they should have one: they have
given them all to themselves. But *the prerequisites* for all earlier goals
are annihilated. Science shows the river, but not the goal. It does,
however, set the preconditions [*Voraussetzungen*] to which the new
goal must respond." [44] Nietzsche, as we shall see, sees his task to be
the establishment of new preconditions which will make the new
goal possible.

The Question of Breeding

The contention that Nietzsche is trying to reground the manner in
which men relate to each other, and to the world, forces us to go
further, into territory which recent work on Nietzsche has generally
avoided. Nietzsche is not (just) talking about a manner of thinking;
since he thinks that men have been changed in their nature by slave

morality, they will also have to be changed if they are to become overmen. It is the most "natural" thing in the world to be slavely moral; indeed, there appears to be nothing else. It will have to appear equally "natural" to be an overman. Hence, I am forced to take very seriously all those bothersome statements which most modern scholars of Nietzsche have simply left out of their analysis in a well-meant reaction to the distortions of the Nazis. The talk about "breeding" and "race" *is* important in Nietzsche's thought, and it simply won't do to pile up the quotations which say nice things about the Jews and nasty ones about the Germans. Nietzsche *is* talking about *developing* men who are not subject to the "human-all-too-human." He repeatedly uses the word *züchten,* which means to breed, raise, rear, grow or cultivate, a word normally used in connection with animals or plants. After leaving Basel, he conspicuously stops using *erziehen,* which has connotations of "bring up" and "educate."

These remarks permit a considerable modification of the usual opinion that Nietzsche was some sort of Lamarckian. He is saying that the effect of constantly repeating an action (of its being "in eternal return") can produce a change in the individual which is only "psychological," not just "second nature" or habit, but rather eventually becomes one's "real" nature, and in so doing expels the "nature" that was present before. In a passage I have had opportunity to cite before, but which now presents itself for the first time in a clear light, Nietzsche writes:

. . . As we are merely the resultant of previous generations, we are also the resultant of their errors, passions, and mistakes, indeed of their crimes. It is not possible to completely free oneself from this chain. Though we condemn the errors and hold ourselves to be free of them, we have not laid aside the fact that we spring from them. . . . We arrive at best at a conflict between our innate, inherited nature and our knowledge, as well as a struggle of a new strong growth against that which has been from the past cultivated and inherited; we plant a new form of life, a new instinct, a second nature which withers the first. It is an attempt to give oneself a posteriori a past from which one might have sprung, as against that from which one does spring — always a dangerous attempt, because it is so difficult to find a limit to the denial of the past, and because the second nature is generally weaker than the first. We stop too often at knowing the good without doing it, because we also know the better but cannot do it. But here and there the victory is achieved and a special conciliation attained by the combatants . . . : to know that this first nature — it, too — was once a second nature and that every conquering second nature becomes a first.[45]

Already in this early essay Nietzsche takes up the concerns that remain central to the rest of his activity. In the past, men *have* changed radically: a number of forms of life have been possible, different from each other even in their most fundamental traits. Men appear to have no way to consciously free themselves from what they have been. Yet, it appears now that they must, for the triumph of slave morality has become well-nigh total. Nietzsche's task is to find a doctrine that replaces nihilism, now man's "first nature," with another "first nature," and to transfigure the "human" into the "over-human."

These considerations allow me to express my variance with the subtle and seductive interpretation of Martin Heidegger and the related one of Gilles Deleuze. The understanding of Heidegger is complex and complicated: complex, because his thought uses many terms which do not always carry an assured philosophical resonance; complicated, because it is a hallmark of Heideggerian interpretation that one should not necessarily be able to clearly separate the interpreter from the interpreted. For Heidegger, the philosophical meaning of a piece of criticism and interpretation must *emerge out* of the interaction of the writer and his subject — it cannot be stated. [46]

I once had some sympathies for this approach; much less now; in any case, this is not the place to elaborate on it. [47] However, it seems to me that in the case of his understanding of Nietzsche, Heidegger makes several important mistakes that keep him from recognizing what Nietzsche is saying to him. His interpretation [48] seems to contain the following points. (1) The experience of truth can be other than historical (i.e., one can "escape" metaphysics by "understanding" the *Grund* of *Sein,* p. 257). (2) The will to power culminates in eternal return (p. 10) which is still historical and metaphysical in kind (p. 9). (3) Nietzsche's thought, even though the "last stage of metaphysics," is still metaphysical in character, and is a metaphysics of pure subjectivity (p. 199). It would then follow that Heidegger must logically conclude that for Nietzsche there can be no change in basic ontology (no historical ontological relativity, cf. p. 259). He is thus led logically to conclude, for instance, that Nietzsche's "racial" thinking must be metaphysical and not biological in nature (p. 309).

I have noted in the previous chapter some important errors in

Heidegger's reading. I find no reason here to set out a full exposition of the differences between my understanding and his. That we share some points of understanding should also be apparent. For instance, Heidegger finds, as I do, that eternal return is not Heraclitean and cannot be a cyclical concept (pp. 11-12). However, the fact that he leaves Nietzsche fully in, if as the culmination of, the *philosophia perennis*[49] means that I must reject his overall understanding. Put bluntly: by trying to reserve for himself the so-called honor of being the first man to "escape" metaphysics, Heidegger is forced to ignore the fact that Nietzsche fully believed that his doctrine would make men really different — not human-all-too-human. Nietzsche's doctrine does admit of a coherent exposition, in Nietzsche's terms, as I have attempted to show. This understanding does, however, imply that distinctions between the biological and the "metaphysical," or more properly, the philosophical, such as Heidegger would have Nietzsche make, are, in fact, not made by Nietzsche. In no way could Heidegger's Nietzsche permit the extreme and radical rejection of the mind-body dualism which Nietzsche seems in fact to have made.

Gilles Deleuze' interpretation[50] I find even more brilliant than Heidegger's. He emphasizes strongly (if somewhat in *la manière des grandes écoles*) the noncyclical nature of eternal return and attempts to relate it to other aspects of Nietzsche's thought (in particular the views on nihilism). He, however, shares with Heidegger the notion that the will to power has something directly to do with eternal return. He and Heidegger seem to see the will to power as *physis,* the dynamic force leading to eternal return. As far as can be determined, there is no direct textual evidence for this. As we have seen, Nietzsche never calls the will to power *physis,* but rather sees it as *pathos,* as a sequence of states of affairs. The will to power seems to be the principle of a life; eternal return, however, is a *doctrine.* Almost never does Nietzsche speak of them in the same text, nor does he address them to the same audience. But Deleuze is led to affirm that eternal return produces a certain kind of orientation toward the world. He feels that, when coupled with the highest stage of nihilism, eternal return produces an "active" state of existence by a sort of "negation of the negation."[51]

My analysis tends to indicate that it works the other way around: a certain form of orientation produces eternal return. This raises far more difficult problems for putting the doctrine into practice. If the process contains no inward logic which makes it happen in and of itself, how is one to arrive at the state of eternal return? Why will men not simply continue to act in the repetition of their present mode of acting; Nietzsche identifies in *The Antichrist* some "families, tribes, or peoples" who have fortunately and accidentally managed this feat. [52] Among them is, obviously, Greece. The problem for contemporary times, however, is so great and the onslaught of nihilism and decadence so overwhelming that man can no longer depend on accidents and lucky hits. Now, and in opposition to the Greeks, man must "make real by plan what happened before by accident." [53] This makes the task much more difficult and Nietzsche queries of those men who must do this: "How can such a man think of eternal return?" [54]

Signs of Eternal Return:
The Failures of the Higher Men

I said above that eternal return is selective, that it allows us to eradicate the history which leads to present "nature" and which pushes us toward nihilism and, finally, that eternal return cannot operate unless one deals with the world in a certain way. The last contention is probably key; until now, I have had to leave it abstract and have only been able to note that the shepherd appears "transfigured," or that Zarathustra still fails to be able to summon eternal return. I turn here, then, to a consideration of exactly what it means to stand in eternal return. What is it that men must, as Nietzsche significantly says, "learn, practice, and translate into flesh and reality, and even into the commonplace." [55] What sort of beings must we be to experience ourselves and the world in a manner made new by the doctrine of eternal return?

In Book Four of *Zarathustra*, we meet examples of men who, despite their efforts, have been unable to live in eternal return. They are the "higher men," examples of the highest types humanity has yet evolved, and all would-be followers of Zarathustra. Notwithstanding all their discipleship, or perhaps because of it, these men are not on the path to *Übermenschlichkeit.* [56] Zarathustra tells them: "When you reach your goal, when you jump off your horse — on your very *height,* you higher men, you will stumble." [57] The failings in these men are such that they will *never* be able to become overmen, for their will to power maintains them ineluctably in the world of the human.

Nietzsche gives a fairly specific account of these failings, which serves as a happy focal point for an investigation of those traits one would have to have to live in eternal return. The higher men themselves have an inkling of their failures. Nietzsche notes that they feel a need for a constant and unselective affirmation, a yea-saying to everything. They celebrate this in their worship of the ass, "the animal," Zarathustra remarks, "with long ears who only says Yes and never says No. Has he not created the world in his own image, namely as stupid as possible?" [58] The ass is to be contrasted to those creatures who have small, discriminating ears, such as Ariadne, into whose ear Dionysos can whisper the secret of eternal return. [59] The path to eternal return, it appears, is labyrinthian and never direct. It is only available to those who are able to deny as well as affirm. If one tries to say "yes" to everything, as do the higher men, one lacks certain abilities, which Nietzsche seems to hold as central to and descriptive of the world of eternal return. These are spelled out in the chapter "On the Higher Man" as the ability to play and gamble (*spielen*), the ability to laugh, and the ability to dance. [60] These are abilities that appear to make it possible to begin the process of learning, practicing, internalization, and transformation which is characteristic of eternal return. Unless one can do these, nothing else is possible.

All of these abilities involve particular attitudes toward the world and a particular way of dealing with oneself, with others, and with the environment. Nietzsche selects them as exemplary of the failures of the higher men because, I believe, they portray a mode of existence different from the "normal," yet generally available to the reader who has experienced them and is able to understand the importance of his or her experience.

Play, the first of these activities, is a form of behavior in which a goal is of little or no importance. The German *spielen* carries with it denotations even more extensive than those accompanying the English "play." Not only does it signify "playing" and "play-acting," but it is also used where an English speaker would say "gambling." With this activity, Nietzsche wants to bring back an attitude he had found central to Heraclitus. What Heraclitus saw, "the teaching of *the law in becoming and play in necessity* must be seen from now on in all eternity. He raised the curtain on this greatest of all possible dramas." [61] For Heraclitus, the world was the gaming table of the divine world-child. It is the affirmation of the accidental necessities of such gaming that attracts Nietzsche. He writes in *Zarathustra:* "If I ever played dice with gods at gods' tables . . . — for the earth is a table for the gods and trembles with creative new words and god-throws: Oh, how should I not lust after eternity. . . ." [62] Gaming combines in one activity the result *created* by the throw, the *accident* of that result, and the *necessity* of the conditions that make the throw possible.

Playing is sufficiently important to Nietzsche that he makes it the characteristic of the self-affirming child who is the final metamorphosis of the spirit in the beginning of *Zarathustra.* [63] What attracts Nietzsche, I believe, is the fact that games and gaming are only made possible by necessities, yet, while playing, one does not experience the necessities as constraint. They are rather the condition of freedom which makes the game possible. For instance, one simply would not know what to say to a chess player who (seriously) claimed to be oppressed by the rule that "bishops move on the diagonals." This and other necessities make chess possible. Nietzsche selects dice as an example because while there is the experience of chance as to what comes up, one would not want to claim at the same time that there was not a necessity to the throw.

In play, then, one's behavior is an affirmation of those rules which, in their necessity, make possible that one plays. Nietzsche claims, for instance, that Zarathustra's kingdom is that of chance, [64] an affirmation of that which happens to be Zarathustra. It is as if in dice one were what one plays, and, if one plays oneself correctly there can be no cause for recrimination, either at the external world (which is "bad conscience") or at oneself (*ressentiment*). The higher men refuse to affirm what they play and seek a reason for failure, or feel ashamed. Nietzsche writes: "Shy, ashamed, like a tiger whose leap has failed: thus I have often seen you slink aside, you higher men. A throw failed you. But you dice-throwers, what does it matter? You have not learned to gamble and jest as one must gamble and jest. Do we not always sit at a big gambling table and jesting table? And, if something great has failed you, does it follow that you yourselves are failures, does it follow that man himself is a failure?" [65] Though they *appear* to play, the higher men do not know how; the game remains a means for them in their misbegotten attempt to attain *Übermenschlichkeit*.

The higher men do not realize that since they fail in their throw, it *does* follow that man is a failure. Instead of looking for reasons, Nietzsche thinks then that they should accept that they are also *schlecht-weggekommene* and wish to perish. "I love him," writes Nietzsche, "who is abashed when the dice fall to make his fortune and asks, 'Am I then a crooked gambler [*falscher Spieler*]?' For he wants to perish." [66] Instead of going under, the higher men seek to stay alive; they are evil, slavely moral players who seek to trap the dice in a web of probability and to profit from an infinite series of chances. This is a very different attitude from that which accepts that one wins because one has the right to win. The other stance is *amor fati,* [67] the love of necessity, which recognizes that perhaps one is entitled *only* to go under. The acceptance of oneself in eternity may require that one perish; above all, Nietzsche says, don't wait for your chance. Statistics are not the path of eternal return.

In *Beyond Good and Evil,* Nietzsche can then refer to a final stage which closes out morality, the *ausser-moralisch,* in which matters will not be judged by their effects, nor their intentions, but rather when "the decisive value of an action lies precisely in what is *unintentional* to it." [68] In such a situation, character would once again be destiny, much as it had been for Aeschylus. In games, too, the intentions of the players (as long as they are playing the game) are of little importance. For instance, excuses and the attendant concept of responsibility do not often occur in a game. Should one kick the ball over the goal in soccer, the plea that "I did not intend to" is not really appropriate; on the other hand, the notion of fault is equally out of place. The game is then a capsule summary for Nietzsche of a life beyond good and evil, beyond utility and the moral antinomies which "normally" shape existence. In a game, properly played, one truly "wills one's *own* will." [69]

Situations such as gaming imply a perfect union between obligation and desire, between what one has to do (play this game) and what one wants to do (play the game). This resembles what Kant thought would be the case with a being both perfectly rational and perfectly moral. Kant, characteristically, found such a life to be impossible; Nietzsche hopes to make one possible. For both men, however, the perfect unity characterizing such a being is one that knows no moral *problems,* that eliminates choice between moral alternatives. The world cannot present (moral) problems, when whatever one might and can do is appropriate. [70] In such cases, one is reminded, as Nietzsche writes in *The Gay Science,* "of the improvising masters of the musical art, to whom even the listeners would fain ascribe a divine *infallibility* of the hand, notwithstanding that they now and then make a mistake as every mortal is liable to do. But they are skilled and inventive, and always ready in a moment to arrange into the structure of the score the most accidental tone. . . . And animate the accident with a fine meaning and soul." [71]

Laughter is the second attitude that leads to eternal return and that the higher men lack. We can appreciate here the leap that has occurred since the world of the *Iliad.* There Achilles accuses Apollo of gaming with him and is furious over it. [72] Nietzsche would have had him laugh. Such laughter, though, was not possible in the shame culture of Homeric Greece. Achilles had been shamed by Apollo and had no means to deal with it, for laughter implies a nobility that transcends the bounds of the heroic.

From *The Birth of Tragedy* to the problems of the higher men, Nietzsche sows his work with affirmations of the necessity of laughter. At the moment of transfiguration which leads to eternal return, the shepherd laughs "not like a man." Man must "learn to laugh," [73] Nietzsche constantly asserts. And laughter will be a characteristic of the transfigured man; a sign of the final approach of eternal return to Zarathustra is the "laughing lion." [74] For Nietzsche, not to laugh is in the end to revere; [75] to revere is to take as permanently deserving of reverence that which is at best transitory. Nietzsche reproaches the higher men for their seriousness: ". . . learn to laugh at yourselves as one must laugh! You higher men, *how much is still possible.*" [76] The higher men do *attempt* to laugh. The magician's *Nur Narr! Nur Dichter!* is a poetically successful though ontologically clumsy attempt at self-mockery, which immediately follows Zarathustra's command to laugh. It is possible to fail in laughter — to laugh in the wrong manner — just as it is possible to game wrongly.

Laughter is not, however, the simple denial of the present situation. It is, if done properly, the sign of a different consciousness, of an existence grounded on some other basis than that which is being laughed at. Thus, the higher men must learn to laugh at themselves.

Laughter is the means by which the suffering in the world is transformed into joy. Zarathustra must "laugh angrily" at himself *before* he realizes that he has overcome the last obstacle to eternal return: pity.

If laughter *transforms* suffering and nausea into joy, it is also symbolic of the affirmation of this joy. Laughter is will to power in that the same basic impulse takes on a plurality of forms on a plurality of occasions. Each laugher affirms a particular instance, but in so doing affirms the power of laughter and ontological height of the laugher. Laughter, as an overcoming of pity, is the means by which the whole question of the past is transformed. It allows men to forget that the whole question of guilt was ever asked. Without the past, there can be no guilt, for guilt implies the existence of the past independent of the actor. Laughter is a sign that the past is willed and is thus contained in the willing individual; it therefore returns as he acts. As in tragedy, this means that the laugher is *by his existence* affirming the responsibility for his acts. Laughter gives men an existence that does not ask the questions of transcendent guilt.

Upon the overcoming of the nauseating version of eternal return, the shepherd is transformed, laughs, and breaks into *dance.* The inability to dance is the third failure of the higher men, for the dance is the symbol of the joyful wisdom: it is that which can only be expressed in activity, but which nevertheless comes welling up out of a conscious innocence. [77]

Some examination of dance as an activity makes clear what Nietzsche was getting at and further fills in the characteristics of eternal return. "Only in the dance," Nietzsche writes, "do I know how to speak the image of the highest things." [78] For Nietzsche, to dance is to signify triumph over the spirit of gravity and over the spirit of *ressentiment.* [79] What seems important to Nietzsche is that dance is a learned activity in the sense that one learns to do all the steps making up a dance, but that, even though learned, it is not thereby reflective. Once one has learned how to do a *tour jêté*, one can do it without a feeling of difficulty or compulsion — almost, I might say, "naturally." As a whole a dance is a plurality, or, as Nietzsche notes in a more exalted language during the time he was figuring these ideas out for the writing of *Zarathustra,* it is the "*impression* upon becoming of the character of being." [80] As with music or a language, a dance is a process, learned, yet nonetheless natural, which appears as a whole.

In dance, then, the dancer manifests in a conscious fashion that which is an acquired instinct. The dance is "learned, practiced, translated into flesh and reality and even into common sense." It is not that Nietzsche wants people to punctuate their walks with occasional *entre-chats* (though we do speak approvingly of "jumping for joy"); he rather chooses dance as a sign of the failure of the higher men to learn a new and complicated form of activity so well that they feel no compulsion, and can do it "naturally." As T. S. Eliot put it some twenty-five years later from a somewhat more Anglican vein:

> The inner freedom from practical desire,
> The release from action and suffering, release from the inner
> And the outer compulsion, yet surrounded
> By a grace of sense. . . . [81]

These reflections incidentally enforce a further modification in the normal interpretation that Nietzsche is some sort of Lamarckian and believes in the inheritance of acquired characteristics. There certainly *is* a manner in which Nietzsche wants to say that the more one practices new forms of activity, the more natural and commonplace the artificially acquired traits become. [82] It is not really important to settle the problem as to whether or not they can be genetically inherited. As is often the case, there is some truth in the designation (here as Lamarckian) given Nietzsche; as usual, the understanding misses its mark.

Eternal Return: A Simple Case

These concepts — playing, laughing, dancing — are highly metaphorical and condensed in resonance. It must be understood, though, that while Nietzsche intends them as metaphors and wishes the reader to be carried back and forth between two worlds, one of which may be familiar, the other rich and strange, he also intends them as descriptive of a particular orientation toward the world. It should therefore be possible to give a description of a person in this state, a state of eternal return. Before moving to Nietzsche's discussion of the historical and social consequences of eternal return, I will essay a description which ties these notions together in an available manner.

In doing so, I must immediately enter a caveat. The example of eternal return that follows is as simple as it can be. It is an example of only a limited activity, not a whole life, where behavior is like that which Nietzsche describes as subject to eternal return. There is the danger that the reader assume that this is "all" that eternal return means. I shall attempt to dissuade the reader from this position as I go along, but my experience has often been that this made no difference.

Since eternal return involves the return of specific forms of life, it cannot be investigated in general. An understanding, though, may be gained from the description of a particular activity. I pick here skiing. In doing so I recognize two things. In the first place, skiing is obviously a limited portion of a human life. It does not imply the sort of complete transformation that Nietzsche was trying to bring about. It does, however, seem to me probable that Nietzsche accepts the possibility of eternal return for a particular portion of a person's life, as long as, during the time the person is engaged in that activity, the activity can or does encompass all of the person's attention. Such is true of skiing, as it is of many other activities. [83] Secondly, it is probable that this discussion will be fully meaningful only to the degree that the reader skis, or is able to substitute a similar activity of his own. Nietzsche notes that "one only understands these things theoretically when they have been achieved in practice." [84] Unless the reader has experienced the sense of freedom and power and the lack of constraint attained when skiing well, or when in more complicated situations, such as playing in a string quartet or making love, the following description may remain in part a mystery.

In skiing, one affirms skills that one has acquired. However, the affirmation of these skills is not reflexive: one does not have to *think* to do a parallel christiania. In fact, to the degree that my parallels are still reflexive, the chances of their execution are diminished. Furthermore, the easier my turns come, the more difficult can be the slope I undertake (and the more likely I will be to undertake them.) If a fall, in this case, it will be because I have made a mistake; that is, I have undertaken something I should not have, or need not have. [85] In this case, however, it is wrong to say, as slave-skiing-morality would have it, either that "something tripped me up," that is, that something inevitable happened, or that I did something not really my fault, for example, "caught an edge." Both of these explanations are possible, but they are not about skiing; they remove the process of skiing from me and ascribe my problems to an outside agency. There is a way in which it makes sense to say that a really good skier gets down anything that is a ski slope. In a happier subcase of having made a mistake, I may also fall, in that I tried to do something I am not capable of. In this case, I may eventually come to master the slope; if I cannot, I should be content with that, or perhaps realize that skiing is not what I am cut out for. "My teaching says," writes Nietzsche, "live such that you must wish to so live again. . . . To whom striving gives the highest feeling [*Gefühl*], let him strive; to whom peace gives the highest feeling, let him be peaceful; to whom ordering, following, obedience give the highest feeling, let him obey. May he only *become conscious* about that which gives him the highest feeling, and not balk at any means. It is a matter of *eternity*. . . ." [86] When I ski, that portion of me which lets me ski "naturally," without reflection, is constantly being actualized. Yet my ability to ski, now so "natural," is an acquired characteristic, which I am no more capable of forgetting than I am capable of not knowing how to ride a bicycle. In my skiing, I have, then, solved the problem that Nietzsche sets as entirely new, "just dawning on the human eye and hardly yet recognizable: *to embody knowledge within ourselves and make it instinctive.*" [87] In a note from the period of *Morgenröte*, Nietzsche seems even to indicate that the change is neurophysiological: "All which has been organized in the nerves lives on in them." (Biochemically, this is, of course, pure hypothesis and speculation. It may not be entirely without reality, however. See note 45 above.)

When I have thus learned to ski, in a certain manner I have also conquered time. That portion of my life which was not-skiing and wanting-to-ski no longer affects me and has been completely eradicated. I am not capable of returning to that form of existence; my skiing ability is now always with me, and will appear whenever I ski. So Wagner was to "make art become natural." [88] As Nietzsche writes, my "new life . . . has slain [my previous life] ; (I) *do not require it anymore,* and now it breaks down of its own accord." [89] For Nietzsche, if an activity of a life is in eternal return, all that might affect this activity or life adversely is destroyed. For instance, when I have learned how to ride a bicycle (or to ski), to go again to the situation of not being able to ride a bicycle will probably require more effort than the acquisition of the ability to ride, and may be impossible. It is, I believe, the situation of having learned how to ride a bicycle and no longer being the sort of person who cannot ride a bicycle, which Nietzsche characterizes in *Morgenröte* as "conscious innocence."

Finally, what one has learned and incarnated in becoming a person-who-can-ski will be manifest in the entire activity for which it is appropriate. As Zarathustra notes: "That which you called world, that must be created first by you: it must itself become your reason, your picture [*Bild*], your will, your love."[90] And thus one will call this situation good. "*Each fundamental character trait* that lies at the bottom of *every* occurrence and finds expression in every occurrence must, if recognized by the individual as *his* fundamental character trait, drive every individual to triumphantly call each instance of the whole existence [*des allgemeinen Daseins*] good. It would in fact come down to this: one happily feels this fundamental character trait in oneself as good and worthwhile, with pleasure."[91] Many of our common expressions carry out the image that Nietzsche conveys here. We say easily, "I was skiing way above my head — that's why I fell." Here we are much like those who wish to go under, for even if we don't fall when skiing "above our head," we know that we are not entitled to that run. In fact, we often feel, I think, a *frisson* of childish pleasure at having gotten away with something. Nietzsche would deny us this by the above citation: we must know that what we are and do shall pervade every part of our activity.

In skiing-eternal return, then, a learned process is constantly and unreflexively manifesting itself in the particular present that is skiing. It is not surprising that Nietzsche notes that there have been homologues to eternal return in the past. Indeed, there are several occasions in history when the immediate life of a man was colored by the constant pressure of a particular dominant notion. For instance, the "prospect of damnation" played such a role in making men examine their acts in terms of something other than the moment.[92] The possibility of eternal damnation is, for Nietzsche, a thought similar to eternal return. That it was a false thought and did not liberate men from their past, is, of course, true. But the effect of this erroneous thought is, in Nietzsche's eyes, still staggering. "Let us examine," he writes, "how the thought that something recurs [*sich etwas wiederholt*] has worked until now (the year, for example, or periodic illness, waking and sleeping, etc. . . .). Even when the coming back again is only a possibility it can stagger and reform us. . . ." [93] It is worth noting here that Nietzsche contrasts his position with this one; for him, living in eternal return is not to function as a simple "possibility," but only as a reality. Nor is his position the *folie circulaire* referred to in *Ecce Homo*. [94] Nietzsche is talking of a life informed by entirely new tones, different in kind from the old ones. I should think it a change, on a vast scale, analogous perhaps to that one feels the first time one knows one is able to ride a bicycle or do a parallel christiania, but whereafter there is, so to speak, a different era. As Nietzsche writes: "From the moment on, when this thought is there, all colors are changed and there is a new history." [95]

Eternal Return and the Times to Come

I have picked a very limited example of an activity that can occur in something like what Nietzsche means by eternal return. In skiing, or riding a bicycle, or indeed, in playing in a string quartet or making love, though these last two examples involve other people and are thus more complicated, one learns to do a very complicated set of actions perfectly well, such that these actions come into play whenever it is appropriate for them to. Once the activity is fully made part of a person, he or she is incapable of not being that sort of person. I, for instance, am incapable of *not being able* to ride a bicycle; whenever I am on a bicycle, the ability to ride naturally comes back and manifests itself. It is true, of course, that riding a bicycle or skiing occupy only a portion of my life. If, however, it should be my whole life, or, as Nietzsche says, my "highest feeling," then everything I did would stand in eternal return and in the joy that comes in feeling no discontinuity between myself and the world in which I act. (Think here of what it is like to ski well, or play an instrument well.)

I realize that my focus on examples such as skiing may prove misleading: as skills, they do not apparently involve a transformation of the whole person. Nietzsche, however, certainly thinks the doctrine of eternal return to have consequences beyond those in a portion of an individual. He writes in a late note: "The coming history: this thought will always conquer more — and those who do not believe in it must eventually, due to their nature [*ihrer Natur nach*] , *die out.* Only he who holds his existence [*Dasein*] capable of eternal return will remain [*bleibt übrig*] ; among such, however, conditions such as no utopian yet has imagined are possible." [96] Eternal return then will provide a doctrine that can eventually inform all existence, much in the way that Socratic Christianity dominates at present. Though Nietzsche gives very little extended discussion of what he has in mind, it is possible to say a bit about the new transvaluation of values.

For the last twenty-four hundred years, Nietzsche says, men have incarnated an error. [97] They have persuaded themselves of the "truth" of the self-destructive illusions of slave morality and have lived them out. We saw in previous chapters how the logic of the genealogy of slave morality leads men inexorably to the vicious circle of nihilism. One might say that the last (slavely moral) men are their own fetishes, their own prisoners in their own errors.

To break out from the prison of our present being is both difficult and dangerous. Nietzsche speaks often of the attractions that his doctrine will have for men and is afraid that men will seize upon it as justification for behavior to which they are not entitled. "Are you prepared?" he demands in a late note. "You must have lived through every degree of skepticism and have desiringly bathed in ice-cold streams — otherwise you have no right to this thought. I must *defend* myself against the easy-to-believe and the enthusiasts." [98] Nietzsche's notes from this period are filled both with his conviction that his doctrine should be spread throughout the world and with his fear of the danger that mankind will not be sufficiently prepared to be able to incorporate the new teaching.

His reason is cautiousness: the soil must be prepared. Success for the doctrine of eternal return, such that it becomes "a great tree, which overshadows all of coming humanity," [99] will require careful husbandry over a long period. Whereas, in the past, some men and peoples may have lived as overmen, they attained it through lucky and only partially successful circumstances, which Nietzsche does not think sufficient for the future. He writes that "success in individual cases is constantly encountered in the most widely different places and cultures: here we really do find a higher type which, in relation to mankind as a whole, is a kind of overman. Such fortunate accidents of great success were always possible and will perhaps always be possible. And even entire families, tribes, peoples can occasionally represent such a bull's-eye." [100] The Greeks were such a success. For the future, however, we can no longer rely on accidents; instead, and this is the source of Nietzsche's concern with "breeding" and "extirpation," the overman must be "bred, willed, and attained" through the doctrine of eternal return. [101]

Conditions must be created such that the doctrine can "sink in slowly," [102] failing which there will be "thirty years *Gloria*, with drums and fifes, and then thirty years of grave-digging." [103] It is true, Nietzsche writes, that the democratization of civilization, which he spends so much time diagnosing in *On the Genealogy of Morals* and *The Antichrist*, makes it possible for the overman to "maintain and develop himself the most easily." [104] But overmen can only exist initially in conjunction with a philosophical ruling class [105] addressing itself to the central political task, without which nothing else will be possible. "The question and at the same time the task is approaching with hesitation, as terrible as fate, but nevertheless inevitable." Nietzsche warns: "How shall the earth as a whole be ruled? And to what end shall man as a whole — no longer as a people or a race — be reared and trained?" [106]

The task of the preparation for the doctrine of eternal return is of central concern to Nietzsche. In a note from 1885, he writes: "Basic idea: the new values must first be created — we shall not be *spared* that! The philosopher must be a lawgiver to us. New types. (As earlier the highest types (e.g., Greeks) were bred: this type of 'accident' to be willed consciously.)" [107] We seem to be in a situation where nothing holds mankind back: there is a danger of a total chaos, in which any and all voices will speak, and none be heard. Nietzsche is then concerned that the earth be prepared for his doctrine, so that he be not misinterpreted. Much as for Zarathustra, Nietzsche's initial problem is to develop an audience able to hear what he says.

To this extent, Nietzsche occasionally refers to the "lords of the earth," who seem to be a dominating and legislative class, and whose role it is to create the conditions that will make meaningful discourse and life possible again on the earth. The "lords of the earth" will have to discover "a whole host of transitory and deceptive measures . . . to this end: slowly and cautiously to liberate . . . a whole host of slandered instincts. . . ." [108] There is no doubt that Nietzsche thinks that the function of this political class will be to reshape what it means to be human.

From now on, there will be more favorable conditions for more comprehensive forms of domination, whose like has never yet existed. And this is not even the most important thing; it is rather the development of the possibility of international species-unions [Geschlechts-Verbänden] which will set themselves the task of rearing a new master race [Herren-Rasse], the future "lords of the earth"; — a vast new aristocracy, based on the most severe self-legislation, in which the will of the philosophical men of power and the artist-tyrants will be given permanence [Dauer] over millennia; — a higher kind of men who . . . will work on "men" themselves as artists. Enough, the time comes, in which one will have to change all one knows about politics. [109]

To bring about this new transfigured world, and put into practice the doctrine of eternal return, will require a change in "all one knows about politics." By this Nietzsche seems to mean that in the past, politics was, as was the case in Greece, an often fearful agon of equals inside an unquestioned arena. Men fought and competed for advantage and superiority. They did not, however, fight to define *what* would make a man superior or give him advantage. In previous politics, Nietzsche is saying, men fought and cooperated to gain more of what there was to get; it is, however, presumed that men knew what they were fighting about. The breakdown of the common world, which Nietzsche sees as a necessary characteristic of modern times, [110] means that men increasingly have no idea of what counts to be fought for. Hence, the new idea of politics must be war to *say what will count,* what the standards by which men will measure themselves shall be. This is politics to *define* the world, not to gain control of a portion of it. (On a far lesser scale, since both the United States and the Soviet Union emerge from a common tradition, Nietzsche would think that there is a right track in the naïve belief that "we are fighting with the communists — or capitalists — to see who will run the world.")

If nihilism was a form of behavior in which one could never rest content with a conclusion, where, as Wittgenstein said, one could not stop philosophizing, the modern world is for Nietzsche a world in which one cannot possibly be content. The will to create a world where on would be, and know, who one is, leads Nietzsche, as it does Max Weber, to occasionally express admiration for the caste system of India. However, he thinks it to be so simplistic a system as to be unworkable ("a school for stupefaction," in which is lacking "nature, technology, history, art, science . . ." [111]). The world which must be made for Europeans and eventually for all men ("mankind wants to become one") must take its own past into account. The eradication of the forms of behavior which men have inherited from Socrates and Christ and which form the basis of Western nihilism does for Nietzsche, require the eradication of what we have meant by the moral point of view. Nietzsche finds that at this time in history, the conjoining of morality and war (the "war of spirits" above) is not only dangerous, but leads nowhere except to insanity. As Stanley Cavell has remarked: "Someday, if there is a someday, we will have to learn that evil thinks of itself as good, that it could not have made such progress in the world unless people planned and performed it in all conscience." [112] One must only add to this that when men lose the ability to call anything good or evil, then *all* must appear, as it does to the higher men, worthy of affirmation.

To the nihilism of universal affirmation, a world taught by the doctrine of eternal return provides an alternative, not a necessary or likely one, nor an immediately available position, but only an alternative. Nietzsche hopes that men will begin to think of life as "an experiment of the thinker — and not as a duty, not a fatality, not a deceit." [113] In such a tentative, the whole science of ethics which evolves from Socrates and which Nietzsche characterizes as "knowledge in service to life" will become simply unnecessary. Such men will not need knowledge to shore up their life; rather, for them, "life is a means to knowledge." They will uncover, or recover themselves, and, as in a game, not have to ask "What should I do?" as a moral question.

Nietzsche, in fact, thinks that his own life has proceeded along such lines. Only that which the language of his life has made knowledge, exists and survives. The rest, the mistakes and the past which might otherwise weigh upon his life, is no more. On his birthday in 1888 he writes a passage to this effect, which stands as epigraph to his autobiography, *Ecce Homo:* "On this perfect day, when everything ripens and not only the grape becomes brown, the eye of the sun just fell on my life; I saw backward, I looked forward,

I never saw so many and so good things at once. It was not in vain that I buried my forty-fourth year today, I had the right to bury it; what was life in it is saved, is immortal. . . . How could I fail to be grateful to my whole life? And so I tell my life to myself." [114]

This is a life beyond good and evil, which has no need of moral problems, where one does what one is, means what one says, where character is destiny. But this is not a claim by Nietzsche that anyone can do anything one wants to, or that morality is simply pablum for the weak. Men who live in eternal return are entitled to live beyond morality. Not anyone can at any time do this, however: one cannot claim to live beyond morality just because one wants to. The transfiguration required is slow and difficult and requires much effort. [115]

Nietzsche's Political Predicament

In the *Republic,* Plato writes of a man who has attained the blessings of philosophy. Such a man, remarks Plato, may be compared to "a man who has fallen in among wild beasts — he will not join the wickedness of his fellows, but neither is he able to singly resist all their fierce natures, . . . and therefore he goes his own way, . . . and will have done a great work before he departs; . . . but not the greatest, unless he finds a state which is suitable for him; for in a state suitable for him, he will have a larger growth and be the savior of his country as well as of himself." [116] At the end of his life in sanity, Nietzsche writes to his old friend and mentor Jacob Burckhardt that he is having the top leadership of Germany done away with; a few days earlier, he had written August Strindberg that he has ordered "a convocation of princes in Rome" and means "to have the young emperor shot." Presumably, these political leaders are those he identifies as keeping him from taking over Europe to prepare the way for the doctrine of eternal return. I have mentioned that to extend the description of eternal return beyond the range of some portions of an individual's life to a whole life, and from there to interpersonal relations and the world is so complex as to defy, I suspect, all attempts. Nietzsche certainly feels it to be necessary, though. The Dionysos he celebrates throughout his life is also "the type of the lawgiver." And, at the very end, he hopes that war will not be necessary, for "there are still other ways to bring physiology to honor [*die Physiologie zu Ehren zu bringen*] besides military hospitals. . . . Well and good, *very* good in fact: after the old god is abolished, I am ready, *to rule the world.*" [117]

There was to be no state for Nietzsche, which is not really surprising; but to call this demented or megalomaniacal misses the point. If, in annihilating the Hohenzollern, Nietzsche claims to be annihilating lies, [118] it is because he understands that changing ideas is, in the end, not possible without changing the lives and habits and indeed the world in which one lives. This theme runs through all of Nietzsche: our moral behavior, our language, our epistemology, our institutions, religions, and political practices are of a loose piece. No more for Nietzsche than for Marx could one make a radical change of opinion without making a change in the *nature* of men, in their lives and world. "Previous philosophers have merely interpreted the world; the problem, however, is to change it," wrote Marx in the last of the *Theses on Feuerbach.* I read this in the same light as the citation of Wittgenstein which serves as an epigraph to this chapter: "The sickness of a time is cured by an alteration in the mode of life of human beings. . . ." [119]   And, it is in this consciousness that we must understand the last letter which, with one foot over the edge into insanity, Nietzsche sends to Burckhardt, on January 6, 1889: "In the end, I would rather be a Basel professor than God; but I have not ventured to carry my private egoism so far as to desist from creating the world on its account." For Nietzsche, unless that world is created and made available, the sickness of the time will not be eradicated.

Chapter X

TEXTS, PRETEXTS, AND THE SUBJECT: PERSPECTIVISM IN NIETZSCHE

Only knowledge of a language that possesses another mode of conceiving the world can lead to the appropriate knowledge of one's own language.

—U. Von Wilamowitz-Moellendorff, *Platon*, vol. I, cited in M. M. Bakhtin, "From the Prehistory of Novelistic Discourse" in *The Dialogic Imagination*

In chapter III I very briefly address the central Nietzschean concept of perspectivism. At the time I wrote that chapter, perspectivism seemed to me naturally to fall into the general area of epistemology. It is noteworthy, however, that perspectivism is mentioned only three times in that chapter (and indeed in the entire book) – almost as if I didn't know what to do with it, as if it did not fit. Indeed, the most extensive discussion comes in a footnote.[1]

It is clear in retrospect why I paid such little attention to the doctrine of perspectivism: it did not fit with a discussion of Nietzsche's epistemology. The pursuit of epistemology was in fact connected to nihilism, as the chapter revealed. Most commentators have assumed that perspectivism is Nietzsche's attempt to give an account of how knowledge of the world is or is not possible. From this shared premise, some commentators judge Nietzsche as successful, in that he establishes a credible epistemological position; for others his position is coherent but incorrect; for still others his is an impossible and self-contradictory enterprise. Each of these responses has a certain plausibility. Nietzsche's doctrine of perspectivism is often textually associated with his remarks on the possibility of truth, with his claims as to the status knowledge can have in human affairs, with his critique of the epistemological writings of other philosophers, and, most notably, with his attacks on Kant's concept of the thing-in-itself.

There is, however, reason to doubt that perspectivism is Nietzsche's version of epistemology. I take epistemology to be that branch of philosophy concerned either to ground knowledge in a realm that is "objective," that is, not affected by the act of knowing, or to establish "objectively" that this aim is impossible in at least certain realms of human experience. In both cases the aim of epistemology is to delineate a realm secure from the phenomenal vagaries of the knower. The benefit for Kant, for instance, was to make room for faith; for early positivists, epistemology served to separate the world of science from the mists of moral judgments.

In any case, epistemology focuses on the attempt to discover a permanent framework for inquiry. More precisely, it consists in an attempt to discover how a thinker comes to be associated with the transcendent pattern that makes "objective" thought possible.[2] Of necessity, epistemology either must seek to establish a knowing self that transcends the vagaries of phenomenal life or it must despair of attaining knowledge at all.

When Nietzsche talks about perspectivism, however, he speaks of it as a doctrine that encompasses epistemology:

What I paid attention to was much more the fact that no epistemological skepticism or dogmatics has ever appeared without ulterior motives; that they had a value of second rank as soon as one considered *what* in fact *compelled* this position.[3]

Fundamental innovation: in the place of epistemology, a perspective theory of affects.[4]

In these and other passages Nietzsche attacks the possibility of achieving a position in which knowledge might be treated as if it were liberated from the knower. Such attacks suggest that the final project of epistemology is ultimately untenable. None of this implies that Nietzsche is, as some have argued, a "noncognitivist," but it does imply that for Nietzsche knowledge cannot be epistemologically grounded.

I wish to argue here that for Nietzsche the whole epistemological enterprise is flawed in that it misconstrues the nature of the self. Perspectivism is Nietzsche's attempt to replace epistemology with an understanding of the self and of knowledge that does not posit any particular position (or self) as final. It teaches us not only that we are always masked but that we must be masked if we wish to know at all. If, as Nietzsche remarks in the first book of *Dawn of Day*, nature is always silent and we are condemned to error when we speak, perspectivism is the solution to that dilemma. It is the recognition that speech and thought are disguises, even and perhaps especially for ourselves, but that they are not to be rejected as lesser for all of that; it is the enforcement on ourselves of the dialectical recognition to the self and to the hearer and reader that we are in disguise. The most aristocratic of modern thinkers deconstructs himself repeatedly into the most democratic.[5]

There is perhaps no better place to begin this investigation than with Alexander Nehamas's paper "Immanent and Transcendent Perspectivism in Nietzsche."[6] Nehamas claims that Nietzsche alternates between or confuses two versions of perspectivism,[7] only one of which is ultimately interesting and philosophically tenable (which come to the same thing here).

In the first version, according to Nehamas, Nietzsche asserts that no one human understanding of the world can coherently claim to be an "ultimate" or "privileged" understanding. This is because Nietzsche understands (almost as well, one might say, as Wilfrid Sellars) that the world is not *given* to human beings and that the activity of knowing is a formulating of the world.[8] Nehamas calls this "immanent perspectivism" and notes that it does not imply that there are not knowable rules as to how humans understand the world nor that the world is without structure or regularity. Rather, immanent perspectivism merely asserts that it is the nature both of understanding and of the world that the world cannot be exhausted by any number of acts of understanding. There always is a first word, but never a last.

Nehamas also sees in Nietzsche a second version of perspectivism, which he calls "transcendent." For Nehamas this view includes two separate propositions: First, that Nietzsche wants to say that there is such a thing as a "human" perspective, understood in the sense of *Gattungswesen*; second, that Nietzsche thinks this human perspective is incommensurable and radically untranslatable into any other possible species-perspective.

Nehamas's central argument is that Nietzsche's two versions of perspectivism are incompatible. The proposition that the world is not exhausted by the knowing of it in no way implies and indeed contradicts the claim that we never know another point of view. Clearly, this argument is logically true; but I believe it commits Nehamas to a number of propositions about Nietzsche, none of which I think correct. The exploration of Nehamas's argument, however, is a fruitful entry into a different understanding of the place of perspectivism in Nietzsche's thought.

The following conclusions seem to me to be entailed by Nehamas's argument. First, transcendent perspectivism lures Nietzsche back into the trap he consistently seeks to escape. The "human" perspective becomes a grounding, by default, it is true; it is an unsatisfactory but paradoxically secure basis for human knowledge.

Second, in this view perspectivism describes something that a subject *has*. For instance, Nehamas assumes that to know another's point of view one must have it. This is a logical imputation: it corresponds to a point of view whereby the world is something that we suffer, and knowledge becomes a kind of burden of the species. It is true, of course, that Nietzsche often speaks of knowledge as suffering; but he does so most often when talking about the kind of knowledge characteristic of a world "infected" by Socratic epistemology or when he suggests that there still lurks a Christian understanding in Kant. As we shall see, this is a view that Nietzsche seeks to undermine, not one that he holds.

Nietzsche spends a good deal of time arguing that it is wrong to think of the world as "appearing" *to* us. In the summer of 1888 he noted that "the apparent world" reduces itself to a specific manner of action on the world, emanating from a "center." He goes on to say that the interaction of all such actions constitutes what we mean by the world. After that, "no shadowy right remains such that one might here speak of appearance. . . . The specific manner of reacting is the only manner of reacting; we do not know how many and what kinds there are in all."[9] The conclusion of this passage is the well-known epigram that the "antithesis of the apparent world and the true world has reduced itself into the antithesis world and nothing." That is, there is only the world, and no thing is "behind" or "above" (or even "below") it.

I do not think that by this somewhat Hesiodic vision Nietzsche wants to say that the world is simply that which we have created in our seeing. Such a facile radical Kantianism still would commit Nietzsche to the claim that all knowledge is knowledge *for* the knower and, therefore, that there is something called a subject *before* there is knowledge. Knowledge would be something one *had* and philosophy would consist, as it has since Socrates, in coming to know oneself.

It is important to note here that a self that had a transcendent perspective would also have to be a self that did not change. That self would involve what it means to be an *x*, where *x* is understood as a species with some kind of permanent enduring characteristics that in turn ensure its definition. Much of the writing from the period during which Nietzsche explores perspectivism – from 1884 onward – is occupied with a critique of the idea of a unitary self.

I think there is an important difficulty with an implication such as Nehamas's that Nietzsche thinks that knowing the world constitutes a reduction of the world to something less than it "is" and that knowledge of the world, therefore, is something flawed. When Nehamas writes that for Nietzsche "physical realities are . . . fundamentally flawed and take us no closer to understanding real nature," both the implication that there is a flaw and the implication that there is a "real nature" are misleading. The passage he is discussing comes in a criticism of the presuppositions of physicists.[10] Nietzsche is arguing that these scientists forget that when they reduce the "apparent world" to atoms, the atoms are themselves constructions. They make this mistake, he indicates, because they have forgotten that it is in the nature of being such a subject (a physicist) to come to such conclusions about the world.

Nietzsche, if I read him correctly, is not saying that physics is per se flawed, but that as a science it cannot, any more than anything else, claim to be a foundation for other knowledge. Physics, like any form of understanding, requires a knowing subject, in this case one whose knowledge is what we call physics. Physicists are what we are in the conversation of humankind when we do physics.[11] (Here I might note somewhat gnomically that Nietzsche speaks of becoming *"what* one is," not *who.*)

This is preliminary reason for the argument that the self may not know itself in any final or complete fashion. When Nietzsche notes in the preface to the *Genealogy of Morals* that "we are unknown to ourselves" as men of knowledge, he is claiming that any self that claims to know itself is necessarily self-defeating. This constant theme in Nietzsche – it already was the burden of the *Birth of Tragedy* to argue against the Aristotelian notion of *anagnorisis* (recognition) – finds a direct expression in another note from early 1888: "First mark of the great psychologist: he never seeks himself, he has not eyes for himself. . . . *We* have neither the time nor the curiosity to rotate about ourselves."[12]

Thus, for Nietzsche there is not only no point of view that is privileged in relation to the outer world (which Nehamas acutely points out is a consequence of immanent perspectivism), but also none privileged in relation to the "inner self," in relation to consciousness. Indeed, the whole relation between outer and inner is denied. There is neither a kind of internal self positing a self – à la Fichte – nor a given noumenal self. Nietzsche remarks: "The apparent 'inner world' is governed by just the same forms and procedures as the 'outer world.' We never encounter facts."[13]

Perspectivism, then, cannot mean that everything is in the eye of the beholder, nor that all is "subjective" – although we might mistakenly think so if we read perspectivism to imply merely that what we see is shaped by our point of view. To such a claim, Nietzsche explicitly responds that "even this is interpretation. The 'subjective' is not something given, it is something added and invented and projected behind what there is. . . . Insofar as the word 'knowledge' has any meaning, the world is knowable . . . ; it has no meaning behind it; it has countless meanings."[14] Nietzsche's point here is that it is a mistake to look behind or underneath the world for its true sense. As he notes in 1888, the world of becoming is of "equivalent value every moment." All we need to know and all we can know is present in the world as we encounter it. This is the meaning of the "Midnight" poem in *Zarathustra*; to paraphrase Robert Frost, all meaning is already ours.[15]

Ever since the sixth book of the *Republic*, a dominant theme and presupposition of epistemology has been that there is one "layer" of the self and of the understanding that is somehow deeper and closer to unchanging "reality" than any other. Nietzsche's response to this is categorical: "The 'subject' is a fiction that many similar states in us are the effects of one substratum; but it is we who first created the 'similarity' of these states; our adjusting them and making them similar is the fact, not their similarity – which had rather ought to be denied." Nietzsche then proceeds to compare the "subject" to a regent at the head of a commonality and never so sure of its position that it can simply ignore the world and wreak its will. Elsewhere, he speaks of the world and the self as centers of power that have entered into alliances with each other. None of this is a denial that there "is" such a thing as a subject, but rather a critique of the presupposition that the subject has a natural and given unity of any kind. Thus, Nietzsche continues and asserts that if our " 'ego' is for us the sole being, there is also good reason to doubt if it be not a 'perspectival illusion,' an 'apparent' unity in which all is gathered as if bonded by a horizon."[16]

If knowledge is possible only by virtue of a "belief in being," this does not imply that for Nietzsche there is no such thing as knowledge, nor that knowledge depends on "point of view," but only that for knowledge to be possible some grounding has been accepted and recognized. Earlier thinkers had assumed that knowledge depended on the nature of the knower; in Nietzsche's *umgedrehter Platonismus*, the nature(s) of knowing produces the self and additional modes of knowing produce additional selves.

What concerns Nietzsche is that for many people the very possibility of a secure and confident knowledge of the world has disappeared – or is in the process of doing so. Their selves, therefore, are also dissolving, such that like those at the end of the *Genealogy of Morals*, they would rather "will the void than be void of will." Many of us, for instance, are or are in the process of becoming what Max Weber called "religiously unmusical." We know what religion is, but it makes no sense for us, we cannot sing in tune. Part of what Nietzsche is trying to accomplish is to impress on us that the subject that might have been religiously musical has been called into radical question. We – some of us – are no longer and can no longer be that person. Although the particular reasons for such a disintegration derive from historical and genealogical factors, the process itself derives from the general nature of the self. Nietzsche writes: "The subject is itself . . .

a construct . . . : a simplification in order to designate [*bezeichnen*] the *force*, which posits, invents, thinks as something distinct from all other particular positings, discoverings, thinkings as such."[17]

With this we can arrive at a new understanding of Nietzsche's advocacy of "having many points of view."[18] In 1884 Nietzsche had noted the following as an "insight":

All estimations of values [*Wertschaetzungen*] are a matter of a definite perspective: the maintenance of the individual, a commonality, a race, a state, a church, a belief, a culture. *Due to the forgetfulness that there are only perspectival evaluations* [my italics], all sorts of contradictory evaluations and thus contradictory drives swarm [*wimmeln*] inside *one person*. This is the expression of the diseased condition in man, in opposition to the condition in animals, where all instincts play particular roles. This contradictory creature has however in his nature a great method of knowing: he feels many fors and againsts – he raises himself up to *justice* – to a comprehension beyond the valuation of good and evil. The wisest man would be the richest in contradictions, who as it were, has feelers [*Tastorganen*] for all kinds of men: and right among them [has] his great moments of *grandiose harmony*.[19]

This is a difficult and important passage. Two broad perspectival categories appear: the first that of "good and evil" (i.e., moral) and the second that of "justice" (i.e., doing that which is appropriate to that which one encounters). The move to justice is something Nietzsche considers to be beyond the valuation of good and evil. Justice itself seems not to depend on the "unity" of a self, but on the ability of an organism to contain what one might call nonantagonistic contradictions within itself.

Nietzsche is engaged in a radical reconceptualization of the subject. We are not to think of the subject as a unity but as a multiplicity, what Nietzsche calls a *Vielheit*.[20] This conclusion clearly is preliminary, as even to assert that the subject is a multiplicity is still to assert that there is something that it is. That said, exploration still is rewarding. Most individuals, and here Nietzsche means both philosophers and the rest of us, assume that the unity of the world is derived from the unity of the architectonics of the faculty that makes knowing possible – from the nature of the self. (This is what Kant had demonstrated.) Such a unity would have its origins in the unity of the self which knows. Against this Nietzsche argues that the unity of the known and the unity of the knower are derived from the activity of knowing. As an activity, knowing – understanding the world – is something that humans and perhaps other species do; perhaps we have done it as a species since, say, the "discovery of the mind" around 1400 B.C., or since the development of what Karl Jaspers called the axial period. For Nietzsche, knowing is not a *consequence* of the self, but rather *productive* of what we have come to call the self. (Part of Nietzsche's repeated strictures against Socrates derive from this source.)[21]

Most people, according to Nietzsche, have "forgotten" that the unity of the world is a double imputation, first from the unity of the knower derived from the act of knowing and then, in turn, by the transfer of the unity of the knower onto the world. "We put value into things," writes Nietzsche in the late summer of 1886, "and this value has an effect on us, after we have forgotten that we were the donors."[22] In those who rise up to justice, the knower remains multiple, even in his or her own understanding. In them life is an "experiment of the thinker . . . not a duty, not a fatality, not a deceit."[23]

We will look more closely at what it means to think of life as an experiment, but let us note here that it does not mean precisely what Jean Granier refers to as "multiple ontologies."[24] Rather, life as a *Versuch* carries all the meanings of *Versuch*: it is an "experiment" and also an "endeavor," but always subject to the "temptation" that one may call oneself finished, given, and final. (One thinks here of Whitman.)[25]

Thus Nietzsche does not alternate between two versions of perspectivism but rather gives us a hierarchy. The perspectivism of morality and that of justice do not correspond to points of view, nor to some kind of natural species differentiation (as in being a bat, or an ant, or a human), but to the differences in the way that a perspective affects the knower's understanding of himself or herself in the world. Some lack the ability to have "a basis, a condition of existence" for their judgments, and their judgments therefore are "chaos." They have no world(s) but simply nothing, even though they may not know it (yet).[26] Some kinds of perspective may ultimately not make sense for the knower but rather produce a lack of sense; indeed, Nietzsche's formulation and critique of nihilism is among the consequences of one such perspective (the moral), perhaps the most important consequence for contemporary Europeans.

It is worth noting in passing here that this is not a theory of false consciousness. False consciousness, as Michael Holquist observes, implies that all claims to knowledge "can never express the actual place they occupy among the reigning myths of their own time and place."[27] Nihilism is not a false consciousness whereby our knowledge of ourselves would be incomplete because of our own involvement in the inevitability of our misrecognitions of our own place in the world. The theory of a hierarchy of perspectives places the emphasis not on "truth" but on the consequences of a perspective on the knower and on what counts as knowledge for the knower. Nietzsche presents far fewer epistemological problems than does Marx.

In any case, it is against a perspective such as that of nihilism that Nietzsche sets this statement: "Task: to see things *as they are*. Means: to look on them from a hundred eyes, from many persons."[28] Given what has been said, Nietzsche must mean by this that things can be seen as they are only if they are seen multiply and as multiple. The more composite a knower is – that is, the less he is subject in a "forgetful" fashion to his own creations and valuations – and the less we insist that each "I" be a unity, the more eyes the "subject" will have, the better to see things "as they are," not as given but as multiple themselves.

The move to justice, furthermore, has no "accomplishment": there can be no *Vollendung*. There is, in fact, a danger that we will want to think or pretend that we have accomplished ourselves. As Nietzsche writes in *Beyond Good and Evil*:

It might be a basic character of existence that those who would know it completely would perish, in which case the strength of a spirit should be measured according to how much "truth" one could still barely endure – to put it more clearly, to what degree one would *require* that it be thinned down, shrouded, sweetened, blinded, falsified.[29]

The (neo-Calvinist?) claim that humans are beings whose nature it is to be limited shapes much of Nietzsche's work. *The Birth of Tragedy* is a text in the theory of understanding; it is the answer to the question of how the Greeks came to be who they were and how they attained that mode of life without falling either into "Asiatic chaos" or into the rigid prose of Rome.[30] From 1872 onward, Nietzsche insists explicitly on the incompatibility of truth and life and of the necessity of "horizons" in making meaning possible. In *Beyond Good and Evil*, he notes: "Let at least this much be admitted: there would be no life at all if not on the basis of perspective estimates and appearances."[31] We are caught, we might say, in danger of establishing what

I might call a "fetishism of persons," in which, as Nietzsche says, we project the "conditions of our preservation as the predicates of being in general."[32]

Perspectivism is then at the center of Nietzsche's understanding of our presence in the world and of its availability to us. To have a perspective is to have horizons, and such limitation is what we mean by life and having a definition as (a) being. The fact that we are alive – and that we die – means that we are unable to do full justice to the world, which would require one to have so transparent a contact with it ("as it is," in all its becoming) that there would be "no simplification of it." We must then accept as a predicate of human existence that it is "unjust." In the 1886 preface to *Human, All-Too-Human*, Nietzsche argues that human beings can never experience the world as other than unjust and that it is a sign of health that one forgo any attempt to conceive of experience in the world as other than tragic. Indeed, already in his 1870 lectures on *Oedipus Rex*, Nietzsche had made the point that tragedy presents the "deepest conflict between life and thought." Greek tragedy consists of the manner in which the Greeks managed to accept the fact that all knowledge, including that of themselves, was perspectival – and yet without calling that acceptance into question.[33]

If there is nothing besides perspective (for humans at least),[34] then the obvious conclusion is not that the world cannot be known but rather that *it is in the nature of the world as we experience it to be known.* There is no action in the world that does not embody all that we need to understand it, providing only that we do not insist on understanding it according to a mistaken and arrogant notion of the subject.[35] Nietzsche warns us against the temptation of assuming that the world is not or cannot be known or that we are not and cannot be known. Knowledge is not flawed, even if it is not perfect.

If the above is true, then everything must be understood in terms of the whole of which it is a part. Yet the characteristic of that whole must be what M. M. Bakhtin has called "heteroglossia": At any given place or time the totality of the conditions that give an utterance meaning will ensure that it will necessarily have a meaning somewhat different at any other time and place. And this is not a flaw.

Such a position is entailed by Nietzsche's conclusion that it is in the nature of the world to be known. Yet Nietzsche has established two fundamental perspectives that characterize attitudes toward the world. For his writing to be successful he must at the same time express both of those perspectives and seek to bring them into an "alliance." On the face of it, this would seem impossible; but a careful exploration of the relation between the doctrine of perspectivism and the will to power shows, I think, the opposite.

The answer as to *why* humans insist on seeing the world as a unit is the subject of Nietzsche's genealogical investigations.[36] The question of what condemns us to experience the world as known and thus ensures that we will experience the world as a self comes in the doctrine of the will to power.

The will to power is in fact the operating principle of perspectivism. As I noted in chapter VIII, all forms of life are/have will to power. The activity of will to power is what Nietzsche calls *interpretation*, "a means to become master of something."[37] The will to power understands/interprets/makes the new in terms of the old; it extends the understanding and the categories of the life and action of a particular being over that which is not yet that being. The will to power is that by which the world has the quality of being intelligible.

The rhetoric of Nietzsche's approach to this topic is important. In the second section of *Beyond Good and Evil*, he notes that "there would be no life at all if not on the basis of perspectival estimates and appearances."[38] Two aphorisms later, he introduces the notion of a "text without an author," and then deepens his earlier statements by suggesting that to view the world as will to power is to view it from the "inside," that is, on its own terms. The perspectival world thus is a text without an author and is "determined and characterized according to its 'intelligible character.'"[39] Hence, when we speak of the world as will to power we mean that the world as it presents itself to us is completely intelligible – that is its "nature," so to speak.[40] The question of what a perspective is cannot be answered or, indeed, even asked because a perspective has no conceptual substance.

Does not, however, the assertion that the world *is* will to power constitute an assertion that there is something that the world is? And can this assertion be without contradiction a perspective? To address this problem requires a detour through the discussion, alluded to above, of a text without an author.

On a preliminary basis, let us note that Nietzsche is aware of this issue. In a note not included in the *Will to Power*, he raises what he calls a "basic question":

Basic question: if the perspectival belongs to essence [*Wesen*] as such? As is not only a form of considering [*Behauptungsform*], a relation between different beings [*Wesen*]? Do the different powers stand in relation, such that this relation is tied to the observations-optics [*Observations-Optik*]? This would be possible if all being [*Sein*] were *essentially* some kind of observation [*Wahrnehmenden*].[41]

Perspectivism thus cannot be understood as the perspective *of* some-thing, for there can be no thing without perspective, which is not a perspective. Indeed, "there would be nothing called knowledge, if thought did not reform the world into 'things.'"[42]

Knowing consists in forming, in making the world, and in making known. (Here the English misses the resonances of *machen*.) In a "complicated" way, Nietzsche explains, knowing makes for "specific-ity." "My notion," he continues, "is that each particular body tries to become master over the whole territory and to expand its strength (its will to power) and to push back all which resists its expansion."[43]

In the "turned-around Platonism" that which is, is the result of human action rather than its premise. Thus: "To *impress* upon be-coming the character of being – that is the highest will to power."[44] Nietzsche emphasizes "impress" (*aufzuprägen*) because the will to power will be the highest when the subject in question actively "im-presses being," that is, takes becoming out of the river of time and gives it being. The aphorism continues: "That everything recurs in the closest approximation of a world of becoming to a world of being." It is precisely because of perspectivism that eternal return is possible. (There are, of course, also different forms of eternal return, which in turn correspond to the different forms of perspectivism).[45]

If the above is the case, there can be no transcendent perspectivism for Nietzsche. We are inevitably meaningful to and for all creatures we encounter. That we want to deny this is the source of the disease of transcendent perspectivism, of the desire to believe that we are unknowable to others. (In fact, for Nietzsche we are meaningful even to the inorganic, given that we cannot on these grounds refuse to make a clear-cut differentiation between such entities and ourselves.) What Nietzsche is struck by is the fact that we make sense all the time, without having to want to, and by how fragile yet compelling is our description of ourselves. There is no need to erect defenses against not making sense, as do, for instance, those scientists who are so pan-icked by the possibility of incalculability that they turn calculability into a general a priori of knowledge.[46]

Is the world (and, indeed, are we ourselves) a text of which we are the continual author? In a later essay Nehamas argues that Nietzsche holds to this position, but that he is wrong, for no life can ever be lived completely in this mode – we cannot be identical as both text and autobiographer.[47] The basis of his argument is akin to that advanced in his earlier essay: We always are more than that which we make of the world; hence, as authors we always are more than the text that we would that ourselves be.

Again, Nehamas's argument provides an important route into Nietzsche. Clearly, for Nietzsche what something "is" is what is made of it (that is, the relations that it enters into). Anything that is the case is just as great as the number of the relations that compose it. Are the interpretations necessarily *of* something, of a text that is not itself an interpretation? Nietzsche's answer appears to be "not necessarily." For instance, he writes of the French Revolution that "the text has disappeared under the interpretations."[48] I take this to mean not that the "facts" have disappeared (in which case a historical accident would have no necessary philosophical consequences), but that the different interpretations of the French Revolution no longer enter into "alliances" with one another. The reasons for this failure are historical and, Nietzsche indicates, have to do with the long and passionate "indignations and enthusiasms" characteristic of later "spectators" of the French Revolution. It is the present impossibility of these alliances that has led to the disappearance of a text.[49]

We remember here that a self that rose up to justice was a self that held together as an alliance of a multiplicity of modes and relations. And yet one of the modes of such a "self" must also be the mode that the "unity" of the self is merely apparent and not given once and for all. This poses the final question about the status of Nietzsche's doctrine of perspectivism – is it not itself a claim to a transcendent position and therefore doomed to self-referential contradiction?

In *Ecce Homo* Nietzsche attempts to bring into an alliance all of his activities, past, present, and future.[50] He proclaims that "I am a one thing [*das Eine*], my books are the other [*das Andre*]."[51] That is, the texts that Nietzsche gives us – his writings, his philosophy – are given in such a way that "Nietzsche" cannot be found in them. When he asserts in *Ecce Homo*, for instance, that he is both a decadent and its opposite, we are meant to take this claim absolutely literally. The consequence is that the unity of his texts is to be found in the reader, and that there is no authorial unity imposed on the text, any more than the subject might impose a unity on the world. Thus, the strictures that Nietzsche applies to his understanding of the subject apply also to his teachings on perspectivism. Perspectivism cannot be a doctrine or a point of view because, properly understood, it makes impossible the epistemological activism that a doctrine requires. This position anticipates the one arrived at in relation to modern texts by Roland Barthes in "The Death of the Author" and extended by Michel Foucault in "What Is an Author?"[52] W. D. Williams summarized his analysis of Nietzsche's style as follows: "Wherever one turns . . . one can find the same tendency to disguise himself while letting the reader know that what is being shown is in fact a disguise."[53]

Perspectivism, then, does not consist in asserting, with becoming pluralism, that I "should" have or support a number of different points of view. It asserts, rather, that "I" am a number of different ways of knowing and that there is no such entity as a permanent or privileged self. An order of rank is found in a "grandiose alliance" such as Nietzsche, for instance, claims for himself in *Beyond Good and Evil* and *Ecce Homo*.[54]

If a "subject" is thus a containing of multitudes, then it can change both in time and in history. Understanding the changes is the task of genealogy. For our purposes, the more important consequence is that whatever actions such a subject engages in must manifest the grandiose alliance that went into making them. Thus, as Williams notes in the passage cited above, Nietzsche's actions (his texts) all by and large constantly call themselves into question even as they prepare the reader for an outrageous, seductive position. "Does not one write books precisely to conceal what one harbors?" Nietzsche asks. "Every philosophy also *conceals* a philosophy; every opinion is also a hideout, every word also a mask."[55] Note his insistent repetition of "also": Philosophy, opinions, words are not *only* concealments, hiding places, and masks but *also* philosophy, opinions, and masks.

What is the importance of the perspectival understanding of the world? Three consequences immediately come to mind. First, it enforces in the writer the necessity for an unrelenting honesty toward self and reader: All pretense must be shown to be pretense. Second, it makes it impossible for the writer to pretend to be the physician of culture – all that one says must also be said about oneself. Finally, no privileged position is available from which to discuss the world as if one were not part of it: Philosophy is praxis. As Nietzsche notes in the preface to the second volume of *Human, All-Too-Human*, "I forced myself, as doctor and patient in the same person, into a diametrically opposite, untried climate of the *soul*, and in particular into a sharpened wandering in foreign parts, in that which is foreign, into a curiosity about every kind of strangeness."[56] *Ecce Homo* is an account of what it took to achieve this:

Need I say after all this that in matters of *decadence* I am *experienced*? I have spelled them backwards and forwards. Even that filigree art of grasping and comprehending in general, those fingers for *nuances*, that psychology of "seeing around the corner," and whatever else is characteristic of me was learned only then, is the true present of those days in which everything in me became subtler.[57]

As a test of the noble soul, the acceptance of perspectivism also provides Nietzsche an indication of what will have to be done successfully to confront the coming century, with its wars "the like of which has never been seen" and its leveling of all distinctions of value. This is the topic of eternal return, as suggested in this passage from 1888: "To value anything to be able to live it, I must comprehend it as absolutely necessarily tied in with everything that is – thus for its sake, I must call all existence [*Dasein*] good and know thanks [*Dank wissen*] for the accident in which such priceless things are possible."[58]

In the end, each part of Nietzsche leads the reader to the other parts: one moves from perspectivism to horizons, to the will to power, and on to eternal return. This may not make him a unified character, but it does describe a grandiose alliance.

EPILOGUE

When the first edition of this book appeared in 1975, it was almost alone in the English language, not only in the limited field of works concerned with Nietzsche and politics but even in the broader field of Nietzsche studies. The bibliography shows only two booklength English language sources first published after 1964, Arthur Danto's *Nietzsche as Philosopher* and an edited volume by Robert Solomon composed in half of previously published pieces. The situation in 1975 had in fact not changed much since I finished a dissertation on Nietzsche (archeological traces of which survive in the present book) some six years earlier.

This is clearly not the case today. Books on Nietzsche appear with almost predictable regularity. If Nietzsche was once the "bad boy of philosophy," as Norman O. Brown called him,[1] serious attempts at domestication have been made in the last decade. On the model of the *Kant-Studien* or *Hobbes Studies*, there is now an annual series, the *Nietzsche-Studien*, and articles on Nietzsche appear even in major journals in analytic philosophy such as the *Philosophical Review*.[2] Books on Nietzsche come out with such frequency that so distinguished a commentator as Sarah Kofman feels the need to defend "yet another book on Nietzsche."[3] We even have metacriticism that establishes categories of Nietzsche interpreters. For what it is worth, this book is probably that of a left/splitter/therapeutic/vitalist.[4]

[310

The reasons for the explosion in Nietzsche studies are twofold. One set of reasons is intellectual-academic; the other sociopolitical. Taken together they give some indication as to "why Nietzsche now?" and as to why the Nietzsche we have now has appeared in the form he has.

The first of the intellectual-academic reasons was the publication in 1961 of Heidegger's lectures on Nietzsche.[5] Heidegger argued that Nietzsche had brought the Western philosophical tradition to an end. While Nietzsche remained for Heidegger within that tradition (if only *malgré lui*), it was now, after Nietzsche, possible to start thought over again, to "think the ground of being."

By the mid 1960s, Heidegger's influence was making itself felt in the writing of some young German philosophers and social theorists, but far more eventful was the emergence in France of a school of Nietzsche interpretation that sought to integrate and then move away from Heidegger. From Gilles Deleuze, Michel Foucault, and Jacques Derrida, we were beginning to receive a "new" Nietzsche.[6] The new-ness consisted in taking Nietzsche seriously, or, as I would now say, at his word. If Nietzsche claimed to break the history of thought in two, the French showed why it might be possible seriously to think that he had, in fact, done so. If he claimed that illusion was more central to life than truth, the French seemed to provide a perspective in which this might be true.

Above all, the new French school of criticism was antifoundation-alist, arguing that Nietzsche had destroyed the *possibility* of providing foundations for claims about the world, that is, of elaborating state-ments whose truth value was beyond rational dispute. Even more strongly, the new French critics argued that there was no *need* to pro-vide an assured epistemological grounding for propositions about the world. Indeed, they suggested that the pursuit of foundations was itself a mistake, part of the *philosophia perennis*.

There were important differences among Deleuze, Foucault, and Derrida, and more nuanced ones among their respective followers. But they all sought to give us a Nietzsche who was not simply the right-wing counter to Marx, but rather (they argued) moved thought beyond where Marx had left it.[7] *Genealogy* suddenly became an oper-ative concept, designating a way of approaching history that was both historical and nondialectical.

The effect of the new French scholarship was perhaps first felt in the United States in literary criticism; soon, however, it made itself felt in the work of philosophers and political theorists. Whether or not they actually appropriated structuralist, poststructuralist, and deconstructionist approaches, they gained a new and different way to respond to a text. Most importantly, the new way of reading responded to the "linguistic turn,"[8] directing scholars to take Nietzsche's rhetoric in a philosophically serious manner. Nietzsche's style, which had previously been praised or excused, was now seen as integral to the content of his work.

As these new approaches continued to percolate throughout British and American universities, the English-language community of Nietzsche scholars suffered the loss of its leading authority. Criticism of Nietzsche in English had been dominated since 1950 by Walter Kaufmann, whose path-breaking *Nietzsche: Philosopher, Psychologist, Antichrist* had first made Nietzsche respectable again in the Western intellectual world. Kaufmann's death, in effect, left an intellectual vacuum, a vacuum determined to some degree by the Nietzsche he had tried to present.

Here it is worth pausing to mention several key attributes of Kaufmann's approach to Nietzsche, for Kaufmann's Nietzsche was *the* Nietzsche for American and British studies, so much so that in 1967 a major figure in American academic intellectual history could say to me that he did not see why I was writing on Nietzsche inasmuch as there seemed little to say after Kaufmann's work. As I indicate in chapter V, Kaufmann sought to give us a Nietzsche who participated in the *philosophia perennis*. Shakespeare, Hegel, Nietzsche – these and others – were the peaks of thought, all in conversation with each other, all distinguished by the common rejection of Christian morality, at least in an immediate sense. This was a Nietzsche fundamentally of the Enlightenment – against authority, against tradition, against any constraints on thought. Had the Kant of *What is Enlightenment?* lived at the end of the nineteenth century, Nietzsche is who he might have looked like.

Kaufmann argued, for instance, that Nietzsche was not an anti-Semite and that, at the most, passages which appeared to be anti-Semitic should be understood as part of the rhetoric of the day. Likewise, when Nietzsche appeared to speak favorably of war, Kaufmann suggested that wars were far less catastrophic in the nineteenth century than in our nuclear age.

Kaufmann appeared to show that the Nazis' appropriation of Nietzsche's themes was unjustified by the texts themselves. "Unfortunate" images in Nietzsche Kaufmann tended to dismiss as "rhetoric"; rather he gave the world a bright, iconoclastic writer, whose serious work challenged the Western mind as did, say, that of Hegel or Sartre. Kaufmann's Nietzsche was an important cultural critic, but not a good philosopher; his was an "interesting," but not a rigorous, mind. Yet for each citation that bolstered Kaufmann's point, one could find another that appeared equally plausibly to contradict it.

In sum, Kaufmann's great and singular achievement was to have made it again legitimate in the Anglo-Saxon world to read Nietzsche. His translations were by and large without peer in English. But the paradoxical consequence of his work was to reinforce the judgment that Nietzsche was at best an inconsistent philosopher. To read Nietzsche seriously, to read his works as an integrated corpus – rather than as a sometimes strained amalgam of little insights and grand claims – was, according to Kaufmann, impossible.

The power of Kaufmann's book, especially when compared with others and when combined with Kaufmann's command of the text and the felicity of his translations,[9] effectively gave him and his supporters control over Nietzsche studies in America. It was not that Kaufmann sought to prevent other writing from coming to publication but that as he was for a long time almost the only writer of distinction in the field, his was the only opinion that would always be sought.[10] He dominated the field in part because there was no real alternative.

Walter Kaufmann died precisely at the time that the North American Nietzsche Society (NANS) was being formed. NANS had its origins in the generalized perception that an English-language "boom" in Nietzsche studies was under way (especially in response to developments in Europe) and that it would be important to academic philosophy. In Kaufmann's absence, it is fair to say, the direction of Nietzsche studies was up for grabs. Following perhaps the lead of their French counterparts, all sorts of American and British academics began to read Nietzsche seriously. Soon an article on Nietzsche in English was as likely to appear in journals of political theory, literature, social theory, or cultural criticism as in any journal of philosophy.

Who were these newcomers? In the academic world, most of the generation of Nietzsche readers responsible for these multiple efflorescences entered their chosen profession during the late 1960s and the early 1970s, though most of those who wrote about Nietzsche did not start to do so until later.[11] What drew them – what drew us – to Nietzsche then? Any answer runs the risk of taking autobiography to be actuality. Still, I may risk such a Proustian fate, if only because it is in the spirit of its subject.

The academic generation of the late 1960s was the first postwar generation which had not directly experienced the Second World War. We were thus the first for whom the authority of the battles fought in the Second World War was sufficiently attenuated as not to govern our conclusions. Bluntly, the importance of being *against* fascism and even perhaps against Stalinism was no longer a sufficient basis for one's politics or one's intellectual life. In this context Nietzsche was attractive for several reasons.

First, Nietzsche raised the question of the health of a society as a whole.[12] Standards of judgment, including moral standards, were analyzed by Nietzsche in terms of structures of domination and power, that is, as political. This was not a reason for rejecting them as flawed (although some read Nietzsche in this way), but it was a reason to raise general questions about the possibility that society as a whole must be changed. In the 1960s cultural revolution was an apparent actuality or at least something of a possibility. Something was happening in America, in Europe, in China and no one knew what it was. This realization allowed readers to grope toward a Nietzsche who was not so much concerned with the free "super-human" individual as he was with societies as a whole.

Second, and more problematically, the attraction to Nietzsche came from an extension of the claim that moral and social structures were disguised structures of domination. We found (or we thought we saw) in Nietzsche a reason to be deeply suspicious of morality as a justification for action.

These suspicions were not the old suspicions that morality might be a kind of personal judgment. It was rather that the categories of "good" and "evil" seemed to be available to almost anyone. Hitler had clearly thought of what he had done as "good." Thus a particular kind of moral relativism developed in the wake of the Second World War. The energy and the apparent clarity of purpose that the Nazis brought to the justification of their enterprise called the very cate-gories of "good" and "evil" – that is, the moral enterprise as a way of organizing human affairs – into radical doubt. The question "What if the Nazis had won?" inescapably suggested that moral categories were relative to success and success relative to power. If that was so, then apparently the only answer to Hitler was power. But power, we knew or thought, was not a moral category.

If the war made possible a kind of moral relativism, I want further to claim that too many people too quickly thought themselves entitled to conclude that what they wanted was good simply because they wanted it. In effect, such people abandoned the notion of morality as a category. But as I argue in this book, Nietzsche understood that not anyone can for any reason, at any time, think him or herself excused from morality. Nonetheless, some readers found in Nietzsche a way to raise the question of the cost of the "moral point of view."

For some, again, moral relativism went only so far as the facile claim of "I-me-mine, and there is nothing anyone can say about it." For others, however, reading Nietzsche made it possible to imagine a life not based on structures of imperatives (explicit or unconscious), structures that Kant had shown to be a necessary component of morality. Nietzsche pointed, that is, to a life "beyond good and evil." In the enthusiasm of liberation, of course, many did not fully appreciate how difficult it is not to live morally; to some degree Nietzsche is responsible for making it appear unrealistically easy and safe (see chapter IX).

Third, at some deep and almost always unspoken level, I think Nietzsche attracted the postwar generation because his texts allowed us to think seriously about the possibility of human extinction.[13] The deepest fact – not the most important, or the most prominent – of our life might be said to be that we can destroy all life on the planet. The significance of this fact is that there are no terms by which to understand human life other than those it makes available to itself. Nietzsche had realized as deeply as anyone that human life had no reference to anything other than itself. This is what "the death of God" means – that from now on we will be able to "play dice with gods at gods' tables, for the earth is a table for the gods."[14]

There is in Nietzsche an insistence, indeed a stridency, that this is *our* world. He means that there is no guarantee that anything we do will have any significance beyond itself in terms of nature, or progress, or a particular group that carries historical significance. We cannot even discuss possible effects on future generations, for there may not be any future generations, let alone significance.[15] This stridency is the basis of his insistence that human beings now confront each other in an entirely new setting.

The present setting, he calls nihilism. In this book I argue nihilism to be the form of human life that corresponds to the recognition that meaning is not to be attained by human effort, all the while not abandoning the attempt to attain meaning. As Nietzsche remarks in the last paragraph of *On the Genealogy of Morals*, humans would rather "will the void than be void of will."[16]

If this is so, then the act of writing must be radically altered. Previously the answer to the question, Why does one write? would be "to make a difference," on the presupposition that "making a difference" was a meaningful category. In this understanding, for this way of being in the world, the act of authoring implicitly presupposes a transhistorical position, at a minimum the givenness of a possible future audience. But Nietzsche tells us that no such position is necessarily available. The author must not then privilege himself from inclusion in any category by which he seeks to understand the world. When Nietzsche suggests at the beginning of the section "Why I write such good books" that he will be born posthumously,[17] he means that he will be born in his readers, as his readers. This is a source of worry to him ("Above all, do not mistake me"), but also the origin of the possibility of doing philosophy in a manner true to this earth and to this earth only.[18]

In "Science As a Vocation," his great essay about how it is possible to know, Max Weber insists in a very Nietzschean mode that the acceptance of the essential ultimate inconsequentiality of scientific achievement is a prerequisite for being able to do science.[19] His problem is Nietzsche's: How does one write, then, so as not to deny precisely that which one is asserting?

What Nietzsche did, as we are now coming to see, is to develop a way of writing philosophy that radically empowered the reader. The unity of all his writings comes precisely in his assurance, ambivalent in *The Birth of Tragedy* and clear-cut by the time of *Zarathustra* and *Beyond Good and Evil*, that his texts are what they are because of their readers. He wants us to encounter these texts as we would encounter another person, based on the acknowledgment of an individual presence. As with another person, we can never start or end with

Nietzsche's texts by claiming that knowing what they mean is all there is. We do not, therefore, if Nietzsche be correct, learn from his texts by determining what they "mean," as though they were a container for a "message."[20] We learn from them by finding ourselves in them, which is precisely the source of authority that Nietzsche had found perhaps too easily in Greek drama and which all his subsequent writings try to make possible in different realms of human existence. Thus the *Genealogy* is among other things an exploration of what it would mean to have morality available in a nonimperative fashion; in *Beyond Good and Evil*, Nietzsche is concerned with various aspects of knowing, what is called *Wissenschaft*; in *Zarathustra* he addresses the varieties of social organization as they have become concretized in human practice; the *Twilight of the Idols* is about authority itself. And it is finally in *Ecce Homo* that Nietzsche explores what it means for an author to explore these topics. *Ecce Homo* is about writing itself and is, in this mode, his autobiography. Thus, he must allow others to find themselves in him and also warn them away from finding a message. He advises his readers that he will be born posthumously, that is, in his readers. "Whosoever had thought he had understood something of me, had made up something out of me after his own image."[21]

If these reflections have validity and meet with any understanding, then we should be approaching a time when we will start reading Nietzsche as he wanted to be read, that is, to read his books as books and not as collections of sayings. Although I now think very little of what I say in this book to be wrong, it is still concerned with topics in Nietzsche, and I do not think that this is the (only) hope that Nietzsche had for his readers. Indeed, this book often struggles against the construction of topics and categories it has taken for itself (a conflict especially noticeable in "The Epistemology of Nihilism," which, as the new chapter X makes clear, is really about nihilism and not epistemology). While we need not abandon the study of topics – after all, we can still write on what Hegel says about "self-understanding" – our frame of attention must be Nietzsche's books, not fragments of them.

In this way, the work of other Nietzsche commentators during the past thirteen years has helped me to understand better what I was trying to do as I wrote this book. I am grateful to those who in the interim have pushed me toward both recovery and discovery in my

KEY TO CITATIONS
FROM NIETZSCHE

A. The following is basically the standard key adopted by Colli and Montinari in their edition of the complete works (see below), which I have supplemented and used.

AC	Der Antichrist	The Antichrist (or Antichristian)
DD	Dionysos Dithyramben	Dionysos Dithyrambs
DS	David Strauss	David Strauss
EH	Ecce Homo	Ecce Homo
FW	Die fröhliche Wissenschaft	The Gay Science
FWg	Der Fall Wagner	The Case of Wagner
GD	Götzendämmerung	The Twilight of the Idols
GM	Zur Genealogie der Moral	On the Genealogy of Morals
GS	Der griechische Staat	The Greek State
GT	Die Geburt der Tragödie, Oder: Griechentum und Pessimissmus	The Birth of Tragedy, Or: Hellenism and Pessimism
HKP	Homer und die klassische Philologie	Homer and Classical Philology
HL	Vom Nutzen und Nachteil der Historie für das Leben	On the Use and Disadvantage of History for Life
HW	Homers Wettkampf	Homer's Contest
JGB	Jenseits von Gut und Böse	Beyond Good and Evil
M	Morgenröte	The Dawn of Day
MAM	Menschliches, Allzumenschliches	Human, All-Too-Human
NW	Nietzsche *contra* Wagner	Nietzsche *contra* Wagner
PTZ	Die Philosophie im tragischen Zeitalter der Griechen	Philosophy in the Tragic Age of the Greeks

RWB	Richard Wagner in Bayreuth	Richard Wagner in Bayreuth
SE	Schopenhauer als Erzieher	Schopenhauer as Educator
VM	Vermischte Meinungen und Sprüche	Mixed Opinions and Maxims (part 1 of Vol. II of MAM)
WL	Über Wahrheit und Lüge im aussermoralischen Sinn	On Truth and Lie in the Extra-Moral Sense
WM	Der Wille zur Macht	The Will to Power
WP	Wir Philologen	We Philologists
WS	Der Wanderer und sein Schatten	The Wanderer and His Shadow (part 2 of Vol. II of MAM)
WWK	Wissenschaft und Weisheit im Kämpfe	Science and Wisdom in Conflict
Za	Also Sprach Zarathustra	Thus Spoke Zarathustra
ZB	Über die Zukunft unserer Bildungsanstalten	On the Future of Our Educational Institutions

B. I have used a number of different German editions of Nietzsche for references in the footnotes. Because it is the most generally available, the Schlechta edition is cited from whenever possible. The German editions are keyed as follows.

> WKG: *Werke.* Kritische Gesamtausgabe. Herausgegeben von Giorgio Colli und Mazzino Montinari. Berlin: Walter de Gruyter, 1967. This edition is divided into "divisions" marked by roman numbers, and the divisions into volumes indicated by arab numeral subscripts.
> Thus: WKG VIII3 p. 57.

> I, II, or III: *Werke in drei Bänden.* Herausgegeben von Karl Schlechta. München: Carl Hanser Verlag, 1954. Most citations are from this edition, which is in three volumes.
> Thus: III 561.

> Naumann and roman volume number: *Werke.* Vols. IX-XIV. Leipzig: Naumann Verlag, 1898.
> Thus: Naumann IX p. 143.

> Kröner and roman volume number: *Die Unschuld des Werdens.* Vols. I and II. Herausgegeben von A. Bäumler. Kröner Verlag: Stuttgart, 1956.
> Thus: Kröner I p. 175.

C. In order to facilitate references to different editions (including those in English), I have referred to a citation first by Nietzsche's title (abbreviated), then by the relevant subdivisions of that work, then by the edition cited, and, finally, by the page of that edition on which the citation may be found. Thus JGB 23, II 587 is *Beyond Good and Evil*, paragraph 23, Schlechta Volume II, page 587.

Letters are cited by addressee and date. With a few noted exceptions, these are found in Schlechta, Volume III. There is a translation of them, with commentary, in *Selected Letters of Friedrich Nietzsche* Ed. Christopher Middleton (Chicago: University of Chicago Press, 1968).

NOTES

PREFACE

1. EH Why I Write Such Good Books 1, II 1100. For an explanation of the notes, see the preceding Key. All italics in quotations, unless otherwise stated, are the original author's.
2. See letter to Overbeck, October 18, 1888.
3. FW 340, II 202.

CHAPTER I: INTRODUCTION: ON APPROACHING NIETZSCHE

1. See Elizabeth Foerster-Nietzsche, *The Nietzsche-Wagner Correspondence* (New York: Boni and Liveright, 1921), pp. 291-298; see also letter to Fuchs, end of July, 1877.
2. EH Why I Write Such Good Books — The Genealogy of Morals, II 1143.
3. Erich Heller, *The Artist's Journey into the Interior* (New York: Random House, 1959), pp. 202-203.
4. Ludwig Wittgenstein, *Philosophical Investigations* (New York: Macmillan Company, 1958), par. 66.
5. EH Why I Write Such Good Books 1, II 1100.
6. See Walter Kaufmann, *Nietzsche: Philosopher, Psychologist, Antichrist* (3rd ed.; Princeton: Princeton University Press, 1968), pp. 287-306.
7. Wittgenstein, *Philosophical Investigations*, p. ix.
8. Nietzsche felt this himself. See the letter to Burckhardt, August, 1882.
9. Letter to Overbeck, April 7, 1884.

10. This is well recognized in Herbert Roeschl, "Nietzsche et la solitude," *Société française des études nietzschéenes,* Bulletin (1958), esp. p. 77.

11. Letter to Burckhardt, January 6, 1889. In his edition of the *Selected Letters of Friedrich Nietzsche,* Christopher Middleton writes "his" for "its," which is probably wrong. For earlier instances of this motif in Nietzsche see Za On the Old and New Tablets 19, II 454-455 and III 921-922 (WM 1040).

12. See the extraordinary book by Pierre Klossowski, *Nietzsche et le cercle vicieux* (Paris: Mercure de France, 1969), and the commentary on Nietzsche in Gilles Deleuze and Felix Guattari, *L'anti-Oedipe. Capitalisme et schizophrénie* (Paris: Editions de Minuit, 1972), pp. 102-103.

13. WKG VIII$_2$ pp. 431-432.

14. FW 125, II 126-127.

15. EH Why I Am a Destiny 1, II 1153.

16. M 103, I 1077.

17. Freud generally despaired of such a possibility. See, for instance, "Analysis, Terminable and Interminable," *Collected Papers,* Vol. V (London: Hogarth, 1953), pp. 316-357. At times, however, he is closer to accepting the possibility of a solution to Nietzsche's problem. See, in the same volume, "Why War," pp. 283-285, and "My Contact with Joseph Popper-Lynkeus," pp. 298-301.

18. HL 3, I 230; see also WKG V$_1$ p. 395.

19. FW 11, II 44.

20. WKG VIII$_2$ p. 433.

21. Immanuel Kant, *The Critique of Pure Reason,* trans. N. K. Smith (New York: St. Martin's Press, 1961), p. 7. My discussion here and in the following paragraph is informed, though not prompted, by Stanley Cavell, *Must We Mean What We Say?* (New York: Charles Scribner's Sons, 1969), pp. 352 ff.

22. GM iii 28, II 900.

23. III 893 (WM 1032).

24. WKG VIII$_3$ p. 289. A slightly different version of this note is given in III 834-835 and in Kaufmann's edition of WM 1041. Kaufmann reads "evaluate" (*abschätzen*) as "depreciate." This translation obscures Nietzsche's contention, made explicit elsewhere, that certain traits lie at the "bottom" of each form of life and, in their own affirmation, give that life its being. Nietzsche, as we shall see, holds this to be true of *all* forms of life; even slave morality "affirms." Hence the problem is not to "depreciate" them, which can't be done, but first to "evaluate."

CHAPTER II: THE NECESSITY AND POSSIBILITY OF TRUTH

1. I owe the expression to Judith N. Shklar's examination of the nineteenth century, *After Utopia* (Princeton: Princeton University Press, 1957).

2. WKG VIII$_2$ p. 339.

3. WKG VIII$_2$ p. 290 (WM 12). See III 548-551 (WM 585).

4. WKG VIII$_2$ p. 298. For an extended consideration see Gilles Deleuze, *Nietzsche et la philosophie* (Paris: Presses universitaires de France, 1962), esp.

pp. 1-3. See also Martin Heidegger, *Nietzsche* (Pfüllingen: Neske, 1961), II, 35-45, and Stanley Rosen, *Nihilism: a Philosophical Essay* (New Haven: Yale University Press, 1969), esp. pp. 94-139. An unconvincing argument against this position is made in Richard Schacht, "Nietzsche and Nihilism," in *Nietzsche,* ed. Robert Solomon (New York: Doubleday & Company, 1973), pp. 58-82.

5. Georg W. F. Hegel, *The Phenomenology of Mind,* trans. J. B. Baillie (London: George Allen & Unwin, 1966), p. 548. See Naumann XIV no. 23, pp. 15-16.

6. JGB 1, II 567.

7. JGB 2, II 567-568; see MAM i 1-2, I 447-448.

8. III 761-762 (WM 271).

9. Robin G. Collingwood's distinction of "absolute" and "relative" presuppositions is a close cousin to mine. See his *An Essay on Metaphysics* (Chicago: University of Chicago Press, 1972); see also Stephen Toulmin, "Conceptual Revolutions in Science," *Boston Studies in the Philosophy of Science,* Vol. III, eds. R. Cohen and M. Wartofsky (Dordrecht: Reidel, 1966), pp. 331-347 for a commentary. Nietzsche comes very close to making this distinction explicitly in WKG VII$_2$ pp. 127-128.

10. Naumann XIV p. 5.

11. This formulation is influenced by Ludwig Wittgenstein, *Philosophical Investigations* (New York: Macmillan Company, 1958), par. 231, and Stanley Cavell, "Existentialism and Analytic Philosophy," *Daedalus,* XCIII (Summer, 1964), 946-974.

12. Collingwood, *An Essay on Metaphysics,* p. 190.

13. The example is drawn from Thomas S. Kuhn, *The Structure of Scientific Revolutions* (Chicago: University of Chicago Press, 1962). My notion of "unquestioned" presuppositions is close to his "paradigms." For material relevant to this and the next chapter see Thomas S. Kuhn, "Reflections on my Critics," *Criticism and the Growth of Knowledge,* eds. I. Lakatos and R. Musgrave (Cambridge, England: The University Press, 1970), and Stephen Toulmin's essay in that volume linking Kuhn and Collingwood, as well as Kathryn Pyne Parsons' essay in *Nietzsche,* ed. Robert Solomon.

14. JGB 6, II 571.

15. HL 1, I 214.

16. Ludwig Wittgenstein, *On Certainty* (New York: Harper & Row, 1969), par. 97.

17. EH Preface 3, II 1066.

18. GD Preface, II 941. See Wolfgang Bartuschat, *Nietzsche: Selbstsein und Negativität; zur Problematik einer Philosophie des sich selbst vollenden Willens* (Inaugural Dissertation, Heidelberg, 1964), p. 166. For the argument that Nietzsche's writing is basically political here, see Erich F. Podach, *Ein Blick im Notizbücher Nietzsches* (Heidelberg: Rothe, 1963), p. 71. See also EH Why I Am a Destiny 1, II 1152-1153.

19. GT 12, I 70. Some limits to both diplomacy and blindness are introduced in Bernard Pautrat, *Versions du soleil: figures et système de Nietzsche* (Paris: Editions du Seuil, 1971), p. 325.

20. III 480 (WM 254).

21. "Corresponds" is Marx's usage (in the "Preface to a Contribution to a Critique of Political Economy"). See on this the important article by Maurice Godelier, "Système, structure et contradiction dans le *Capital*," *Les temps modernes*, XXII (November, 1966), 828-864.

22. SE 4, I 317. See HL 3, I 229.

23. JGB 61, II 621 is not a counter example. The "selective and cultivative influence" referred to there is designed to make a change in genealogy. See Chap. IX below.

24. Nietzsche's dealings with his own past are best examined in Pierre Klossowski, *Nietzsche et le cercle vicieux* (Paris: Mercure de France, 1969).

25. See Karl Hotter, *Das Bildungsproblem in der Philosophie Nietzsches* (Inaugural Dissertation, München, 1958), pp. 1-58.

26. The "museum" designation is Maurice Merleau-Ponty's in *La prose du monde* (Paris: Gallimard, 1969), p. 153. See HL 2, II 219.

27. Naumann XIV no. 204, p. 348.

28. For an example, obviously in other terms, see Hegel, *The Phenomenology of Mind,* p. 145.

29. HL 3, I 229.

30. III 779 (WM 257); GM Preface 2, II 764.

31. William Arrowsmith, "Nietzsche on the Classics and the Classicists," *Arion,* II (Winter, 1963), 7.

32. This pamphlet and the other relevant ones (Rohde's and Wagner's responses to Wilamowitz) are conveniently collected in Karlfried Grunder, ed., *Der Streit um Nietzsches Geburt der Tragödie* (Hildesheim: Olms Verlag, 1969). In his Introduction Grunder suggests that there was more involved in the acrimony of the dispute than simple philologica. Nietzsche was a student of Ritschl, the leader of one of the two prominent German schools of classical philology. The other school was lead by Otto Jahn, whose student Wilamowitz was. A version of this affair seems to be set forth in Za On the Teachers of Virtue, II 295-297. See also GD What I Owe to the Ancients 3, II 1029-1030.

33. Rohde's counterattack, for instance, was quite correctly responded to by Wilamowitz with the statement that whatever Rohde was defending, it was not what Nietzsche had said (see, for example, Grunder, *Der Streit* . . . , p. 122). Overall this is probably an accurate understanding of Rohde's appreciation of Nietzsche. There are, however, many traces (unmentioned) of Nietzsche's influence in Rohde's major work *Psyche.*

34. Arrowsmith, "Nietzsche on the Classics and the Classicists," p. 10.

35. GT 19 and 24, I 105 and 129 (my italics).

36. GT 21, I 113-114.

37. Wittgenstein, *Philosophical Investigations,* par. 90. Stanley Cavell is probably the first to see the link of this passage to Kant. See his *Must We Mean What We Say?* (New York: Charles Scribner's Sons, 1969), pp. 64-65. I have been much influenced by Cavell's reading of Wittgenstein.

38. I mention Rousseau here with the full knowledge that Nietzsche often directed very sharp attacks at him. Rousseau is a "moral tarantula," a romantic,

full of *odor femina*, etc., etc. Nietzsche seems to have accepted the conventional romantic understanding of Rousseau, based mainly on *La nouvelle Héloise, Les réveries du promeneur solitaire, Les confessions.* I suspect that if Nietzsche had paid equal attention to the *Discours sur l'origine de l'inégalité* and *Du contrat social* he would have had to come up with a more favorable understanding. So much has been persuasively argued by William D. Wiiliams, *Nietzsche and the French. A Study of the Influence of Nietzsche's French Reading on His Thought and Writing* (Oxford: Blackwell, 1952), esp. pp. xxi, 10-11, 130. The quote from Claude Lévi-Strauss is in his *Structural Anthropology* (Garden City: Doubleday Anchor Books, 1967), p. 22. The link of Rousseau, Lévi-Strauss and Nietzsche is made in Paul DeMan, *Blindness and Insight* (New York: Oxford University Press, 1971), pp. 138-165. He draws heavily on Jacques Derrida, *De la grammatologie* (Paris: Editions de Minuit, 1967), pp. 149 ff.

39. III 805 (WM 479). See also Eugène Fleischman, "L'esprit humain selon Claude Lévi-Strauss," *Archives européens de la sociologie*, Vol. VII, no. 1 (1966) 27-57, esp. p. 37.

40. GT 1, I 22.

41. HL 6, I 247. See also EH Why I Write Such Good Books ii, II 1099-1101. See Wittgenstein, *Philosophical Investigations*, p. 193 and Sec. II, par. xi.

42. WKG IV₁ p. 173.

43. JGB 260, II 730.

44. Kröner II No. 875, p. 305.

45. III 548-550 (WM 585A). See Martin Heidegger, *Nietzsche* (Pfüllingen: Neske, 1961), I, 33. See F. Assaad-Mikhail, "Heidegger, interprète de Nietzsche," *Revue de métaphysique et de morale*, LXIII (January-March, 1968), 16-55 and esp. p. 18: "*Le but (est de) créer une vie du questionnement qui force l'être à se découvrir.*"

46. This is not to say that there are no stopping places, only that they cannot be found. Compare Wittgenstein, *Philosophical Investigations*, par. 29.

47. III 499 (WM 486). See III 863 (WM 473). Jürgen Habermas, in his *Knowledge and Human Interests* (Boston: Beacon Press, 1970), chap. 11, attacks precisely this point in Nietzsche from the point of view of a Kantian who has assimilated the historical lessons of Marx. His attack is well formulated and would be telling if, in fact, the positivism he accuses Nietzsche of were the only alternative to the critical rationalism he (Habermas) proposes. See, however, the discussion of Kant below.

48. I shall investigate this shortly. See Bernhard Bueb, *Nietzsches Kritik der praktischen Vernunft* (Stuttgart: Klett, 1970), pp. 9-10, 19-23.

49. Naumann XIV no. 55, p. 29. See WL 1, III 314: "What then is truth? A mobile army of metaphors, metonyms, anthropomorphisms, in brief a sum of human relations which have been enhanced . . . and which, after long use seen firm, canonical, obligatory to a people: truths are illusions of which one has forgotten that that is what they are. . . ."

50. FW 357, II 225-229.

51. Immanuel Kant, *The Critique of Pure Reason*, trans. N. K. Smith (New York: St. Martin's Press, 1961), p. 7.

52. FW 357, II 225-229.

53. Kant, *Critique of Pure Reason,* p. 435.

54. See III 884-886 (WM 530).

55. There is a similar but more disparate account in Karl Löwith, *From Hegel to Nietzsche* (New York: Holt, Rinehart and Winston, 1964), pp. 6-7.

56. WKG IV₁ pp. 208-209. See Bueb, *Nietzsches Kritik der praktischen Vernunft,* p. 19.

57. III 884 (WM 579).

58. Kröner II no. 18 p. 8. See JGB 3, II 569: "Not just man is the measure of all things." Nietzsche is not Protagoras; see Chap. VI below and III 760-761 (WM 458).

59. Kröner I no. 144 p. 67.

60. III 564 (WM 571). See JGB 11, II 576.

61. WKG V₁ p. 430.

62. WKG VIII₂ p. 295. Earlier editions (WM 477) omit the title and the "as that" in the clause between dashes. See also Naumann XIV no. 74 p. 36 and III 733-735 (WM 423).

63. Compare Wittgenstein's notion that the Sèvres meter neither is a meter long, nor is not a meter long.

64. Kröner I no. 131 p. 63.

65. III 499 (WM 505). The color example seems to be directed against Kant.

66. III 883-884 (WM 579). See III 548-551 (WM 585) and III 717-720 (WM 586).

67. III 556 (WM 507).

68. III 706 (WM 567). See III 769-770 (WM 568).

69. This is not to suggest that these are the same concepts, merely that they have the same relation to the "empirical world."

70. Kröner II no. 375 p. 305.

71. III 726 (WM 584). See WKG VIII₂ p. 291.

72. III 925 (WM 256).

73. Naumann XIV no. 17 p. 14.

74. HL 1, I 214, 213.

75. Wittgenstein, *Philosophical Investigations,* par. 1.

76. See below and Joan Stambaugh, *Untersuchungen zum Problem der Zeit bei der Philosophie Nietzsches* (Den Haag: Nidjhoff, 1959), p. 174. See Wittgenstein, *On Certainty,* par. 163.

77. Kröner II no. 56 p. 24.

78. III 915 (WM 535). See Stambaugh, *Untersuchungen zum Problem der Zeit bei der Philosophie Nietzsches,* pp. 58-59. An interesting discussion is in Arthur Danto, "Semantical Theory and the Limits of Nihilism," *New Essays in Phenomenology,* ed. J. Edie (Chicago: Quadrangle, 1969), p. 162.

79. WP, WKG IV₁ pp. 164-165.

80. WKG IV₂ p. 119.

CHAPTER III: THE EPISTEMOLOGY OF NIHILISM

1. For an interesting discussion drawing these relations see Bernard Pautrat,

Versions du soleil: figures et système de Nietzsche (Paris: Editions du Seuil, 1971), pp. 156-265.

2. MAM i 11, II 453.

3. WKG VIII₂ p. 152. That the relations of signs to signified is not unilateral should no longer require mention. The *locus classicus* is Ferdinand de Saussure, *Cours de linguistique générale* (Paris: Payot, 1967). For additional arguments see Jerrold J. Katz, *The Philosophy of Language* (New York: Harper & Row, 1966), esp. pp. 186 ff. Compare Karl Marx and Friedrich Engels, *The German Ideology* (New York: International Publishers, 1961), p. 122.

4. See Stanley Rosen, "Nihilism," *New Essays in Phenomenology*, ed. J. Edie (Chicago: Quadrangle Books, 1969), pp. 151-158. See also his *Nihilism: a Philosophical Essay* (New Haven: Yale University Press, 1969), esp. pp. xii-xx.

5. See Martin Heidegger, *On the Way to Language* (New York: Harper & Row, 1970), esp. pp. 1-57. This is the foundation of the interpretation of Pierre Klossowski, *Nietzsche et le cercle vicieux* (Paris: Mercure de France, 1969). Pautrat, *Versions du soleil*, pp. 358-361, also finds that this is what Nietzsche is doing, but thinks it impossible.

6. III 862 (WM 522). See GM Preface 7, II 769: "Gray is the most important color" for the genealogist. See ZB 2, III 196-213 for Nietzsche's less mature thoughts on language and culture.

7. Martin Heidegger, *Nietzsche* (Pfüllingen: Neske, 1961), II, 378. Danto has argued the same from the point of view of analytic philosophy. See his *Nietzsche as Philosopher* (New York: Macmillan Company, 1965) and his "Semantical Theory and the Logical Limits of Nihilism," *New Essays in Phenomenology*, ed. J. Edie (Chicago: Quadrangle, 1969), pp. 159-176. For a short commentary on some of the problems in Danto's approach, see note 22 below.

8. EH Why I Write Such Good Books 1, II 1100.

9. This essay is not included in the Schlechta volumes. See "On Words and Music," *The Complete Works of Friedrich Nietzsche*, ed. Oscar Levy (New York: Macmillan Company, 1914), II, 30-31. See also Kröner II, no. 143 p. 201, and Ludwig Wittgenstein, *Philosophical Investigations* (New York: Macmillan Company, 1958), par. 301.

10. GT Attempt at a Self-Critique *passim* and esp. 3 and 7, I 9-18, esp. 11 and 17.

11. Kröner II no. 92 p. 41.

12. WS 11 (MAM ii), I 878-879 (my italics).

13. JGB 20, II 584 (my italics). See Nietzsche's proposal at the end of the first essay in GM for a prize to be offered for the best essay on the question "What light does linguistics and especially the study of etymology throw on the history of the evolution of moral consciousness?" The school of anthropological linguistics associated with Edward Sapir and Benjamin Lee Whorf has advanced virtually identical hypotheses. See Edward Sapir, *Language: an Introduction to the Study of Speech* (New York: Harcourt, Brace & World, 1969), *passim.* Benjamin L. Whorf, *Language, Thought and Reality* (Cambridge: M.I.T. Press, 1964), esp. "Language and Logic," pp. 233-245. For a good criticism of Whorf's oversimplifications see Claude Lévi-Strauss, *Structural Anthropology* (Garden

City: Doubleday Anchor Books, 1967), pp. 66-95. For Nietzsche's position see WL 1, III 313. The link of Nietzsche and Sapir-Whorf is made explicitly in H. Wein, "Métaphysique et antimétaphysique," *Revue de métaphysique et de morale,* LXIII (October-December, 1958), 385-411. Nietzsche and Whorf use the same illustration of the reifying qualities of the subject-object distinction (lightning). See GM i 13, II 789 and p. 243 in the Whorf essay cited above.

14. WL 2, III 320. See Georg W. F. Hegel, *The Phenomenology of Mind,* trans. J. B. Baillie (London: George Allen & Unwin, 1966), p. 105.

15. JGB 268, II 740 (my italics). The following Wittgenstein citation is *Philosophical Investigations,* par. 19.

16. GD Reason in Philosophy 5, II 960. On "truth as a woman" see JGB Preface, II 565.

17. GD Skirmishes of an Untimely Man 5, II 993.

18. GM iii 27, II 898.

19. See Tracy B. Strong, "Hold on to Your Brains: An Essay in Meta-Theory," *Power and Community,* eds. P. Green and S. Levinson (New York: Pantheon, 1970).

20. RWB 5, I 387.

21. WKG VIII₂ p. 291 (WM 12).

22. There rages a sharp debate among Nietzsche scholars as to whether or not Nietzsche "had" an epistemology. Karl Jaspers and Karl Schlechta maintain that he didn't. They seek to show a Nietzsche who criticizes and destroys the prejudices of his time. They argue that since there can be for Nietzsche no "true" knowledge, there can also be no epistemology. Against this Arthur Danto and E. R. Dodds try to show that Nietzsche had a coherent epistemology (which Danto refers to as "non-cognitivism"). Danto's conclusion depends, however, as Kurt R. Fischer points out in "Review," *Journal of Philosophy,* Vol. LXIV, No. 18 (1967), 564-569, on the presumption that the reason Nietzsche never formulated his epistemology is that he never got around to it. Danto then sees himself as merely reconstructing what Nietzsche would or could or should have done. He never asks himself why Nietzsche didn't. Danto is suspect on two other grounds. As Walter Kaufmann points out (in his edition of the GM, p. 22, n. 5), Danto (a) finds no significant difference between those works that Nietzsche saw to press and those he didn't, and (b) often uses truncated quotations. In any case both those pro and con epistemology seem to me to share a common flaw: they assume that epistemology means for Nietzsche *an* epistemology. They thus retain the Kantian view that either there is or there isn't a pure epistemology and that this antinomy exhausts the alternatives.

23. See Heidegger, *Nietzsche,* II, 378.

24. GM i 13, II 789-790. See Whorf, *Language, Thought and Reality,* p. 243: "We are constantly reading into nature fictional acting entities, simply because our verbs have substantives in front of them. We have to say 'it flashed' or 'a light flashed,' setting up an actor 'it' or 'light' to perform an action 'to flash.' Yet the flashing and the light are one and the same." Such considerations in Nietzsche make it difficult to hold with Kaufmann that Nietzsche's conception of the will to power resembles Shakespeare's understanding of strength in *Measure for Measure,* Act II, scene ii, lines 107-111, when Isabella asserts:

> O, it is excellent
> to have a giant's strength; but it is tyrannous
> to use it like a giant.
> *Lucio:* That's well said.

I have added the line for Lucio. The apparently sardonic context, in my reading, casts some doubt on the seriousness of Shakespeare's intention. In any case it is not Nietzsche's position, though there is no doubt that Kaufmann finds it to be so. He writes in his *From Shakespeare to Existentialism* (Garden City: Doubleday, Anchor Books, 1960), p. 249: "This is Nietzsche in a nutshell." Perhaps the final comment on this is Shaw's in *What I Really Said About the War:* "I think that it is good to have a giant's strength and not at all tyrannous to use it like a giant, providing you are a decent sort of giant." For an elaboration of these problems see John Silber, "Being and Doing," *Chicago Law Review* (Autumn, 1967), pp. 47-91; Sigmund Freud, "Criminality from a Sense of Guilt," *Collected Papers* (London: Hogarth, 1953), IV, 341-344; and Za The Pale Criminal, II 303-305. See Chap. VIII below.

25. III 733 (WM 529).

26. MAM i 2, I 448; WKG IV$_1$ pp. 20-21. See also MAM i 1, I 447 and WKG IV$_1$ p. 19.

27. Naumann XII no. 230 p. 129.

28. WKG IV$_4$ p. 305.

29. MAM i 18, I 460.

30. WS 11 (MAM ii), I 878.

31. III 862 (WM 522).

32. WS 55 (MAM ii), I 903. See also WS 10 (MAM ii), I 878 and esp. EH Why I Write Such Good Books 1, II 1100.

33. JGB 19, II 582-583.

34. See my "Dramaturgical Discourse and Political Enactments: Towards an Artistic Foundation for Political Space," in a forthcoming book edited by Stanford Lyman and Richard Brown. See Chap. VII below.

35. III 876 (WM 667).

36. JGB 21, II 585.

37. FW 374, II 249-250. See FW 112, II 119-120.

38. III 490 (WM 631).

39. GD The Four Great Errors 5, II 975.

40. III 540 (WM 552).

41. III 767-768 (WM 551). On the atom as "super-added" cause see JGB 12 and 17, II 577 and 580-581; letter to Gast, end of August, 1883. See III 541 (WM 552): "There are no opposites, only from logic do we have the concept of opposites — and from there they are falsely carried over to things." See Wittgenstein, *Philosophical Investigations,* par. 81; see also W. V. O. Quine, "Two Dogmas of Empiricism," *From a Logical Point of View* (New York: Harper & Row, 1963), pp. 20-46.

42. FW 357, II 225-229. See III 504 (WM 650).

43. III 768 (WM 551).

44. JGB 16, II 579-580.

45. GD Four Great Errors 3, II 972-973.

46. JGB 23, II 587. See Immanuel Kant, *The Critique of Pure Reason*, trans. N. K. Smith (New York: St. Martin's Press, 1961), pp. 7-8.

47. III 501 (WM 550).

48. This link is also drawn in Pautrat, *Versions du soleil*, pp. 235 ff.

49. FW 58, II 77-78.

50. III 543 (WM 517). See III 501 (WM 628 and 550).

51. WL i, III 314.

52. FW 11, II 44.

53. FW 58, II 78.

54. III 770 (WM 568).

55. M 210, I 1161.

56. FW 11, II 44.

57. See Naumann X p. 190: "Wir kennen nur eine Realität, die der Gedanken."

58. HL 10, I 280-281. See Chap. VIII below for a fuller discussion.

59. III 491 (WM 575).

60. WKG VIII$_1$ pp. 215-216 (WM 5). Walter Kaufmann refuses (as did Martin Heidegger) to take Nietzsche's biological language seriously. Thus he uses the figurative "inveterate" for *eingefleischt*. The literal translation is "incarnate." "Inveterate" is a possible meaning but loses the physiological possibilities of *eingefleischt*, as in *der eingefleischte Gott*, "God incarnate."

61. Za On the Old and New Tablets 8, II 447-448.

62. FW 344, II 207.

63. WKG VIII$_2$ p. 290. See also WKG VIII$_2$ pp. 287, 292. See III 550 (WM 585): "Overcoming of philosophers through the destruction of the world of being: intermediary period of nihilism: before there is yet present the strength to reverse values and to deify becoming and the apparent world as the only world and to call them good."

64. Rainer Maria Rilke, "Letter to Witold von Hulewicz, November 13, 1925," *Letters, 1910-1926*, trans. Jane Bannard Greene and M. D. Herder (New York: W. W. Norton & Company, 1948), pp. 374-375.

65. The best pieces I know are Erich Heller, "Nietzsche and Wittgenstein," *The Artist's Journey into the Interior* (New York: Random House, 1959); Stanley Cavell in some of the essays in *Must We Mean What We Say?* (New York: Charles Scribner's Sons, 1969); Robert Goff, "Aphorism as Lebensform in Wittgenstein's *Philosophical Investigations*," *New Essays in Phenomenology*, ed. J. Edie, pp. 58-71.

66. Wittgenstein, *Philosophical Investigations*, p. 226.

67. Ludwig Wittgenstein, *On Certainty* (New York: Harper & Row, 1969), par. 559.

68. See Wittgenstein, *Philosophical Investigations*, par. 217. The quotations from *On Certainty*, above and following, par. 95.

69. Wittgenstein, *On Certainty*, par. 378. See Cavell, *Must We Mean What We Say?* pp. 238-266.

70. Wittgenstein, *Philosophical Investigations*, par. 122. Wittgenstein con-

tinues on and, in parentheses, asks: "Is this a *Weltanschauung?*" Stanley Rosen (*Nihilism,* chap. 1) picks up the Nietzsche-Wittgenstein link. But in his determination to make them both radical exponents of the German idealist tradition, he leaves off the parentheses and assumes that Wittgenstein's answer is unproblematically "Yes." Wittgenstein does not equate *Weltanschauung* with *Lebensform,* however; he may see a family resemblance in them, but that is only the beginning of a problem.

71. Wittgenstein, *On Certainty,* par. 152. See pars. 96, 136, 401, 402.

72. Wittgenstein, *Philosophical Investigations,* par. 50. Peter Strawson's criticism of this in his review of the *Philosophical Investigations,* reprinted in *Wittgenstein's Philosophical Investigations,* ed. George Pitcher (Garden City: Doubleday Anchor Books, 1966), seems to me to miss Wittgenstein's point. What matters is not whether or not we use the Sèvres meter or a light-wave length as the basis of measure. Wittgenstein is making a point about the relation of a proposition ("X is a meter long") to its grounds ("We know where to look to find out what a meter is").

73. *Philosophical Investigations,* par. 178. See par. 92.

74. *Ibid.,* par. 115.

75. *Ibid.,* par. 89; pars. 371-373.

76. *Ibid.,* par. 50.

77. *Ibid.,* par. 103. See pars. 98-102. See Ludwig Wittgenstein, *Blue and Brown Books* (Oxford: Blackwell, 1969), p. 109: "Language makes things the same."

78. Wittgenstein, *Philosophical Investigations,* par. 593.

79. *Ibid.,* pars. 109, 115, 309.

80. *Ibid.,* pars. 118, 194. Hanna Fenichel Pitkin has argued to me that the relation here and in this whole paragraph must be the other way around, that our "urge to misunderstand" bewitches our intelligence. I am not sure which is true for Wittgenstein — he seems to talk both ways. For Nietzsche, it is, I think, the way I have it.

81. *Ibid.,* par. 109. See par. 299. See Ludwig Wittgenstein, *Zettel* (Berkeley and Los Angeles: University of California Press, 1967), par. 690.

82. Wittgenstein, *Philosophical Investigations,* par. 133. See par. 255: "The philosopher's treatment of a problem is like the treatment of an illness."

83. Stanley Rosen (*Nihilism*) picks up this link, but he fails to recognize that nihilism is also a historical stage.

84. III 550 (WM 585).

85. By "ordinary language philosophy" I mean what Wittgenstein does; less so what, for example, Ryle or Weldon do. Granted that this is perhaps an idiosyncratic nomenclature. But ordinary language philosophy, as Stanley Cavell has noted, is about the words that are meant and said by particular men and the fact that "to understand what they (the words) mean you must also understand what they (whoever is using them) mean." *Must We Mean What We Say?* p. 270.

86. Wittgenstein, *Philosophical Investigations,* par. 129.

87. Thus J. O. Urmson's remarks about ordinary language and analytic philosophy simply don't apply to Wittgenstein's enterprise. He says: "Should it

be accomplished for English, one will still have to determine in what degree its conclusions might apply to other languages," Colloque de Royaumont, *La philosophie analytique* (Paris: Editions de Minuit, 1962), p. 39. My translation. Also cited in Rosen, *Nihilism*, p. 49. See Stanley Cavell, "Existentialism and Analytic Philosophy," *Daedalus*, XLIII (Summer, 1964), 946-974, and *Must We Mean What We Say?* pp. 97-114.

88. Wittgenstein, *Philosophical Investigations*, par. 130.

89. Wittgenstein also calls "language games" such activities as praying, a coronation, telling jokes, etc., or generally any form of discourse that has its particular practices and rationality.

90. *Philosophical Investigations*, pars. 131 and 109. Compare Thomas S. Kuhn, "A Function for Thought Experiments," *Mélanges Alexandre Koyré* (Paris: Hermann, 1964), II, 329-334.

91. Wittgenstein, *ibid.*, p. 230; see p. 56n.

92. HL 6, I 247 (my italics).

93. HL 10, I 282-283.

94. Wittgenstein, *Philosophical Investigations*, par. 119. See par. 464.

95. Ludwig Wittgenstein, *Remarks on the Foundations of Mathematics* (Cambridge: M.I.T. Press, 1966), p. 57. See Chap. IX below for a complete development of this point.

96. For instance, pars. 99-106.

97. Wittgenstein, *Remarks on the Foundations of Mathematics*, p. 157; Za Preface 5, II 283; Wittgenstein, *Philosophical Investigations*, par. 66.

CHAPTER IV: THE PSYCHOSOCIOLOGY OF ETHICS: THE BASIC TREND OF MORALITY

1. See Nietzsche's discussion, WKG VIII3 p. 89.

2. Arthur Danto, "Semantical Theory and the Logical Limits of Nihilism," *New Essays in Phenomenology*, ed. J. Edie (Chicago: Quadrangle Books, 1969), pp. 61-62. See also his *Nietzsche as Philosopher* (New York: Macmillan Company, 1965), p. 159.

3. Erich Heller *The Artist's Journey into the Interior* (New York: Random House, 1959) and Stanley Rosen *Nihilism: a Philosophical Essay* (New Haven: Yale University Press, 1969) share this position.

4. See Karl Jaspers, *Nietzsche: An Introduction to His Philosophical Activity*, trans. Charles Walratt and Charles J. Schmitz (Tucson: University of Arizona Press, 1965), esp. p. 288. Karl Schlechta, *Der Fall Nietzsche* (München: Carl Hanser Verlag, 1958), snares this position.

5. Lucien Goldman calls this the "genetic structuralism of moralities" in his "The Subject of Cultural Creation," *Boston Studies in the Philosophy of Science*, Vol. IV, eds. R. Cohen and M. Wartofsky (Dordrecht: Reidel, 1969), pp. 241-260.

6. GM ii 12, II 817-818.

7. GD The Four Great Errors 6, II 975-976.

8. III 831 (WM 262). See MAM i 40, I 481.

9. III 925 (WM 256). The argument against La Rochefoucauld is made in III 461 (WM 362).

10. FW 345, II 210. See also III 512 (WM 95).

11. See III 480 (WM 399); GM Preface 6, II 767-768.

12. III 484 (WM 253).

13. M 230, I 1168.

14. III 546 (WM 724).

15. MAM i 68, I 494. See FW 84, II 92-93.

16. JGB 225, II 689. See letter to Gersdorff, February 4, 1872: "I fear that we are not born to be happy."

17. GM i 3, II 774.

18. GM i 2, II 772.

19. JGB 228, II 691-693.

20. III 484 (WM 253).

21. JGB 190, II 648, See GT Attempt at a Self-Critique 4, I 13.

22. GD The Four Great Errors 5, II 975. See WKG VIII$_2$ p. 87.

23. WKG VIII$_2$ p. 154. See pp. 151-157.

24. WS 44 (MAM ii), I 900. See GM ii 1, II 799 and WKG IV$_3$ p. 211.

25. Stanley Cavell, *The World Viewed: Reflections on the Ontology of Film* (New York: Viking Press, 1971), p. 59. See GT 3, I 29-30 where Nietzsche recounts the legend of the encounter between the satyr companion of Dionysos, and King Midas. To the question of what is the best and most desirable for men Silenus is first silent, then answers: "O wretched and ephemeral race, children of chance and misery, why do you compel me to tell you what it would be best for you not to hear? What is best of all is beyond your reach: not to be born, not to be, to be nothing. But the second best for you — is to die soon." See the discussion of Dionysos and the dionysian in Chaps. V and VI below.

26. JGB 201, II 658.

27. MAM i 71, I 495.

28. WKG VIII$_2$ p. 156. The line is omitted in Schlechta, given in a footnote in Kaufmann's WM 786. In addition, WKG VIII$_2$ p. 207 is entitled *Ein tractatus politicus von F. N.*

29. MAM i 92, I 501-502.

30. GM ii 9, II 812. On the etymological point, see Emile Benveniste, *Le vocabulaire des institutions indo-européenes,* (Paris: Editions de Minuit, 1969), I, 190-191.

31. See GM ii 20, II 830-831. See M 13, I 1022: "One has pushed the insanity so far as to understand existence itself as a punishment." For an interesting and broad investigation see John Wikse, "On Possession" (Ph.D. thesis, University of California, Berkeley, 1973).

32. WKG VIII$_2$ p. 311. See p. 331.

33. GM ii 21, II 833.

34. See esp. MAM i 39, I 479-481; III 745 (WM 288).

35. M 128, I 1098. The Freud essay is in *Collected Papers* (London: Hogarth, 1953), V, 154-157.

36. M 128, I 1098. See MAM i 39, I 479-481.

37. WS 33 (MAM ii), I 893. See Ludwig Wittgenstein, *Philosophical Investigations* (New York: Macmillan Company, 1958), par. 65.

38. GM ii 14, II 822.

39. WS 33 (MAM ii), I 893. See WS 28 (MAM ii), I 890-891 and GM ii 4, II 804-805.

40. See Freud, "Criminality from a Sense of Guilt," *Collected Papers*, IV, 341-344; and "Dostojewski and Parricide," V, 222-242. The same basic idea seems present to me in Durkheim's notion of anomie. See his *Suicide* (Glencoe: Free Press, 1962), esp. pp. 241-276. In general see Za The Pale Criminal, II 303 and WKG VIII₃ pp. 82-83.

41. M 202, I 1149.

42. *Ibid.*

43. Similar dynamics are analyzed in the writings of Gregory Bateson and Ronald D. Laing and form the basis for much contemporary "radical" psychiatry.

44. M 202, I 1149.

45. WKG VIII₂ p. 432.

46. Fyodor Dostoyevsky, *The Brothers Karamazov*, trans. Constance Garnett (New York: New American Library, 1957), pp. 230-231.

47. Freud thus accuses Dostoyevsky ("Dostojewsky and Parricide") of becoming a "gaoler" of mankind rather than an "apostolic" liberator — even though this is a role Freud refuses for himself at the end of *Civilization and Its Discontents* (New York: W. W. Norton & Company, 1962), p. 104. See also Søren Kierkegaard, *The Present Age* and *Of the Difference Between a Genuis and an Apostle* (New York: Harper & Row, 1962), esp. pp. 81-83, 101, 107. See Nikolai Berdayev, *Dostojewsky,* trans. W. Lowrie (New York: Meridian Books, 1957), pp. 64, 82, 96. The same point is made in very different language by Georg Simmel, *The Sociology of Georg Simmel,* ed. K. Wolff (Glencoe: Free Press, 1950), pp. 123, 136. According to Simmel the two basic forms of social relationships are the dyad and triad. In the former, "each of the two feels himself confronted by the other only, and not by a collectivity above him. . . ." The dyad therefore does not attain that superpersonal life that the individual feels to be independent of himself. The relations of the dyad are characterized by intimacy, meaning, and fragility. The triad, on the other hand, acquires a "third element, or . . . a social framework that transcends both members." This allows for the incorporation of many more people with a subsequent loss in meaning and intensity, but a gain in stability. Hence to be drawn by the desire for permanence, no matter what the nobility of one's morality in the moment, is ultimately and perhaps necessarily to contribute to the victory of the mediocre, in fact to the encouragement of the mediocre. Simmel wrote a rather good book on Nietzsche which reflects some of these concerns, *Schopenhauer und Nietzsche* (Leipzig: Duncker und Humboldt, 1911). The only commentator I know of who deals with the link of Simmel and Nietzsche is Walter M. Salter, *Nietzsche the Thinker* (New York: Holt and Co., 1917), p. 378.

CHAPTER V: WHO IS DIONYSIAN? THE PROBLEM
OF THE IMMORALIST

1. WKG VIII$_2$ p. 349.

2. Letter to Elizabeth, December, 1888. There are many passages of a similar self-consciousness. See, for instances, EH Preface, II 1065-1068; letters to Gast, December 16, 1888; to Fuchs, December 18, 1888; to Overbeck, December 28, 1888; etc.

3. M 9, I 1019. See RWB 11, I 431.

4. EH Why I Am A Destiny 8, II 1158 (my italics).

5. M Preface 3, I 1013. See n. 38, Chap. II above.

6. M 9, I 1020. See WWK, WKG IV$_1$ p. 184.

7. GD Skirmishes of an Untimely Man 45, II 1022.

8. Best known is Richard Oehler, *Nietzsche und die Vorsokratiker* (Leipzig: Dürr'schen Buchhandlung, 1904). Oehler is hostile to Socrates. There are also those who accept the view of Nietzsche as simply opposed to Socrates and use it to attack Nietzsche. Thus E. Sandvoss, *Sokrates und Nietzsche* (Leiden: E. J. Brill, 1966) sees Nietzsche as an ideologist and Socrates as a "philosopher in the service of God" (p. 136). Hermann-Josef Schmidt, *Nietzsche und Sokrates. Philosophische Untersuchungen zu Nietzsches Sokratesbild* (Meisenheim am Glan: Hain, 1969), contains a good attack on Sandvoss (pp. 2-6). His conclusions would seem to effectively criticize also Karl Jaspers' views of Nietzsche as a world-historical sacrifice for our time. Schmidt's is by and large the best full-length criticism available; for some of his criticism, see note 12 below.

9. WKG IV$_1$ p. 173.

10. III 519 (WM 274). See GT 15, I 82-87.

11. Walter Kaufmann, *Nietzsche: Philosopher, Psychologist, Antichrist* (3rd ed.; Princeton: Princeton University Press, 1968), p. 398. The best example of this might be Nietzsche's attack on the "cultural philistine," David Strauss. See EH Why I Write Such Good Books — Untimely Considerations 2, II 1114; on Nietzsche's *Kriegspraxis,* EH Why I Am So Wise 7, II 1092, and the letter to Gersdorff, February 11, 1874.

12. Schmidt, *Nietzsche und Sokrates,* p. 4. Schmidt also points out (pp. 23-24) that Nietzsche transforms the *sophia-amathia* distinction in the *Apology* to that between consciousness and instinct. Schmidt's conclusion, however (p. 354), that Socrates is used by Nietzsche only as a *Demonstrations-Objekt* for Nietzsche's various antipodes, is far too narrow. It neglects the whole historical perspective. See below, and Chaps. VI and VII.

13. JGB 295, II 755-756; FW 340, II 201. See also EH Why I Write Such Good Books — Beyond Good and Evil, II 1142.

14. Kaufmann, *Nietzsche,* p. 411.

15. Za On the Three Metamorphoses, II 293-294. The Hegel-Wagner link is made specifically in FWg 10, II 924.

16. Letter to Cosima, January, 1889. See Erich Podach, *L'effondrement de*

Nietzsche (Paris: Gallimard, 1931), pp. 109-129. esp. p. 127. The literature on Nietzsche and Ariadne is varied and tortuous. The most important things seem to me to be said in Gilles Deleuze, *Nietzsche et la philosophie* (Paris: Presses universitaires de France, 1962), pp. 213-217. For a standard interpretation, see Karl Reinhardt, *Nietzsches Klage der Ariadne* (Frankfurt: Klostermann, 1936), esp. pp. 66 ff.

17. III 758 (WM 430).

18. GD The Problem of Socrates 9, II 954. See WKG VIII$_3$ p. 60.

19. Naumann X p. 125.

20. Naumann IX p. 157.

21. This can be problematic, for though we often assume that Socrates always wins, and certainly Plato often appears to want us to think so, at a deeper level, Socrates often does not win, especially in the major dialogues with Sophists (*Gorgias, Protagoras*).

22. III 732 (WM 441).

23. III 760 (WM 431).

24. See WWK, WKG IV$_1$ p. 182 and GD The Problem of Socrates 12, II 956. Appropriately enough, in arguing to Crito that he should stay in Athens, thus ensuring his death, Socrates quotes a passage from the *Iliad* where Achilles sees his choice as between growing old, or dying young and remaining "famous forever." (*Crito* 44b).

25. GT 8, I 52-53; GT 17, I 94. See NW Wagner as a Danger 1, II 1043 and NW Epilogue 2, II 1061.

26. GT 13, I 77. See III 758 (WM 430).

27. GT 23, I 127.

28. GT 13, I 77; GT 23, I 125.

29. GD The Problem with Socrates 10, II 955.

30. See WWK, WKG IV$_1$ pp. 180-181. In NW Where Wagner Belongs, II 1050, Nietzsche speaks of Wagner as a "virtuoso . . . born enemy of the straight line."

31. GD The Problem of Socrates 9, II 955.

32. WKG IV$_1$ p. 180 (my italics).

33. Za The Song of Melancholy 3, II 533-536. See Za The Awakening 2, II 547; The Ass Festival 1, II 548-549; On the Three Metamorphoses, II 293.

34. WWK, WKG IV$_1$ p. 180. See WKG VIII$_3$ p. 29; AC 29, II 1190-1191.

35. Perhaps the most interesting collection of these are the notes from the period Nietzsche was working on *The Antichrist*. See WKG VIII$_2$ pp. 396-409, 333-359.

36. JGB 60, II 620-621. Incomprehensibly, Walter Kaufmann thinks this refers to Moses.

37. JGB 164, II 638. See JGB 153, II 637: "Whatever is done from love always occurs beyond good and evil."

38. WKG VIII$_2$ p. 350; III 830 (WM 158). See III 639, 642-643, 656-657, 658 (WM 159, 165, 169, 168). See WKG VIII$_3$ pp. 36-37.

39. AC 33, II 1195-1196.

40. III 654 (WM 166).

41. WKG VIII$_2$ p. 338.

42. AC 39, II 1200. "Christianity is possible only as the most private form of life." See also III 660 (WM 179).

43. JGB 269, II 743-744.

44. See AC 29, II 1191. See AC 32, II 1194: "To negate is the very thing that is impossible to [Christ] ."

45. AC 33, II 1195.

46. AC 44, II 1207.

47. AC 35, II 1197. See the ironic despair of AC 38, II 1200: "Whom does the Christian negate?"

48. AC 34, II 1196.

49. AC 39, II 1200. See WKG VIII$_2$ p. 404.

50. AC 43, II 1205.

51. AC 43, II 1205 (Nietzsche's italics).

52. WKG VIII$_2$ p. 409.

53. VM 94 (MAM ii), I 772. See also Naumann XIV p. 115: "Plato says the dead in Hades are true philosophers; he means saved from their bodies."

54. FW 340, II 201-202. In *The Portable Nietzsche* (New York: Viking Press, 1954), p. 101, Walter Kaufmann cites part of this passage. His selectivity is noteworthy for he chooses the third of the aphorism most conducive to his own interpretation of Socrates. He leaves out the part about "life as a long sickness," and the exclamation that "Socrates suffered from life," ending his selection with the line that Socrates "was not only the wisest talker [*Schwätzer*, which means something like 'prattler' — TBS] who ever was, he was just as great in his silence." The next sentence, not given by Kaufmann, begins: "I would that in the last moment of his life he had remained silent — then he would have belonged to an even higher order of spirits."

55. III 773 (WM 1052).

56. Karl Jaspers, *Nietzsche and Christianity*, trans. E. B. Ashton (Chicago: Gateway Editions, 1961), p. 90.

57. Albert Camus, *The Rebel*, trans. A. Bower (New York: Vintage Books, 1957), pp. 9-10.

58. Søren Kierkegaard, *The Present Age* trans. A. Dru and W. Lowrie (New York: Harper & Row, 1962), p. 42. See Georg W. F. Hegel, *The Phenomenology of Mind*, trans. J. B. Baillie (London: George Allen & Unwin, 1966), p. 114.

59. GD Skirmishes of an Untimely Man 51, II 1026.

60. AC 34, II 1196 (my italics).

61. WKG VIII$_2$ p. 336.

62. It is sometimes argued that an early opposition of Socrates and Dionysos is replaced in Nietzsche's later thought by a truer opposition of Christ and Dionysos. In Kaufmann's view, in fact, the new Dionysos has incorporated much of Socrates into himself; hence, the earlier opposition is inappropriate. I find little textual evidence for this. It has been the burden of this chapter to argue that Socrates and Christ represent opposite ends of a continuum which Nietzsche finds in its entirety disastrous. Their respective effects will ultimately be the same. Dionysos represents something else: he is not a synthesis of previously operative situations.

63. Za On Reading and Writing, II 305; GM Preface 8, II 770.

64. The analogy of Parzival and "answers in search of questions" is suggested by Claude Lévi-Strauss, *The Scope of Anthropology*, (London: Jonathan Cape, 1964), pp. 37-38.

65. JGB 164, II 638.

66. Za On Reading and Writing, II 305. Ludwig Wittgenstein, *Philosophical Investigations* (New York: Macmillan Company, 1958), p. x.

67. JGB 295, II 754.

CHAPTER VI: WHAT IS DIONYSIAN? NIETZSCHE AND THE GREEKS

1. Most prominent in the United States are Hannah Arendt, Eric Voegelin, Leo Strauss and his followers.

2. WP, WKG IV$_1$ p. 159.

3. HL 10, I 284.

4. PTZ Preface, III 351. See SE 8, I 353: "I hold as useless each written word behind which there does not stand a summons to action."

5. Naumann X, p. 410.

6. WKG IV$_1$ p. 173.

7. William Arrowsmith, "Nietzsche on the Classics and the Classicists," *Arion,* II (Winter, 1963), 9. On p. 8, Arrowsmith writes that Nietzsche seeks to "refresh classical experience and thereby invigorate contemporary culture." My analysis indicates this to be potentially misleading in that it implies a version of the "return" thesis.

8. See Naumann XIV p. 116 and WKG IV$_1$ p. 109.

9. GT Attempt at a Self-Critique 3, I 12.

10. GT Attempt at a Self-Critique 5, I 14. See III 792 (WM 1050). This characteristic feature is especially manifest, as Vincent Scully brilliantly demonstrates, in the architecture and choice of site in the temples dedicated to Apollo (as well as those dedicated to other deities). See his *The Earth, the Temple and the Gods. Greek Sacred Architecture* (New Haven: Yale University Press, 1962), pp. 100-131, especially his discussion of *entasis* in columns (p. 104) and of the temple at Ptoon (pp. 107-108). The relation to Dionysos is considered on pp. 114-117.

11. Nietzsche's phrase is about Schopenhauer, but appropriate here.

12. GT 7, I 48-49. Most of Nietzsche's language is drawn directly from the "To be or not to be" soliloquy and the soliloquy at the end of *Hamlet,* Act II.

13. A good summary of the usual positions is in Martin Vogel, *Apollonisch und Dionysisch. Geschichte eines genialen Irrtums* (Regensburg: Bosse, 1966), pp. 11-36. In English, see Walter Kaufmann, *Nietzsche: Philosopher, Psychologist, Antichrist* (3rd edn.; Princeton: Princeton University Press, 1968); George Morgan, *What Nietzsche Means* (Cambridge: Harvard University Press, 1941), pp. 215-222. The main exceptions are Gilles Deleuze, *Nietzsche et la philosophie* (Paris: Presses universitaires de France, 1962), pp. 1-41, and Joan Stambaugh, *Untersuchungen zum Problem der Zeit bei der Philosophie Nietzsches* (Den Haag: Nidjhoff, 1959), pp. 3-16.

14. Naumann IX, p. 323, p. 183. See also pp. 38, 53, 166. See Stambaugh, *ibid.*, pp. 5-6.

15. GT 10, I 61. See Naumann X pp. 80-83. See III 791-792 (WM 1050). See Werner Jaeger, *Paideia* (Oxford: Blackwell, 1965), I, 294.

16. Thus Erwin Rohde, Nietzsche's closest friend, was able to write in his *Psyche,* trans. W. B. Hillis (New York: Harper & Row, 1962), II, 422: "The eventual opposition of character and destiny which places both the poet and his hero, another Hamlet, in a position of direct hostility to the mythological background can never become the rule. It is the business of the poet as far as possible to assimilate and make his own the spirit that actually called forth the cruel and dark legend of the past, while remaining true to the mode of perception proper to the time. He must manage to leave undistributed the full primitive sense of the mythical story and bring it about that by its marriage with the spirit of another age, its meaning is not destroyed, but deepened. He is committed to the search for adjustment between the mental attitudes of an older and newer age."

17. See Jack Stein, *Richard Wagner and the Synthesis of the Arts* (Detroit: Wayne State University Press, 1960), for a brilliant analysis of Wagner's music and theory. He shows what truth there is in Nietzsche's contention that Wagner's music changes. See Richard Wagner, *On Music and Drama,* eds. A. Goldman and E. Sprinchhorn (New York: E. P. Dutton & Co., 1964), esp. pp. 68-69, 77-94, 179-238.

18. Kröner I p. 136. See Naumann IX p. 38. See FWg 5, 8, 10, II 913, 920, 924. Compare to GT 6, 18, 21, I 41-42, 99-102, 119-120.

19. WKG VIII$_3$ p. 17. Nietzsche is discussing the GT and refers to himself as "Nietzsche" (given as "I" in other editions.)

20. GT 21, I 114.

21. On the antiquity of Homer see GT *passim;* WKG IV$_1$ p. 154, and esp. letter to Rohde, September 16, 1872. Books sharing the same general premise as GT include Eric R. Dodds, *The Greeks and the Irrational* (Boston: Beacon Press, 1957); Jaeger, *Paideia;* W. K. C. Guthrie, *The Greek Philosophers from Thales to Aristotle* (New York: Harper & Row, 1960); A. W. H. Adkins, *From the Many to the One* (Ithaca: Cornell University Press, 1970); and the work of Nilsson, Friedlander, and of course Rohde. Most of those who were influenced by Nietzsche, especially during his lifetime, acknowledge him not at all. Burckhardt, for instance, ceases praising Nietzsche to other friends after the Wilamowitz affair. The last letter mentioning Nietzsche appears to be to Van Preen, October 12, 1878, noting the appearance of MAM. Burckhardt does attack what is being done to Nietzsche after he went insane in a letter to Van Pastor, January 13, 1896. The debate about GT still goes on in other guises. See, for instance, Kurt Latte, "The Coming of the Pythia," *Harvard Theological Review*, XXXIII (January, 1940), 9-18 and the works cited in Phillip Slater, *The Glory of Hera* (Boston: Beacon Press, 1968).

22. GT 3, I 26.

23. GM iii 25, II 892. See Jacob Burckhardt, *A History of Greek Culture* (New York: Unger, 1963), p. 107.

24. See Adkins, *From the Many to the One*, pp. 23-40, 276 ff. Adkins

considers the one case where Ulysses appears to decide between moral alternatives and shows it not to correspond at all to our notions of moral reasoning (p. 21).

25. The only exception is Thersites the buffoon, who is made to appear a despicable character, an ape among heroes. The gods are similar to the heroes. There is a possible exception in Hermes, but Norman O. Brown has shown in his *Hermes the Thief: the Evolution of a Myth* (New York: Vintage Books, 1969), esp. pp. 80-81, that Hermes' character is of late development and characteristic of slave morality, not of the Olympus.

26. Compare Albert Einstein, "Autobiographical Note," *Einstein,* ed. P. A. Schilpp (New York: Harper & Row, 1961), p. 23. See also Reinhard Bendix, *Social Science and the Distrust of Reason* (Berkeley and Los Angeles: University of California Press, 1951). Bendix' argument is drawn from Hans Barth, *Wahrheit und Ideologie* (Erlenbach: Rentsch, 1961), esp. pp. 207-282.

27. HKP, III 162.

28. WKG VIII$_3$ pp. 16-17. See WKG IV$_1$ pp. 154-155.

29. Dodds, *The Greeks and the Irrational,* pp. 38 ff.

30., Homer, *Iliad,* trans. R. Lattimore (Chicago: University of Chicago Press, 1961), Book X, lines 318-320. See Book XXII, lines 104-107.

31. MAM i 114, I 525-526.

32. III 425 (WM 940). See Za On the Three Metamorphoses, II 293 ff.

33. GM ii 23, II 835 (last italics mine). See WKG IV$_1$ p. 157.

34. HW, III 292.

35. WKG IV$_1$ p. 154.

36. MAM i 262, I 609.

37. WKG IV$_1$ p. 154.

38. See J. M. Robinson, *An Introduction to Early Greek Philosophy* (Boston: Winthrop, 1968), p. 4. (This is an immensely helpful book, except for some fanciful statements about Hesiod. Thanks to John Cooper for calling my attention to it.)

39. HW, III 292.

40. HW, III 293. See Norman O. Brown's Introduction to Hesiod, *Theogony* (New York: Bobbs-Merrill Company, 1953), pp. 18 ff.

41. HW, III 293-294.

42. MAM i 261, I 605-606.

43. WWK, WKG IV$_1$ p. 180. See pp. 177-178.

44. PTZ 3, III 363. See WKG VIII$_2$ p. 410. D. J. Stewart, in a brilliant article to which I owe much, notes the same phenomenon but ascribes the achievement mainly to Plato. See his "Hesiod and the Birth of Reason," *Antioch Review,* XXI (Summer, 1961), 213-231. The process starts much earlier, though it is certainly not accomplished by Plato's time. See Francis M. Cornford, *Thucydides Mythhistoricus* (London: E. Arnold, 1907), p. x, and Jean Pierre Vernant, *Mythe et pensée chez les grecs* (Paris: Maspéro, 1965) and Bruno Snell, *The Discovery of the Mind* (New York: Harper & Row, 1960). See also Aristophanes, *The Clouds,* Act I, lines 240 ff.

45. WWK, WKG IV$_1$ pp. 178-179. See PTZ 3, III 361-365.

46. WWK, WKG IV$_1$ pp. 178-179. See MAM 261, I 605.

47. The existing plans for its completion include Socrates. Kaufmann makes much of this, but it would appear (a) that Nietzsche intended to show that something new starts with Socrates (see WWK, WKG IV$_1$ pp. 174, 178, 181, 183), (b) that in any case, there is no overall evaluation of the group, and (c) that Nietzsche often claims to prefer Plato to Socrates (see Naumann X pp. 149-150).

48. PTZ Preface, III 353-354.

49. PTZ Preface, III 351. Unless otherwise noted, all subsequent citations in this section are sequentially from PTZ. My text is an elaborated paraphrase of Nietzsche's with no other sources unless noted.

50. This is also Aristotle's understanding and probably misreads what Thales means by "all is. . . ." This is the *only* sentence to come down to us from Thales and there is great difficulty in getting any understanding of what he is about. I am indebted for many of these, and subsequent specific comments, to conversations with Alexander Nehamas.

51. The attempt to make the "indefinite" equivalent to a *Ding an sich* is potentially misleading. Anaximander calls the "infinite" the source of all existing things, that is, that out of which they come. Since Nietzsche understands this, the reference to the *Ding an sich* only makes sense because we can understand no predicates of either it or the "infinite." (This had been Nietzsche's understanding of Kant.) If Nietzsche is claiming more than this, he is mistaken. In my reading, he does not seem to be.

52. PTZ 5, III 372 draws a specific link between this and Hesiod's good *eris.*

53. Nietzsche barely mentions Heraclitus' notion of the *logos* and seems to see it as the "fire," calling Heraclitus, in this, still the "disciple of Anaximander."

54. This is already in Parmenides, though Nietzsche does not note it.

55. The objections that Anaxagoras raises do not really meet the Parmenidean problem; perhaps this is why Nietzsche calls them *ad hominem* or *ex concessis.* Anaxagoras should have dealt with the question of contradiction between the process of inference and the senses. See Robinson, *An Introduction to Early Greek Philosophy,* pp. 194-195. Melissus appears to have met Anaxagoras' objections before the fact. See the citation in Robinson, p. 140.

56. Aristotle indicates (see Robinson, *ibid.,* p. 175) that Empedocles may have written before Anaxagoras. Nietzsche, for obvious genealogical reasons, wants to end up with Empedocles.

57. Naumann X pp. 90-103 (PTZ).

58. Naumann X p. 136.

59. Naumann X pp. 149-150. See p. 132. See Jaeger, *Paideia,* I, 429, n. 34.

60. Dodds, *The Greeks and the Irrational,* p. 40. See Jaeger, *Paideia,* I, 245. See Rohde, *Psyche,* II, 421-422.

61. Kröner I no. 11 p. 6. See WKG IV$_1$ p. 206; Naumann IX p. 212.

62. GT 23, I 125.

63. GT 7, I 47. See Naumann IX pp. 210-211. The material cited on this and the preceding pages is all from GT 7, 8, 21. In addition, I have greatly benefited

from reading Stanley Cavell, *Must We Mean What We Say?* (New York: Charles Scribner's Sons, 1969), pp. 212-237 and 266-353, as well as Maurice Merleau-Ponty, *La prose du monde* (Paris: Gallimard, 1969), pp. 66-160.

64. Considerable doubt has been raised about Nietzsche's account of the ancestry of the chorus. William Ridgeway, *The Dramas and Dramatic Dances of Non-European Races in Special Reference to the Origin of Greek Tragedy* (Cambridge, England: The University Press, 1915), and following him, Arthur Wallace Pickard-Cambridge, *Dithyramb, Tragedy and Comedy* (Oxford: Clarendon Press, 1966), seem to me to have demonstrated that the facile equation that Nietzsche, following Aristotle, makes between the chorus and satyrs, is wrong. Ridgeway argues that ceremonies for the dead are a much more likely source. Neither man, however, investigates what difference, if any, this might make, nor exactly what it means to relate tragedy to ceremonies for the dead instead of to dionysian rituals. In any case, I do not think that the analysis of the audience, which is Nietzsche's central concern throughout GT, is changed by the question of the origin of the chorus.

65. The citation is GT 8, I 51. Some of my language here is drawn from Cavell, *Must We Mean What We Say?*

66. GT 21, I 119. Walter Kaufmann translates *Gleichnis* as "parable" instead of "metaphor"; this is appropriate only in a religious context and seems to me to lose a lot given Nietzsche's other writings about metaphor. In addition, despite a note to the contrary in his edition of GT (p. 34), he gives "feeling" for *Schein: erweckt . . . den Schein* becomes "deceives into feeling" rather than, as in my version, "awakes . . . the illusion." I do not think Nietzsche wants to suggest that something is put over on the spectator.

67. Naumann IX p. 53.

68. Naumann IX p. 179.

69. *The Eumenides*, trans. R. Lattimore, in *Greek Tragedies*, eds. D. Grene and R. Lattimore, Vol. III (Chicago: University of Chicago Press, 1960), lines 464-469. See *Agamemnon*, lines 1286-1290. This scene in *The Eumenides* leads to the trial where the relation of "young laws" (obedience to deity) to "old laws" (prohibiting matricide) is weighed in the balance. In an argument that Nietzsche would accept, I suspect, H. D. F. Kitto has demonstrated that it is likely that Athena was one of the twelve jurors and not an external force, thus part of the polis and not granting a decision from on high. She can vote for Orestes and against the Erinyes because she "has no mother." Kitto can then argue that the nature of the polis is such that it is occasionally necessary for the mother principle to die, or at least be reconciled to the new structures of (paternal) authority. See H. D. F. Kitto, *Form and Meaning in Drama* (London: Methuen & Co., 1956), pp. 65 ff.

70. Naumann IX p. 37. See Jaeger, *Paideia*, I, 258.

71. See Naumann IX pp. 51-52.

72. Hermann-Josef Schmidt, in *Nietzsche und Sokrates. Untersuchungen zu Nietzsches Sokratesbild* (Meisenheim am Glen: Hain, 1969), p. 22, considers the idealization of Euripides which makes Nietzsche's judgments possible.

73. Thucydides, *The Peloponnesian War,* trans. R. Warner (Baltimore: Penguin Books, 1966), Book III, par. 81.

74. Naumann X pp. 150, 147.

75. William Arrowsmith, "A Greek Theater of Ideas," *Arion,* II (Autumn, 1963), 33, 38.

76. The transition figure is obviously Sophocles. In Naumann IX p. 186, Nietzsche indicates that whereas in Aeschylus the hero fights against the world, and in Euripides the hero recognizes the pointlessness of it all, in Sophocles the hero accepts the world, while fighting against it. See also Naumann IX p. 52. This and the material in the text is about all that Nietzsche says about Sophocles.

77. Arrowsmith, "A Greek Theater of Ideas," p. 43. See Nietzsche's parody of this in Za On Redemption 1, II 392-393.

78. GT 11, I 69. Material in this section, unless otherwise noted, is from GT 11-12, I 64 ff.

79. It is true that much of what Nietzsche makes of this relationship is an idealized piece of his artistic imagination. Euripides was in fact ten years older than Socrates and had formulated his art in its mature style long before their relationship evolved. Against this objection (fundamentally that of Wilamowitz) remains the fact that the Greeks of the time (Aristophanes being only the most prominent example) made the link, as did the oracle at Delphi.

80. GT 14, I 81.

81. Stanley Cavell, *Must We Mean What We Say?* p. 71.

82. Compare Hanna Fenichel Pitkin, *Wittgenstein and Justice* (Berkeley and Los Angeles: University of California Press, 1972), pp. 34-35.

83. Naumann IX p. 38.

84. Naumann IX pp. 39-40.

85. Naumann X p. 125.

86. Sheldon S. Wolin, *Politics and Vision* (Boston: Little, Brown and Company, 1962), chap. 3.

87. See Jean Granier, *Le problème de la vérité dans la philosophie de Nietzsche* (Paris: Editions du Seuil, 1966), p. 43.

88. III 331. I am indebted to my friend Bruce Payne for much of the analysis of *Protagoras* that follows. Not for the conclusion which I draw, however: we, too, fight at every turn.

89. This is arrived at through a series of arguments which Socrates accepts from Protagoras even though he knows them to be false. For instance, in 329d and following, he argues that the parts of virtue must be identical, because "everything has but one contrary." In 346d, however, he calls "ridiculous" the proposition that all that is not black is white. See also the funny and phony exegesis of a poem by Simonides in 345.

90. JGB 3, II 569.

91. *Theatetus* 161c, trans. B. Jowett (New York: Random House, 1956).

92. JGB 3, II 569. See Kröner I no. 1326 p. 427.

93. This conclusion seems to be shared by Leo Strauss, *Socrates and Aristophanes* (New York: Basic Books, 1966), Introduction.

94. See Jaeger, *Paideia*, p. 380: "The art of Euripides could not give Athens what Aeschylus had given his countrymen in their sore need. And nothing else could save Athens at that critical moment. Therefore Dionysus is finally compelled to choose Aeschylus."

95. See Francis M. Cornford, *The Origin of Attic Comedy* (London: E. Arnold, 1914), esp. pp. 83-100.

96. GT 23, I 127.

97. *Ibid.*

98. FW 340, II 202. See GD The Problem of Socrates 9, II 954-955.

CHAPTER VII: PARABLES OF THE SHEPHERD AND THE HERD: NIETZSCHE AND POLITICS

1. Attempts to investigate Nietzsche on politics are few and not very good. One can note however the following. Karl Löwith, *From Hegel to Nietzsche* (New York: Holt, Rinehart and Winston, 1964), pp. 257, 260, 283-286. Frank A. Lea, *The Tragic Philosopher: A Study of Friedrich Nietzsche* (London: Methuen & Co., 1957), pp. 295-299. John E. McNees, "Nietzsche as a Political Philosopher" (Bachelor's thesis, Harvard University, 1960). Charles Baroni, *Nietzsche, éducateur de l'homme au surhomme* (Paris: Buchet, 1961), esp. pp. 224-228. Karl Jaspers, *Nietzsche: An Introduction to His Philosophical Activity*, trans. Charles Walraff and Frederick J. Schmitz (Tucson: University of Arizona Press, 1965), esp. pp. 252-283. Walter M. Salter, *Nietzsche the Thinker* (New York: Holt and Co., 1917), esp. pp. 70-83. Walter Kaufmann, *Nietzsche: Philosopher, Psychologist, Antichrist* (3rd edn.; Princeton: Princeton University Press, 1968), Part III. Glen O. Robinson, "New Parables for the Modern Age: The Moral and Political Philosophy of Nietzsche" (Bachelor's thesis, Harvard University, 1958). Henry Kariel, "Nietzsche's Preface to Constitutionalism," *Journal of Politics*, XXIV (May, 1963), 211-255. William Arrowsmith, "Nietzsche on the Classics and the Classicists," *Arion*, II (Winter, 1963), 2-31. Hans Barth, *Wahrheit und Ideologie* (Erlenbach: Rentsch, 1961). Hans Peter Hohn, *Die metaphysische und anthropologische Voraussetzungen der Politik bei Friedrich Nietzsche* (Inaugural Dissertation, Bonn, 1959).

2. For an index, see Hohn, *ibid.*, pp. 170-175.

3. JGB 211, II 676. See GD Skirmishes of an Untimely Man 39, II 1015-1017.

4. This is the general theme of Hannah Arendt, *The Human Condition* (Garden City: Doubleday Anchor Books, 1959).

5. HL Preface, I 209.

6. See Hannah Arendt, *The Human Condition*; Leo Strauss, *Natural Right and History* (Chicago: University of Chicago Press, 1963); Eric Voegelin, *The New Science of Politics* (Chicago: University of Chicago Press, 1962); Sheldon S. Wolin, *Politics and Vision* (Boston: Little, Brown and Company, 1962).

7. See WKG IV$_1$ p. 159.

8. Kröner I no. 57 p. 28. See Bruno Snell, *The Discovery of the Mind* (New York: Harper & Row, 1960), p. 261.

9. MAM i 439, I 666; GS, III 279.

10. HL 1, I 214.

11. Arendt, *The Human Condition*, p. 177. See Jean Pierre Vernant, *Mythe et pensée chez les grecs* (Paris: Maspéro, 1965), p. 170.

12. JGB 258, II 728. See Snell, *The Discovery of the Mind*, pp. 244, 277 f.; A. W. H. Adkins, *Merit and Responsibility* (Oxford: Clarendon Press, 1960), chap. 9.

13. Vernant, *Mythe et pensée chez les grecs*, p. 131. See III 765-766 (WM 437), and Snell, *The Discovery of the Mind*, pp. 227-245.

14. GM i 4-6, II 774-778. Adkins, *Merit and Responsibility*, esp. chaps. 6-8, has carefully traced the changing relations of word and object in Greek moral thought. See also Naumann IX p. 279: "Der Genius hat die Kraft die Welt mit einem neuen Illusionsnetze zu umhängen."

15. Naumann X p. 125. Martin Heidegger, in *Nietzsche* (Pfüllingen: Neske, 1961), II, 71, has argued that the very word "category," the existence of which is necessary to permit Socratic discourse, derives from *kata-agora*, to look down on the public place, hence, to be outside the agora. Alasdair MacIntyre has, in his usual delicate manner, reminded me that Liddell and Scott's authoritative *Lexicon* gives no support to this notion.

16. Kröner II no. 1041 p. 369; Kröner I no. 8 p. 5. See also Hohn, "*Die metaphysische* . . . ," p. 89. In Naumann XII p. 103 Nietzsche notes that the agon turns "thoughts of combat away from the state."

17. GS, III 281.

18. GS, III 282. See GS, III 279. On fathers and sons see MAM i 455, I 673.

19. Julius Binder, *Nietzsches Staatsauffassung* (Göttingen: Dieterischen Universitäts-Buchdruckerei, 1925), p. 39. This notion is fully criticized in Hohn, "Die metaphysische . . . ," pp. 84-85.

20. WKG IV$_1$ p. 194.

21. GT 23, I 125.

22. III 631 (WM 889). See MAM i 474, I 684 and Hohn, "*Die metaphysische* . . . ," p. 89.

23. MAM i 450, I 671; MAM i 439, I 666. See Max Pohlenz, *Freedom in Greek Life and Thought* (Dordrecht: Reidel, 1966), pp. 8-9.

24. GS, III 280. On this whole question see GM i, esp. 7, 10-16, II 771-798, esp. 778-780, 782-797. See Gilles Deleuze, *Nietzsche et la philosophie* (Paris: Presses universitaires de France, 1962), pp. 127-136. See Chap. VIII below for a full discussion of the will.

25. III 658 (WM 718). See III 698 (WM 143) and MAM i 57, I 491.

26. III 635 (WM 717). See GM i 13, II 789-791.

27. III 658 (WM 718). See Kröner II no. 5 p. 4.

28. Za On Redemption, III 393-394. Compare Karl Marx, *Capital* (New York: International, 1967), I, 418-427.

29. Naumann X p. 153.

30. WWK, WKG IV$_1$ pp. 184-185. See also pp. 140, 183, 193-194, 332-333. See Naumann X p. 153. For supporting historical data see Pohlenz, *Freedom in Greek Life and Thought*, pp. 22 ff.

31. An ancillary comment should be added for the purposes of intellectual history. Nietzsche's concept is, of course, remarkably similar in dynamics to plans such as William James' "moral equivalent of war" and similar attempts to set up harmless and even productive ways to drain off the "reservoir" of psychic energy. This was not in the long run Nietzsche's solution, any more than it was Freud's, but the analogy holds well here. For instance, Nietzsche writes: "The English of today, who appear on the whole to have renounced war, adopt other means in order to generate anew those vanishing forces; mainly dangerous exploring expeditions . . . nominally undertaken for scientific purposes, but in reality for bringing home surplus strength from adventures and dangers of all kinds. Many other substitutes for war will be discovered, but . . . such a highly cultivated and therefore necessarily easily enfeebled humanity . . . not only needs wars, but the greatest and most terrible wars . . . lest by means of culture, it should loose its culture and its very existence" (MAM i 477, I 678-688). Nietzsche's notion of the psyche, though inverted, appears to be of the same form as that in James.

32. GS, III 282 (my italics). See GS, III 280-281.

33. For Nietzsche's comments on Bismarck, see MAM i 453, I 672; Kröner II no. 1174 pp. 426-427 ("Parliamentarism is his new means"); JGB 254, II 722. Nietzsche writes to Gersdorff (February 16, 1868) some months after the Schleswig-Holstein crisis, that "politics is now the organ of general thinking [Gesamtdenkens] . . . Bismarck makes me immeasurably happy. I read his speeches like strong wine." This is the period during which Nietzsche hopes that Bismarck might bring about the cultural unity of Germany. Later, when Bismarck had made clear his preference for Kleindeutschpolitik, Nietzsche writes to Rohde (July 19, 1870) that the Franco-Prussian War is disastrous, and, at the end of his life, with one foot already over the edge of insanity, writes to Burckhardt that he is having "Wilhelm, Bismarck, and all anti-Semites shot." See JGB 256, II 724; Naumann X, p. 402. The differences between Nietzsche and Bismarck are perhaps too strongly argued in Theodor Schieder, Nietzsche und Bismarck (Krefeld: Scherpe Verlag, 1963), esp. p. 29, and glossed over in H. Fischer, Nietzsche, apostata, oder die Philosophie des Ärgernisses (Erfurt: K. Stenger, 1931), esp. pp. 18-23. For a similar analysis of Bismarck, see Henry Kissinger, "Reflections on Bismarck: The White Revolutionary," Daedalus, XLVII (Summer, 1968), 888-924.

34. III 420 (WM 725). See MAM i 441, I 667 and Naumann X p. 337.

35. GM ii 2, II 801; SE 4, I 313.

36. III 474 (WM 783). See III 820-824 (WM 765).

37. JGB 203, II 661 (my italics). See Kröner I no. 1331. See WKG VIII$_2$ p. 333, "The little bit of politics left to us. . . ." Compare Wolin, Politics and Vision, chaps. 9 and 10.

38. MAM i 472, I 680. Compare the account in Numa Denis Fustel de Coulanges, The Ancient City (Garden City: Doubleday & Company, 1956).

39. III 659 (WM 207). Compare Wolin, Politics and Vision, chap. 3.

40. MAM i 472, I 681. The envelope is noted in WKG IV$_4$ p. 228.

41. On the pun see AC 58, III 1228. The citation is III 588 (WM 211) (my

italics). On Zarathustra see Za Prologue 2, III 278-279. See also III 665 (WM 30) and AC 43, II 1205-1206. The importance of refusing to tell someone something is noted in Stanley Cavell, *Must We Mean What We Say?* (New York: Charles Scribner's Sons, 1969), pp. xxviii and (I gather) 352-353.

42. III 822-824 (WM 765). See Henri Birault, "En quoi nous sommes encore pieux," *Revue de métaphysique et de morale,* LXVII (January-March, 1962), pp. 25-64, esp. 64.

43. MAM i 472, I 681-682. See Phillip Rieff, *The Triumph of the Thera-peutic* (New York: Harper & Row, 1966), pp. 52-57. See also JGB 242, II 707-708; WKG IV$_2$ pp. 414-415.

44. III 605 (WM 784). See Za The Convalescent, II 461-462; MAM i 436, I 665-666. See Za The Sign, II 561; WKG IV$_2$ p. 401; Hohn, *"Die meta-physische . . . ,"* p. 96. For a full discussion of the ascetic priest, see the next chapter.

45. Za The New Idol, II 313-314.

46. *Ibid.* See III 906 (WM 275).

47. III 426 (WM 750). See MAM i 481, I 690-691; SE 8, I 351 ff.; MAM i 438, I 565. Plato has a similar account in *Statesman, 275.*

48. JGB 228, II 692. See JGB 212, II 678. Thanks to Robert Eden for reminding me of these passages.

49. See Henri Lefebvre, *Nietzsche* (Paris: Editions sociales internationales, 1939), pp. 143 ff.

50. FW 40, II 65-66. See III 474-475 (WM 783).

51. III 604 (WM 784). See WKG IV$_3$ p. 243.

52. WKG IV$_2$ p. 557.

53. Here again Nietzsche shares with Marx the appreciation that the whole basis of the system must be changed. Marx writes, for instance in *The Holy Family,* that capitalist and proletarian are equally alienated, though the former "profits from the fruits of its alienation." The point is that neither for Marx, nor for Nietzsche, are individuals at fault qua individuals. The particular form of life is.

54. WKG IV$_2$ p. 579.

55. MAM i 473, I 683-684.

56. III 439 (WM 752). See III 420 (WM 725); III 419 (WM 941).

57. JGB 256, II 724.

58. MAM i 475, I 685.

59. GS, III 283-284 (my italics). This is an early essay. At the end of his life, Nietzsche seems to think that the doctrine of eternal return may provide a way to avoid such wars. See WKG VIII$_3$ pp. 458, 460 under *Letzte Erwägung,* "Last Consideration." See Chap. IX below. Compare to WKG IV$_2$ pp. 414-415.

60. EH The Case of Wagner 2, II 1148.

61. MAM i 481, I 690. See MAM i 442, I 667-668.

62. Schieder, *Nietzsche und Bismarck,* p. 29. See JGB 254, II 722; III 529 (WM 87).

63. On the "spectacle," GM iii 27, II 899. On "unevenness," JGB 208, II 671-672.

64. JGB 208, II 671-672.

65. III 521 (WM 898).

66. III 504 (WM 960).

67. MAM i 472, I 683.

68. III 505 (WM 960).

69. GM iii 28, II 899; WKG IV$_1$ p. 251.

70. EH Why I Am a Destiny 1, II 1152-1153. See Naumann XII p. 110, where Nietzsche wants "war for the leadership of the earth to be carried out in the name of basic philosophical principles [*philosophische Grundlehre*]."

71. GM iii 28, II 899. See III 621 (WM 28).

72. Hannah Arendt, "Truth and Politics," *Between Past and Future* (New York: Viking Press, 1968), p. 259.

73. The following is influenced by Martin Heidegger, *Nietzsche*, Vol. II, and Pierre Klossowski, *Nietzsche et le cercle vicieux* (Paris: Mercure de France, 1969).

74. Kröner II no. 1044, pp. 370-371.

CHAPTER VIII: THE WILL TO POWER

1. Not surprisingly it has been the French who have developed the best understanding of Nietzsche, e.g., Deleuze, Klossowski, Granier. Nietzsche would have been pleased.

2. See EH Why I Write Such Good Books 1, II 1100-1101.

3. *Ibid.* – Thus Spoke Zarathustra 1, II 1128.

4. WKG VIII$_3$ p. v. It thus postdates "eternal return."

5. Martin Heidegger, "Who is Nietzsche's Zarathustra?" *Review of Metaphysics*, XX (March, 1967), 412.

6. Naumann XII p. 216.

7. Reading *das hiesse mir erst Erlösung* as carrying the passive connotation rather than, with Kaufmann, as "that alone should I call redemption."

8. Heidegger, "Who is Nietzsche's Zarathustra?" p. 422.

9. GM iii 28, II 900.

10. Za On the Old and New Tablets 16, II 452. Charles Andler points out that "Pour Nietzsche, la vraie découverte de Schopenhauer est: il a détroné le rationalisme comme interprétation de l'homme." See Charles Andler, *Nietzsche: sa vie et sa pensée* (Paris: Gallimard, 1958), I, 85.

11. Naumann XI (*Sorrentiner Papiere*) pp. 37-38. See also Kröner I p. 226.

12. Jean Granier, *Le problème de la vérité dans la philosophie de Nietzsche* (Paris: Editions du Seuil, 1966), p. 386.

13. WKG IV$_3$ p. 476. See Georg Simmel, *Schopenhauer und Nietzsche* (Leipzig: Duncker und Humboldt), pp. 9-11. See VM (MAM ii) 5, I 746.

14. III 746 (WM 289) (my italics).

15. Frederick R. Love, *Young Nietzsche and the Wagnerian Experience* (Chapel Hill: University of North Carolina Press, 1963), p. 63, has convincingly shown that this opera, and not *Tristan und Isolde*, was the most influential on Nietzsche.

16. FWg first postface, II 929. See WKG VIII₃ p. 35: "Who will redeem us from the redeemer?"

17. The changing influence of Schopenhauer on Wagner is well set out in Jack Stein, *Richard Wagner and the Synthesis of the Arts* (Detroit: Wayne State University Press, 1960). See also the last chapter of Morse Peckham, *Beyond the Tragic Vision* (New York: Braziller, 1962).

18. Kröner I p. 145. See also GT Attempt at a Self-Critique 6, I 16; letter to Rohde, August 10, 1868; to Gersdorff, February 27, 1873; to Wagner, April 18, 1873; and Naumann XIV p. 375. This conclusion is born out by Nietzsche's correspondence, even in the edition put out by his sister to show that it isn't.

19. WKG VIII₃ p. 43.

20. WKG VIII₂ pp. 279-280.

21. WKG VIII₃ p. 152 (WM 702).

22. WKG VIII₃ p. 51 (WM 635) (my italics).

23. FW 317, II 185.

24. Martin Heidegger, *Nietzsche* (Pfüllingen: Neske, 1961), I, 26, attempts to link the will to power with *physis* and his own notion of *Seiendes* in one group, and eternal return, *ta on*, and his notion of *Sein* in another. This seems illegitimate, given my analysis. It does allow him to make the will to power an ontological principle and the center of his interpretation of Nietzsche. Thus in his *Nietzsche*, II, 259: "Der Wille zur Macht ist das Wort für das Sein des Seienden." See also *Nietzsche*, II, 284-290. There is a good analysis of this problem in F. Assaad-Mikhail, "Heidegger, interpréte de Nietzsche," *Revue de métaphysique et de morale*, LXXIII (January-March, 1968), 16-55. On *physis* see Arthur W. H. Adkins, *From the Many to the One* (Ithaca: Cornell University Press, 1970), pp. 92 ff.

25. WKG VIII₂ p. 259.

26. III 712 (WM 702).

27. III 480 (WM 254). See also JGB 13, II 578.

28. III 489 (WM 643).

29. GM ii 18, II 828.

30. Kröner II, p. 68.

31. GM iii 14, II 863 f.

32. HL 3, I 229-230 (my italics).

33. In Hegel's *Phenomenology of Mind*, the most obviously related dichotomy is lordship and bondage. For Hegel, the question arises during a consideration of self-consciousness and dependency, that is, of the possible kinds of relations that men can have with each other. He maintains, much as Sartre was to in *Being and Nothingness*, that men recognize themselves through mutual acceptance. Each accepts the self-recognition of the other and is in turn recognized by him. In other words, an individual's identity depends on his acceptance of others and on theirs of him. For Hegel, this element of reciprocity is precisely what is lacking in the relationship between the lord and bondsman. The lord "relates himself to the bondsman immediately through the independent existence, for that is what keeps the bondsman in thrall." Georg W. F. Hegel, *The Phenomenology of Mind*, trans. J. B. Baillie (London: George Allen & Unwin,

1966), p. 235. Hegel is saying that the lord does not act toward the bondsman in the same way that he acts toward himself. Conversely, the bondsman does not act toward others (especially the lord) in the manner his servitude makes him act toward himself. All reciprocity becomes impossible.

This does not make the master the ultimate historical victor for Hegel. Far from it. As Rousseau says: "Tel se croit le maître d'autrui, qui ne laisse pas d'être plus esclave d'enx," Jean Jacques Rousseau, "Du contrat social," *Oeuvres Complètes*, Vol. III (Paris: Pléiade, 1964), p. 363; and "La liberté consiste . . . à ne pas soumettre la volonté d'autrui à la notre," "Lettres de la montaigne, 7," Vol. III, p. 813. Hegel thus says: "The truth of the independent consciousness is accordingly the consciousness of the bondsman. . . . Just as lordship showed its essential nature to be the reverse of what it wants to be, so too bondage will, when completed, pass into the opposite of what it immediately is: being a consciousness repressed within itself, it will enter into itself and change round into real and true independence." Hegel, *Phenomenology* p. 237.

What are we to make of this? Alexandre Kojève in *Introduction à la lecture de Hegel* (Paris: Gallimard, 1947), and following him John Plamenatz, *Man and Society* (New York: McGraw-Hill, 1963), II, 219-269, tend to give Hegel a highly "Marxian" interpretation. The bondsman, in his oppression, becomes the progressive force in history. George A. Kelly, "Notes on Hegel's Lordship and Bondage," *Review of Metaphysics*, XX (June, 1965), picks up Kojève on this and cites his *Introduction:* "The slave alone is able to transcend the world as it is (in thrall to the master) and not perish. The slave alone is able to transform the world of his own making where he will be free" (p. 782). This is the "Marxian" interpretation. Kelly continues: "In more humble language, the future belongs to the once terrorized producer progressively liberated by the spiritualized quality of his own labor, not to the seemingly omnipotent consumer, who treats both the servant and his product as dead things. Effectively the slave releases history from nature and it is the slave's satisfaction that brings history to a close. Thus . . . Kojève . . . tends to regard forms of servitude as epiphenomena of the relations of production" (p. 783).

Kojève's interpretation tends to make Hegel overly concrete. The conclusions he draws are simply not drawn by Hegel. The reason for Kojève's mistake seems to be his overlooking of the fact that Hegel holds lordship and bondage to be types, not concrete social entities in the manner that Marx saw classes. Hegel himself denies that production (concrete social phenomena) is the key to his discussion of the relations of lordship and bondage. "The thing is independent for him (the bondsman) and in consequence he cannot, with all his negating, get so far as to annihilate it outright and be done with it; that is to say *he merely works on it.* . . . The aspect of its independence (is left) to the bondsman, who labors upon it." Hegel, *Phenomenology*, pp. 235-236. This is the basic point about the Hegelian dialectic which separates him from Nietzsche. For Hegel, advances and finality come about through the combination of both partners in the dialectic, not by the replacement of one by its opposite. The freedom of the slave is jointly the freedom of the master. Lord-bondsman relations do occur for Hegel inside history and are a manifestation of the greater development of freedom (*Phenomenology,* pp. 238-239), but they do not in and of themselves create the dialectic. For Nietzsche, on the other hand, master and slave do not stand in a dialectical relationship to each other (they do not depend on each other, though they may interact), nor are they helped in their interaction by some force or principle exterior to them.

34. It is remarkable how closely indebted these two works are to the *Genealogy.* In *From Max Weber,* eds. H. Gerth and C. W. Mills (New York: Oxford University Press, 1958), pp. 270 ff., Weber speaks of two kinds of religious attitudes with specific reference to Nietzsche and sees the triumph of the second in stages which correspond exactly to Nietzsche's. Freud's delineation of the tricks men use to get around or alleviate the discontents of civilization could have been footnoted to Nietzsche.

35. JGB 260, II 730.

36. Citations on this and the next page are from GM ii 17-18, II 826-829.

37. Reading *aus . . . geschafft* as "created out of" and not with Kaufmann as "expelled from one's path." Nietzsche goes on to speak of this instinct for freedom as in the world, which indicates to me that he is saying that the masters create freedom from the world, and that the badly conscienced slaves turn this inward.

38. GM ii 19, II 829.

39. JGB 260, II 730.

40. MAM i 45, I 483.

41. JGB 260, II 732.

42. GM i 11, II 785.

43. III 745 (WM 288). See MAM i 39, I 479.

44. Compare Za On the Old and New tablets 3, II 445: "From the sun I learned this, as it set overrich: it pours gold into the sea out of inexhaustible riches, so that even the poorest fisherman rows with golden oars."

45. I follow Nietzsche's account here. Gilles Deleuze, *Nietzsche et la philosophie* (Paris: Presses universitaires de France, 1962), pp. 131 ff., does the same.

46. GM i 13, II 790. See n. 24, Chap. III above.

47. For an application of this principle in action to America see the astonishing speech of Abraham Lincoln, "Speech to the Young Man's Lyceum at Springfield," *Collected Works of Abraham Lincoln,* ed. R. P. Basler (New Brunswick: Rutgers University Press, 1953), I, 108-114.

48. GM i 10, II 782.

49. GM i 10, II 784-785 (my italics).

50. Kröner II, pp. 68-69.

51. Kröner II p. 13.

52. Kröner II p. 68. See also HL 1, I 211-212. For a less historically oriented analysis see Deleuze, *Nietzsche et la philosophie,* p. 131.

53. See, e.g., GD Skirmishes of an Untimely Man 14, II 998-999. Arthur Danto, *Nietzsche as Philosopher* (New York: Macmillan Company, 1965), p. 224, seriously mistakes the nature of Nietzsche's challenge by referring to him as "merely a punning anti-Darwinian."

54. GM ii 16, II 824. All citations following are from this section. See also

Kenneth Burke, *A Grammar of Motives* (Berkeley and Los Angeles: University of California Press, 1969), p. 20.

55. GM ii 21, II 832. See AC 18, II 1178: "The deteriorization of a God: God become the thing-in-itself."

56. Compare Hegel, *Phenomenology of Mind,* pp. 806-807, 233.

57. Karl Marx, "Introduction to the Critique of Hegel's Philosophy of Right," *Early Writings,* ed. and trans. T. B. Bottomore (New York: McGraw-Hill, 1967), pp. 42-43.

58. Especially Bruno Bauer, who had read Nietzsche. See EH Why I Write Such Good Books — The Untimely Considerations 2, II 1114. See also letters to Taine, July 4, 1887 and Brandes, December 2, 1887. Nietzsche also knew Max Stirner. The influence of Nietzsche on Marxists does not really show up until the twentieth century, for instance in Georg Lukacs and Antonio Gramsci.

59. See Naumann XI p. 209: "History is the development of the design in time."

60. AC 7, II 1168.

61. GM iii 17, II 871.

62. All of this is drawn from GM iii 17-18, II 871-877.

63. EH Why I Am a Destiny 8, II 1159. *Folie circulaire* is the psychiatric term of the time for what we might call manic-depressive.

64. GM iii 18, II 876. See also GM iii 15, II 866-869 and GM i 13, II 790.

65. GM iii 23, II 886.

66. GM iii 25, II 891-892. See FW 344, II 206-208 and M Preface 4-5, I 1014-1016.

67. For example, Callicles and Nietzsche are often linked in the history of thought with the same basic idea, that of the right of the strong to make laws. See Dodds's Introduction in Plato, *Gorgias,* ed. E. R. Dodds (Oxford: Clarendon Press, 1959), p. xiii. Callicles argues, as Dodds points out, that might *is* right; the argument that it leads to right is only a preliminary notion. However, such a notion of self-indulgence is quite contrary to anything that Nietzsche ever called morality in others or even thought of as a good principle for the overman. In JGB 188, II 645 he says: "What is essential and inestimable in every morality is that it constitutes a long compulsion. . . ." This is related specifically to the most general fact of human history which is "obedience." Callicles had argued that natural justice was the will of the most strong. But it is precisely this correlation of nature and morality which causes Nietzsche to argue that *laissez-aller* could never be considered moral. It is not for slaves, and not for masters, as "Old and New Tablets" and my argument have, I hope, made clear. Callicles is a very slavely moral person, and mistaken besides.

68. III 677-678 (WM 12).

69. EH Why I Write Such Good Books — Thus Spoke Zarathustra 6, II 1136.

70. Za The Awakening 1, II 545 ff.

71. Za The Spirit of Gravity 2, II 441-442.

72. MAM i 107, I 514 (my italics).

CHAPTER IX: THE DOCTRINE OF ETERNAL RETURN

1. This was, for instance, Peter Gast's opinion. I use "eternal return" rather than "eternal recurrence" because "return" seems to me to convey more of a sense of action than does "recurrence." Compare, in French, *retour éternel.*

2. EH Why I Write Such Good Books — Thus Spoke Zarathustra 1, II 1128. See WKG VIII₃ pp. 397, 420; Kröner II p. 313; III 916-917 (WM 1067). I recognize that there is a potential problem in my tacit identification of Nietzsche and Zarathustra here. The important thing to remember is that Zarathustra is not the *Übermensch*, but much more of a John the Baptist figure, a herald. So perhaps also is Nietzsche. See Martin Heidegger, "Who is Nietzsche's Zarathustra?" *Review of Metaphysics*, XX (March, 1967), 411-431.

3. FW 11, 54, 303, 324, II 44, 73, 178-179, 187-188. Even earlier, see WKG IV₂ p. 502 and HL 2, I 222. See also Kröner II, pp. 299-301. See Martin Heidegger, *Nietzsche* (Pfüllingen: Neske, 1961), II, 284 ff. for an interesting discussion.

4. Za Prologue 5, II 283. See EH Why I Write Such Good Books 1, II 1100.

5. H. Wein, "Métaphysique et anti-métaphysique," *Revue de métaphysique et de morale*, LXIII (October-December, 1958), 391. This is also the conclusion of Arthur Danto, *Nietzsche as Philosopher* (New York: Macmillan Company, 1965), especially the last chapter. See WKG IV₂ pp. 392 ff.

6. Walter Kaufmann, *Nietzsche: Philosopher, Psychologist, Antichrist* (3rd edn.; Princeton: Princeton University Press, 1968), pp. 323, 332. Kaufmann makes a link between Nietzsche and Vaihinger on pp. 356 ff. See Hans Vaihinger, *The Philosophy of As-If* (London: Routledge and Kegan Paul, 1968), Epilogue. See Karl Jaspers, "Nietzsche and the Present," *Partisan Review*, XVIII (January-February, 1952), 20.

7. It is significant that this announcement be made to sailors since the news of the death of the god of tragedy was also first made to sailors. See GT 11, I 64. A good interpretation of these symbols, and in general, can be found in Eugen Fink, *La philosophie de Nietzsche* (Paris: Editions de Minuit, 1965).

8. The meaning of these symbols is complex and not essential to my argument here. In WS 450 (MAM ii), II 1107-1108, the dog is identified with the shadow of the wanderer and he in turn with Zarathustra. Later the shepherd is called part of Zarathustra also. See Za The Convalescent 2, II 463. On the serpent, see Za Prologue 10, II 290 and especially WKG IV₂ p. 510. On animal symbolism in Za, see Kröner II no. 1364 p. 489 and Donna Jean Hayes, "Nietzsche's Eternal Return: a Prelude to Heidegger," *Journal of Existentialism*, VI (Winter, 1965-1966), 189-196, esp. p. 192.

9. Kaufmann notes this in his *The Portable Nietzsche* (New York: Viking Press, 1954), pp. 260-263.

10. Za The Convalescent 1, II 461.

11. *Ibid.*, II 462-463.

12. See HL 4, I 230; GM ii 1, II 799.

13. Kröner II p. 475.

14. Naumann XII p. 118. In Kröner II p. 473 there is an assertion that eternal return will spread to "one, then many, then all. . . ."

15. Kröner II p. 447.

16. Naumann XII p. 118.

17. See the remarkably similar description in Henry Thoreau, *Walden* (New York: W. W. Norton & Company, 1969), p. 11 (chapter on "Economy") and p. 66 ("Where I Lived and What I Lived For"). There is much to be written on Thoreau and Nietzsche. William Arrowsmith and Timothy Gould first pointed me to the relevance of *Walden*.

18. See "The Will and the Problem of the Past," in Chap. VIII above.

19. See Za On the Vision and the Riddle 2, II 408; Kröner II no. 1324 p. 469. See Ludwig Wittgenstein, *Blue and Brown Books* (Oxford: Blackwell, 1969), p. 53, for a specific consideration mentioning Nietzsche.

20. Naumann XII p. 129.

21. Naumann IX p. 77.

22. This struggle with himself is especially noticeable in the notes of the period September, 1888 to January, 1889, his last four months of sanity. See WKG VIII₃ pp. 346-461, esp. p. 421 with a compulsive repetition of a paragraph on "thou shalt not kill." Reading this material makes me astonished at the effort required to produce something of the coherence of *Antichrist, Ecce Homo, Nietzsche* contra *Wagner.*

23. The formulation is that of Gilles Deleuze in a personal communication. I take this opportunity to note how much I have profited from his work.

24. This is true, for instance both of *Zarathustra* and of the drama about the re-creative mission of Empedocles. *Zarathustra* was apparently to end with the Persian jumping into the Etna — the traditional death of Empedocles. See Charles Rammoux, "Les fragments d'un Empédocle de Friedrich Nietzsche," *Revue de métaphysique et de morale,* LXX (April-June, 1965), 199-212. See also EH Why I Write Such Good Books — Beyond Good and Evil 1, II 1141.

25. Karl Löwith and Hans Vaihinger, for example. See Eugène Fleischman, "De Weber à Nietzsche," *Archives européens de la sociologie,* Vol. XIV, no. 2 (1964), 190-238. Nietzsche himself draws attention to this possibility. In the Preface to the *Genealogy,* he asks himself what is his "a priori — that, alas, so anti-Kantian, enigmatic 'categorical imperative' which spoke through it and to which I have listened since more and more closely and not merely listened" (GM Preface 3, II 765; see JGB 5, II 570). It is probably not misleading to see the whole of the *Genealogy* as a book written both in content and organization to counter the *Critique of Pure Reason,* much as *Zarathustra* is, among other things, a counter to Hegel's *Phenomenology of Mind.* The categorical imperative is emblematic of nihilism for Nietzsche and "*riecht nach Grausamkeit*" (GM ii 6, II 806).

26. III 809 (WM 63): "In my own way I am attempting a justification of history."

27. Kröner II no. 1383 p. 499.

28. WKG VIII$_2$ pp. 14-18.

29. GM iii 15, II 866. As seen in the previous chapter, the third essay in *Genealogy* is devoted to the psychology of the priest. Such forces occur in a similar fashion in morality (pity) and politics (nationalism).

30. GM iii 13, II 862.

31. III 855-856 (WM 55). By *schlecht-weggekommene* Nietzsche has in mind psychophysiological cripples, not political misfits. They are the products of centuries of slave morality. A modern political man is rather an "inverse cripple." See Za On Redemption, II 392-393.

32. III 854-855 (WM 55).

33. III 855 (WM 55).

34. Za Prologue 3, II 279. Gilles Deleuze develops this in *Nietzsche et la philosophie* (Paris: Presses universitaires de France, 1962), p. 79.

35. III 856 (WM 55). See Kröner II no. 1296 p. 461.

36. WKG VIII$_2$ pp. 312-313.

37. III 826-827 (WM 54). On kinds of negation in Nietzsche with an enlightening comparison to Hegel, see Erica Sherover, "Nietzsche: On Yea- and Nay-Saying," *Journal of Existentialism*, V (Summer, 1965), 423-426.

38. Za The Awakening, II 544-548.

39. Za The Three Metamorphoses of the Spirit, II 294.

40. Kröner II no. 1336 p. 475.

41. Analogues to this have been described in some of the anthropological literature dealing with the effect of myths. Claude Lévi-Strauss investigates, for instance, the nature of organic cures effectuated by Shamans. He describes such a cure as a process of "stimulating an *organic* transformation which would consist essentially in a structural reorganization, by inducing the patient intensively to live out a myth — either received or created by him — whose structures would be at the unconscious level analogous to the structures whose genesis is sought on the organic level...." *Structural Anthropology* (Garden City: Doubleday Anchor Books, 1967), p. 197.

42. Immanuel Kant, *The Critique of Pure Reason*, trans. N. K. Smith (New York: St. Martin's Press, 1961), p. 7.

43. It is not surprising, however, that a number of the early twentieth-century positivists (e.g., Neurath and Schlick) recognized a sort of second cousin in Nietzsche.

44. Kröner II pp. 453-454. See Za On the Thousand and One Goals, II 322-344.

45. HL 3, I 230. Ronald D. Laing and Aaron Esterson, in *Sanity, Madness and the Family* (New York: Basic Books, 1971), p. 19, have hypothesized, for instance, that precisely this occurs in the repeated exposure of children to "insane" family situations, and is the ultimate source of both the physiological and psychological phenomenon known as schizophrenia. See also Jean Piaget, "Problems of Genetic Psychology," *Six Psychological Studies* (New York: Random House, 1967), pp. 117-118. Such problems seem to be on the order of that recently proposed only slightly waggishly by Sir Francis Crick as to the relation between praying a lot and longevity, i.e., are there physiological consequences to

particular types of repeated activity? See on this score Gareth Matthews, "Bodily Motions and Religious Feelings," *Canadian Journal of Philosophy,* I (September, 1971), 75-86. If I understand him properly, these concerns are central to Stanley Cavell, *The World Viewed: Reflections on the Ontology of Film* (New York: Viking Press, 1971), esp. pp. 60-68 and 126-160.

46. Heidegger, *Nietzsche,* II, 262.

47. See Tracy B. Strong, "Hold on to Your Brains: An Essay in Meta-Theory," *Power and Community,* eds. P. Green and S. Levinson (New York: Pantheon, 1970), esp. pp. 349-351.

48. Page references are to Heidegger, *Nietzsche,* Vol. II.

49. As does also Jean Granier, *Le problème de la vérité dans la philosophie de Nietzsche* (Paris: Editions du Seuil, 1966).

50. Deleuze, *Nietzsche et la philosophie.*

51. Deleuze, *Nietzsche et la philosophie,* pp. 80-81.

52. AC 4, II 1166.

53. WKG IV$_1$ p. 119.

54. III 856 (WM 55).

55. FW 301, II 177.

56. Za On the Higher Man 3, II 523.

57. *Ibid.* 10, II 526.

58. Za The Awakening, II 547.

59. DD Ariadne's Lament, II 1259. See EH Why I Write Such Good Books 2, II 1102: "Ich bin der Anti-Esel *par excellence."*

60. Za On the Higher Man 14-20, II 528-531.

61. PTZ 8, III 381.

62. Za The Seven Seals 3, II 474.

63. See the commentary on this passage in Gilles Deleuze, *Logique du sens* (Paris: Editions de Minuit, 1968), p. 75.

64. Za On the Honey Offer, II 480, See ZB 1, III 191.

65. Za On the Higher Man 14, II 528.

66. Za Prologue 4, II 282.

67. See EH Why I Am so Wise 10, II 1098, and NW Epilogue 1, II 1059.

68. JGB 32, II 597.

69. Za On the Three Metamorphoses, II 294. These considerations are close to those in Stanley Cavell, *Must We Mean What We Say?* (New York: Charles Scribner's Sons, 1969), pp. 1-43. I am grateful to Ingrid Lorch Turner for helping with my understanding of play.

70. See Hanna Fenichel Pitkin, *Wittgenstein and Justice* (Berkeley and Los Angeles: University of California Press, 1972), pp. 264-279.

71. FW 303, II 178. Nietzsche was known for his ability to improvise at the piano.

72. Homer, *Iliad* xxii.

73. FW 1, II 34.

74. Za The Sign, II 559.

75. See WKG IV$_1$ pp. 256-257.

76. Za On the Higher Men 15, II 528.

77. FW To the Mistral, II 273.

78. Za The Grave Song, II 369.

79. Za The Dancing Song, II 364.

80. III 895 (WM 617). I read *aufprägen* as "impress," rather than, as Kaufmann does, "impose."

81. T. S. Eliot, *Burnt Norton,* II. Eliot is talking about dance also.

82. See Heidegger, *Nietzsche,* II, 509.

83. This is at the outset a psychological doctrine (see JGB 23, II 586) and it is thus likely that just as both master and slave morality elements can be present in the same person (see JGB 260, II 730), so also can elements of eternal return.

84. Naumann IX p. 77.

85. On mistakes, see Cavell, *Must We Mean What We Say?* pp. 105-107, and Paul Ricoeur, *The Symbolism of Evil* (New York: Harper & Row, 1967), pp. 211-238.

86. Kröner II pp. 474-475.

87. FW 11, II 44.

88. RWB 9, I 415.

89. FW 307, II 181.

90. Za On the Blessed Isles, II 344.

91. III 854 (WM 55).

92. Kröner II p. 476. See WKG V$_1$ p. 411.

93. Kröner II no. 1338 p. 475. Thus, though potentially misleading, it is not inaccurate to call eternal return "the new religion *wissenschaftlich begrundet,*" as does Hans Barth in *Wahrheit und ideologie* (Erlenbach: Rentsch, 1961), p. 248. See Karl Jaspers, *Nietzsche: An Introduction to His Philosophical Activity* trans. Charles Walraff and Frederick J. Schmitz (Tucson: University of Arizona Press, 1965), pp. 363 ff. See Kröner II pp. 472, 477.

94. EH Why I Am a Destiny 8, II 1159.

95. Kröner II p. 476.

96. Kröner II p. 476.

97. FW 11, II 44.

98. Kröner II p. 479. See FW 338, II 198-201.

99. Kröner II p. 478.

100. AC 4, II 1166.

101. AC 3, II 1166.

102. Kröner II p. 478.

103. Kröner II pp. 478-479.

104. III 610 (WM 887).

105. III 447 (WM 978).

106. III 467 (WM 957).

107. III 447 (WM 979).

108. III 468 (WM 957). See III 432 (WM 958). See Naumann IX p. 342 on how Nietzsche had hoped that Wagner might do this. See III 469 (WM 980): "Such an educator is beyond good and evil, but no one must know this."

109. III 504-505 (WM 960).

110. See Chap. VII above.

111. WKG VIII$_3$ p. 178. See also GD The Betters of Mankind 3, II 980, and AC 56, II 1224-1225.

112. Cavell, *Must We Mean What We Say?* p. 136. Cavell continues: "Nietzsche was not crazy when he blamed morality for the worst evils, though he may have become too crazy about the idea. This is why goodness, in trying to get born, will sometimes look like the destruction of morality. I am scarcely to be taken as presenting a theory of Nazism, any more than of the acquiescence to world destruction, so it would be irrelevant to point to other considerations which help explain human involvement in events of such catastrophe. . . ." See WKG VIII$_3$ p. 452.

113. FW 324, II 187-188.

114. EH Frontispiece, II 1069. In WKG VIII$_3$ pp. 422-423, Nietzsche continues a draft of his passage with a reference to "lived books."

115. As such the position seems to be close to that adopted by Stanley Cavell in his "The Claim to Rationality" (Unpublished Ph.D. thesis, Harvard University, 1962), pp. 352-354. He argues that the competence of morality "as judge of conduct and character is limited. This is what Kierkegaard meant by the 'teleological suspension of the ethical' and what Nietzsche meant by defining a position 'beyond good and evil.' What they meant is that there is a position whose excellence we cannot deny, taken by persons we are not willing or able to dismiss, but which, *morally,* would have to be called wrong." Morality, continues Cavell, "provides *one* possibility of settling conflict, a way of encompassing conflict which allows the continuance of personal relationships against the hard and apparently inevitable fact of misunderstanding, mutually incompatible wishes, commitments, loyalties, interests and needs, a way of healing tears in the fabric of relationship and of maintaining the self in opposition to itself and others. Other ways of settling or encompassing conflict are provided by politics, religion, love and forgiveness, rebellion and withdrawal. . . . But although morality is open to repudiation, either by the prophet or the raging and suffering self, or by the delinquent or the oldest and newest evil, and though it cannot assure us that we will have no enemies, nor that our actions are beyond reproach even when they pass all moral tests, *not just anybody, in any way, can repudiate it.*" (My italics at the end.) Cited from Pitkin, *Wittgenstein and Justice,* pp. 151-152.

116. *The Republic,* 496c-497a, trans. B. Jowett (New York: Random House, 1956).

117. WKG VIII$_3$ p. 420.

118. WKG VIII$_3$ p. 461.

119. Ludwig Wittgenstein, *Remarks on the Foundations of Mathematics* (Cambridge: M.I.T. Press, 1966), p. 57. Hanna Fenichel Pitkin (*Wittgenstein and Justice*) ends her book on Wittgenstein with the same point, which was hers, as it was mine, before we knew or read each other.

CHAPTER X: TEXTS, PRETEXTS, AND
THE SUBJECT: PERSPECTIVISM IN NIETZSCHE

1. See chapter III, note 22. To that discussion, one may add John T. Wilcox, *Truth and Value in Nietzsche: A Study in His Metaethics and Epistemology* (Ann Arbor: University of Michigan Press, 1974). Wilcox describes Nietzsche as holding both noncognitive ("destructive") elements and cognitive elements ("appraising"), which together are "transcognitive" (creative); but, as Wilcox notes (p. 201), Nietzsche does not say much about this.

2. See Richard Rorty, *Philosophy and the Mirror of Nature* (Princeton: Princeton University Press, 1979), esp. pp. 380ff.

3. WKG VIII₁ pp. 141–42 (WM 410).

4. WKG VIII₂ p. 6 (WM 462).

5. I have developed this general theme in two essays: "Nietzsche's Political Aesthetics," *Toward New Seas: Nietzsche on Politics, Philosophy, and Poetry*, Michael A. Gillespie and Tracy B. Strong, eds. (Chicago: University of Chicago Press, 1988) and "The Deconstruction of the Tradition: Nietzsche and the Greeks," *Nietzsche and Nihilism*, T. Darby et al., eds. (Toronto: University of Toronto Press, 1988).

6. Alexander Nehamas, "Immanent and Transcendent Perspectivism in Nietzsche," *Nietzsche-Studien*, XII (Berlin: Gruyter, 1983), pp. 473–490, and see my comment there, immediately following. See also Nehamas, *Nietzsche: Life As Literature* (Cambridge, Mass.: Harvard University Press, 1985), pp. 42–73.

7. There is a relative to Nehamas's distinction in Jean Granier, *Le problème de la vérité dans la philosophie de Nietzsche* (Paris: Seuil, 1966), p. 322.

8. See Wilfrid Sellars, "Empiricism and the Philosophy of Mind," *Science, Perception and Reality* (London: Routledge and Kegan Paul, 1962).

9. My translation differs from Kaufmann's, which does not add "in all": "Wir wissen nicht wie viele und was für Arten es Alles giebt."

10. WKG VIII₃ p. 165 (WM 636).

11. See my *The Idea of Political Theory*, chapter 3 (Notre Dame: University of Notre Dame Press, forthcoming).

12. WKG VII₃ pp. 22–23 (WM 426).

13. WKG VIII₂ p. 295 (WM 477).

14. WKG VIII₁ p. 323 (WM 481).

15. It is Thoreau's burden in *Walden* to make this point manifest to his readers. In this sense, as Stanley Cavell notes (*The Senses of Walden* [New York: Viking Press, 1972]), *Walden* can be said to provide a "transcendental deduction of the category of the thing-in-itself" (p. 140n).

16. WKG VIII₁ p. 104 (WM 518); WKG VIII₃ pp. 165–166 (WM 636). See WKG VIII₁ pp. 102–103 (WM 561 and 486).

17. WKG VIII₁ p. 12 (WM 556).

18. *Die Unschuld des Werdens*, A. Bäumler, ed. (Stuttgart: Kröner Verlag, 1956), II, 24.

19. WKG VII₂ pp. 179–180 (WM 259). Cf. Martin Heidegger, *Nietzsche* (Pfüllingen: Neske, 1961), I, 632ff.

20. WKG VII₃ p. 382 (WM 490). Nietzsche thus is willing to deconstruct the

subject in the manner of Derrida, but not to destroy the subject – as I think Derrida suggests Nietzsche does; see *Eperons/Spurs* (Chicago: University of Chicago Press, 1979). See my "The Deconstruction of the Tradition."

21. See, for instance, Bruno Snell, *The Discovery of the Mind* (New York: Harper & Row, 1960). See my discussion in chapter VI. For a more sociological discussion, see my discussion in chapter II and also Johannes Goudsblom, *Nihilism and Culture* (Oxford: Blackwell, 1979).

22. WKG VII₁ p. 196 (not in WM). See also WL.

23. WKG V₂ p. 232 (FW 324).

24. Granier, *Le problème de la vérité*, pp. 357–366.

25. See George Kateb, "Thinking About Human Extinction: (I) Nietzsche and Heidegger," *Raritan* 2 (Fall 1986), 1–28; "Thinking About Human Extinction: (II) Emerson and Whitman," *Raritan* 3 (Winter 1987), 1–22.

26. WKG VII₁ p. 695 (WM 667).

27. Michael Holquist, "The Politics of Representation" (unpublished typescript), p. 19.

28. Nietzsche, *Gesammt Ausgabe* (Leipzig: Nauman, 1898), XII, p. 13 (#22).

29. WKG VI pp. 52–53 (JGB 39). One thinks here also of Max Weber, who, in response to a question as to why he learned so much, answered, with probably a conscious echo of this aphorism: "I want to see how much I can bear." See Marianne Weber, *Max Weber: Ein Lebensbild* (Tubingen: Mohr, 1976). See also W. D. Williams, *Nietzsche and the French. A Study of the Influence of Nietzsche's French Reading on His Thought and Writing* (Oxford: Blackwell, 1952), pp. 96–98; cf. WKG V₂ pp. 19–20 (FW Vorrede 4). Paradoxically, Nietzsche shares something like the old Calvinist understanding. Calvin had argued that one could/should never pretend to know the world as it is – such was only for God. Human knowledge was necessarily from a point of view – that of the creaturely sinner. In this light, Nietzsche's last letter to Burckhardt, in which he claims identification with "all names in history," makes chilling sense. *Vollendung* is, in fact, madness. For a further discussion, see my "Oedipus As Hero: Family and Family Metaphors in Nietzsche," *boundary 2: a journal of post modern literature* (Spring/Fall 1981), 311–336.

30. WKG III₁ p. 129 (GT 21); see also A. Kremer-Marietti, *L'homme et les labyrinthes* (Paris: Seuil, 1972), pp. 77ff.

31. WKG III₁ p. 248 (HL 1); WKG VI₂ p. 49 (JGB 34).

32. WKG VIII₂ p. 17 (WM 507). Part of the force of Nietzsche's critique of historicism, which dominated the thought of his time, was that it saw human beings as necessarily prisoners of a past that they had in fact made. To the degree that one cannot free oneself from the mold of the past [WKG VII₁ p. 545 (not in WM)] – one's own past – one is destined not only to repeat it, but finally to be annihilated in it. The past is always in danger of being taken for truth. Thus, "man must have, and from time to time use, the strength to break up and dissolve a past, in order to be able to live" [WKG III₁ p. 261 (HL 3)].

33. WKG IV₂ p. 14 (MA 1886 preface 6). See Nietzsche, *Einleitung zu den Vorlesen ueber Sophocles' "Oedipus Rex," Gesammelte Werke* (Munich: Musarion, 1920–1929), II, p. 257. See also my discussion of the chorus in chapter VI.

34. WKG VI₂ p. 99 (JGB 150).

35. WKG V₂ pp. 308–309 (FW 374).

36. Nietzsche suggests various factors as productive of this syndrome. The most general is in WKG VIII₂ p. 277 (WM 708), as the "hypothesis of being" (*Hypothese des Seienden*); at other times he suggests the subject-object distinction.

37. WKG VIII₁ p. 159 (WM 254). See also VI₂ pp. 21–22 (JGB 13). For a comparison between the will to power and Freud's doctrine of eros, see F. A. Lea, *The Tragic Philosopher: A Study of Friedrich Nietzsche* (London: Methuen, 1957).

38. WKG VI₂ p. 49 (JGB 34).

39. WKG VI₂ p. 51 (JGB 36).

40. This is the source of Heidegger's analysis of the will to power as *physis*. For discussion and a criticism, see below.

41. WKG VIII₁ p. 192 (not in WM). This seems to me to show the essential fallacy in the claim of R. H. Grimm, *Nietzsche's Theory of Knowledge* (Berlin and New York: Gruyter, 1977) to the effect that if there were to be a theory of knowledge that was more encompassing than the will to power, Nietzsche would welcome it as a confirmation of his theory rather than a disproof. Grimm's position has been extended, unsuccessfully I think, in Philip J. Kain, "Nietzsche, Skepticism and Eternal Recurrence," *Canadian Journal of Political Science* (September 1983), 365–387.

42. WKG VII₁ p. 353 (WM 574).

43. WKG VIII₃ p. 165 (WM 636).

44. WKG VIII₁ p. 230 (WM 617).

45. See the discussion of active and passive return in Gilles Deleuze, *Nietzsche et la philosophie* (Paris: Presses Universitaires de France, 1962), and my argument in chapter IX.

46. WKG VIII₁ p. 192 (not in WM).

47. Alexander Nehamas, "How One Becomes What One Is," *Philosophical Review* XXCII, 3 (July 1983), 485–517. Bernd Magnus has suggested that the world for Nietzsche is a kind of pentimento of interpretations. Nehamas's "Immanent and Transcendent" argues against this on the grounds that, even if a lost Aristotelian text for us has become its transcriptions and interpretations, there was nonetheless an original text. See my argument about this problem below. See Bernd Magnus, *Nietzsche's Existential Imperative* (Bloomington and London: Indiana University Press, 1978) and his "Nietzsche's Mitigated Skepticism," *Nietzsche-Studien*, IX (Gruyter: Berlin and New York: 1980), pp. 260–267. See also Nehamas, *Life as Literature*, passim. I am conscious here of the influence of W. Isel, *The Art of Reading* (Baltimore: Johns Hopkins University Press, 1978).

48. WKG VI₃ p. 263 (EH Why I am so wise, 1); see also the earlier version in WKG VII₃ p. 442.

49. See WKG VIII₃ pp. 165–166 (WM 636). Helene Keyssar has suggested that this failure should be seen in light of the position advanced in Walter Benjamin's "The World of Art in an Age of Mechanical Reproduction," in his *Illuminations*. What, one might ask, is the status of the "text" if there can exist a potentially unlimited number of identical copies? Certainly they are not interpretations.

50. Cf. WKG VI₃ p. 318 (EH Why I write such good books – Untimely Consid-

erations, 2); WKG V₂ pp. 224–225 (FW 307); WKG VI₂ pp. 56–58 (JGB 44); see Nehamas, "How One Becomes What One Is," p. 416.

51. WKG VI₃ p. 296 (EH Why I write such good books, 1).

52. Roland Barthes, "The Death of the Author," *Image–Music–Text* (New York: Hill and Wang, 1977), pp. 142–148; Michel Foucault, "What Is an Author?" *Language, Counter-Memory, Practice* (Ithaca: Cornell University Press, 1977), pp. 113–138, esp. pp. 131ff.

53. Williams, *Nietzsche and the French*, p. 102

54. WKG VI₂ pp. 241–242 (JGB 283–284).

55. WKG VI₂ p. 244 (JGB 289).

56. WKG IV₃ p. 9 (MAM ii, Vorwort 5).

57. WKG VI₃ p. 263 (EH Why I am so wise, 1); see also the earlier version in WKG VIII₃ p. 442.

58. WKG VIII₂ p. 179 (partly in WM 907). See EH epigraph. As I have come (dangerously) close to anthropology, see here Clifford Geertz, "From the Native's Point of View: On the Nature of Anthropological Understanding," *Meaning in Anthropology*, K. Basso and N. Selby, eds. (Albuquerque: University of New Mexico Press, 1967), pp. 236–237. Peter Winch has advanced a position like that which Nehamas attributes to Nietzsche; see Winch, "Understanding a Primitive Society," *American Philosophical Quarterly* (October 1964), 307–324. For a critique of Winch's position similar to my defense of Nietzsche, see Hanna F. Pitkin, *Wittgenstein and Justice* (Berkeley and Los Angeles: University of California Press, 1972), and, to a lesser extent, Alasdair MacIntyre, "Rationality and the Explanation of Action," *Against the Self-Images of the Age* (London: Duckworth, 1971), pp. 244–259. For a slightly different point of view, see Robert Eden, *Political Leadership and Nihilism* (Gainesville: University of Florida Press, 1984).

EPILOGUE

1. In a pamphlet urging summer reading for incoming freshpeople to the University of California at Santa Cruz.

2. I believe the first such article was Alexander Nehamas, "How One Becomes What One Is," *Philosophical Review* XXCII, 3 (July 1983), pp. 485–517.

3. Sarah Kofman, *Nietzsche et la scène philosophique* (Paris: Galilée, 1986), p. 1.

4. See Alasdair MacIntyre, *After Virtue* (London: Duckworth, 1981), p. 108 ("Left"); Bernd Magnus, "Nietzsche's Philosophy in 1988: The Will to Power and the Ubermensch," *Journal of the History of Philosophy* XXIV, 1 (January 1986), 82 ("Splitter"); Magnus, "Nietzsche and the Project of Bringing Philosophy to an End," *Nietzsche as Affirmative Thinker,* Yirmiyahu Yovel, ed. (Dordrecht: Nijhoff, 1986) ("Therapeutic"); and Gianni Vattimo, "Nietzsche and Contemporary Hermeneutics," ibid. ("Vitalist").

5. Martin Heidegger, *Nietzsche* (Pfullingen: Neske, 1961); English translation by David Farrell Krell (New York: Harper and Row, 1979).

6. Gilles Deleuze, *Nietzsche et la philosophie* (Paris: Presses Universitaires de France, 1962); Michel Foucault, *Language, Counter-Memory and Practice* (Ithaca:

NOTES TO PAGES 311-316 [365

Cornell University Press, 1977); Jacques Derrida, *De la grammatologie* (Paris: Editions de Minuit, 1967) and *Eperons/Spurs* (Chicago: University of Chicago Press, 1978). See also the collection by David Allison, *The New Nietzsche* (New York: Dell, 1977).

7. There are some odd parallels here with the understandings that Leo Strauss and his followers advance about Nietzsche. Sometimes Nietzsche is presented as "a man of the right" (the phrase is Allan Bloom's in conversation), a kind of counter to Marx; sometimes he is taken to have been (perhaps *malgré lui*) a progenitor of what is seen as the nihilism of the sixties (again Bloom, in *The Closing of the American Mind* [New York: Basic Books, 1987]). Strauss, however, tends to see himself as close to Nietzsche (cf. S. Drury "The Esoteric Philosophy of Leo Strauss," *Political Theory* XIII, 3 (August 1985), 315–338) and to think that Nietzsche "points to a way of thinking and living that transcends historicism" (Strauss, *Studies in Platonic Political Philosophy* [Chicago: University of Chicago Press, 1983], p. 188). Some of the difficulties with this claim can be seen in Werner Dannhauser, *Nietzsche's View of Socrates* (Ithaca: Cornell University Press, 1974). What the Straussians seem to hold against Nietzsche is that he apparently said publicly that which only a few (those able to bear it) should hear. The moralism of this claim ("should hear") seems to me to lie counter to everything that Nietzsche tried to make available.

8. The phrase is Gustav Bergmann's in Richard Rorty, ed. *The Linguistic Turn: Recent Essays in Philosophical Method* (Chicago: University of Chicago Press, 1967).

9. Kaufmann's translations are both accurate and felicitous; however, like all translations, they are the product of a particular understanding of the text. For some examples (not of mistakes), see chapter I, note 24 and chapter VI, note 66.

10. I should add here, to be perfectly honest, that the manuscript of this book was first sent to Walter Kaufmann, who recommended against publication in a fourteen-page single-spaced critique. His subsequent correspondence with me reveals a proud and generous man; we never met.

11. A fact also noted, although put to very different use, by Bloom in *Closing of the American Mind*.

12. See WKG V₁ pp. 176–178 (M 202) and my discussion on pp. 104–107.

13. George Kateb has brilliantly realized this theme in "Thinking About Human Extinction: (I) Nietzsche and Heidegger," *Raritan* 2 (Fall 1986), 1–28, and "Thinking About Extinction: (II) Emerson and Whitman," *Raritan* 3 (Winter 1987), 1–22.

14. WKG VI₁ p. 284 (Z The Seven Seals, 3).

15. See Reinhard Bendix and John Seery, "An Exchange of Letters Between the Author and a Graduate Student," *Force, Fate and Freedom*, Reinhard Bendix (Berkeley and Los Angeles: University of California Press, 1984).

16. WKG VI₂ (GM iii, 25), my translation. See my discussion on pp. 16–18 and in chapter III.

17. WKG VI₃ p. 296 (EH Why I write such good books, 1).

18. See my "Nietzsche's Political Aesthetics," *Towards New Seas: Nietzsche on Politics, Philosophy, and Poetry*, Michael A. Gillespie and Tracy B. Strong, eds. (Chicago: University of Chicago Press, 1988).

19. Max Weber, "Science As a Vocation," *From Max Weber*, H. Gerth and C. W. Mills, eds. (New York: Oxford, 1958). See also Robert Eden, *Political Leadership*

and Nihilism (Gainesville: University of Florida Press, 1984). The relation of Nietzsche to Weber is a topic to be pursued; Eden has laid some of the groundwork.

20. See the discussion by Stanley Fish in the appendix to *Self-Consuming Artifacts* (Berkeley and Los Angeles: University of California Press, 1974).

21. WKG VI$_3$ 296 (EH Why I write such good books, 1). I have explored this problem at great length in "Nietzsche's Political Aesthetics," and "The Deconstruction of the Tradition: Nietzsche and the Greeks," *Nietzsche and Nihilism*, T. Darby et al., eds. (Toronto: University of Toronto Press, 1988). It is the problem of authority.

BIBLIOGRAPHY

A war wages among Nietzsche scholars not only as to which edition is the best, but, in fact, even as to what are the criteria for the best Nietzsche edition. I have very little to add to this conflict except to note the following.

In *all* editions there are enough correct pages to permit (though certainly not ensure) an accurate understanding.

While there are dangers in assuming that *The Will to Power* is organized along lines Nietzsche would have approved of (see Chap. VIII above), there is, as far as I can tell, no ordering of the vast material from which *The Will to Power* was drawn (the *Nachlass*) which helps the reader any more than any other. This includes the order in which Nietzsche happened to set his thoughts down. (A partial exception to this are the first 206 pages in the Colli and Montinari edition, Vol. VIII$_2$.)

While the Schlechta edition is the most accessible, the Colli and Montinari edition offers even in the present state of its completion (as I write, twelve volumes of a projected twenty-eight, not counting the letters) the most useful edition for scholars. The one volume of critical apparatus which has thus far appeared is superb.

I. Editions of Nietzsche in German

Due to the fact that I have worked on this book in many places, and that no complete edition of Nietzsche is available to the public for purchase, I have used several editions. These are listed above in the Key, Section B.

II. Editions of Nietzsche in English

The translations of Walter Kaufmann comprise eleven books written by Nietzsche. His translations not only are the best available, they are really the *only* ones that the English-speaking student of Nietzsche should use. Contrary to most other translations, Kaufmann's work is not only accurate, but also stylistically close (or as close as possible) to the original; and what is of great importance, they are philosophically informed. Kaufmann's translations have been of tremendous assistance to me, for, though I have worked from the German, I have not hesitated to consult his versions to determine the happiest rendering of particular passages.

A. Translations by Walter Kaufmann

The Birth of Tragedy and *The Case of Wagner*. New York: Vintage Books, 1967.
Beyond Good and Evil. New York: Vintage Books, 1966.
On the Genealogy of Morals and *Ecce Homo*. New York: Vintage Books, 1967.
The Portable Nietzsche. New York: Viking Press, 1954. This volume contains, as
    well as extensive material from other works of Nietzsche, the following:
        Thus Spoke Zarathustra
        Twilight of the Idols
        The Antichrist
        Nietzsche Contra Wagner
The Will to Power. Trans. with R. J. Hollingdale. New York: Random House,
    1967.
The Gay Science. New York: Random House, 1974.

B. Other Translations

With the exception of the first, these are generally stylistically unfortunate and often inaccurate.
Selected Letters of Friedrich Nietzsche. Ed. and trans. Christopher Middleton.
    Chicago and London: University of Chicago Press, 1969.
Philosophy in the Tragic Age of the Greeks. Trans. with an Introduction by
    Marianne Cowan, Chicago: Henry Regnery Company, 1962.
Schopenhauer as Educator. Trans. James W. Hillesheim and Malcolm R. Simpson
    with an Introduction by Eliseo Vivas. Chicago: Gateway Editions, 1965.
The Use and Abuse of History. Trans. Adrian Collins with an Introduction by
    Julius Kraft. ("Library of Liberal Arts.") New York: Bobbs-Merrill Company,
    1957.
The Complete Works of Friedrich Nietzsche. Ed. Oscar Levy. New York:
    Macmillan Company, 1914. Old and generally awful translations.

III. Secondary Literature

A. For the reader first approaching the secondary literature on Nietzsche, I give here those books in English which form the most important and accessible commentary. Inevitably, this list is shaped by my understanding of Nietzsche.

Danto, Arthur. *Nietzsche as Philosopher.* New York: Macmillan Company, 1965. Danto is an American philosopher trained in analytic philosophy. He focuses mainly on Nietzsche's ethics and epistemology, trying to show that they are related and form a consistent position. He then attempts a criticism of Nietzsche's position.

Jaspers, Karl. *Nietzsche: An Introduction to His Philosophical Activity.* Tucson: University of Arizona Press, 1965. Jaspers is a European philosopher of great renown, associated with phenomenology and existentialism. He tries to show that Nietzsche's philosophical activity is characterized by the refusal to let a proposition stand without asserting its contrary. He thus makes a virtue out of what many have found a problem in Nietzsche, namely, that he appears to contradict himself.

Kaufmann, Walter. *Nietzsche: Philosopher, Psychologist, Antichrist.* 3rd edn. Princeton: Princeton University Press, 1968. Kaufmann is the man most responsible for bringing Nietzsche back to the center of public attention in America. His book, originally published in 1950, places Nietzsche squarely in the tradition of Western humanist philosophy.

Lea, F. A. *The Tragic Philosopher: A Study of Friedrich Nietzsche.* London: Methuen & Co., 1957. To my mind, one of the best general introductions. Lea's book contains some interesting comparisons to Marx and Freud and generally sees the sociological element in Nietzsche's work.

Love, F. R. *Young Nietzsche and the Wagnerian Experience.* Chapel Hill: University of North Carolina Press, 1963. The best book in English on the relations of Wagner and Nietzsche. Love knows and understands music, which he uses to good advantage.

Williams, W. D. *Nietzsche and the French.* Oxford: Clarendon Press, 1952. A very sound study of the influence of French thought on Nietzsche's work.

The best work on Nietzsche is now being done by the French, especially in the work of Deleuze, Granier, Klossowski, Pautrat, and Wahl. Works of most interest to the student of what Nietzsche says specifically about politics are cited at the beginning of Chapter VII above.

B.   There exists a Nietzsche index which contains 3973 items in 27 languages: *International Nietzsche Index.* Eds. H. W. Reichert and Karl Schlechta. Chapel Hill: University of North Carolina Press, 1960.

What follows from this is obviously not exhaustive. I have divided it into two categories. In the first, I have placed works that deal directly and (almost) only with Nietzsche. I have included those works that shaped my thinking (either actively or reactively) enough to merit mention. Some effort has been made to include the significant material coming after 1960.

In the second part that follows, I have cited two kinds of works. Firstly, those which deal with Nietzsche, but in terms of some broader scope. For instance, Habermas' *Knowledge and Human Interests* has two chapters on

Nietzsche in the context of a discussion of critical rationality and nineteenth-and twentieth-century social theory. Secondly, those that deal with the sorts of problems that Nietzsche also deals with. Sometimes not. But in both cases they have helped or jarred my understanding.

Good capsule summaries of the main literature on Nietzsche are given in J. Granier, *Le problème de la vérité dans la philosophie de Nietzsche*, pp. 21-27, and generally in C. Baroni, *Nietzsche, éducateur de l'homme au surhomme*. Most major interpretations are considered in the text of this book. The best biography is probably Halévy's book, but the best sense of Nietzsche's life is probably gained from reading Middleton's edition of the letters.

1. Works on Nietzsche

Andler, Charles. *Nietzsche: sa vie et sa pensée.* 3 vols. Paris: Gallimard, 1958.

Arrowsmith, William. "Nietzsche on the Classics and the Classicists," *Arion,* II (Spring, Summer, Winter, 1963), 5-12, 5-27, 5-31.

Assaad-Mikhail, F. "Jaspers, interprète de Nietzsche," *Revue de métaphysique et de morale,* LXXI (July-September, 1966), 307-338.

————. "Heidegger, interprète de Nietzsche," *ibid.,* LXXIII (January-March, 1968), 16-55.

Baroni, Charles. *Nietzsche, éducateur de l'homme au surhomme.* Paris: Buchet, 1961.

Bartuschat, Wolfgang. *Nietzsche: Selbstsein und Negativität: zur Problematik einer Philosophie des sich selbst vollenden Willens.* Inaugural Dissertation, Heidelberg, 1964.

Berthelot, René. *Un romantisme utilitaire: étude sur le mouvement pragmatiste.* Vol. I, *Le pragmatisme chez Nietzsche et Poincaré.* Paris: F. Alcan, 1911.

Bianquis, Geneviève. *Nietzsche devant ses contemporains.* Monaco: Du Rocher, 1954.

Binder, Julius. *Nietzsches Staatsauffassung.* Göttingen: Dieterischen Universitäts-Buchdruckerei, 1925.

Birault, Henri. "En quoi nous sommes encore pieux," *Revue de métaphysique et de morale,* LXVII (January-March, 1962), 25-64.

A Brassard, Werner. *Untersuchungen zum problem des Übermenschen bei Friedrich Nietzsche.* Freiburg: Müller, 1962.

Brinton, Crane. *Nietzsche.* Cambridge: Harvard University Press, 1941.

Bueb, Bernard. *Nietzsches Kritik der praktischen Vernunft.* Stuttgart: Klett, 1970.

Bulhof-Rutgers, B. *Apollos Wiederkehr, eine Untersuchung der Rolle des Kreises in Nietzsches Denken über Geschichte und Zeit.* s'Gravenhage: Nidjhoff, 1969.

Colloque philosophique internationale de Royaumont. *Nietzsche.* Paris: Editions de Minuit, 1967. Conference transcript.

Copleston, Frederick, S.J. *Friederich Nietzsche: Philosopher of Culture.* London: Burns, Oates & Washburn, 1942.

Danto, Arthur. *Nietzsche as Philosopher.* New York: Macmillan Company, 1965.

Deleuze, Gilles. *Nietzsche et la philosophie.* Paris: Presses universitaires de France, 1962.

Deussen, Paul. *Erinnerungen an Friedrich Nietzsche.* Leipzig: F. A. Brockhaus, 1901.

Dickopp, Karl-Heinz. *Nietzsches Kritik des Ich-denke.* Inaugural Dissertation, Bonn, 1965.

Fink, Eugen. *La philosophie de Nietzsche.* Paris: Editions de Minuit, 1965.

Fischer, H. *Nietzsche, apostata, oder die Philosophie des Ärgernisses.* Erfurt: K. Stenger, 1931.

Fischer, Kurt R. "Review of Danto," *Journal of Philosophy,* Vol. LXIV, No. 18, 564-569.

Fleischman, Eugène. "De Weber à Nietzsche," *Archives européenes de la sociologie* Vol. XIV, No. 2 (1964), 190-238.

Foerster-Nietzsche, Elizabeth. *The Nietzsche-Wagner Correspondence.* New York: Boni and Liveright, 1921.

Friedman, M. "Friederich Nietzsche: Father of Atheistic Existentialism," *Journal of Existentialism,* (Spring, 1966), 269-279.

Garnier, Paul-Louis. *Reflexions sur Nietzsche.* Paris: Ermitage, 1902.

Granier, Jean. *Le problème de la vérité dans la philosophie de Nietzsche.* Paris: Editions du Seuil, 1966.

Grunder, Karlfried, ed. *Der Streit um Nietzsches Geburt der Tragödie.* Hildesheim: Olms Verlag, 1969.

Halévy, Daniel. *Nietzsche.* Paris: B. Grasset, 1944.

Hayes, Donna Jean. "Nietzsche's Eternal Return: a Prelude to Heidegger," *Journal of Existentialism,* VI (Winter, 1965-1966), 189-196.

Heidegger, Martin. *Nietzsche.* 2 vols. Pfüllingen: Neske, 1961.

————. "Who is Nietzsche's Zarathustra?" *Review of Metaphysics,* XX (March, 1967), 411-431.

Heller, Erich. *The Artist's Journey into the Interior.* New York: Random House, 1959.

Hohn, Hans Peter. *Die metaphysische und anthropologische Voraussetzungen der Politik bei Friederich Nietzsche.* Inaugural Dissertation, Bonn, 1959.

Hotter, Karl. *Das Bildungsproblem in der Philosophie Nietzsches.* Inaugural Dissertation, München, 1958.

Huan, Gabriel. *La philosophie de Friederich Nietzsche,* Paris: Editions du Boccard, 1917.

Jaspers, Karl. *Nietzsche and Christianity.* Trans. E. B. Ashton. Chicago: Gateway Editions, 1961.

————. "Nietzsche and the Present," *Partisan Review,* XVIII (January-February, 1952), 19-30.

————. *Nietzsche: An Introduction to His Philosophical Activity.* Trans. Charles Walraff and Frederick J. Schmitz. Tucson: University of Arizona Press, 1965.

Kariel, Henry. "Nietzsche's Preface to Constitutionalism," *Journal of Politics,* XXIV (May, 1963), 211,225.

Kaufmann, Walter. *Nietzsche: Philosopher, Psychologist, Antichrist.* 3rd edn. Princeton: Princeton University Press, 1968.

Klossowski, Pierre. *Nietzsche et le cercle vicieux.* Paris: Mercure de France, 1969.

Knight, Arthur Harold John. *Some Aspects of the Life and Work of Nietzsche and Particularly of His Connection with Greek Literature and Thought.* Cambridge, England: The University Press, 1933.

Kofman, Sarah. *Nietzsche et la métaphore.* Paris: Payot, 1972.

Kremer-Marietti, Angèle. "Nietzsche et la verité," *Revue de métaphysique et de morale,* LXXII (October-December, 1967), 486-496.

————. "Nietzsche et quelques un de ses interprètes actuelles, *ibid.,* LXXIV (October-November, 1969), 457-468.

Lea, Frank Alfred. *The Tragic Philosopher: A Study of Friedrich Nietzsche.* London: Methuen & Co., 1957.

Lefebvre, Henri. *Nietzsche.* Paris: Editions sociales internationales, 1939.

Love, Frederick R. *Young Nietzsche and the Wagnerian Experience.* Chapel Hill: University of North Carolina Press, 1963.

Löwith, Karl. *From Hegel to Nietzsche.* New York: Holt, Rinehart and Winston, 1964.

————. "Nietzsche," *Revue de métaphysique et de morale,* LXI (July-September, 1956), 328-345.

Ludovici, Anthony Maria. *Nietzsche and Art.* London: Constable and Co., 1911.

McNees, John Earl. "Nietzsche as a Political Philosopher." Unpublished Bachelor's thesis, Harvard University, 1960.

Mann, Heinrich. *The Living Thoughts of Friederich Nietzsche.* London: Cassell and Company, 1946.

Mann, Thomas. *Nietzsches Philosophie im Licht unserer Erfahrung.* Berlin: Suhrkamp, 1948.

Manthez-Zorn, Otto. *Dionysus: The Tragedy of Nietzsche.* Amherst: The College Press, 1956.

Morawa, H. *Sprache und Stil von Nietzsches Zarathustra.* Inaugural Dissertation, Berlin, 1958.

Morgan, George Allen, Jr. *What Nietzsche Means.* Cambridge: Harvard University Press, 1941.

Oehler, Richard. *Nietzsche und die Vorsokratiker.* Leipzig: Dürr'schen Buchhandlung, 1904.

Pautrat, Bernard. *Versions du soleil: figures et système de Nietzsche.* Paris: Editions du Seuil, 1971.

Pfeffer, Rose. "Eternal Recurrence in Nietzsche's Thought," *Review of Metaphysics,* XVIII (December, 1965), 276-300.

Podach, Erich Friedrich. *Ein Blick im Notizbücher Nietzsches: Eine schaffensanalytische Studie.* Heidelberg: Rothe, 1963.

————. *L'effondrement de Nietzsche.* Paris: Gallimard, 1931.

Rammoux, Charles. "Les fragments d'un Empédocle de Friedrich Nietzsche," *Revue de métaphysique et de morale,* LXX (April-June, 1965), 199-212.

Reinhardt, Karl. *Nietzsches Klage der Ariadne.* Frankfurt: Klostermann, 1936.

Reinhardt, Kurt. *Tradition und Geist.* Göttingen: Vandenhoeck und Ruprecht, 1960.

Ries, Wiebrecht. *Grundzüge des Nietzsche-Verständnisses in der Deutung seiner Philosophie. Zur Geschichte der Nietzsche-Literatur in Deutschland, 1932-1963.* Inaugural Dissertation, Heidelberg, 1967.

Robinson, Glen Osmond. "New Parables for the Modern Age: The Moral and Political Philosophy of Nietzsche." Unpublished Bachelor's thesis, Harvard University, 1958.

Roeschl, Herbert. "Nietzsche et la solitude," *Société francaise des études nietzschéenes.* Bulletin, 1958.

————. *Nietzsche, poète de la solitude.* Paris: Minard, 1960.

Salter, Walter MacIntyre. *Nietzsche the Thinker.* New York: Holt and Company, 1917.

Sandvoss, E. *Sokrates und Nietzsche.* Leiden: E. J. Brill, 1966.

Schieder, Theodor. *Nietzsche und Bismarck.* Krefeld: Scherpe Verlag, 1963.

Schlechta, Karl. *Der Fall Nietzsche.* München: Carl Hanser, Verlag, 1958.

Schmidt, Hermann-Josef. *Nietzsche und Sokrates. Philosophische Untersuchungen zu Nietzsches Sokratesbild.* Meisenheim am Glan: Hain, 1969.

Seillière, Ernest. *Apollon ou Dionysos. Etude critique sur Friedrich Nietzsche et l'utilitarisme imperialiste.* Paris: Plon-Nourrit et Cie., 1905.

Sherover, Erica. "Nietzsche: On Yea and Nay Saying," *Journal of Existentialism,* V (Summer, 1965), 423-426.

Simmel, Georg. *Schopenhauer und Nietzsche.* Leipzig: Duncker und Humboldt, 1911.

Solomon, Robert, ed. *Nietzsche.* New York: Doubleday & Company, 1973.

Stambaugh, Joan. *Untersuchungen zum Problem der Zeit bei der Philosophie Nietzsches.* Den Haag: Nidjhoff, 1959.

Vogel, Martin. *Apollonisch und Dionysisch, Geschichte eines genialen Irrtums.* Regensburg: Bosse, 1966.

Wahl, Jean André. "Le cas Nietzsche," *Revue de métaphysique et de morale,* LXVI (July-September, 1961), 306-311.

————. *L'avant dernière pensé de Nietzsche.* Paris: Centre de documentation universitaire, 1961.

————. *La pensée philosophique de Nietzsche des années 1885-1888.* Paris: Centre de documentation universitaire, 1959.

Weichelt, H. *Zarathustra Kommentar.* Leipzig: Baustein, 1922.

Wein, H. "Métaphysique et anti-métaphysique," *Revue de métaphysique et de morale,* LXIII (October-December, 1958), 385-411.

Williams, William David. *Nietzsche and the French. A Study of the Influence of Nietzsche's French Reading on His Thought and Writing.* Oxford: Blackwell, 1952.

2. Other Importantly Relevant Works

Adkins, Arthur William Hope. *From the Many to the One, a Study of Personality and Views of Human Nature in the Context of Ancient Greek Society, Values and Beliefs.* Ithaca: Cornell University Press, 1970.

————. *Merit and Responsibility,* Oxford: Clarendon Press, 1960.

Arendt, Hannah. *Between Past and Future.* New York: Viking Press, 1968.

————. *The Human Condition.* Garden City: Doubleday Anchor Books, 1959.

Arrowsmith, William. "A Greek Theater of Ideas," *Arion,* II (Autumn, 1963), 32-56.

Baier, Kurt. *The Moral Point of View.* Ithaca: Cornell University Press, 1958.

Barth, Hans. *Wahrheit und Ideologie.* Erlenbach: Rentsch, 1961.

Bendix, Reinhard. "Industrialization and Ideologies," *American Sociological Review,* XXIII (October, 1959), 613-623.

————. "Social Stratification and the Political Community," *European Journal of Sociology,* Vol. X, Nos. 1-2 (1960).

————. *Social Science and the Distrust of Reason.* Berkeley and Los Angeles: University of California Press, 1951.

Benveniste, Emile. *Le vocabulaire des institutions indo-européenes.* 2 vols. Paris: Editions de Minuit, 1969.

Berdayev, Nikolai. *Dostojewsky.* Trans. W. Lowrie. New York: Meridian Books, 1957.

Brock, Werner. *Contemporary German Philosophy.* Cambridge, England: The University Press, 1935.

Brown, Norman O. *Hermes the Thief: the Evolution of a Myth.* New York: Vintage Books, 1969.

Burckhardt, Jacob. *A History of Greek Culture.* New York: Unger, 1963.

————. *The Letters.* Ed. A. Dru. London: Routledge and Kegan Paul, 1955.

Burke, Kenneth. *A Grammar of Motives.* Berkeley and Los Angeles: University of California Press, 1969.

Colloque philosophique internationale de Royaumont. *La Philosophie analytique.* Paris: Editions de Minuit, 1962. Conference transcript.

Camus, Albert. *The Rebel.* Trans. A. Bower. New York: Vintage Books, 1957.

Cavell, Stanley. "Existentialism and Analytic Philosophy," *Daedalus,* XCIII (Summer, 1964), 946-974.

————. *Must We Mean What We Say? A Book of Essays.* New York: Charles Scribner's Sons, 1969.

————. *The World Viewed: Reflections on the Ontology of Film.* New York: Viking Press, 1971.

Collingwood, Robin George. *An Autobiography.* Oxford: The University Press, 1939. 2nd. edn., 1964.

————. *An Essay on Metaphysics.* Chicago: University of Chicago Press, 1972.

Cornford, Francis Macdonald. *The Origin of Attic Comedy.* London: E. Arnold, 1914.

————. *Thucydides Mythhistoricus.* London: E. Arnold, 1907.

Danto, Arthur. "Semantical Theory and the Logical Limits of Nihilism," *New Essays in Phenomenology.* Ed. J. Edie. Chicago: Quadrangle Books, 1969.

Deleuze, Gilles. *Logique du sens.* Paris: Editions de Minuit, 1968.

Deleuze, Gilles, and Guattari, Felix. *L'anti-Oedipe. Capitalisme et schizophrénie.* Paris: Editions de Minuit, 1972.

Deman, Paul. *Blindness and Insight.* New York: Oxford University Press, 1971.

Derrida, Jacques. *De la grammatologie.* Paris: Editions de Minuit, 1967.

Dodds, Eric Robinson, ed. Plato's *Gorgias.* Oxford: Clarendon Press, 1959. See the Appendix.

————. *The Greeks and the Irrational.* Boston: Beacon Press, 1957.

Dostoyevsky, Fyodor. *The Brothers Karamazov.* Trans. Constance Garnett. New York: New American Library, 1957.

Durkheim, Emile. *Suicide.* Glencoe: Free Press, 1962.

Einstein, Albert. "Autobiographical Note," *Einstein.* Ed. Paul Schilpp. New York: Harper & Row, 1961.

Fleischman, Eugène. *"L'esprit humain selon Claude Lévi-Strauss,"* *Archives européenes de la sociologie* Vol. VII, No. 1 (1966), 27-57.

Foucault, Michel. *Les mots et les choses. Une archéologie des sciences humaines.* Paris: Gallimard, 1966.

Freud, Sigmund. *Civilization and Its Discontents.* New York: W. W. Norton & Company, 1962.

————. "Criminality from a Sense of Guilt," *Collected Papers.* London: Hogarth, 1953. Vol. IV, pp. 341-344.

————. "Dostojewski and Parricide," *Collected Papers.* London: Hogarth, 1953. Vol. V, pp. 222-242.

————. "Moral Responsibility for the Content of Dreams," *Collected Papers.* London: Hogarth, 1953. Vol. V, pp. 154-157.

Fustel de Coulanges, Numa Denis. *The Ancient City.* Garden City: Doubleday & Company, 1956.

Godelier, Maurice. "Système, structure et contradiction dans le *Capital,*" *Les temps modernes,* XXII (November, 1966), 828-864.

Goff, Robert. "Aphorism as Lebensform in Wittgenstein's *Philosophical Investigations,*" *New Essays in Phenomenology.* Ed. J. Edie. Chicago: Quadrangle Books, 1969.

Goldman, Lucien. "The Subject of Cultural Creation," *Boston Studies in the Philosophy of Science.* Vol. IV. Eds. R. Cohen and M. Wartofsky. Dordrecht: Reidel, 1969. Pp. 241-260.

Guthrie, William Keith Chambers. *The Greek Philosophers from Thales to Aristotle.* New York: Harper & Row, 1960.

Habermas, Jürgen. *Knowledge and Human Interests.* Boston: Beacon Press, 1970.

Hegel, Georg W. F. *The Phenomenology of Mind.* Trans. J. B. Baillie. London: George Allen & Unwin, 1966.

Heidegger, Martin. *On the Way to Language.* New York: Harper & Row, 1970.

Hesiod. *Theogony.* Ed. with an Introduction by N. O. Brown. New York: Bobbs-Merrill Company, 1953.

Homer. *Iliad.* Trans. R. Lattimore. Chicago: University of Chicago Press, 1961.

Jaeger, Werner. *Paideia.* Oxford: Blackwell, 1965. Vol. I.

Kant, Immanuel. *The Critique of Pure Reason.* Trans. N. K. Smith. New York: St. Martin's Press, 1961.

Katz, Jerrold J. *The Philosophy of Language.* New York: Harper & Row, 1966.

Kaufmann, Walter. *From Shakespeare to Existentialism.* Garden City: Doubleday Anchor Books, 1960.

Kelly, George A. "Notes on Hegel's Lordship and Bondage," *Review of Metaphysics,* XX (June, 1966), 774-791.

Kierkegaard, Søren. *The Present Age* and *Of the Difference Between a Genius and an Apostle.* Trans. A. Druand W. Lowrie. New York: Harper & Row, 1962.

Kissinger, Henry. "Reflections on Bismarck: The White Revolutionary," *Daedalus*, XCVII (Summer, 1968), 888-924.

Kitto, Humphrey David Findlay. *Form and Meaning in Drama*. London: Methuen & Co., 1956.

Kojève, Alexandre. *Introduction à la lecture de Hegel*. Paris: Gallimard, 1947.

Kuhn, Thomas S. "A Function for Thought Experiments," *Mélanges Alexandre Koyré*. Vol. II. Paris: Hermann, 1964.

————. "Reflections on my Critics," *Criticism and the Growth of Knowledge*. Eds. I. Lakatos and R. Musgrave. Cambridge, England: The University Press, 1970.

————. *The Structure of Scientific Revolutions*. Chicago: University of Chicago Press, 1962.

Laing, Ronald D. *The Divided Self*. Baltimore: Penguin Books, 1965.

————. *The Politics of Experience*. New York: Ballantine Books, 1969.

Laing, Ronald D., and Esterson, Aaron. *Sanity, Madness and the Family*. New York: Basic Books, 1971.

Latte, Kurt. "The Coming of the Pythia," *Harvard Theological Review*, XXX (January, 1940), 9-18.

Lévi-Strauss, Claude. *The Scope of Anthropology*. London: Jonathan Cape, 1964.

————. *Structural Anthropology*. Garden City: Doubleday Anchor Books, 1967.

Marx, Karl. *Capital*. Vol. I. New York: International Publishers, 1967.

————. "Preface to a Contribution to a Critique of Political Economy," *Selected Works*. Vol. I. Moscow: Foreign Languages Publishing House, 1951.

Marx, Karl, and Engels, Friedrich. *The German Ideology*. New York: International Publishers, 1961.

Matthews, Gareth, "Bodily Motions and Religious Feelings," *Canadian Journal of Philosophy*, I (September, 1971), 75-86.

Merleau-Ponty, Maurice. *La prose du monde*. Paris: Gallimard, 1969.

Peckham, Morse. *Beyond the Tragic Vision*. New York: Braziller, 1962.

Piaget, Jean. *Six Psychological Studies*. New York: Random House, 1967.

Pickard-Cambridge, Arthur Wallace. *Dithyramb, Tragedy and Comedy*. Oxford: Clarendon Press, 1966.

Pitcher, George, ed. *Wittgenstein's Philosophical Investigations*. Garden City: Doubleday Anchor Books, 1966.

Pitkin, Hanna Fenichel. *Wittgenstein and Justice*. Berkeley and Los Angeles: University of California Press, 1972.

Plamenatz, John. *Man and Society*. Vol. II. New York: McGraw-Hill, 1963.

Plato. *The Complete Dialogues*. 2 vols. Trans. B. Jowett. New York: Random House, 1956.

Pohlenz, Max. *Freedom in Greek Life and Thought*. Dordrecht: Reidel, 1966.

Quine, Willard Van Orman. *From a Logical Point of View*. New York: Harper & Row, 1963. See Chap. II, "Two Dogmas of Empiricism," pp. 20-46.

Ricoeur, Paul. *History and Truth*. Evanston: Northwestern University Press, 1965.

Ridgeway, William. *The Dramas and Dramatic Dances of Non-European Races in Special Reference to the Origin of Greek Tragedy*. Cambridge, England: The University Press, 1915.

Rieff, Phillip. *The Triumph of the Therapeutic*. New York: Harper & Row, 1966.

Rilke, Rainer Maria. *Letters, 1910-1926*. Trans. Jane Bannard Greene and M. D. Herder Norton. New York: W. W. Norton & Company, 1948.

Robinson, J. M. *An Introduction to Early Greek Philosophy*. Boston: Winthrop, 1968.

Rohde, Erwin. *Psyche*. Trans. W. B. Hillis. 2 vols. New York: Harper & Row, 1962.

Rosen, Stanley. "Nihilism," *New Essays in Phenomenology*. Ed. J. Edie. Chicago: Quadrangle Books, 1969. pp. 151-158.

_____. *Nihilism: a Philosophical Essay*. New Haven: Yale University Press, 1969.

Said, E. "Linguistics and the Archeology of Mind," *International Philosophical Quarterly*, XI (March, 1971), 104-134.

Sapir, Edward. *Language: an Introduction to the Study of Speech*. New York: Harcourt, Brace & World, 1969.

Saussure, Ferdinand de. *Cours de linguistique générale*. Paris: Payot, 1967.

Scully, Vincent. *The Earth, the Temple and the Gods. Greek Sacred Architecture*. New Haven: Yale University Press, 1962.

Shklar, Judith N. *After Utopia*. Princeton: Princeton University Press, 1957.

Silber, John. "Being and Doing," *Chicago Law Review* (Autumn, 1967), pp. 47-91.

Simmel, Georg. *The Sociology of Georg Simmel*. Ed. K. Wolff. Glencoe: Free Press, 1950.

Slater, Phillip. *The Glory of Hera*. Boston: Beacon Press, 1968.

Snell, Bruno. *The Discovery of the Mind*. New York: Harper & Row, 1960.

Stein, Jack M. *Richard Wagner and the Synthesis of the Arts*. Detroit: Wayne State University Press, 1960.

Stewart, D. J. "Hesiod and the Birth of Reason," *Antioch Review*, XXI (Summer, 1961), 213-231.

Strauss, Leo. *Natural Right and History*. Chicago: University of Chicago Press, 1963.

_____. *Socrates and Aristophanes*. New York: Basic Books, 1966.

Strong, Tracy B. "Hold on to Your Brains: An Essay in Meta-Theory," *Power and Community*. Eds. P. Green and S. Levinson. New York: Pantheon, 1970.

Thoreau, Henry David. *Walden and Civil Disobedience*. New York: W. W. Norton & Company, 1969.

Thucydides. *The Peloponnesian War*. Trans. Rex Warner. Baltimore: Penguin Books, 1966.

Toulmin, Stephen. "Conceptual Revolutions in Science," *Boston Studies in the Philosophy of Science*. Vol. IV. Eds. R. Cohen and M. Wartofsky. Dordrecht: Reidel, 1966.

Vaihinger, Hans. *The Philosophy of As-If*. London: Routledge and Kegan Paul, 1968.

Vernant, Jean Pierre. *Mythe et pensée chez les grecs.* 2 vols. Paris: Maspéro, 1965.

Voegelin, Eric. *The New Science of Politics.* Chicago: University of Chicago Press, 1962.

Wagner, Richard. *On Music and Drama.* Eds. A. Goldman and E. Sprinchhorn. New York: E. P. Dutton & Co., 1964.

Weber, Max. *From Max Weber.* Eds. E. Gerth and C. W. Mills. New York: Oxford University Press, 1958.

Whitehead, Alfred North. *Process and Reality.* Cambridge, England: The University Press, 1929.

Whorf, Benjamin Lee. *Language, Thought and Reality.* Cambridge: M.I.T. Press, 1964.

Wikse, John. "On Possession." Unpublished Ph.D. thesis, University of California, Berkeley, 1973.

Wittgenstein, Ludwig, *Blue and Brown Books.* Oxford: Blackwell, 1969.

————. *On Certainty.* New York: Harper & Row, 1969.

————. *Philosophical Investigations.* New York: Macmillan Company, 1958.

————. *Remarks on the Foundations of Mathematics.* Cambridge: M.I.T. Press, 1966.

————. *Zettel.* Berkeley and Los Angeles: University of California Press, 1967.

Wolin, Sheldon S. *Politics and Vision.* Boston: Little, Brown and Company, 1962.

Addendum to the Bibliography, 1988 Edition

Works on Nietzsche

Allison, David, ed. *The New Nietzsche.* New York: Dell, 1977.

Dannhauser, Werner. *Nietzsche's View of Socrates.* Ithaca: Cornell University Press, 1974.

Derrida, Jacques. *Eperons/Spurs.* Chicago: University of Chicago Press, 1979.

Grimm, Rüdiger. *Nietzsche's Theory of Knowledge.* Berlin and New York: Gruyter, 1977.

Kain, Philip J. "Nietzsche, Skepticism and Eternal Recurrence," *Canadian Journal of Political Science* (September, 1983), 365–387.

Kofman, Sarah. *Nietzsche et la scène philosophique.* Paris: Galilée, 1986.

Kremer-Marietti, Angèle. *L'homme et les labyrinthes.* Paris: Seuil, 1972.

Magnus, Bernd. "Nietzsche's Philosophy in 1988: The Will to Power and the Ubermensch," *Journal of the History of Philosophy*, XXIV, no. 1 (January, 1986), 78–100.

Nehamas, Alexander. "How One Becomes What One Is," *Philosophical Review*, XXCII, no. 3 (July, 1983), 485–517.

————. "Immanent and Transcendent Perspectivism in Nietzsche," *Nietzsche-Studien: Internationales Jahrbuch für die Nietzsche-Forschung*, XII, 473–490. Eds. Ernst Behler and Mazzino Montinari. Berlin: Gruyter, 1983.

————. *Nietzsche: Life as Literature.* Cambridge: Harvard University Press, 1985.

Strong, Tracy B. "The Deconstruction of the Tradition," *Nietzsche and Nihilism*. Eds. T. Darby et al. Toronto: University of Toronto Press, 1988.

———. "Nietzsche's Political Aesthetics," *Towards New Seas: Nietzsche on Politics, Philosophy and Poetry*. Eds. Michael A. Gillespie and Tracy B. Strong. Chicago: University of Chicago Press, 1988.

———. "Oedipus as Hero: Family and Family Metaphors in Nietzsche," *boundary 2: a journal of post-modern literature* (Spring/Fall, 1981), 311–336.

Wilcox, John T. *Truth and Value in Nietzsche: A Study in His Metaethics and Epistemology*. Ann Arbor: University of Michigan Press, 1974.

Yovel, Yirmiyahu, ed. *Nietzsche as Affirmative Thinker*. Dordrecht: Nijhoff, 1986.

Other Importantly Relevant Works

Barthes, Roland. *Image-Music-Text*. New York: Hill and Wang, 1977.

Bendix, Reinhard. *Force, Fate and Freedom*. Berkeley and Los Angeles: University of California Press, 1984.

Bloom, Allan. *The Closing of the American Mind*. New York: Basic Books, 1987.

Cavell, Stanley. *The Senses of Walden*. New York: Viking, 1972.

Drury, S. D. "The Esoteric Philosophy of Leo Strauss," *Political Theory*, XIII, no. 3 (August, 1985), 315–338.

Eden, Robert. *Political Leadership and Nihilism*. Gainesville: University of Florida Press, 1984.

Fish, Stanley. *Self-Consuming Artifacts*. Berkeley and Los Angeles: University of California Press, 1974.

Foucault, Michel. *Language, Counter-Memory, Practice*. Ithaca: Cornell University Press, 1977.

Kateb, George. "Thinking About Human Extinction: (I) Nietzsche and Heidegger," *Raritan* 2 (Fall, 1986), 1–28.

———. "Thinking About Human Extinction: (II) Emerson and Whitman," *Raritan* 3 (Winter, 1987), 1–22.

MacIntyre, Alasdair. *Against the Self-Images of the Age*. London: Duckworth, 1971.

———. *After Virtue*. London: Duckworth, 1981.

Rorty, Richard. *Philosophy and the Mirror of Nature*. Princeton: Princeton University Press, 1979.

Sellars, Wilfrid. *Science, Perception and Reality*. London: Routledge and Kegan Paul, 1962.

Strauss, Leo. *Studies in Platonic Philosophy*. Chicago: University of Chicago Press, 1983.

Weber, Marianne. *Max Weber: Ein Lebensbild*. Tuebingen: Mohr, 1976.

Index

(Boldface page numbers refer to important discussions)

[381